LONERGAN'S RETRIEVAL OF
THE NOTION OF HUMAN BEING

Clarifications of and Reflections on the Argument of Insight, Chapters I–XVIII

Frank Paul Braio

UNIVERSITY
PRESS OF
AMERICA

Copyright © 1988 by

University Press of America,® Inc.

4720 Boston Way
Lanham, MD 20706

Library of Congress Cataloging-in-Publication Data

Braio, Frank Paul, 1948–
Lonergan's retrieval of the notion of human being : clarifications of and
reflections on the argument of Insight, chapters I-XVIII / Frank Paul Braio.
p. cm.
Bibliography: p.
1. Lonergan, Bernard J. F. Insight. 2. Knowledge, Theory of. I. Title.
BD161.L613B73   1988   121—dc 19   87–34587 CIP
ISBN 0–8191–6851–3 (alk. paper)

All University Press of America books are produced on acid-free
paper which exceeds the minimum standards set by the National
Historical Publications and Records Commission.

ψυχῆς πείρατα οὐκ ἄν ἐξεύροιο,
πᾶσαν ἐπιπορευόμενος ὁδόν.
οὕτω βαθὺν λόγον ἔχει.

Heraclitus
Fragment 235

ἐδιζησάμην ἐμεωυτόν.

Heraclitus
Fragment 249

δίκαιος δὲ καὶ σώφρων ἐστὶν οὐχ ὁ ταῦτα πράττων
ἀλλὰ καὶ ὁ οὕτω πράττων ὡς καὶ οἱ δίκαιοι
καὶ οἱ σώφρονες πράττουσιν.

Aristotle
Nicomachean Ethics II, iv. 4-5

ACKNOWLEDGEMENTS

Grateful Acknowledgement is made to the following for permission to reprint selected passages from Lonergan's previously published and/or as yet unpublished texts.

Longmans, Green and Co., Ltd.: from **Insight: A Study in Human Understanding,** by Bernard Lonergan, 1957. Reprinted with the permission of the Longman Group.

Lonergan Research Institute: from **Lectures on Existentialism, Lectures on Education,** and **Horizon,** by Bernard Lonergan, 1957, 1959, 1963, respectively. Printed with Permission.

The Edwin Mellen Press: from **Understanding and Being,** by Bernard Lonergan, edited by Mark and Elizabeth Morelli, 1980. Reprinted with permission.

TABLE OF CONTENTS

PREFACE

The title of this study is "Lonergan's Retrieval of the Notion of Human Being: Clarifications of and Reflections on the Argument of Lonergan's Insight, Chapters I-XVIII." But to preface the more systematic outline attempted in the Introduction, I would briefly explicate the sense of this title and the central limits and aims of the project it names.

First, then, to retrieve a thought is to (1) call it back from the obscurity into which its content has fallen; (2) recall it as a possibility for critical human judgement and resolute, responsible decision. But obscurity is the state into which a content has fallen when the thinking which queries it (1) is uncritical; (2) has failed to raise itself to the level of the times; (3) takes the "truth" of its content for granted and, therefore, as unworthy of further thought, assessment, decision.

Secondly, by a "notion" is meant that which one already possesses and pre-understands in thought when a particular content has become an issue. Thus, remotely, it is what is intended by the coming of the given issue into question. Again, the intention is for that which meets the issue of query in all its relevant respects and, therefore, in all its relevant contemporary dimensions.

But, thirdly, according to our title, that which has fallen into obscurity but remains at issue for "contemporary" thought is the Being of the human.

But, fourthly, a clue is ventured us in recalling this issue. It is the fact that the one who raises it, the one who, therefore, already has a notion of the content which is at issue, is also, simultaneously, the Being in question. But it is to retrieve the notion and, therefore, the issue of human Being in exactly this sense and its full, contemporary context, that we must follow up on this clue.

Fifthly, one contemporary who has ventured this clue and, in our opinion, uniquely, thoughtfully, and reflectively plumbed its issue is

Bernard Lonergan. Hence, we study his venture to help us in our own attempts to plumb the issue.

Sixthly, in one etymological sense an "argument" is that which calls something by name and asks it to stand forth into the open so that a decision may be rendered. But it is the contention of this study that Lonergan's Insight is best interpreted as a venture in naming the issue of the Being of the human and letting it come out into the open where decision is to be rendered. Thus, to take up Lonergan's venture in "retrieving" the "notion" of human Being, we "reflect" upon the "argument" of his work Insight.

But, seventhly, such reflection is laden with implications for the performance, performer, and "subject matter" of "human" studies.

Eighthly, the original intention of this study was to take up the development of Lonergan's approach to the issue by successively interpreting his major works. The project was put off as overly ambitious. On the other hand, because of its importance in beginning this or any contemporary anthropological project, the text of Insight was chosen as the major focus. That the issue might be more rigorously engaged and rendered more suitable for study by a philosopher, and so that efforts would not be reduplicated, it was decided to confine attention to Chapters I–XVIII of Insight. Finally, to insure that even this more limited study would not become excessively unwieldly, it was decided to abstract from important but non-"foundational" themes, e.g., the scholarly differentiation of consciousness.[1] It was also decided not to take up such disputed questions as whether and/or to what extent Lonergan, in Insight, had already discovered and posited a "fourth" or "fifth level" of intentional consciousness, transcended or transposed the limitations of "faculty psychology," etc. Still it was hoped that the present, more limited study, would render future efforts to address these issues more tractable and worthy of greater thought.

Ninthly, the author has (1) struggled but failed to find any

---

[1]Cf. Insight, XVIII.3, etc. Thus, we will explicitly discuss neither the critical hermeneutics which Lonergan articulates in Insight, XVIII.3, nor the additional "historical" light its application would shed upon its own "foundations," those of human Being generally.

adequate way of restructuring the English language that reverses the male bias of its pronouns; (2) opted to retain "man" when it is to be understood generically. He asks that his failure neither be mistaken for his endorsement of sexism of any kind nor confused with an attitude of linguistic resignation on the matter.

Tenthly, in certain sections of this work, the author has been forced to employ an augmented outline form. But this has only been done in cases in which (1) adequate treatment of the material would have called for independent, book length consideration; (2) interpretation is necessary if some approximation to the proceeding argument is to be accomplished. It is hoped that these sections will reward study without either sacrificing or obscuring essentials (cf. Chapter V, Section B9, below). Again, the author has sometimes used underlining and bolding in an unconventional manner. His purpose has only been to provide the reader with possibly relevant visual cues for reading when what is relevant may be in question.

Eleventhly, this study does not propose to be the last word on either the proper interpretation of Lonergan's Insight or on its implicit anthropological issue. We think, however, that we have gotten hold of something at least relatively and presumptively invariant, and set the "data" on human Being in a heuristically expansive and extremely fruitful explanatory perspective. Still, in several senses, the import of this labor has been and could only be the discovery of just how much still remains to be done.

Twelfthly, we must acknowledge even if we cannot repay our debts. I would like to specially thank my sister Christine Braio who originally typed and then word processed the original drafts of this work. I would also like to thank Dr. Charles Betros, and Tahira A. and Patricia C. Williams for helping me edit this work into its final form; and Gloria F. Kopechy and Frank Borchardt for their administrative assistance. Again, I thank Joseph Lalino and Lillian Fields for their generous technical advice on operating the necessary computer technology. I am grateful to Dr. Gerald Quinn, Associate Vice President of Academic Affairs at Fordham University, for his confidence in my ability to complete this study. I am also grateful to Tom Beckett and Sister Anne

Tubman for encouraging me to finish this project. I owe a debt of gratitude to the staff and, especially, the library staff of Fordham University. I would like to thank the Rev. Michael Shields, S.J. and the Lonergan Research Institute of Regis College of Toronto, Ontario; Boo Riley and the Lonergan Center of Santa Clara University, Santa Clara, California; and the Rev. Jose Cruz, S.J. and the Lonergan Center of Ateneo de Manila Universidad, Manila, Philippines for their permission to use Lonergan's published and unpublished manuscripts and their collections of secondary literature. I am grateful to Fred and Sue Lawrence, and the succession of discussion leaders and lecturers of The Lonergan Workshop of Boston College, Boston, Massachusetts for their summer workshops. They stimulated and appreciably accelerated my efforts in this study. My attempts at thought have been guided, quickened, and encouraged by conversations with Hannah Arendt, Lawrence Azar, Frank Boehme, Justus Buchler, Rickard Donovan, Don Idhe, Steven Ippolito, Joseph Charles Lalino, Anthony Loftus, Ron McKinney, Walter Murray, George Pepper, the Rev. Bill Richardson, S.J., Loretta Richter, Arthur Seifert, Socrates Tello, H.S. Thayer, Joseph Trompeter, Ernst Vollrath, Walter Watson and, especially, the Rev. J. Quentin Lauer, S.J., K. Irani, and my father Angelo Braio. I would like to thank Dominick Balestra, Robert Johann, and Robert Roth for their considerable efforts in studying and offering their constructive criticisms of the drafts of this text. I am greatly indebted to the Rev. Frederick Crowe, S.J., for the many hours he has spent helping me interpret elusive Lonerganian texts and his willingness to share his unpublished and published manuscripts. I am especially grateful to Jim Marsh and Pat Byrne for introducing me to the originality and radicalness of Lonergan's accomplishment; Phil McShane for seminally, brilliantly, and consistently furthering their introductions. Again, in composing this study, I have been greatly benefited by the intellectual generosity and friendship of the Rev. Patrick H. Heelan, S.J.; the patient teaching, incisive criticism, personal depth and constant encouragement of the Rev. W. Norris Clarke, S.J. I wish to acknowledge a very great debt to the Rev. Vincent J. Potter, S.J. Without his unstinting and prolonged editorial efforts, his example and support, his belief in the author and theme of this study, we could never have brought this project to completion. I owe a great debt of gratitude to Bernard Lonergan, S.J. His accomplishments have sustained and expanded my own Self-discovery over the last decade. Finally, I owe the deepest and greatest debt of gratitude to my wife Ann Braio who has seen me through the entire project.

INTRODUCTION

A. General Considerations

In the only recently recovered "Original Preface of Insight,"[1] Lonergan notes that what was "so new," i.e., the Renaissance "ideas that fostered . . . [the] genesis" of our "twentieth century" world, have been "discredited by its maturity," have become "so old" (M, 4b). Thus, being educated" is no longer a matter of speaking Latin and writing Greek." The art and technology, the rise of non-European developing nations, the nearly "Utopian" frame of the modern political discussion, the re-emergence of theological speculations under the guise of existentialist thought and the rebirth of interest in logic all would have astounded and/or puzzled our renaissance forebears. Again, Einstein's work has unseated Galileo's and Heisenberg's Laplace's. Furthermore, the higher viewpoint that has transformed the natural sciences:

> cannot but affect profoundly the methods that were transferred with so sedulous fidelity to the human sciences (M, 3, 4b).

So has "a new world . . . been bequeathed us" out of the limitations and contradictions of the old. Yet we, "the heirs of the Renaissance," we who "know too much in too many fields," who "have witnessed too much suffering in too many unexpected quarters," lack the thought necessary to make sense of it. And that failure has left the contemporary subject without the "spirit of . . . venturesome assurance" (M, 5b) which marked his renaissance counterpart. It has left him with a sense of bewilderment, of unease in the face of what has, unexpectedly, been wrought by it. Nor has the "basic question" been missed. Thus, in his famous essay, Ernst Cassirer asked:

---

[1]This has appeared in Method, 3 (1985), pp. 3-7. Further references to this text will be abbreviated by citing M and the relevant volume and page numbers.

(j)ust what is man?[1] Answers, he remarked, have been worked out by theologians and scientists, by politicians and sociologists, by biologists and psychologists, by ethnologists and economists. But not only do the many answers not agree, not only is there lacking some generally accepted principle that would select one and reject the others, but even within specialized fields there seems to be no method that can confront basic issues without succumbing to individual temperment and personal evaluations (M, 3, 5b).

Again, given the "widespread disorientation" characteristic of the modern age:

man's problem of **self**-knowledge ceases to be simply the **individual** concern inculcated by the ancient sage. It takes on the dimensions of a social crisis. It can be read as **the** historical issue of the twentieth century. If in that balance human intelligence and reasonableness, human responsibility and freedom, are to prevail, then they must be summoned from the dim and confused realm of latent factors and they must burst forth in the full power of self-awareness and self-possession. If such is the urgency of personal appropriation of rational self-consciousness, the difficulty of achievement should not discourage attempts at making a beginning (M, 3, 5b-c, emphases mine).

First, then, the thesis of this study is that Lonergan's Insight[2] should be read as an attempt to address "**the** historical issue," the "basic question." Thus, the question which guides the sequence of Chapters I through X of Insight, the question which intends the shift of the reader's attention towards his own conscious acts as "data" and, therefore, towards "Insight as Activity," is the question of a once "naive" subject, lost in "externals" and alienated from Self-questioning. It is the question of a disoriented and uneasy subject now become at issue for himSelf and uttering the **question for intelligence** "**What am** I?," "**What** does it mean to **be** fully human?" It is the question which, for Lonergan, must provoke the turn to "interiority" as its adequate contemporary response. The following, then, is offered as re-phrasing of Lonergan's original question:

What is the noetic structure integrating and determining the ordered sequence of my conscious operations insofar as it is fully

---

[1] Cassirer, Ernst, An Essay on Man (London: Yale University Press, 1944).

[2] Lonergan, Bernard, Insight (London: Longmans, Green, and Co., revised student edition, 1958). The reader should note that this study will confine itself to Insight's **pre**-theological reflections.

human and insofar as it is analogously operative within different regional strata, within different "patterns" of my consciousness?

Again, implicit in this question is its inverse.

What is the pattern to my conscious activity insofar as this noetic structure is noteworthy by its absence, insofar as it has been put out of play, fails to perform its integrative function?

But we contend that the ensuing interpretations of the biological,[1] aesthetic,[2] common sense,[3] dramatic,[4] intellectual,[5] and ethical[6] patterns" of the subject's experience recover and integrate the successive partial answers to the question which Lonergan posed, the successive fruits of the journey of Self-inquiry, Self-discovery and Self-expression which it called forth in him.

And it is our further contention that it is the **challenge** of such a Self-recovery that Lonergan's Insight poses to the twentieth century reader, in the expectation of reawakening and affording guidance for his own "inner" journey. On pain of incompleteness the journey points towards the further question for **reflection** "Is this, in essence, what I **am**?"[7] This question is raised and answered proximately but decisively in Chapter XI of Insight. And the paradox of the asking and of the inquiry and pro-pective answer which preceded it, is that the asking itself is the clue and unflankable evidence for: (1) its proper answering; (2) excluding the questionless, "biological" pattern of naive extroversion as the essential element in its proper answering.

---

[1] Cf. Chapter I, below. The reader should note that the inverse aspect of the "basic question" is being addressed here. The reader may also wish to consult Chapter V, Section B10, below.

[2] Cf. Chapter II, below.

[3] Cf. Chapter III, below.

[4] Cf. Chapter IV, below.

[5] Cf. Chapters V and VI, below. They deal with the respective scientific and philosophic differentiations of the intellectual pattern of human experience.

[6] Cf. Chapter VII, below.

[7] This issue guides the reflections of Chapter VI.

Again, upon the paradox of that proper answering and the "invariant structures" of human consciousness which it "grounds," Lonergan is able to "construct" a Metaphysic. But the upshot of that construction is the metaphysically mediated expression of the achieved Self-knowledge of the subject. Again such an expression "sets" the Self-knowing subject within the "Horizon" of Being. And it fills out the original account of human Being by relating it to its underlying conditions, the dynamic of history and of community, etc., etc.

Again, if the subject's decision implicitly initiated, conserved, and effected his fidelity to the question of his own Being, the answering holds itself up for the subject's explicit and pellucid Self-choice. Thus, in Chapter XVIII of Insight, the subject's further, fundamental question of responsibility comes up. Having come to know himSelf in his human Being, the subject asks of himSelf, fundamentally, "Is this the Self whom I ought deliberately to bring forth?" "Is it to the good that I thus give mySelf to mySelf as such a project?" "Is this the Self into which, through my own choices, I ought deliberately to make mySelf?"[1] But any but an afffirmative answer involves the subject's default upon the extension of his Self-knowledge into action, upon himSelf as "rationally Self-conscious."

Again, the question of the "implementation" of the subject's judgment of Self-"worth" raises the further issue of his effective freedom to implement it, actually to put it into practise. And this issue, in turn, is tied up with his ability so to symbolize the dynamic to the Self he has affirmed and would "implement" that his sensitivity aligns itself with, comes to motivate and reinforce, to make effective his fundamental Self-option.[2] But, finally, then, the "basic question" of the subject only actually comes to term with its "invitation" to its subject, e.g., the reader, to opt fundamentally and resolutely for his own possibility of rational Self-consciousness, for himSelf as

---

[1] This is the question underlying the brief reflections concluding Chapter VII, below.

[2] The role of the symbol in human life is taken up in Chapter VI, Section 11, below and, again, briefly, in the reflections concluding and appending Chapter VII, below.

effectively free. But this is to invite his transformed manner of living in the universe of Being.

Secondly, it is the intent of this study to recover the implicit "Man—heuristic" of Insight.[1] Thus, a "heuristic" or "intentionality" structure is composed of the two "aspects" or "poles" informing some determinate "attitude" of human consciousness. The two "poles" or "aspects" are correlative to each other and can, therefore, only be defined by their mutual relations. In the general case, the "noetic" or "subject"-pole to the structure comprises an open field of questions of a specifiable type which are addressed to "external" or "internal" human experience.[2] The "noematic" aspect or "object"-pole[3] to the structure comprises a response of a certain kind which is pre—figured in outline by the "noetic" component. Again, once the "subject" and "object"-poles of the given structure have been specified, the "hori-zon" of the underlying attitude of consciousness they represent has been made determinate.[4] But the whole thrust of Insight is critically

---

[1]Two points must be made here.

First, the recovery is most strikingly and formally accomplished in Chapter V, Section B8, below. Its essential and presumptive "grounds," however, wait for Chapter VI. Again, there is a sense in which each of the chapters and sections of this inquiry fill out, clarify, and deepen the heuristic conception set forth in Chapter V.

Secondly, some of the ensuing chapters are broken up into divisions, e.g., Division "A," Division "B," etc. References to sections within such divisions will be abbreviated. Thus, "B8" refers to Section "8" of Division "B" within a specific chapter. Again, "B8e" refers to Subsection "e" within "B8."

[2]In the exceptional, deficient case, the "subject"-pole of the structure may admit determination, may address itself to experience, from a pre-questioning attitude of consciousness. But, then, the "expanse" linking "noesis" and "noema" is a "horizon" in only a deficient sense. Finally, this qualification will not be introduced into the body of ensuing analyses (cf. Chapter I, below).

[3]The "object"-pole of a given attitude of consciousness may also be called its "field" or "formal object."

[4]The general strategy of Lonergan's "horizon" analyses is reflectively to enucleate the "noetic" aspect of the relevant, fundamental attitude or pattern of human consciousness. On the basis of the constant "noetic" features which his analyses uncover, he can

to "ground" a "Man-heuristic," that is, a basic set of terms and relations through which the activity of any human subject can be understood and explained in the fullness of its humanity. It is a set of terms and relations which, along its essential lines, is so fundamental that it will hold its ground, admitting only minor revisions or expansions. It is the further contention of this study, then, that to bring out this thrust would afford theoretical, collaborative and incipiently dialectical efforts in the "sciences of man" with a relatively invariant paradigm by which their ongoing and diverse findings can find adequate, ongoing, integration.[1] Thus, Lonergan says:

---

specify the constant features of its correlative "field." But from there he can argue to the "horizon" of the given attitude of consciousness in general. Again, the general strategy of analysis will be clarified in the course of the successive contexts of its application. And it will be nuanced in Chapter V, Section B8. Finally, Lonergan refers to his approach in Insight as a "generalized empirical method." Thus, as the "data of sense" stand to empirical method, so do the "data of consciousness" stand to such a generalized procedure. Again, consciousness is only the initial data of such a method. Thus, the compass of relevant data will expand to include the relations between: (1) different conscious subjects; (2) conscious subjects and their milieu or environment; (3) consciousness and its neural base (I, 244a).

[1]Lonergan's Insight first appeared in print in April of 1957. Writings and lectures which date from within a year or two of that time will be cited to shed light on Lonergan's intentions in Insight. Thus, in August of 1958, Lonergan delivered a set of ten lectures on Insight, following roughly the order of the original text. These have been edited and published by Elizabeth and Mark Morelli under the title Understanding and Being (New York and Toronto: The Edwin Mellen Press, 1980). Reference to this text will be abbreviated by UB. We will also cite, when necessary, from the following works of Lonergan: De Constitutione Christi Ontologica et Psychologica (Rome: Gregorian University Press, 1956); Lectures on Education, unpublished, (Cincinnati: Xavier University, 1959); Lectures on Existentialism, unpublished, (Boston: Boston College, 1957), etc. Again, reference to these texts will be abbreviated, respectively, by DCC, LED, LE. Citations will also appear from later works of Lonergan, such as Method in Theology (New York: Herder and Herder, 1972). Again, this work will be abbreviated by MT. Still these later works will be cited more cautiously and only if their intent is clearly consistent with their correspondents in Insight. Again, our study has tried to remain

> (t)horoughly understand what it is to understand, and not only will you understand the broad lines of all there is to understand but also you will possess a fixed base, an invariant pattern opening upon all further developments of understanding (I, xxviiib).[1]

This study would preserve the thrust of his remark but reverse the axis along which it travels. And it would do this to crystallize the full implications of its meaning:

> thoroughly understand what it is to be human and not only will you understand the broad lines of all that there is to understand about human being and community in the world, but also you will possess a fixed base, an invariant pattern opening upon all past and future developments of human Self-understanding, Self-knowledge, Self-enactment and providing the underlying structures and methods relevant to every area of human studies.[2]

Finally, abstracting from its inverse, the Self-discovery which the following discussions clue admits simple formulation. It is that human subjects develop "intentionally" and that development is, minimally, intellectual and moral and, in fact, historical and communal. That development is conditioned by their advance, by stages, from processes of "experience" to "understanding," from "understanding," to "judgment," and from "judgment" to "decision," etc. But human "experience," the "sensitive" or "psychic" and "intersubjective" components of human consciousness are themselves subject to development. They have, proximately, organic conditions which are themselves

---

perfectly faithful to the meaning and intent of Lonergan's Insight. Still, it has attempted, as far as this is possible, to interpret it in light of the larger context opened in Method in Theology. Finally, the terms "reflective" and "reflection" are used in two broad contexts in what follows. On the one hand, they refer to an operation on the "third" level of the subject's consciousness. Thus, the subject "reverts" to the "phantasm" to "grasp" whether or not, for instance, her content coincides with or only approximates to the "virtually unconditioned." On the other hand, they refer to the process by which the subject turns to the data of her own consciousness in order to properly grasp, affirm, and implement its underlying "structure." The reader is asked to distinguish the two senses from the given contexts of their application.

[1] The initial small letter concluding page citations refers to the paragraph of the citation.

[2] This is my own gloss upon and re-casting of the preceding quotation.

subject to maturation. Again, they contribute conditions which are continually integrated and re-integrated by the unfolding theories, precepts, and syntheses of human understanding, judgment and decision. Thus, to simplify later discussions, Section B1, below, introduces essential characteristics of the "tri-fold unity" of human development. Again, in Section B2, further determination is added to the notion of a "pattern" of human experience, a notion which recurs throughout this study.

B. Specific Considerations

1.   The Tri–fold Unity of Human Development: The Neuro–Organic Base, the Sensitive and Intellectual Flows of Consciousness

When the operations of "(i)nquiry and insight, reflection and judgment, deliberation and choice" supervene upon the sensitive flow of human consciousness, they constitute it as <u>human</u> and represent the higher <u>dynamic</u> integration of what in the animal is mere sensitive process (<u>I</u>, 266b). The "patterns" of sensitive experience in and by which these operations occur are several and will be distinguished in subsequent sections. But the "sensitive flow of consciousness" is itself a higher <u>dynamic</u> integration of lower organic and neural processes. The plant is not only an aggregate of cells but an "intelligible unity" distinguishable by determinate states and laws of development of its own. Similarly, the animal is an intelligible unity at a next "higher" level. It "exploits" events left undetermined by the laws of organic integration as "materials" for the higher dynamic systematization of "biological consciousness," of <u>conscious</u> stimulus, condition and response (<u>I</u>, 264b). A sketch of the nature and relation of neuro–organic and sensitive processes will serve to introduce discussion of the <u>higher</u> patterning of the sensitive flow of psychic contents through the mediation of the operations of "inquiry and insight," etc.

The organism assembles and arranges its cells in a series of more or less determinate stages. These stages involve the differentiation of organs. Organic differentiation underlies the emergence of a sequence of organic <u>functions</u> whose full range of organic diversity is <u>not</u> effectively realized at the level of plant life. With the emergence of animal life, organic growth includes the differentiation of neural tissues. These provide a <u>material base</u> for a <u>series</u> of increasingly complex forms of perceptual–motor and appetitive "consciousness." Thus, the "irritability" manifested at the cellular–organic level remains only a possibility neglected by plant life. The same possibility is exploited by animal life to become the substrate for the sensitivity of touch, etc.

On the other hand, the emergence of sensitive process in the animal forms a dynamic "higher system" for meeting sequences of (increasingly) determinate demands issuing from its organic and neural base of operations (I, 266b).

> Hence, while chemical elements appear as dominated by the manifolds that they systematize, a multicellular structure is dominated by an idea that unfolds in the process of growth, and this idea can itself be subordinated to the higher idea of conscious stimulus and conscious response (I, 264b, emphases mine).

Thus, the dynamic "sensitive system" manifest in animal life will successively integrate sequences of coincidental manifolds of events on the neuro—organic level without disrupting the lower level's own laws and stages of development.

Sensitive system will itself develop along two complementary lines. First, a multiplicity of particularized nerve endings grounds the possibility of increasingly differentiated sensible impressions and sensitively guided elements of movement. Thus, the emergence of rods and cones at a neural level makes "seeing" possible. The evolution of the deep radial and ulnar nerves makes the conscious "flexing" of the thumb possible. Both possibilities have become concretely probable and actual in the course of time. Secondly, an ascending hierarchy of nerve centers grounds the possibility of higher perceptual integrations of these impressions and ever more diversified coordinations of response. Thus, the evolution of the brain makes possible the operation of a center on which external stimuli can converge and a base from which integrated response can emanate. This possibility, too, became probable and actual in the course of time. In these two ways, neural development in animal organisms supplies the underlying coincidental manifold for psychic development.

> The latter [e.g., psychic development] is conditioned by the former [e.g., neuro—organic development] but it consists neither in neural tissues nor in neural configurations nor in neural events but in a sequence of increasingly differentiated and integrated sets of capacities for perceptiveness, for aggressive or affective response, for memory, for imaginative projects, and for skilfully and economically executed performance (I, 456b, emphases mine).

"Psychic development," then, is this higher, dynamic, sensory-responsive integration of neural events. It is "on the move," in two complementary directions dictated by the properties of the events and processes of the nervous system with its afferent and efferent branches and central core. Sensitive process develops <u>laterally</u> increasingly to differentiate conscious events. The latter development integrates particular afferent and efferent neural impulses and demands. The <u>limit</u> of this line of development is prescribed by the "multiplicity and diversity of nerve endings" (<u>I</u>, 468b). Sensitive process develops <u>vertically</u> towards "increasing proficiency in <u>integrated</u> perception and <u>appropriate</u> and <u>coordinated</u> response." The <u>limit</u> of this line is set by:

    (1) the operationally significant set of combinations of different nerve endings; and

    (2) the existence of higher nerve centers at which such combinations can be integrated and coordinated (<u>I</u>, 468b).

By studying the integrated activity of the animal at any given stage of its sensory-mobile development, the flexible, empirically specifiable "schemes of recurrence" patterning and regularizing its operation can be identified. From such data, deeper, non-observable laws of a "classical" kind which simultaneously explain the data and set it in the context of its underlying physical, chemical and neuro-organic conditions can be specified. Their presupposed sets of implicitly defined conjugate forms would account for "habitual types of perceptiveness and response" at particular stages of development. In so doing they:

> would seem to be emergent in [successively] underlying neural configurations or dispositions <u>as insights are emergent in images and functions in organs</u> (<u>I</u>, 468c, emphases mine).

Again, determination of the principles, e.g., the "operator(s)" which account for the <u>succession</u> to these stages, for the "development" of the animal's perceptual-motor life, would "explain" that existence in its dynamic aspect. But even as the sensitive flow <u>provides</u> a "dynamic" higher integration for underlying neural manifolds, so it <u>offers</u> successive coincidental manifolds of conscious events for ordering at the level of the laws of <u>human intelligence</u>. And it is under the dynamic control of, and in dynamic correspondence with, these operations that human sensitivity and perceptiveness, imaginative power and acquired skill reach their greatest differentiation and higher integration. Thus, the "common sense attitude" of human intelligence forms the dynamic basis for the generation of a series of increasingly differentiated and re-integrated forms of perceptual and sensory-motor skills. This series remains in correspondence with the increasingly determinate series of underlying organic and neural events and impulses, while introducing series of determinations "beyond" the reach of their immanent laws. In an ongoing circle of intentional development, and through an ongoing series of interactions with significant adults, peers, situations in home, school, work, etc., the subject accumulates, corrects and clusters the insights concerning local patterns of perception and skill.

At certain points, the learning process is "short-circuited" by "sensitive routine" (I, 554b). In this way, intelligence can focus on the learning and mastery of significantly different or higher order skills. Differentiated possibilities of performance can now be grouped in various ways and at "sequences" of successively higher levels. This latter possibility normally converges towards the ability of the subject to perform the sets of tasks necessary to take up and discharge a "social role." Analogous circles of developmental learning and interaction will be operative in art, mathematics, science and philosophy, etc. and not only in the exercise of common sense and practical intelligence. In each case, higher intellectual operations will dynamically order coincidental elements of the sensitive and responsive flow at levels beyond the reach of the laws of "sensitive psychology," even as sensitive process supervenes upon coincidental elements to organic and neural development.

Thus, human development moves on at least three interlocking levels (I, 470a). Each has its own laws, schemes of recurrence, conjugate forms. Each preceding level would offer materials to be ordered by its successor in series of stages and each successive level would provide higher successive integrations and, hence, just the modification of its predecessor which "calls forth" its successor. From this vantage point, the unconscious organic-neural base of this tri-fold development can be interpreted as:

an upwardly directed dynamism seeking fuller realization, first, on the proximate sensitive level and, secondly, beyond its limitations on higher artistic, dramatic, philosophic, cultural, and religious levels. Hence it is that insight into dream symbols and associated images and affects reveals to the psychologist a grasp of the anticipations and virtualities of higher activities immanent in the underlying unconscious manifold (I, 457a, emphasis mine).

2. Patterns of Experience: Neuro–Organic Base and Sensitive Integration

Lonergan points out that acts of sense experience never occur in isolation from some content, from other such acts, and from a "dynamic context" which relates acts and contents. Likewise, conscious experience is never independent of a "bodily basis" in the organism and a systematic link to its bodily movements.

> Thus, without eyes, there is no seeing; and when I would see with my eyes, I open them, turn my head, approach, focus my gaze (I, 181e).

On the other hand, the sensitive flow of consciousness involves not only the temporal succession of its manifold contents but also "conation, interest, attention, purpose" (I, 182b), i.e., human "concern." Both human bodily movements and sensations are subject to an "organizing control" by this "immanent" conscious factor. Thus, patterns of change reflecting an external situation and occurring in the human optic nerve and cerebrum, and also in the statoacoustic nerves and temporal lobe of the cortex may lead to and condition corresponding acts of seeing and hearing. But that amidst all the other street sights and sounds I see a friend and hear only her words testifies to the selectivity of consciousness and the variability of human concern which controls it. Thus, the sensitive stream of consciousness is of variable direction. The orientation determines how: (1) the subject will become sensitive to the series of "demands" for attention issuing from her environment and mediated by the neuro-organic substrate of her waking consciousness; (2) her sensitive contents will be selected, organized, "patterned," and dealt with.

Human consciousness, in effect, "floats upon,"[1] and is not determined by, the series of demands on its attention exerting themselves with varying degrees of intensity and duration, and in

---

[1]Cf. Lectures on Education, Chapter III.4.1.3, p. 73a.

various directions from below the threshold of awareness. In animal consciousness, these organic demands will "dominate" sensitivity and "lock" it into a biological pattern. **Generically**, then, a "pattern of experience" is a set of intelligible relations, discernible within the sensitive flow of consciousness, which dynamically "links together" its sequences of sensory and affective sensitive contents (i.e., sensations, desires, fears, emotions, images, memories, anticipations, bodily movements, etc.) in a determinate, identifiable way. **Specifically**, with respect to human consciousness, a pattern of experience is defined as a structure, i.e., a set of "intelligible relations," which orders the conscious flow of sensitive–imaginative presentations and active responses, by its relations to the immanent and variable orientation of human "concern." But as the orientation of the subject's concern is a variable, so will her consciousness move, not only from one thematic "object" to another, but through a variable, specifiable series of patterns within which thematization occurs. Finally, in several of the patterns, the sensitive flow to the consciousness of the subject may be so "ordered" as to facilitate the emergence, survival and/or implementation of insights, reflections, deliberations of the relevant kind.

CHAPTER I

THE BIOLOGICAL PATTERN OF EXPERIENCE

ANALYSIS

Principally in Insight, Chapter-Sections VI.2.2, VII.2.3, and VIII.2, Lonergan lays out his reflectively grounded discovery of the biological "pattern" and underlying attitude of human subjectivity. His exposition moves through five groups of examples to highlight, first, the "subjective" and then, increasingly, the "objective" features or correlative "field" of the "Horizon" this attitude structures. His fifth example "returns to the subject" in a new way.[1]

Again, given that his first three examples are selected from the pre-human domain of living things, and his fifth from a genetic psychologist's reconstruction of the character of the awareness of the human child, the question arises of whether Lonergan should have so eschewed examples drawn from the biological pattern of adult human experience.[2] Nevertheless, the purport of the examples Lonergan did

---

[1]Lonergan's first example thematizes the relation of "quarry and prey" to determine the nature of the "cognition" of the subject of the biological pattern. His second example thematizes the experience of the animal rising from slumber to clarify the nature of his "objectivity." His third example considers a kitten lapping at a painting of a saucer of milk to bring out the notions of "reality" and "value" of the biologically patterned subject. His fourth example singles out the lived experience of, for example, the human smile and family to concretize the notion of "intersubjective community." In a final example, Lonergan turns to the experience of a child to expand upon the Self-"notion" of the subject of the biological pattern of experience.

[2]This question is implicitly answered in Chapter V, Section B10, below, where the notion of dialectic comes under analysis.

16

give is summed up in the first. He notes, then, that in our:

> endeavor to understand the sudden twists and turns both of fleeing quarry and pursuing beast of prey, we ascribe to them a flow of experience not unlike our own (I, 182d, emphases mine).

Thus, to understand the "delicately co-ordinated" interplay of these two animals, we affirm the movement and intersection of two outwardly directed loci of "inner," conscious life. The latter comprises an ordered flow of perceptual data, conations, motile responses, anticipations, emotions, memories and images, etc. But in this developing flow of sensitive events, a flow "not unlike our own," there is a recurring pattern and attitude of operation to be grasped. And Lonergan claims that the grasp of the generic keys to that pattern sheds light on the attitude and field of one "partial" and "intermittent" orientation of the global flow of adult conscious life, of its "cognition, operation and motivation."

The point of Lonergan's examples, then, is not that either "kitten," quarry or infant can be made to "understand and describe [or explain] its spontaneity" (I, 251d). The point is rather to offer images and clues which advance the purposes of the adult subject in pursuit of Self-understanding. And that pursuit advances when, through them, he learns to pick out reflectively in himSelf and, thereby, to recognize in others:

> a merely biological and non-intelligent response to [a] stimulus (I, 251d 3-4, emphases mine);
>
> the elements in a non-conceptual [and non-rational] knowing (I, 251d 4-7, emphases mine);

a never fully eradicable tendency to lapse back into such an attitude of response and "cognition" from series of higher, intelligently and reasonably integrated performances. That pursuit advances, then, when its subject has learned to discern the **absence** of a fully intentional engagement with his, with "one's" "object."[1] Furthermore, the

---

[1]The subject's discovery is that some anticipated intelligibility and, in this case, some requisite instance of his intelligence, reasonableness, and/or responsibility, is neither present nor forth-

analysis is important because the adult subject's cognitional, ontological and Self-reflections tend to be based upon images, metaphors, and locutions drawn from examples patterned upon this performative attitude of his subjectivity.   But if the biological pattern of experience is valid within its own limits—as is evidenced by the survival and development of animal species (cf. I, 252c)—its hermeneutical and ontological paradigmatization is, minimally, incompatible with the subject's Self-questioning, his intelligent pursuit of acts of understanding and his pursuit of correct Self-understanding and understanding of Being.

Reflecting on the already cited first example, Lonergan concludes that the manifold acts (e.g., of pursuit and/or flight) and contents (e.g., images, anticipations, etc.) of sensitive consciousness are unified in each animal by their orientation towards ends with immediate "biological significance."[1]   Thus, the sensitive flow of the consciousness of the "subject" of the biological pattern of experience, whether animal or human, tends to:

> converge(s) upon terminal activities of intussusception or repro-
> duction or, when negative in scope, self-preservation (I, 183b).

Thus, in the biological pattern, pre-set "vital anticipation(s)" (I, 388a, emphasis mine) structure the awakening, pursuit and consummation of the subject with respect to his object.   And, in its mature form, this structuring represents a fairly routinized, relatively inflexible order of conation, stimulus, and response.

---

coming.   It is the occurrence of an "inverse insight" into the procession of the "data" of his own consciousness, or into the other's, or possibly into his community's conscious activity or its fruits. Again, such a discovery sets the stage for the occurrence of the direct insights whose expression sets forth, in what follows, the lower order "structure" of the conscious acts or their fruits which is actually taking place.   Finally, the notion of "inverse insight" is discussed in Chapter V, Section A3, below.

[1] Many of the themes taken up in what follows are clarified in Lonergan's "Cognitional Structure."   It appears in Collection (New

Comparing plant and animal life, Lonergan's second example involves his note that many strictly biological functions such as cell metabolism, the chemistry of digestion, etc., are fulfilled organically without the benefit of conscious control (I, 183c, emphases mine). Thus, whereas none of plant living is spent in wakefulness, a part of the animal's is. Rising from its slumber, it acts intermittently to restore or correct disturbed, unconscious functioning, but recurrently to: "deal rapidly, effectively, and economically with external situations . . ." (I, 183c, emphases mine). Thus, when the external object "fails to stimulate" his desire:

> the subject [of the biological pattern] is indifferent; and when [his] non-conscious vital process has no need of outer-objects, the subject dozes and falls asleep (I, 184b, emphases mine).

Lonergan's implicit point is that the subject of the biological pattern of experience sensitively "constitutes" his "field" of objects (cf. V, 7b). Thus, he gathers his "stimulating" object on a purely "sensitive" basis, "completely on the level of experience" (I, 252b), purely in its immediately integrable "relations to us." But since the sensitive subject cannot fully reflect upon himSelf, his "object" is always already to be pre-"understood" as exterior to himSelf, as fully constituted in itself at a merely spatio-temporal and sensitive level of integration, and only to be carefully glared at, manipulated, listened to, etc. to be fully "grasped."

Thus, biologically patterned consciousness grasps its object by "turning-outward-towards" what lies spread out before and around it, spatially separate from itself. This constitutive extroversion of attitude "underpins the confrontational element of consciousness itself" (I, 184b). Thus, subject and object, stimulus and response, are faced off in this attitude, dyadically "opposed," "ever against." Sensitively absorbed in externality, in exterior "unities" of sight, sound, smell, touch, etc., confronting without question a surrounding

---

York: Herder and Herder, 1967), pp. 221-239, where the interested reader should attend to pp. 231b-236b. Henceforth, this paper will be abbreviated by CS, and this book by Cl.

world of immediacy,[1] the vital anticipations of the conscious subject begin (have already begun?) to trace opportunities and structure means to biologically desirable ends.

But if the biological extroversion of sensitive consciousness is construed as the paradigm of human intentionality and the sense of sight is singled out as the paradigmatic formality under which the world of "objects" is to be gathered, a fundamental "counter-position"[2] can be construed concerning human cognition:

> Knowing can be conceived as intrinsically or essentially a matter of confrontation, of [the subject's] taking a look, seeing what is there, **intuition**. Since knowing, on this account is what comes from the look, anything that comes from the subject [e.g., his questions, insights, reflections, the principle of sufficient evidence, of non-contradiction, etc.] is not [a component in] knowing at all; and if it comes from the subject that just means it [e.g. what he is doing] is not knowing. Knowing is what is given in the look, [and its "object" is] what is out there to be looked at and seen when . . . [the subject] looks (UB, 196c–197a, emphases mine).

> For example, naive [epistemological] realists say that they know that this very obvious mountain is real because with their eyes they can see it, with their feet they can tread on it, with their hands they can handle it, and since to them the matter is so patently clear, they will attribute either to silliness or perversity every effort to find or urge or offer, any further ground for their conviction (WN, 132).[3]

In the intellectual pattern of experience, one starts out from the otherness of the subject (in pursuit of understanding) and the unknown

---

[1]Cf. Method in Theology, p. 238c ff.

[2]Three brief points should be made here.
First, such a "counter-position" will represent a first determination of the "subject-pole" of the "horizon" of the biologically patterned consciousness of the subject.
Secondly, the issue of the nature of the "counter-positions" will be taken up in Chapters V and VI, below.
Thirdly, Don Ihde brilliantly diagnoses the counter-positional attitudes toward and in human speech and auditory phenomena, generally, in his Listening and Voice: A Phenomenology of Sound (Athens, Ohio: Ohio University Press, 1976). Still, he fails adequately to uncover or embrace the "positions."

[3]Four points should be made here.
First, the preceding reference is to Conn O'Donovan's translation from the Pars Dogmatica (pp. 17–112) of De Deo Trino. It is published under the title The Way to Nicea (Philadelphia: The Westminster Press,

"object" (not yet but to-be-known). In the best case, this otherness is converted into an intentional identity, the "objectivity" of the process is fully achieved, in the reflective act of understanding, in the grasp of the virtually unconditioned which initiates the term of the inquiry.[1] In the biological pattern, however, one starts out from the otherness of extroversion between its subject and his object. But "objectivity" can have two senses here. On the one hand, it can mean, seeing what is there clearly, seeing all that is there to be seen, seeing it distinctly, leaving out nothing which is there to be seen. In this sense, then, the extroversion of sensitive consciousness is not transcended but, rather, comes into its own. On the other hand, the biological subject's equivalent for the intellectual subject's intentional conversion of otherness into identity can be specified. It would consist in his physical manipulation, his labor upon and consequent consumption, his ultimate physical assimilation of his

---

1976). Reference to this work is abbreviated by WN.

Secondly, the naive epistemological realist's quoted sayings, above, bring out neither the role of "direct" nor "reflective" understanding in his knowledge. The effect of this is to confine his intentionality to no more than a pre-explanatory, descriptive horizon.

Thirdly, besides the "looking" based on the human "eyes," besides an "empirically intuitive" model of the cognition of the subject, there: "is also [his] spiritual looking. It looks at the content of acts of conceiving, thinking, supposing, defining, considering" (I, 496a, emphases mine). On this model, then, there are: "looks with one's intellect, interior and spiritual x-rays that penetrate the essence of things and see the essence that is there" (UB, 197a, emphases mine). From such an "intellectually intuitive" model of the cognitional operation of the human subject the great ontological idealist counter-positions can be constructed with their, minimally, implicitly dualistic conceptions of human being. Thus, specific philosophic and philosophically anthropological constellations can be generated from the "first transposition" of the biological attitude of the subject. And if these constellations are "dialectectically opposed" to their originals, they remain counter-positions since they retain their essentially intuitive model of cognition and its object.

Fourthly, for classic criticism of the intuitive model of cognition in both of its dialectically opposed forms, see Charles Peirce's "Questions Concerning Certain Faculties Claimed for Man" and "Some Consequences of the Four Incapacities," Collected Papers, ed. C. Hartshorne and P. Weiss, vol. V (Cambridge, Mass.: The Belknap Press, 1965), pp. 135-152 and 156-185, respectively.

[1]Cf. Insight, p. 552c.

object in fulfillment of his vital, organically aligned anticipations!
The "objectivity" of the biologically patterned subject in this
"second" sense can be further determined if we recall that his "world"
comprises the totality of immediately present or sensitively integrable
"objects," the totality of the things in their relationships "to us."
Such a subject is:

> a centre in the world of sense operating (S)elf-centredly [e.g., in
> accord with the pre-set, organic orientation of his conscious
> concern] (I, 474a, emphases mine);

> content to orientate . . . [himSelf] within . . . [his] visible and
> palpable environment and to deal with it successfully [e.g., to
> secure such ends as survival, etc.] (I, 474b, emphases mine).

But, then, the "necessary and sufficient conditions" of the objectivity
of the subject in such a "world of immediacy" consist in his being "a
successfully functioning animal [in a habitat]" (MT, 263c, emphases
mine).

Combining the two senses, then, the "objectivity" of the subject
of the biological pattern can be described as "a property of [his]
vital anticipation, [his] extroversion, and [his] satisfaction" (I,
388a).[1]

Lonergan's third example considers "a kitten." It is awake and
its stream of consciousness flows in the biological pattern (I, 251b).
He begins by recapping the point of the preceding examples by
thematizing the "outwards" orientation of sensitive consciousness
towards "vital ends" which "satisfy appetites" (I, 251b). But the
"extroversion" of the consciousness of the biological subject is now
further determined. It is, first, spatial. Thus, its palpably

---

[1]The identification by the reflecting subject of his
"objectivity" with an attitude of, minimally, "extroversion" represents
a second fundamental "counter-position" upon the fully human cognition
of the subject. It also represents a second determination of the
"subject-pole" of the biological "horizon" of human subjectivity.
Again, the sense of objectivity as manipulative and assimilative may
account for the philosophic identification of human action with
"labor." Cf. Karl Marx, Economic and Political Manuscripts of 1844;
John Locke, The Second Treatise on Government, etc. On this specific
point, then, the "thinking" of Martin Heidegger's "Letter on Humanism"
and the transcendental analysis of Bernard Lonergan would seem to be in
accord.

extended operations, e.g., of eye, head, and limb, etc., employ a physical spread of means, e.g., a stone, a basket, a branch, etc. to manipulate "extended" objects which are remote or in proximity "to him." It is, secondly, temporal. Thus, both its acts and the objects upon which they open manifest "duration" and so are surrounded by a double fringe of memories and anticipations. Hence, the biologically patterned subject's cognition cannot (or cannot fully) "pivot" beyond its own or its "object's" dispersal in time (and space). It is, thirdly, not concerned with the mere "appearances" but with the "real." Such concern, however, is evidenced by:

> a realistic painting of a saucer of milk [which] might attract a kitten's attention, make it investigate, sniff, perhaps try to lap; but it could not lead to lapping and, still less, to feeling replete; [thus,] for the kitten, painted milk is not **real** (I, 251b emphases mine).

But if, through the analogy with animal sensitivity, the meaning of the "knowing" and "objectivity" of the biologically patterned subject have been indicated, the nature of the reality intended by human consciousness in this attitude requires further elaboration. Lonergan's procedure is to name the unknown object of the subject's extroverted attitude "body" and work out its "generic" properties or field—characteristics on the basis of his immanent, if implicit, anticipations. Thus, he describes his "body"–object as "already–out–there–now–real."

First, it is "already": the fully constituted sensible integration of the potential totality of its appearing or accessible aspects; assimilable by his extroverted sensible "cognition;" the potential locus of his vital desires and primitive fears.

Secondly, his object is always "out" where he can peer at, pursue or avoid, find or lose it. Thus, the subject of such an outwardly oriented consciousness is: (1) ignorant of the demand of his own questioning for understanding and reflection if he is to meet his "object" cognitionally on its own terms, on its own proper level of intelligible unity; (2) not explicitly aware of the "inner" intelligent ground of his proper access to his object; (3) always only aware of his object as spatially "distinct from" and other than himSelf; (4) not cognizant of the fact that the "object's" real distinction from the cognitional act by which it is known is <u>not</u> equivalent to its spatial exteriority.

Thirdly, his object is always **"there"** and **"now,"** and, consequently, a physical, spatio-temporal unity. But if unity is only spatio-temporal in character, then real distinction is reduced to physical separability in space and time (cf. <u>I</u>, 494c); relations are either unreal or, <u>per impossibile</u>, spatially extended third terms linking other body-relata; causality is reduced to efficiency, to the analogue of the felt outcome of bodily effort, to mechanical process or to regular, antecedent consequent conjunctions.

Fourthly, his object is **"real"** if, in addition to satisfying conditions one to three, above, it is relevant to the subject's "biological success or failure, pleasure or pain" (<u>I</u>, 251b). Thus, the "reality" of milk is "known" and to be distinguished from its mere appearance, when, as already noted, a sense of repletion has followed upon successful lapping.

Finally, the "goodness" of the object for the subject of the biological pattern will be "convertible" with its "reality." Thus, when the "object" of spontaneous, sensitive desire "is attained, it is experienced as pleasant, enjoyable, satisfying." Lonergan names it the "particular good," the "good of appetite."[1] But the sensitive subject:

> experiences aversion no less than desire, pain no less than pleasure, and so on this elementary level, the good is coupled with its opposite, the bad (<u>I</u>, 596b, emphasis mine).

Thus, even as the biological subject at least implicitly identifies his knowing with "taking a look," his objectivity with "extroversion," and reality as the "already-out-there-now," so also does he spontaneously

---

[1] The identification by the reflecting subject of the Being of her "object" with its character as "already-out-there-now-real" and its Good with the latter's capacity to satisfy sensitive desire, constitutes the <u>third</u> and <u>fourth</u> fundamental "counter-positions" inherent in her biologically patterned performance. Again, it also represents a determination of the "field" or the "object"-pole of the biological subject, the "formal viewpoint" within which her "object" gives itself to his consciousness. Finally, then, when the first and second counter-positions are conjoined to the third (and fourth), they specify, respectively, the mutually determining "subject"- and "object"-poles of the biologically patterned "Horizon" of the subject.

identify the good with the "particular object" of his extroverted vital anticipations and consummations.

Lonergan's fourth example pertains to the community of the subject of the biological pattern, to his "being-with" the "other." Thus, the subject of the biological pattern (the subject whose experience is centered around the organic goals not only of intussusception and self-preservation but also of reproduction) is prereflectively aware that his experiencing and desiring are **not** solitary. He is aware, then, that they are immediately open to, patterned by, and communicative of relations with: (1) a common, **inter**-subjective field of "objects" out-there-now; (2) a common "intersubjective" "world" with other similarly patterned subjects. Lonergan brings out his point in two steps. Thus, Lonergan offers two descriptions which would intimate this doubly intersubjective phenomenon. Then, he traces it back to its pure, historical form, reflects from that basis on its nature and the nature of its subject, thereby clarifying its experience in and for contemporary subjectivity.

First, then, Lonergan notes that "prior" to his question, insight, judgment, deliberation or artistry, and almost as if "we" were always already "members of one another prior to our distinctions each from others," the subject spontaneously reaches out to keep a passerby from slipping. Again, his smile or frown "expresses [to him] intersubjectively . . . [his] feeling as it is [being] felt [by him]" (MT, 63d, emphasis mine).

Secondly, he notes that in primitive fruit-gathering communities, the subject's elemental "cognitions," i.e., his "perception" mediated by "hunger" and "thirst," are linked to their desired "object" (i.e., to the "real," particular good they want) by a relatively undifferentiated and "simple sequence of bodily movements." Such movements might include operations of foraging, picking, sucking, swallowing, etc. But so are they also informed by spontaneous, relatively undifferentiated forms of fellow-feeling and cooperation. These "links" are almost "too obvious to be [brought out,] discussed, or criticized . . . ."

> The bond of mother and child, man and wife, father and son, reaches into a past of ancestors to give meaning and cohesion to the clan

or tribe or nation. A sense of belonging together provides the dynamic premise for common enterprise, for mutual aid and succour, for the sympathy that augments joys and divides sorrows (I, 212b, emphases mine).

Thus, it is precisely because such community is predominantly and deeply rooted in the elemental, intersubjective bonds of human sensitivity that the experience, the imagination, the symbolizations, the energies, the hopes and fears, the actions "of each [incarnate subject in local community] resonate with that of every other" (I, 215a, emphasis mine). It is for this reason that each of its subjects is spontaneously led both to "satisfy . . . [his] own appetites . . . and to help [the] others in the attainment of their satisfaction" (I, 219a, emphasis mine).

Again, the social arrangements which intelligently expand upon the spontaneities which intersubjectivity "structures" do so but with only a minimum of complexity and indirectness. Again, the center of the biologically patterned concern of the subject is split and tends to shift between himSelf and his local community. Still, even as his sensitivity is invested in and attached to the "present, immediate, palpable" context of the "objects" of his, of his community's desire, so his:

> intersubjectivity radiates from the self [and its local community] as from a centre, and its efficacy [as a spring of co—operative sense and action] diminishes rapidly with distance in place or time (I, 219c).

Furthermore, even after more differentiated social forms have emerged in history, the specific intersubjectivity of the subject's community survives. It survives, minimally, in his experience of the family:

> with its circle of relatives and its accretion of friends, in customs and folk—ways, in basic arts and crafts and skills, in language and song and dance, and most concretely of all in the inner psychology and radiating influence of women (I, 212b).

Finally, it has been pointed out that the subject of the biological pattern spontaneously and implicitly identifies his knowing with "taking a look," etc., etc. Similarly, in the light of the previous phenomena, he will tend, equally spontaneously, to identify his community with the other as "intersubjective" and, therefore, local, attached, territorial, possibly ethnic or ethnic in inspiration, and relatively exclusive.[1]

Fifthly, having in the third example, above, sketched the principle "heuristic"[2] features of the "body" intended by "an intelligence that is grasping not intelligent procedure, but merely [its own] biological and non-intelligent response to [a] stimulus" (I, 252), Lonergan proceeds variously to exemplify the philosophic relevance of his analysis. He does this by outlining how, on its basis, there can be constructed the positions of: (1) Galileo on the reality of primary qualities;[3] (2) the "decadent Aristotelians" and the subject of common sense on the reality of secondary qualities;[4] (3) Descartes on the identity of material substance and spatial extension;[5] (4) Kant on the exclusively phenomenal range of the application of the categories of substance, existence, and reality;[6] (5) the hedonist in ethics;[7] etc. He only completes his exemplification, however, in a footnote which concludes the summary of his argument in its main section (I, 254 n). This example sheds further light on the Self-interpretation of the subject of the biological pattern and must now be considered.

---

[1]The identification, by the reflecting subject, of her "community" with the "other" as "intersubjective," may be regarded as a derivative counter-position inherent in the "fundamental" counter-positions of her biologically patterned performance. Thus, it represents a further determination of the "horizon" of her thus patterned, conscious activity.

[2]The term is analyzed in Chapter V, below.

[3]Cf. V. Potter, The Philosophy of Knowledge (New York: Fordham University Press, 1987), pps. 82c-85c.

[4]Cf. ibid., pps. 79c-82b.

[5]Cf. Insight, pp. 388e-389a.

[6]Cf. Insight, p. 414a.

[7]This last point is not made in the text in Insight, pp. 250b-254a, with which I am here dealing. It comes up, rather, on pages 606b and 624b.

Harry Stack Sullivan, in his The Interpersonal Theory of Psychiatry,[1] describes the root of the experiences underlying the human child's notion of the Self, a notion which tends to survive into his adulthood. Lonergan uses this to show that the infant's notion of "my body," which emerges from these roots, exemplifies the sense of body as "already-out-there-now" when the latter is transposed from the objective to the subjective "pole" of the biological horizon of consciousness. Thus, there emerges in the oral zone of the child of six months:

> a need to suck, to manipulate with the lips, and so forth, quite irrespective of the need or satisfaction of hunger and thirst (ITP, 135a).

By this time, the infant's ability to coordinate or group manual operations, i.e., to transport from "hand to mouth" by kinaesthetic sense and to suck "anything presented to the mouth," is well advanced.

> But in the infant's experience, of all that which is thus grasped, transported and manipulated, only the parts of his own body which he can get into his own mouth, generally his thumb, uniformly and invariably feel sucked and orally manipulated.

> . . . the thumb is the only . . . [thing transported to his mouth] that feels sucked at the same time that the mouth 'feels sucking' (ITP, 138a, emphases mine).

In this sense, the thumb is "self-sentient."

> It is discovered not by the hand but by the mouth, or rather by hand-mouth cooperation. The mouth feels the thumb, and the thumb feels the mouth; that is self-sentience (ITP, 141a).

The child's physical needs are recurrently dawning into his awareness. He is, likewise, aware first, that his anticipation of satisfaction (by his mother's nipple or a bottle) is not inevitably actually satisfied. He is aware, secondly, that actual satisfaction relies upon the co-operation of some "other" for completion. But this other does not feel sucked when it is sucked. Thus, by mid-infancy, the child's

---

[1]Cf. The Interpersonal Theory of Psychiatry (New York: The Norton Library, 1953). In what follows, this text will be abbreviated ITP. Also cf. "The Illusion of Unique Individuality," Psychiatry, 13:317-332, 1950, reprinted in The Fusion of Psychiatry and Social Science (New York: The Norton Library, 1964), pp. 198-216.

manual exploration of all "reachable" parts of his life-space, leads to a sensitive division of objects into "two grand divisions, the self-sentient and the non-self-sentient" (ITP, 141a). With respect to the former:

> the thumb-in-lips situation is the first we have encountered in which two zonal needs are satisfied by one adequate and appropriate activity that the infant can perform without cooperation of a chronologically more mature person—in which there is no need for evoking the good mother and no danger, at this particular stage, of evoking the bad mother. It is the first situation in which there is an invariant coincidence of the felt need and the foresight of its satisfaction by a certain activity which is always adequate and appropriate, with the satisfaction of the two zonal needs (ITP, 139b-140a, emphases mine).

Sullivan continued:

> This is . . . a kind of experience that will be organized in a pattern . . . [and] evolve into a symbol . . . .
>
> . . . and this sign is the organization of data to which one refers as "my body" and which may include . . . practically everything to which "my" is applied seriously;
>
> . . . it is this pattern, "my body," which has so much to do with the [the child's, with the adult subject's] very firmly entrenched feelings of independence, of autonomous entity . . . (ITP, 140b).

But this achievement is pre-intelligent and pre-rational. It represents the subject's merely sensitive integration of a multi-zonal manifold of Self-sentience and operation. It represents his merely "sensitive" Self-differentiation from the non- or other-Self-sentient "objects" of sensitive integration. These objects are "already out there" "around" the body-subject as center "already-in-here-now."

> In such a fashion, clearly, there can arise an empirical conscious-ness of [one's Self as] a centre of power and self-satisfaction (I, 254 n, emphases mine).

Again, when reflectively appropriated by the "anthropologist," the uncritical and uncriticized survival in the adult of such a Self-"apprehension," of the underlying attitude of subjectivity which it reflects and implies, can be seen as animating empiricist, positivist, utilitarian and, to some extent, pragmatist explications of the being of man. The spelling out of the details and variations of such critical mis-appropriation must be left to a further work. Here it must be added that Sullivan, himself, recognized the inadequacy of such a Self-"conception." Further, he regarded it as:

> a great handicap to the development of a grasp of interpersonal relations, and . . . [the central notion lying] behind . . . [the adult subject's] delusion of unique individuality [e.g., of solitariness, isolation, unbridgable "distance" from the "other"] (ITP, 140b).

But these human mis-Self-conceptions are inevitable as long as the reality-notion of "body" is not transcended and an adequate, reflectively grounded notion of the nature of the "thing"[1] is not achieved. Thus, Lonergan suggests that:

> the empirically conscious self is just as intractable within a field theory of interpersonal relations [Sullivan's ultimate word on "man"] as the old-style atom within modern physical theory; and so, as Cassirer attacked the notion of thing [e.g., body] Sullivan attacks the delusion of unique individuality. Both views have the same merit [i.e., they reject the notion of body] and, I suggest, the same defect (I, 254 n, emphases mine).

Such a common defect is their failure to reappropriate and re-conceive of the dynamic unity of the full human subject in terms of an adequate notion of the "thing" in general. Thus, they fail to "understand" that proportionately, existential uniqueness and distinction and, therefore, "real" identity and "real" relatedness are correlatives. Thus, one cannot be denied without excluding the other. And this is no less true in the case of a community of human beings than in the case of finite Being generally.

Finally, then, insofar as the subject is "in" the biological pattern of experience:

(1) only those aspects of her "object," will be admitted into consciousness which reveal "biological opportunities and dangers." Thus the subject will recall pleasures, anticipate fears, emotionally vent somatic pressures, and unlock the kinds of "delicately coordinated" sequences of acts adequate for negotiating organically vital needs in a "world of sense;"

---

[1]Lonergan "defines" the thing as an existing "unity-identity-whole" in a relevant set of data. Again, he claims that this notion cannot be adequately comprehended without an "insight into insight." Thus, the authentic notion of the thing is "beyond" the "horizon" of the biologically patterned subject and her notion of "body." Finally, Lonergan's explication of the notion of the thing is thoroughly interpreted in Chapter V, Section B8, below.

(2) the process implicit in her cognition will be assimilated to
that of "taking a look." It will satisfy philosophic variants
upon "intuitive" theories of cognition whether of an empiricist
or, in a first displacement, a rationalist kind. In its
fundamental sense, the "objectivity" of the subject will be
assimilated to the radical "extroversion" of her conscious
attitude. Again, the "object" of the extroverted "gazing at"
of the biological subject will be "body." And the "field" or
"formal viewpoint" within which she "perceives," desires,
and/or pursues her "object" will be that of the "already-out-
there-now-real." This "formal viewpoint" represents the
vitally circumscribed, organically allied "field of 'vision',"
action, intersubjective concern and co-operation of the
consciousness of the subject. It determines as ultimately
illusory and insignificant any claims to meaning, value, or
community which would transcend its "limits" and, therefore,
appeal to intelligence, the intelligible, etc. Again, since
these notions of cognition, objectivity, reality, etc.,
determine the mutually determining subject- and object-"poles"
of the subject's biologically patterned performance, the
preceding analysis represents Lonergan's explication of the
"horizon" of such performance. But, then, from this horizon,
the intellectual development of the subject, her maturing
powers of inquiry and understanding, of rational reflection,
deliberation, evaluation and choice, will be interpreted as
exterior, as incidental or posterior to her "knowing" and
"valuing" of reality, to her "community" with the "other," etc.
Again, such development is irrelevant and unnecessary precisely
because it is only incidentally proportionate to the cognition,
valuation, etc., of what is "out-there." Thus, the
"intelligibility," whether of the natural or social worlds,
will be thought of as, ultimately, extrinsic to the "objects"
"intended," desired, or achieved by subjects within this
pattern;

(3) her activity will be, essentially, inflexible despite the
complex and finely coordinated series of behavioural and

intersubjective maneuvers of which it is capable and despite the developmental stages through which it passes. Thus the animal remains "locked from birth into natural routines of stimulus and response." Again, in the human subject of this attitude, these routines leave: "small capacity for **learning** new ways and for mastering other than native skills" (I, 189b, emphases mine);[1]

(4) she will tend to interpret herSelf, as well as her "object" as "body;" she will see herSelf as well as the "other," as, at root, a sensitive, incarnate unity of "power and satisfaction;" she will think of her community with the other as "inter-subjective" and of her good as "particular;"[2]

(5) she will stand ever in **tension** with the conditions of her properly intellectual, moral, sensitive and social development. She will stand in conflict with the "positions" which reflectively Self-possessed consciousness must achieve if it is to remain faithful to its own inevitable and no less spontaneous possibilities of questioning, of understanding and affirming what is, of motivation by value, etc. She will stand ever in tension with those other patterns of experience within which the positions can be made and are fully operative, reflectively grasped or deliberately extended into the realm of action and cooperation.

---

[1]Thus, in the animal organism, the subordination of neural process to the advancing selectivity of sensitive consciousness can reach a "high degree of complexity." This complexity will: "ensure large differentiations of response to nuanced differences of stimuli. None the less, this complexity, so far from being an optional acquisition, seems rather to be a natural endowment and to leave the animal with a relatively small capacity for learning new ways and for mastering other than native skills" (I, 189b).

[2]It is here that the anthropologist may discover the origins of the "mythic attitude" and correlative myths of human consciousness. For example, then, the adoption of such an attitude is the source of the the inadequate anthropomorphic images and stories of the deities (cf. I, 539–540; Chapter VI, Section 11, below).

CHAPTER II

THE AESTHETIC PATTERN OF EXPERIENCE

ANALYSIS[1]

The "experience" of the human subject spontaneously slips into an aesthetic pattern, and this fact both presupposes <u>and</u> evidences a <u>twofold</u> "liberation" of his conscious living in the world.

In the **first** place, presence "in" the aesthetic pattern represents the liberation of the **sensitive consciousness** of the subject from the inertial "drag" of extroverted, organically motivated purposiveness. It represents, in effect, the "untying" of the intentional "cord" which integrates sequences of: (1) perceptual, imaginative, recollective and anticipatory acts in terms of the biologically patterned motives of desire and/or fear, pleasure and/or pain, etc.; (2) responses in terms of their relations to quasi-instinctive fight-flight mechanisms and the instrumentalized, organically motivated routines of common sense living, etc.; (3) sensitive "contents" as "body"-objects "already-out-there-now," etc. The "untying" is equivalent to the initiation of a turn-about in the conscious living of the subject. It is his "release" from his biologically determined, practically instrumentalized, and socially assimilated Self. It is simultaneously a "revelation" of and a "freeing" of himSelf for expanded possibilities of existing and developing: (1) "beyond" the confines of his everyday living; (2) "in"

---

[1]The following analysis draws on relevant parts of Chapter IX of Lonergan's <u>Lectures on Education</u> and Chapter III, Section 3 of his <u>Method in Theology</u> to shed interpretive light on the challenging text of <u>Insight</u>, Chapter VI, Subsection 2.3. It is <u>not</u> the goal of this chapter, however, exhaustively to interpret the former two texts.

a "transformed" and enriched concrete "world."[1] At the same time it opens the subject to the "questions" with which such a freeing must always task him: "What am I to be?;" "Why?"[2] Finally, it exhibits an inviting, underlying attitude of **wonder** at the freedom of his consciousness towards the being of the world, a freedom wherein the totality of questions has its "source and ground."[3] Thus freed, the sensitivity of the subject to his "object" becomes, for itself, a "joy."[4] It is experienced as something "self-justifying" whose deepening is to be valued "for its own sake" and not merely for its results. Again, this freedom is the "origin" of that revelation of and further possibility of evoking such "liberation" which is the "art-work."[5]

In the **second** place, presence in the aesthetic mode liberates the **intelligence** and **reasonableness** of the subject for the possibility of artistic creation. This second liberation of the aesthetic subject [now of, minimally, the second and third levels of his consciousness] is itself twofold in character.

First, the "intentionality" of the aesthetically "released" subject does **not** anticipate the discovery of abstract, conceptual terms and relations ordering coincidental elements with mathematical precision. It does **not** want the theoretical systems which would unify

_____

[1] Cf. Lectures on Education, Chapter IX.2.2, p. 204e f and, Method in Theology, p. 63a-b.

[2] Cf. Insight, p. 185c.

[3] Cf. Insight, p. 185b.

[4] Cf. Insight, p. 184c.

[5] The "look" or "objectifying stare" thematized by phenomenological literature (cf. Jean-Paul Sartre, Being and Nothingness, trans. Hazel E. Barnes (New York: Philosophical Library), pp. 252-302) admits explanation by the subject's explicit or implicit adoption of the biological pattern of experience. Thus, such an adoption involves an attitude of "extroversion" towards the "other" which may find expression in the "stare." Again, it may involve interpreting and, therefore, relating to the other as: a "body;" a possible "object" of sensitive Self-satisfaction; an item of stock to be dominated,

ranges of empirical data.   Rather, developing artistic "intelligence"
would, by stages, uncover by **exhibiting** the "ever novel forms that
unify and relate [i.e., constitute the "sense" of] the contents and
[conscious] acts of [the recently liberated!] aesthetic experience [of
the subject]" (I, 184d).[1]

Secondly, the subject's validation of and "judgment" upon "the
artistic idea" **is** "the artistic deed." Thus, the artistic subject:

> establishes his insights, not by [heeding the "wearying
> constraints" of] proof and verification but by skillfully embodying
> them in colours and shapes, in [the spontaneous and instrumentally
> augmented] sounds and movements [of human subjects], in the
> unfolding situations of fiction (I, 185a, emphasis mine).

Again, the process of validation through the creative, ongoing
incarnation of aesthetic meaning, augments the "spontaneous joy of [the
aesthetic subject's] conscious living" with "the spontaneous joy of
[his] free intellectual creation" (I, 185a).

But if the "validation" of artistic meaning lacks the strict
reflexivity ventured in conceptual-theoretical contexts, still the
evaluation of the artwork has its own immanent criteria. And if they
defy adequate, explicit formulation, still their violation is palpable
and generates dis-"satisfaction."   That dissatisfaction is shaped by

---

manipulated, exploited, mastered, assimilated, etc.   But whether
explicit or implicit, such an interpretation and the relationship it
entails is an "objectification" or "negation" of the other as full
intentional subject. Thus, the "untying" or "release" which we have
associated with presence in the aesthetic pattern is an initiation of:
the overcoming of such an "objectification" of the other;   the
possibility of taking "joy" in and adopting an attitude of
respectfulness towards his being and presence. Again, in the preceding
chapter, the pre-reflective or "intersubjective" dimension of human
community was brought out.   Here we would suggest that this
pre-reflective community: (1) admits an aesthetic as well as a
biological patterning; (2) is never without an underlying biological
"component;" (3) will manifest a different character and, respectively,
be cooperative and uncooperative with the demands of human intelligence
and reasonableness depending on which pattern is predominant. Finally,
Lonergan's identification and analysis of a "dramatic" pattern of human
experience **may** be speaking to this point (cf. Chapter IV, below; also
cf. I, 723b).

[1]Four brief points should be made here.

the subject's aesthetically heightened sensitivity to the "things" exhibited as well as the tradition and community of artistry within which that exhibition and its content are situated. If critical, that dissatisfaction is of the nature of a **"judgment"** that something is wrong, i.e., something that should be present is not or something that is present should not be. Perhaps not all the relevant factors have been taken up, there are avoidable limitations in form or content, or relevant tensions are neither discharged nor exhibited, etc.

First, there is "meaning" or "sense" merely on the level of the aesthetic "experience" of the subject. Such meaning is "elemental" since it: is neither conceptualized nor expressed in any other manner; "precedes" the conceptual distinction of "subject" and "object" (cf. LED, IX.2.2, p.205 ff; MT, 63b–c, 67b, 74b).

Secondly, there are the "forms" grasped and set forth by artistic intelligence. The "grasp" of such forms involves the subject's insight into her aesthetic experience. Her ability "adequately" to "set forth" the form grasped presupposes a period of "learning." The learning will probably involve her: (1) apprenticeship to a "master;" (2) her accumulation of the relevant nucleus of practical insight into her skills; (3) gradual evolution of a style that is distincly her own. Again, the "forms," as exhibited in the art-work, would be "pre"–theoretical in character. They would be post-biological, i.e., they represent something "more" than the biological subject is capable of adequately "grasping" or bringing out and, hence, an "enrichment" of the "elemental" meaningfulness of aesthetic "experience."

Thirdly, the **artist's** "grasp" upon and expression of such "forms" pertains to the "second" level of human consciousness. Again, the "evaluation," "validation," and "judgment" of the exhibited form involves a reference to the "third" level of human consciousness. But this facet of the process of artistic creation and criticism is taken up in the ensuing paragraphs.

Fourthly, Lonergan's inclusion, in the preceding citation, of "conscious acts" among the contents integrated by the "ever novel forms" of the artwork is noteworthy. His point seems to be that there is a "reflective" dimension to all creations worthy of the name art and that, more or less explicitly, this dimension brings to the fore the character of the aesthetically liberated, intentional consciousness of the incarnate, creative, artist-subject. But, then, "represention" of the "already–out–there–now" is, either, per se, alien to the authentic art-work and its artist or typical of an elementary phase in artistic development. And the level of "reflective" development of the artist-subject will determine and be interpretable by the character of her art. Again, these considerations: (1) make "genetic" and "dialectical" considerations intrinsic to the interpretation of the history of art (cf. Chapter V, Sections B9 and 10, and Chapter VI, Section A11, below;

Such a "judgment" "withdraws"[1] the artist-subject from his "object" as exhibited and throws him reflectively back upon the original aesthetic **"experience"** whose "sense" motivated and called forth his work. From that withdrawal, the subject "re-turns" to his work with deepened sensitivity to and **"understanding"** of the limitations and/or aberrations of his historically and socially situated achievement. He also "returns" with a deepened appreciation for the essential integrity of the "experience" which he would less inadequately express, and perchance, with clues for just how to do this. And with what was so won is he able to bring out the succession of increasingly apt drafts of chapters, or oil studies of a particular landscape or social situation, or versions of a wind solo, or couplets of a poem, etc. And each of these in turn will again invite acts of detached and distanced evaluation, reflection, **judgment**, etc. Thus, there is, minimally, a tri-fold, self-complementing, self-correcting structure immanent in the conscious process to the aesthetic-creative intentionality of the subject.[2]

Furthermore, the subject's exhibition of his artwork for the "experience" of his audience wants their critical "assent." The exhibited artwork seeks this assent by inviting their "participation"

---

(2) imply that the "position"-"counter-position" distinction, to be drawn in Chapter VI, Section A6 and expanded in Section A11, has its analogue in art (cf. LED, VIII.1, p. 171).

[1]Two points should be made here.
First, in his Lectures on Existentialism, pp. 26 ff, Lonergan takes up Arnold Toynbee's notion of a creative "withdrawal" from active life for the purpose of uncovering the insights which make a "return" to it fruitful. Such a movement of "withdrawal" and "return" is also evidenced in the artist's "withdrawal" from society for the sake of the aesthetic recovery of possibilities of meaning relevant to everyday living and its world (cf. LED, IX.2.2, p. 205c ff. ff). I am expanding Lonergan's transposition of this notion to explicate his suggestions concerning the artist's and his audience's "judgment" of the possibilities whose recovery the work of art exhibits.
Secondly, the unfavorable or, even, favorable "judgment" which intitiates the artist's "creative withdrawal" from the everyday world may derive from the "other," e.g., some member of his audience.

[2]In light of the preceding footnote, we must add that such an intentional process is always, in fact, historically and communally

in the artist-subject's aesthetically liberated experience of his "object," in what his work would reveal, would bring to the fore. Again it does this through the "reenactment of . . . [his] inspiration and intention" (I, 185b). If the member-subjects of the audience do not refuse, if they accept this invitation, their reflective "withdrawal" into their own conscious "depths" is brought on. In the best case, the withdrawal is their starting afresh, their exploration of fresh possibilities for a greater fullness in conscious living and experience, and an interior trying out of the possibilities gathered. Thus, "withdrawal" is followed by a "release" of sensitivity and insight, as well as a concrete evaluation, or judgment upon the contents released. Reflection is itself followed by a "return" to the specific, routinized sensitivity and correlative, socio-historically conditioned situation "out" of which the subject had been momentarily carried by the artwork. Still, this return is now "mediated" by a deepened understanding of oneself, the immanent possibilities of one's world, one's "origins."

Again, the authentic art-work of the artist-subject as well as the "experience" whose pre-reflectively and pre-theoretically differentiated "truth and value" his art-work brings out, is "symbolic." Still, "what is symbolized [remains] obscure"[1] (I, 185b, emphasis mine).

Finally, it should be noted that it is the two-fold liberation of the consciousness of the aesthetic subject which, first, conditions the

---

mediated.

[1]For an analysis of "Mystery" as the obscure "object" of human "symbolization," the reader must wait for Chapter VI, Section A11. There an analysis of Insight, XVII.1 is performed. That analysis will, indirectly, shed new light on the meaning and purpose of the above remarks, the role of the aesthetic and artistic in human life. Again, a creative reading of that analysis will suggest clues for construing the "distortion" of the artistic intention and the operation of a "dialectic" in the history of art. Finally, if we must prescind from interpreting the issue in this study, Lonergan seems to significantly deepen his notion of symbol in his post-Insight works (cf. LED, IX.2.6, ff, MT, 64–69, etc.).

possibility of his art-work and, secondly, emerges as the principle theme revealed in it. Thus, it is precisely this twofold liberation of human consciousness which the artwork would have the members of its audience experience, discover, "affirm," and freely bring forth for themselves. Again, structuring the expression and underlying the operation of the two-fold liberation of the aesthetic subject is: (1) a dynamic, intentional structure unfolding on, minimally, the levels of his experience, understanding, and judgment; (2) the wonder which pervades and orients that structure towards a "world" of "things" that is more than merely "out-there-now;" (3) the "freedom," the "What?-" and "Why shall I be?" of the thus structured, thus opened subject; (4) the communal and historical situation of (1)-(3), above.

In conclusion, then, the artwork is simultaneously the revelation of, and authentic response by, the subject to the question of her human being in the surrounding world. It is the cipher through which she may perpetually effect and undergo the re-recovery in successively transformed social and historical contexts, of her awareness of the freedom of her own conscious Being. It is a reminder of the possibilities of development which that freedom holds out, the questions with which it elementally tasks each human subject, and the wonder, the correlative, enriched "world" which underscores and situates them both. Again, it is a clue that may reveal the subject's need to pivot beyond the aesthetic pattern of her development. And it may lead to a certain, not totally inauthentic, reflective and explanatory account of the phenomena with which the aesthetic subject is already in touch, which she has already called upon manifold media to exhibit, and which she would, thereby, equally nourish, sustain, and develop. Finally, if they presuppose and bring out the liberation of his sensitivity, the preceding reflections are not those of either the aesthetic or artistic subject. They represent, rather, the conceptual fruit of the subject's deepening reflective Self-revelation, her discovery of her transcendence of the "horizon" of her biologically patterned existence.

CHAPTER III

THE NATURE OF COMMON SENSE: ATTITUDE AND OBJECT

Introduction

In Chapters VI, VII, and X.2-.5 of Insight, Lonergan sets down the conclusions to his reflections upon the nature and "field" of the consciousness of the subject in the attitude of common sense. Commenting on these chapters in Understanding and Being, Lonergan indicates that, in general, the nature of the common sense of the subject was "something very difficult to get hold of with precision" (UB, 106b). He notes that to a considerable extent he could only determine it by contrasting it with more mature differentiations of human consciousness. Thus, it can be "defined" by contrast with the reflectively appropriated initiatives of both the scientific subject's "specialized pursuit of knowledge" and those of the rationally Self-conscious, fully ethical subject. He suggests that non-comparative, positive analysis should be regarded as:

> convincing in the measure that . . . [its author, e.g., Lonergan] can be, in . . . [his] description(s), suggestive, evocative, bringing to people's mind something of their familiarity with ordinary human affairs (UB, 106b).

As thus convincing, Lonergan's descriptions would bring to mind the pre-scientific "intellectual" development of the subject. This development is oriented to "the field of particular matters of fact" (I, 419c) and not to "universal laws." It is pre-philosophic and pre-"reflective." Thus, it may do the good without being able to define it or being aware that it is doing so. It is concerned with the proximate but not the remote "practical possibilites" (cf. I, 417b) which arise in "making and doing" (I, 207a). It would fit its subject with requisite repertoires of behaviour, with substantive skills, with "practical" wisdoms, with "maxims" or "clues" for how to go on learning

40

when the need arises. Such an orientation, such a purpose, such a "fitting," then, condition the subject's creative, "successful" action amidst the environmental and socio–cultural manifolds with which his concrete situation regularly tasks him. Thus, Lonergan's analysis attempts to capture the complexity and heterogeneity of the common sense subject's living–intelligently–in–the–concrete. And since such living proceeds on a less articulate and "critical" basis than more mature differentiations of human consciousness, it should come as no surprise that it would be "very difficult to get hold of with precision."

Still, if its particularities are difficult to pin down with precision, Lonergan argues that the general structure of the common sense performance of the subject is not. He argues that, in fact, it is "structured" on three distinct but interlocking "levels." He claims that the levels "within" this structure can be associated in various ways with the recurrence of acts of "experiencing," "understanding" and "judging." He argues that the specific common sense "patterning" of the "basic," three–fold structure is common to the everyday living of every human subject. And, finally, he contends that it is recognizable and, also, "verifiable" in the course of the intellectually patterned Self–reflection of each one of them.

On the other hand, Lonergan argues that if the **structure** to the attitude of common sense learning is, in fact, invariant, the **content** that it generates and situates is not. Thus, such a content is that "understanding" of "Self" and "world" which **differs** with each subject's village, neighborhood, city, or locale and thus is only conditionally secure. Such differences will correspond to or admit further differentiations by the given craft and trade of their subject, by the given specializations of intelligence and talent to the tasks and roles ingredient in their society with the other. Finally, intelligence in mathematics and empirical science does not merely consist in the mechanical erection, application, and extension of formally systematic languages. It also involves the wealth and fecundity of "understanding" that mediates and complements questions with learning, with inquiry, discovery, and critical reflection. But the common sense subject is "intelligent" in his own right, and so manifests an "insightfulness" of a non-scientific kind. Thus, his everyday living manifests his proficiency "in catching on, in getting the point, in seeing the issue, in grasping implications, in acquiring know how" (I, 173a).

In light of the preceding preliminary comments, then, the issue of this chapter can be clearly stated. This chapter will interpret Lonergan's analysis of the essential content of both the "structural" and the "field" characteristics of the subject's distinctively common sense attitude. To do this, the following explication proceeds in two major steps.

Division A will focus on the structure of the cognitional or "intellectual" development of the common sense subject and then upon the "field" dimension upon which it opens out. This initial focus is advanced in four sections. First, the self-correcting process of common sense development is sketched in general terms and related to the three levels of human consciousness. Secondly, the specific character of the "understanding," of the "intellectual" or "second" level of the consciousness of the common sense subject is defined. It is defined "negatively" in terms of its differences from parallel aspects of the scientific subject's "second level" performance. It is defined "positively" in terms of the uniquely common sense orientation characterizing the underlying cognitional structure of the subject's acts. Thirdly, the character of the "reflective understanding," of the "rational" or "third" level of the consciousness" of the subject of common sense is analyzed. The analysis is made possible by outlining the structures which implicitly define the subject's operations on the "third" level of consciousness independent of the given pattern of his experience. It concludes with an analysis of the "two sources" of the knowledge of the common sense subject. Fourthly, the features of the "field" or "formal object" intended by and answering to the common sense attitude of the subject are brought out. But an "horizon" is composed by a "subject"-pole or "intention" and its mutually determin-ing and determined "field." Thus, the preceding four stages of analysis complete the determination of the "horizon" of the advancing cognition of the common sense subject.

Division B of this chapter, complements Division A and, thereby, sets these reflections within their proper limits by a further analysis of the "practise" of the subject of common sense.[1] Again, the analysis is advanced in four sections. First, the particular good and intersubjective community corresponding to the "sensitive" or biologically patterned "first" level of the consciousness of the practical subject are defined.[2] Secondly, the good of order and civil community corresponding to the "intelligent" or "second" level of the consciousness of the practical subject are set forth.[3] Thirdly, the notions of value and cultural community corresponding to the "value judgment" and "rational choice," or "third" level of the consciousness of the practical subject are defined.[4] Fourthly, the features of the "field" or "formal object" intended by and answering to the now analyzed "practise" of the common sense subject are brought out.[5] Thus, the preceding four stages of analysis complete the determination of the "horizon" of the developing "practise" of the common sense subject.

Finally, Divisions A and B of this chapter are complements. Together, then, they lay bear the, respectively, "intellectual" and

---

[1] There is a further sense in which the ensuing explication of the horizon of the developing practise of the common sense subject is set within its limits by the analysis of his cognitional development.

[2] As the reader will recall, these issues were taken up in Chapter I of this study. Also cf. Chapter II, pp. 34-35 n5, above.

[3] Again, this sketch recalls the analysis in Division A, above, of the "understanding" of the subject of the "intellectual" component of common sense.

[4] Again, this sketch recalls the analysis in Division A, above, of the "judgment" of the subject of the "intellectual" component of common sense. And it foreshadows explication in Chapter VII, below, of the decisiveness of his fully ethical achievement.

[5] In his unpublished "Horizon" lecture, Lonergan indicates that his distinction between the "horizon," subject-"pole" and "field" of human consciousness represents a development of the scholastic, metaphysical notions of potency and formal object. The two sets of distinctions differ, first, in that while Lonergan starts by defining

"practical" components of the "Horizon" of the common sense subject. But this signals the completion of the task of this chapter and the need for the "Concluding Remarks" of Division C.

---

the object–pole of the "horizon" in terms of the intentional acts of the subject: "the Scholastic concept concentrates on the object and considers it, at least commonly, in abstract fashion as the ratio sub qua obiectum attingitur" (H, 1g, emphases mine).

They differ, secondly, in "concreteness": "the concrete subject vs. the potency; the totality of objects vs. the usually abstract ratio . . ." (H, 1h, emphasis mine).

They differ, thirdly, since Lonergan's "horizon" notion has no scholastic counterpart, since it speaks out: "the whole constituted by both conscious subject and concrete totality of objects" (H, 1h, emphasis mine). Again, Lonergan notes that his own philosophic sense of the "horizon" can be approached from its pre–philosophical meaning as the "bounding circle" to the "apprehension" or "appetition" of the subject, of his community. Thus, for different "standpoints" there are "different horizons." For different horizons, there are "different totalities of visible objects" (H, 1k–m).

Finally, in this chapter, the issue is the essence of the "relative" horizon of the subject, of his community, e.g., the horizon corresponding to the developing standpoint of his common sense. In Chapter VI, below, the issue pertains to the "absolute" horizon of the subject, of the utmost, insurmountable limit of his incarnate, intentional consciousness. It should be noted, then, that if it has its historical antecedents, the notion of horizon in Lonergan's precise sense has only recently given itself as a content to be thought. Also cf. p. 99 n, paragraph c, below.

A. The "Intellectual Component"[1]

1. The Subject of Common Sense: The Self-Correcting Intentionality to Learn

A given subject has achieved some relatively mature level of development in the attitude of common sense. She is, therefore, operating with routine "mastery" in a social world of artifacts, things, and other people. But there inevitably comes a break in expectations[2] and the emergence of a further "question." Such a question evokes her "inquiry." It eventually issues in "insight" into the unexpected particularities and/or exigences of her situation. It spontaneously finds "expression" in "thought, word, deed." And when reflection upon the situational adequacy of these expressions again brings out the shortcomings with which "experience" challenges her expectations, a further round of inquiry is called forth. Such a process recurs and converges to a "limit" at which the subject's

---

[1] Two points should be made here.

First, Division A within this chapter corresponds, approximately, to Chapters VI.1, IX, and X.1-.5 of Insight. The relationship between Lonergan's title for Chapter VI and our own in this chapter division can be explained as follows. Thus, insofar as the "structure" of the "intellectual" development of the common sense subject is unveiled, the focus of the discussion is "Common Sense and its Subject." Again, unlike Lonergan's more fragmented presentation, our own discussions in A as well as B, below, explicitly and integrally incorporate the sensitive, intellectual and rational dimensions of the subject of the common sense attitude.

Secondly, despite the focus of this and the next four sections of this study on its "intellectual component," the common sense of the subject is a unified whole into which functional distinctions may be introduced. It is not composed of two separable parts. Thus, it is not surprising that it has proven impossible completely to abstract from the "practical component" of common sense in analyzing its intellectual component and vice versa. Again, the problem proved especially intractable in the just initiated Section A1 of this chapter. It might better be read as an extension to the introduction of Chapter III as a whole.

[2] The point here is that the spontaneities of the common sense subject's intellectually and rationally informed acts are brought up, come up short in the face of refractory experience.

expanded powers of intelligence, judgment and, possibly, action or interaction have re-acquired their forfeited mastery.[1] Thus, they converge upon a "limit" at which judgments can again be truly and recurrently pronounced, at which action or co-operation can again be spontaneously and efficaciously undertaken. In this manner, then, the series to the subject's conscious acts is unified by its relationship to the initial "question" which called it forth. It is further unified by its relationship to the accumulated set of tested, trial-validated insights to which the initial "question" looks foreward and by which a situated, common sense virtuosity is regained. Turns to the "circle" of experience, inquiry, reflection and action preceded the initial situation of the subject to generate and sustain the context in which her further experience would throw her intelligent judgment of the situation into question. So, then, does the "circle" continue to turn after her specific turn has reached its proximate limit, after her own contributing initiative has been made, possibly to break or modify the routine, the expectations of others, or to call forth her own further developments. Lonergan refers to this dynamic as "the self-correcting process of learning" and likens it to a "circuit" (I, 174b). In the individual, the circuit finds proximate closure with the subject's achievement of unbiased judgment and/or rational action. But the closure which the latter afford comes at the term of a process. It is one of learning. And it is one in which the expression of and/or action upon insight into the "data in their bearing upon human living" has revealed its limitations only to call forth the further relevant accumulations of insight.

Again, the subject of common sense, no less than his mathematical or scientific counterpart, is not solitary. And, as noted, the immanent structure of the subject's engagement of the circuit is fixed

---

[1]As will become increasingly clear in the course of the proceeding exposition, "mastery" does not refer to a relation of dominance in any of its forms. It pertains, rather, to the subject's ability to answer a set of relevant questions or display a set of relevant competencies, to secure the relevant, open-ended closure with respect to a situation.

by the three levels of consciousness through which it unfolds.[1] Still, that unfolding plays itelf out within a dynamic <u>social</u> matrix of relationships of communication, collaboration, and institution, etc. Within this matrix, and despite series of lags, the work, the talk, and the myriad interactions of subjects of common sense generate a "communal"[2] development of intelligence. This communal development involves a <u>common</u> "understanding" of a <u>common</u> "experience," a <u>common</u> "judgment" of this common understanding and experience and, possibly, a common action on its basis., Still, this development is merely a function of further turns of the intentional circuit of human intelligence and reasonableness in its concrete <u>social</u> situation (cf. <u>I</u>, 175a).

---

[1]Again, these three levels informing the previous exposition are abbreviable as experience, intelligence, and either rationality or rational action.

[2]Such a development can be community–wide or relevant only to the group whose task has become specialized.

2. "Understanding" and the Cognitional Subject of Common Sense: Contrasts and Clarifications

In this section, six respects in which the "understanding" of the subject of common sense differs from that of his empirically scientific counterpart are specified and rapidly explicated. First, the common sense "understanding" of the subject emerges from and is only relevant to his "concrete situation." Secondly, it involves his gathering of a central "nucleus" or "core" of insights. Thirdly, its operation is always historically and socially prior to the emergence of, search for, and development of the ideal of systematic, complete understanding. Fourthly, its expression is limited to "describing" the data and, therefore, only avails itself of the relevant "experiential conjugates." Fifthly, its manner of communication is "concrete." And, sixthly, if the "field" of the common sense of the subject undergoes a kind of "specialization," this will tend to be along practical lines.

First, from within the scientific attitude, the subject methodically anticipates and, with serially converging degrees of approximation, attains both the "natures" of things and the "ideal frequency norms" from which the actual frequencies of their occurrence do not systematically diverge. Terms are univocally defined and employed. A technical language of definitions, postulates and inferences formulates the "general knowledge" attained in systematic, "universal" terms. On the contrary, common sense is a "specialization of intelligence in the particular and the concrete" (I, 175b). Hence, to ask for a systematic or axiomatized account of what it understands is to ask the wrong question. From within the scientific attitude, the circuit of inquiry is traversed as many times as is necesary to yield a sufficient set of exhaustively formulated insights. Again, the set is sufficient if it enables its subject to deal universally "with all possible situations of a given type" (UB, 107b).

Secondly, the subject of the common sense "circuit" of learning generates a noetic "nucleus," a habitual "core" of understanding. This "core" emerges and develops in response to his multiple and advancing engagements with his situation. It expresses itself in the repertoire of gestures, concepts, linguistic capacities, skills, etc. which fit him for judging and dealing with it.[1] Such a nucleus, as well as the concepts and usages it has spawned "remains incomplete" (I, 175b) unless it is applied. And its proper application has only been learned when its subject can, with the addition of the minimum number of further insights, adjust the "nucleus" to address intelligently "any of the concrete situations that arise in his [ordinary] living" (UB, 109b). The nucleus, then, does not grasp any concrete situation in its utterly unique particularity. It does not grasp any perfectly abstract generalization or general rule. Rather, it moves in the interstices between the two extremes. And it remains mute and disfunctional until the concrete situation yields up the further complementary insights which deliver its full contextual complement of meaning.

Thirdly, in the genesis of societies as well as the human individuals they relate, the world founded and conserved upon the "basis" of such commonly amassed, nucleic acts of common sense understanding is temporally first. It is into such a "world" that the scientific subject's ideal of "universally valid knowledge" (I, 176c) has to be introduced. It is from within such a "world" that it must be accepted and intentionally implemented, and in which it works its consequences. If the drama of Socrates' life and death suggests that this ideal is not spontaneously acceptable to the more palpable concerns of common sense, there is more to the story. Thus, the ideal

---

[1] First, then, since the words manifesting the conceptual and linguistic capacities of the common sense subject become determinate only through the true judgments in which they figure and, since they express the relevant facets of the developing core of insight into his situation, they will have no meaning outside the field of context, of situation dependent statements in which they figure (cf. I, 307f). Such statements "come first" in the determination of the meanings of their words. Thus, a dictionary is composed: "not by the Socratic art of definition, but by the pedestrian, inductive process of listing sentences in which each word occurs in good usage" (I, 308a, emphasis mine).

Secondly, the "mind" of the subject does not develop: "in the same fashion as the wall of a house is built. Prior to concepts there are insights. A single insight is expressed . . . by uttering several concepts. They are uttered in conjunction, and reflection pronounces whether the insight and so the conjunction is correct. The isolation and definition of concepts is a subsequent procedure and common sense does not undertake it" (I, 308b, emphases mine).

of logical system is suggested by the Platonic dialectic, laid down in Aristotle's Posterior Analytics, achieved in Euclid's Elements, reemergent in the aspiration of the medieval Summa, the accomplishment of Newtonian physics, and the continuing scientific exigency to "sustain the logical properties of abstract truth." And, the history of the ideal suggests that it remains an intentional exigency of human subjectivity, one which human subjects will perennially re-discover and re-activate, and transcend the attitude of common sense to achieve (cf. UB, 105a).

But human situations remain particular. And it is the problems that they pose in their particularity that common sense meets. And it does this neither by the formation of an abstract system, nor by the recommendation of a four year course of university training. It does this, rather, through its pre-methodologically controlled acquisition of a "nucleus" of understanding and the relevant additions of insight.

Fourthly, "experiential conjugates" are descriptive concepts or predicates. They are, then, "general" terms expressing the similarities of the things in their relations "to us," to our senses. Their meaning is expressed, at least in the last analysis, by appealing to:

> either a content of [the subject's] experience, such as seeing red or touching extension, or a correlative to such a content, for instance, red as seen or extension as touched, or finally, a derivative of such correlatives, as would be the red that could [potentially] be seen or the extension that could [potentially] be touched (I, 80e, cf. 37i, emphases mine).

Thus, to learn or define the meaning of such terms as "color," "sound," "heat," or "force," the common sense subject spontaneously appeals to his own visual and auditory experiences, as well as those of "effort, resistance or [tactile] pressure" (I, 79f). He will understand "ammonia" to be whatever "smells like this" and has this palpable influence on bathroom grime. He will understand "far away" in relation to the many paces he must stride if he is to negotiate a touch.[1]

---

[1]Two points must be made here.
First, it would seem that the engagement of experiential

Likewise, "duration" and "extension" are experiential conjugates. And
their meaning is fixed by the subject's "elementary," "familiar" and
reflectively verifiable experiences of "looking, moving, grasping,
etc." (cf. I, 142e–143a ff).[1]

Again, the experiential conjugates of common sense function
significantly within the empirical inquiry of the <u>scientific</u> subject.
They provide the initial differentiations of the being whose "unknown
nature" the scientific subject projects in heuristic anticipation.
They provide the differentiation of the data upon which the scientific
subject's efforts to verify his discoveries will converge. Again, from
the vantage point of the subject's shift into the scientific attitude,
the "ordinary [descriptive] language" of the common sense subject
"quickly proves inadequate." Thus, a <u>selection</u> is, in fact, made of
"the <u>relations</u> of things <u>to us</u> that lead more directly to knowledge of
the relations between things themselves" (<u>I</u>, 292b, emphases mine).

Again, once these relations have been selected, the scientific
subject learns a special, "technical terminology" (<u>I</u>, 292b) and the

---

conjugates presupposes the existence of a common sense subject who,
under the appropriate conditions and within the relevant linguistic
context, is able truly to utter a claim such as "This is red." "This"
refers to some concrete unity present "here and now." Its reference
could be any of the potential totality of individuals which would
sustain the truth of the subject's claim. "Red" classifies "this." It
presupposes the occurrence of the subject's <u>insight</u> into the conceptu-
alizable, generalizable relations of the things "to us." Again, reflecting on the judgment "This is red" and the original experience of
"seeing red" which it, in turn, presupposes, the subject can gain insight into, form concepts of: (1) his own <u>act</u> of "seeing red" in distinction from its correlative content "red <u>as</u> seen;" (2) the potential
acts and contents actualized in, first, "seeing red" and, "secondly,"
in his judgment that "This is red;" (3) "red" as what would so appear
were the relevant conditions and potentialities actualized; (4) "red"
as reflecting "real," experientially validatable relations; (cf. V.
Potter, <u>The Philosophy of Knowledge</u>, Chapter III; VII, pp. 155b–159b).
    <u>Secondly</u>, the reader should note that sets of experiential
conjugates <u>do</u> represent a degree of abstraction from the concrete since
they: "<u>prescind</u> from all aspects of [the] data except some single
[observable] quality such as 'red' or 'hot'" (<u>I</u>, 245c, emphasis mine).

[1]The issue of the nature of the temporality of the human subject
will be briefly rejoined in Chapter VII, below.

means to implement its more refined descriptions. Finally, at the term of his inquiring the scientific subject would approximate to or actually attain the relevant set of "pure or explanatory conjugates." Such conjugates are "correlatives":

> defined [not by their relations to the horizon of the subject's immediate experience but] . . . by empirically established correlations, functions, laws, theories, systems (I, 80b).

At the term of scientific inquiry, then, "heat might be defined implicitly by the first law of thermodynamics" (I, 80c), or, less spectacularly, ammonia by "NH3." Again, by the pure conjugates of such purported definitions is "mean(t) no more than [what] is implicit in the meaning of such verified equations [or formulas]" (I, 80d). And the "verification" of implicitly defined pure conjugates is only related to the descriptive realm of experiential conjugates through the mediation of "combinations of combinations, etc., etc., etc., of [technically described and measured] experiences" (I, 80e).[1]

Fifthly, the subject of the common sense attitude literally has "no use for" the exhaustive, universal, explanatory expression of his understanding. In this attitude, the intelligence of the subject is allied to "the possibilities and exigences of concrete tasks of self-communication." But communication is always to someone. It is always in a certain situation. It always has a certain history. It is always at a certain moment in the business, drama, and history of human existence. Thus, the "I" of common sense grasps what the other "has yet to grasp." What "act or sight or sign," what resource available to this "incarnate intelligence" will make him grasp it? I fumble for the expression. And when I understand what is missing, as I am about to

---

[1]Explanatory conjugates, then, understand similars similarly by abstracting completely or converging upon complete abstraction from the relations of the things to the perceptual-motor time/space of the subject. They grasp or head for grasp of the verifiable relations of the things to each other. Thus, for the subject: "to employ an explanatory conjugate is [for him] to turn attention away from all directly perceptible aspects [of the object] and direct it to a non-imaginable term that can be reached only through a series of correlations of correlations of correlations [with what is imaginable or experienced]" (I, 245c, emphases mine).

fill the gap of silence with speech, my expression is undertaken as a "work of art." Such speech avails itself of all the resources of language. These resources are sustained by modulations of:

> tone and changing volume, the eloquence of facial expression, the emphasis of gestures, the effectiveness of pauses, the suggestiveness of questions, the significance of omissions (I, 177b).

Thus, the common sense subject takes up the sensitive-intersubjective underpinnings of human communication, e.g., the pre-reflective concourse of mother and infant, of those who have long lived and worked together, etc., to a "higher level." And it does this without becoming any: "disembodied thing that rests upon technical language aiming at universality" (UB, 107b).

Finally, the process to such expression is intelligent and reasonable although "no set of general rules" can keep pace with it. Operating in a manifold of co-operating subjects, it guides the manner of their interaction in the situation of their social world.

Sixthly, the specialization of human scientific inquiry is by field. Thus, the progressively shifting scientific problematic of the last three hundred years has spawned results coalescing along the relatively autonomous lines of research associated with university departments of physics, chemistry, etc. Consider, on the other hand, the "common sense" of a primitive, predominantly intersubjective community. It is, with only minor variations, exemplified in the behaviour of any of the mature subjects of the group. It is both rudimentary and relatively unspecialized. It is passed on with only minor innovations from generation to generation. It possesses a specific "quality" which differentiates it from the equally rudimentary and unspecialized common sense of, say, its neighboring intersubjective community.

In fact, however, inter- or intra-communal co-operation eventually becomes differentiated. The agent of this differentiation is the division and the consequent need to group human labor. But, then, whether within or among such groups, different "departments" of "common sense" are called forth and continue to differentiate themselves. These advancing differentiations of the rudimentary common sense of the community become increasingly specialized. These specializations are "to" and "for" the varying tasks, roles, situations, environments, institutions, geographies, climates, etc., to which the invariant circuit of the intelligence of the common sense subject both adjusts and contributes. But, then, specialized "common sense intelligence" does not exist <u>as a single whole</u> in anyone's mind. Rather, it remains "divided up and parcelled out among the men and women familiar with its several parts" (<u>I</u>, 419c–420a). Furthermore, it remains a relatively secure achievement <u>only</u> with respect to its particular milieu. Thus, further turns of the intentional "circuit" of learning are required when the situations, environments, climates, tasks, institutions, sensibilities, etc., to which common sense development has become proportioned regress, change, develop. Finally, with these turns, there is also generated:

> those minute differences of viewpoint and mentality that separate men and women, old and young, town and country until, in the limit, one reaches the cumulative differences and mutual incomprehension of different strata of society, different nations, different civilizations, and different epochs of human history (<u>I</u>, 180a).[1]

---

[1]There is need, then, of a method by which such differences can be interpreted and related (cf. <u>I</u>, XVII.3). Again, the import of such a method would be "communication" among the subjects of such differences. Finally, then, the accomplishment of such a communication will call for a development of human intelligence that transcends the attitude of common sense.

3. The Rational Consciousness of the Common Sense Subject

The reflections of the preceding section represent the subject's understanding of his own common sense "understanding," of his own "second level" or "intellectual" consciousness in this intentional attitude. But this very accomplishment opens the question of his no less spontaneous and, initially, unreflected pursuit of the "truth value" of what he has understood and formulated. But such a pursuit traverses questions and further acts of a higher order. And it only fully comes to term when the subject's consideration of the "evidence" for his prospective judgment calls forth his "reflective understanding" and warrants his ensuing "judgment." Thus, the task of this section is twofold. It must trace the common sense of the subject back to its "proximate source" in the subject's "judgment" of the concrete situation. Then, it must trace it back to its "remote source" in the "judgment" of the socio-historical collaboration of common sense subjects.[1]

To carry out this twofold task, two prior steps must be taken. First, the general nature of the subject's "reflective understanding" and "judgment," of his "rational consciousness" must be sketched. Secondly, that general structure must be allowed to shed light on the "judgment" of the subject of common sense. Specifically, his judgment of "concrete matters of fact," of "insights into his concrete situation," and concrete "generalizations and analogies" will be taken up.

---

[1] In so doing, then, this subsection will be completing the stage setting for the explication of the ontological correlate or "formal viewpoint" upon which the immanently and socio-culturally informed judgment of the common sense subject opens out.

a) The Rational Consciousness of the Subject: The General Structure

If he is always already committed to acts on the third or
rational level of human consciousness, the end of their reflective
analysis by the subject of chapters IX and X of Insight is the
discovery of their essential terms and relations, of the essential
nature of his own performance on the third level. Thus, the subject's
question for reflection, his "Is it so?," marks the transition from the
second level to his conscious performance to the third. Again, the
subject's explicit or implicit posing to himSelf of the question of
"whether" his expressed insight "is so?" constitutes his formulation a
"prospective judgment" (I, 280d).[1] The latter looks forward,
proximately, to its conjunction, its link with a relevant set of
conditions. These conditions seal its, e.g., p's, conditioned status.
Again, once they are "fulfilled," they constitute the relevant
"evidence" for p. Thus, their fulfillment turns the conditioned, e.g.,
p, into a "virtually unconditioned."

Again, once these conditions are fulfilled they look forward, on
the basis of his "grasp" of the virtually unconditioned, to the
subject's positing of p and to his attainment of truth. Finally, the
"grasp" of the virtually unconditioned is the function of a "reflective
act of understanding." By such an act the subject reverts from his
prospective judgment to its conditions and, in the appropriate case, is
able to tell whether they are fulfilled. Thus, the subject's affirmative judgment, his "Yes!" or "It is!" follows by rational necessity
from his reflective grasp of the "virtually unconditioned." Again, the
subject's denial, his "No!" or "It is not!" follows by rational
necessity from his reflective discovery that the preponderance of the
evidence is that the conditions are not fulfilled. Finally, if his
discovery is that the evidence is not sufficient to ground this
reflective understanding, then he has rational grounds for neither

---

[1] In what follows, "p" will stand for this prospective judgment.

affirmation nor denial but only the re-institution of his inquiry, etc.[1]

In the first and decisive case, then, the subject meets the question rising upon reflection by transforming the state of his expressed insight from a conditioned to a virtually unconditioned. The meeting is mediated by his dicovery that the uncovered evidence is uniquely relevant to, and sufficient for, the completion of the trans-formation. And Lonergan's point is that whether it be adverted to or not, the dynamic structure of the reflective consciousness of the subject, of his consciousness on its third level of operation, involves a grasped link between conditions and a conditioned. It at least intends the discharging of these conditions in awareness. The "operator" of the process is the subject's question for reflection and its rational term is judgment.

Finally, Lonergan further determines the notion of the subject's judgment in terms of its "content." Thus, he distinguishes its:

(1) derived content: this is the prospective "synthesis" or "p" which has now been affirmed;[2]

(2) proper content: this is the "Yes" or "No," the "It is!" or "It

---

[1] If the unconditioned admits syllogistic expression in which the link between the conditions and the conditioned supplies the major premiss and the fulfillment of the conditions supplies the minor (cf. Insight, X.1 ff), still its function is not to "eliminate" but only to "facilitate" for the conscious subject "the occurrence" of the "relevant reflective act of understanding." Thus, if external "signs in a syllogistic pattern" can be set forth by a parrot, an electronic computer, or a somnambulist "neither can grasp the virtually unconditoned . . . . Inversely, when . . . [the subject] pronounces a judgment . . . it is not because of a syllogism nor even because he accepts the premises of a syllogism but only because the syllogism has helped him grasp the virtually unconditioned in his acceptance of the premises" (I, 710e, emphasis mine).

[2] Two points should be added here.
First, Lonergan speaks of this synthesis as "judgment's matter," as, therefore, in potency to determination by the subject's judgment (UB, 140b).
Secondly, in the same paragraph, Lonergan refers to this content as "borrowed." But (3)-(4), below, represent Lonergan's account of the "borrowed" content of judgment in Insight. So the term "derived" is used to refer to this "content" of the subject's judgment.

is not!" by which the subject's judgment transforms his synthesis, his "object of thought" into an "object of knowledge"
(cf. (UB, 140b);

(3) direct borrowed content: this is the specific "question for
reflection" which initiates and norms the pursuit of "what is
so" (cf. I, 275g);

(4) indirect borrowed content: this is the "It is true" which is
co-present in the subject's positing of any synthesis: "Truth
is the implicit [e.g., the indirect borrowed] content of every
judgment [he makes]" (UB, 140b, cf. I, 276a). Again, the
implicit content grasped may be, on the one hand, "coincident
with" the virtually unconditioned and, therefore, "certainly
true" (I, 707c) or "a certainty" (I, 550e). On the other hand,
it may be an approximation to an ideal content that would be
virtually unconditioned and, therefore, "probably true" (I,
707c) or "a probability" (I, 550c);[1]

(5) contextual and historical content: the given content is
"situated" both with respect to the past judgments which remain
and continue to inform the habitual cognitive orientation of
the subject. It is also situated by the proximate and remote
future judgments which will correct, complement, or augment his
present ones (cf. I, 277c).

---

[1]Two points should be made here.

First, the reader should note that if the truth of p is
ontologically immanent in the subject's conscious acts of assent or
dissent, that it is intentionally **independent** of, for instance, the
subject's specific intentional acts, the place and time of their
occurrence and, consequently, resident in the "virtually
unconditioned," in what "is so." Thus, the truth of p is "detachable"
from the act in which it was posited as well as the spatio-temporal
conditions under which it is uttered. It is, furthermore,
"communicable" even if the contextual character of all judgment may
make such a process difficult, to say the least (cf. S, 3; C2, 194b).

Secondly, it is clear that Lonergan is claiming that "certainty"
and "probability" are properties of the content of the subject's
judgment. When he adds that such contents can be held "with certitude
or probability" he might be closer to unclarified ordinary usage, the
latter's sense that these pertain to the conviction of the subject, not
the content of his judgments (cf. I, 708c 1-3; cf. Potter, p. 6 ff).

b) The General Structure Applied

In Insight X.2, Lonergan reflects upon the process by which the common sense subject arrives at a concrete judgment of fact. His reflection is concrete. It employs terms and presupposes the relations set forth in the preceding general analysis. And it is based upon and interspersed with reflections upon the following example.

Returned from work and seeing the condition of his flat, a homeowner asks himSelf whether something happened? But "something happened," just in case "the same set of things exhibits different data at different times" (I, 301a). It is the subject as intelligent, as operating on the second level of consciousness, who understands that the common, self-identical referent(s) of his perception and memory, of the two sets of data they represent is one, e.g., his house. Again, it is a structural inevitability of the subject's intelligent consciousness that, minimally, a unity enduring through a series of relevant, concrete variations is a "thing." Another is that the grasp of the same "thing" at different times in different data constitutes its change.[1] But if change has occurred, then "something happened." Finally, the conditions for the fulfillment of the prospective judgment lie in the subject's "present and/or remembered data" (I, 301a), in both his direct perceptual awareness of "smoke in the air and water on the floor" (I, 281c) and his memory of its earlier appearance. Thus, since a difference has been detected, and since, ex hypothesi, the subject's perceptual and recollective processes are functioning without aberration, etc., "there are the [requisite] grounds for [his] asserting change" (I, 301a).

Thus, in this deliberately simple case, the subject has been impelled by the unexpected experience of fire and smoke to understand how things stand with his house. He wants his answer to reflect concrete fact and not fancy. And his "want" is culminated through the

---

[1]Again, should the subject deny these structures, the "things" become unintelligible not just in a given instance but universally. Hence, they are not deniable. Cf. Chapter V, below.

process of reflective understanding which, in settling his judgment, mediates the concrete reality of his situation to the subject. In more complicated cases, the fulfilling conditions for judgment could be:

> any combination of data from the [subject's] memories of a long life, and their acquisition may have involved [his assimilation of] exceptional powers of observation. The cognitional structure [involved] may suppose the cumulative development of [his] understanding exemplified in the man of experience, the specialist, the expert (I, 283b).

Still, if in such cases, reflective analysis:

> can indicate the general lines along which . . . [the subject's] intellect proceeds to the concrete judgment of fact, it can never do [full] justice to the full range of its resources and to the delicacy of its discernment (I, 711b).

Thus, both "complex data" and a "complex structure":

> may combine to yield a virtually unconditioned that . . . [the reflective] analysis [of the subject] could hardly hope to reproduce accurately and convincingly (I, 283b).[1]

In Insight X.3, Lonergan shifts to the question of how the subject can pronounce upon the correctness of insights into:

> **concrete situations** that diverge from . . . [the informed] expectations [of his common sense] and by that divergence set up a problem (I, 283e, emphases mine).

Lonergan responds that an "operational" distinction is "prior to the conceptually explicit distinction between correct and mistaken insights. Again, this prior distinction always already obtains within the spontaneous flow to the cognitional awareness of the subject. It is the distinction between his "vulnerable" and "invulnerable" insights. Failing to meet an issue squarely, the subject's understanding is vulnerable. Thus, further questions emerge that are relevant and that reveal to him its unsatisfactoriness. These questions in turn evoke further insights. These further insights may complement it, modify its presuppositions and implications and,

---

[1] Lonergan implicitly attaches the same proviso to the analysis of each and every one of the kinds of judgment whose structure he sets forth.

possibly, revise or set in a new light the original issue to be met. Meeting an issue squarely, the subject's understanding is invulnerable. Thus, since no further relevant questions remain to be asked, no further insights emerge to challenge the initial position or to complement, modify, or revise the original "approach and explanation."

Lonergan's insight, then, is that there is a spontaneously operative, dynamic structure governing the subject's judgment in general, and his judgments of his concrete situation in particular. Through such an intentional structure, conditions are implicitly **linked** to the conditioned, prospective judgment. And they are discharged when, upon reflection, the subject discovers that the conditioned admits of "no further pertinent questions." Again "no further pertinent questions" is not equivalent to "no further questions occur to me" (I, 284f). For example, the subject's attentiveness to the concrete and practically motivated issue at hand may be interfered with, may be distracted or stifled by interests or drives, by desires or fears other than his pure, disinterested desire to know and learn. Nor does it mean that "the very possibility of further questions has to be excluded" (I, 284g, emphasis mine). How, in his concrete situation, is the subject of common sense to strike this "happy balance" between rashness and indecision? How is he to achieve the "good judgment" necessary to operate well the immanent conscious criterion of relevant questioning?[1] If neither a formula nor a recipe is possible, several factors relevant to a general solution can be specified.

First, the subject must permit the further relevant questions which his prospective judgment leaves unanswered both to come to the fore and find their adquate answering. For this, in turn, to occur, the subject has to have already developed sensitively and volitionally. Such development is necessary if he is to hold fast to the inner exigences of his question, if he is to pursue it to the proximate exclusion of other demands upon his attention and action. Furthermore,

---

[1] The reader should note that the answer to this question has general and crucial relevance for the issue of the rational reflection and judgment of the subject throughout the entirety of this study.

he must have developed intellectually and rationally to the point at which he can, for example, sift his prospective judgment for both its internal consistency as well as its coherence with the at least provisionally founded context of his knowledge and belief. It is necessary if he is to be able to project his prospective judgment into his or any proximately similar situation and experiment with it in thought under "trial" conditions of "success and failure" (I, 285c 10, 286b 12). It is necessary if he is to be able to test it in:

> ventures that gradually increase in moment and scope to enlighten . . . [the subject] by [his] failure and to generate confidence [in him] through [his] success (I, 286b).

Finally, for the common sense subject, the above or similar processes do not take place after the "explicit, deliberate, and elaborate" fashion of the scientific inquirer. Rather, they take place but in an analogous manner marked by his:

> intellectual alertness, . . . [his] taking . . . [of his] time, . . . [his] talking things over, . . . [and his] putting [of] viewpoints to the test of action (I, 285c).[1]

Secondly, to set up the question of the correct understanding of concrete situations, Lonergan started with a noteworthy presupposition. Thus, he assumes the existence of a subject who has already learned. This subject, then, already correctly understands, already knows his way around in the social and/or environmental situation at issue and, therefore, knows what is to be expected from it. On this assumption, Lonergan can define a valid "problem" in terms of the divergence of the situation from the subject's "normal" expectations, and let this divergence serve as the criterion of the pertinence of his further questions. This makes the subject's "good judgment" in respect of his understanding depend upon the "large number of other, connected,

---

[1]The point is that the application of the criterion of no further relevant question is an extremely delicate, nuanced, and non-mechanical affair, that in at least some cases all of the relevant conditions for the truth of a given proposition could not be explicitly specified. Those interested may wish to relate the point to Newman's notion of informal inference. Cf. The Grammar of Assent (Garden City: Image Books, 1955), Part II, Chapter IX, Section 2, and Chapter VIII, Section 2.

correct insights" (I, 285e) he has already acquired.

But how shall the truth of those prior insights be gathered without correct judgment? Lonergan's answer to the seemingly vicious circle is the conscious, self-correcting process of learning. It is by such a process that the subject gradually and by stages attains a limit of familiarity and mastery with the situation of his questioning (cf. I, 305, 300c). During the process, the subject's judgment is in abeyance, is being fitted for "independent exercise" (I, 286b).   The elements of this process are now familiar. There is the subject's advancing understanding. There is his purer fidelity to the developing exigences of his question. There is the increasing coherence among his newly emerged insights and between them and the provisionally secure context of his ulterior beliefs. There is his readiness to concretize and give trial to his advancing understanding until the uneasiness of failure gives way to a confidence born of successful execution and cognitional performance.[1] Thus, the already operative prior insights which inform the subject's ability to judge, are correct not because they have all been individually and infallibly certified but because:

> (t)hey occur within a self-correcting process in which the short-
> comings of each prior insight provoke further questions to yield
> complementary insights (I, 286c).

Thus, the dynamic to the consciousness of the subject of common sense grows and expands. It, in fact converges upon a limit of habitual ability. At this limit, the flow to his conscious judgments

---

[1]Lonergan's topic has been the subject's judgment upon the "correctness" of his insights into the concrete situation. He has been making two major points. His first is that the link between such an insight and its conditions is that the insight is correct if it is invulnerable, if it, therefore, puts an end to all the relevant questions that arise. His second point, made above, is that the fulfillment of the conditions lies in the self-correcting process to the subject's learning. Thus, when it has reached the requisite limit of familiarity and "mastery" of the situation, it qualifies him to declare with warrant that "there are no further relevant questions." At the heart, then, of, for example, his "good judgment" concerning what is so in his concrete situation, is the subject's intellectual development, his faithfulness to the cord of learning, to the pull of the further question, his genuineness, etc. Finally, similar considerations inform the preceding account of the subject's concrete

"oscillate(s) about a central mean" (I, 287c). At this limit, the subject's familiarity with a recurring cycle of eventualities and a knowledge of what is to be expected from it has been achieved. Operating at this limit, the conscious subject greets the divergence of the concrete from his expectations with a grasp of "just what happened and why and what can be done to favor or prevent such recurrence . . ." Again, in the fact of an unexpected event that is quite novel, the subject will refuse to judge. He will know that he should and how he ought to "recommence the process of learning." In short, he will be able to:

> recognize when, once more, that self-correcting process reaches its limit in familiarity with the concrete situation and with easy mastery of it (I, 286c-287a).

Thus, the subject's understanding of his concrete situation is "true" when reflective insight grasps it as a conditioned, grasps a link between it and its conditions and discovers that these conditions are, in fact, fulfilled. The latter conditions are discharged when:

> the given insight does put an end to further, pertinent questioning and . . . this occurs in a mind that is alert, familiar with the concrete situation and intellectually master of it (I, 287d).[1]

In Insight, X.4, Lonergan reflects upon the process by which the subject of common sense arrives at, correctly affirms, and applies "generalizations" and "analogies." He notes that the supposition of such a process is that its subject is to understand or has already

---

judgments of fact (cf. the third from the last quotation in the third preceding paragraph). And they are, in fact, built into the way in which Lonergan has framed the notions of reflective understanding, e.g., in relation to the maturing field of the subject's questions, and judgment, e.g., in relation to the subjects grasp of the virtually unconditioned, etc. Again, "correctness" has nothing to do with comparing an "Idea" and its "object." All criticisms of this notion based on such a misapprehension have thoroughly and simply missed their desired mark.

[1] The point is that this structure is always already at least implicitly operative whether it has been reflectively analyzed and appropriated by the subject of common sense or not.

understood, respectively, <u>all</u>, or <u>some</u> similar situation(s) in the same fashion (cf. <u>I</u>, 287f–288a). This supposition, in turn, rests upon the immanent heuristic principle of human consciousness that, unless differences are significant, similars, are to be similarly understood (<u>I</u>, 288b). Again, both the subject's generalization and analogy, etc., presuppose:

(1) his correct understanding of some basic, initial situation.

> But, as we have seen, [for the subject] to know . . . [that his] insights are correct presupposes a process of learning [on his part] and . . . [his consequent] attainment of familiarity [with] and mastery [over the relevant considerations] (<u>I</u>, 288d);

(2) that the initial situation is <u>similar</u> to all or at least some similar situation(s). Thus, <u>significant</u> dissimilarity between them would imply <u>further</u> relevant questions and the need for the emergence of further complementary or revisionary insights;

(3) his native or cultivated ability to discern significant differences between the relevant situations. Thus, unless two situations are similar in all respects, the subject's:

> familiarity with one does <u>not</u> enable . . . [him] to tell whether or not further questions arise when . . . [his] insight is transferred to the other [situation] (<u>I</u>, 289a, emphasis mine).[1]

Again, Lonergan suggests that the human subject spontaneously generalizes, forms analogies, and applies them. He argues that this is so because he "cannot help understanding similars similarly," because generalization and analogy are, in some sense, valid if non–deductive forms of inference. But if they are, in some sense, valid forms:

---

[1]Lonergan's point in the material I have recounted here is, minimally, twofold.

First, the link between, say, the subject's prospective generalization and its conditions is the cognitional principle that similars are similarly understood (cf. Chapter V, Section B3, below).

Secondly, he claims that the conditions for such a generalization are fulfilled when "further, pertinent questions no more arise in the general case than in the correctly understood particular case" (<u>I</u>, 315b).

> when their basis is [the common sense subject's] . . . insight into
> a concrete situation, the conditions of their proper use can become
> so stringent as to render them almost useless (I, 289b, emphasis
> mine).

Conditions are so stringent precisely because, if he would still spontaneously understand similars similarly, nevertheless, the "concrete situations [of the subject's common sense living] rarely are similar."

> Because things fall away from the Pole Star in the northern
> hemisphere, it does not follow that they will do so in the
> southern. Because within the range of human vision the earth is
> approximately flat, it does not follow that the integration of all
> such views will be a flat surface (I, 297a, emphases mine).

Because life in a given city is fast, competitive, bureaucratic and cold, it doesn't follow that life in all cities is. But the common sense subject is always already at least implicitly cognizant of the above stated fact these examples illustrate. Thus, it is not surprising to find him "avoiding" (I, 297b5) and being "perpetually on . . . guard against [faulty or highly abstract] analogies and generalizations." Thus, the subject of common sense aims at:

> [retaining] the insights [he has] gained in former experience and
> . . . [adding] the complementary insights needed in fresh
> situations;
>
> building up a core of habitual understanding that is to be adjusted
> by further learning in each situation that arises (I, 297a).

Finally, the subject's mindfulness of the above-cited fact, of the aim to which it commits him, is evidenced in the proverbs, fables, stories, paradigms, examples, the valuable pieces of advice, the limited generalizations and analogies to which he attends. These he invokes "not as premises for [rigorous] deduction" but as helpful guides for his judgment "in further situations," as "possibly relevant rules of procedure" (I, 297b). Again, their meaning in their "concrete generality" is, neither adequately formalizable logically nor susceptible of mechanical application. And they become "proximately relevant" to his situation only when "a good look around has resulted in the needed additional insights " (I, 176a). Thus, the subject of common sense can "operate directly" on his situation with the insights he has accumulated. In correspondence with:

> the similarities of a situation [the subject] can appeal to an incomplete set of insights;
>
> the significant differences of situations, . . . [he] can add the different insights relevant to each (I, 176a).

c) The "Sources" of the Common Sense Judgment of the Subject

In Insight, X.5, Lonergan reflects upon the proximate and remote "sources" of the common sense subject's judgment. First, its proximate source is two-fold. It lies first, then, in the procedures inherent in his making of true:

(1) concrete judgments of fact;

(2) judgments of his insights into concrete situations;

(3) judgments with respect to his concrete generalizations and analogies or their applications.

But these were described in the preceding section. It lies, secondly, in the dynamic, self-correcting and self-complementing intentionality to question and learn by which the subject of common sense:

(1) accumulates related insights;

(2) progressively revises, modifies, improves and/or transcends the insights, the contexts of insight he has already accumulated;

(3) corrects or complements instances or contexts of judgment of the kind listed under numbers (1)-(3), immediately above (cf. I, 174b, 289d 11).

But as already noted, the proximate sources of the subject's common sense do not unfold, are not brought to act "in isolation." Thus, the subject's "conversation" is a "basic human art" (I, 174a). By it he reveals his manifold wisdoms, reveals what he knows and is up to, but also "provokes from others the further questions" that bring out his own misunderstandings and misinterpretations, the uncritical assessments and ventures that he needs to amend, enhance or remove. Some masterfully arrived at diagnosis and judgment of a situation, some masterfully performed act excites the subject's admiration. He "attends" to and begins to "understand" how it was arrived at or done. He tries it himself only to "attend" again in order to discover the "oversights" that led to his failure, what further "questions" he needs to be able to ask and answer to do it himself. Thus, teachers have already mastered some relevant seriation of acts of understanding and judgment. They are, then, able to methodically help their students to learn. They can set forth for them the relevant questions and clues which will hasten their development to serially higher stages of intelligence and reasonableness in some field. But a similar if less methodic and reflective process underpins the apparent spontaneities of the common sense subject's communicative interactions. Thus, the judgments upon which his intelligence unfolds, spontaneously circulate among the members of his and other, connected groups. There they are informally "tested," questioned and reflected upon, agreed with, corrected, or improved and enhanced, perchance to recur to and excite the further development of their originating subject. And it is such a process which formal teaching tremendously accelerates. Thus, at a first approximation, the relatively spontaneous communication and co-operation of human subjects in the attitude of common sense, is also, simultaneously, the communal genesis, transmission, and advance of the intellectual and rational development of the common sense of the subject. Such a process goes forward "in the family, the tribe, the nation, the race" (I, 175a). Through this communal process, the discoveries of one common sense subject enter a "single, cumulative [socio-historical] series" (I, 290a). The fruit of this inevitable and spontaneous collaboration is a "common," incomplete, if expanding "fund" of tested, complemented and corrected common sense "understanding."

Thus, and **secondly**, the **remote** source of the judgment of the subject of a common sense is also two-fold. First, at any specifiable stage or sub-stage of the socio-historical development of a community's common sense, there is a tested fund of corrected understanding fitted with a set of procedures necessary to adjust and complement it before its subject passes judgment in his concrete situation. Secondly, there is the dynamic of the self-correcting intentionality to learn, now enlarged, unified, and transformed into a socio-historical collabora-tion of mutually contributing, mutually checking human subjects. This is the common intentionality by which the fund was originally amassed and by which its contents will be corrected, enriched, and withdrawn.

It should be recalled at this point that, for Lonergan, the relevant evidence, familiarity, and mastery necessary for the rendering of correct common sense judgments is available only to "individual judges in individual situations" (I, 299a). But it is into a socio-historical world whose very character and existence is mediated by such a local fund of judgment and action-informing meanings and procedures, that the individual human subject is born. And it is within the concrete situations of such a historical "world" and under the already constituted conditions it holds out that his desire to know and learn is called forth. He learns from it how and, by stages, what and what not to question and question further. By it his common sense development is shaped, tasked, and oriented, and, thereby, either augmented, retarded, or distorted. From the advancing sediment of this fund, each human subject, in the spontaneity of the social situation and context of his communication, questioning, and learning, makes his own withdrawal. Each, then, draws "his share [of common sense understanding, of reflective and evaluative competence and facility, of proverbial wisdom, etc.] measured by his capacity, interest and energy" (I, 175a). Each makes his own "appropriation": "inasmuch as [he] intelligently and critically . . . believes the truths which others have grasped" (I, 707d, emphasis mine).[1] And it is to this mediating fund that the subject may contribute "inasmuch as he grasps the virtually unconditioned" (I, 707d, emphasis mine), that he may, thereby, augment the process by which "the achievement of each successive generation [is] the starting point of the next" (I, 175a).

But, human subjects share, not only the "intellectual curiosity" that generates a community of learning along a normative, self-correcting line. It is also involved in "more earthly passions [and corresponding] prejudices." Thus, the drives of human subjectivity have a "mixed character." They distort the process of his common sense learning and judgment and, thereby, introduce an element of inauthenticity into these operations. These can generate:

> a common [e.g., a community-wide] deviation from the product of intelligence [which learning intends] and even a common dishonesty in refusing to acknowledge the effectiveness of further, pertinent questions (I, 290c).

---

[1]The important issue of belief will not be systematically treated in this study. Still, many of the central aspects of the issue are treated informally in this discussion.

These, in turn, will generate unintelligent and uncritical belief, and
so will foul the fund from which members of the community draw and
learn. And this will introduce distortions into the process of further
social development.[1]

Again, if the common sense subject is intelligent and reasonable,
still "human apprehensions and interests" (I, 292b), "practical
considerations and pragmatic sanctions," considerations of "success and
failure" (I, 293b), are at the center of his concern. And since such a
concern is narrower in scope than his pure desire to know and learn, it
will inevitably introduce further aberrations into socio-historical
process (cf. Chapter V, Section B11, below). Thus, the socio-
historical collaboration of subjects in the attitude of common sense:

> not only offers enormous benefits and advantages but it also
> intertwines them with more than a danger of deviation and
> aberration. Nor do we ourselves [e.g., the author or reader] stand
> outside this collaboration as spectators. We were born into it.
> We had no choice but to become its participants, to profit by its
> benefits, and to share in its errors. We have no choice about
> withdrawing from it, for the past development of one's own
> intellect can no more easily be blotted out than the past growth of
> one's body, and future development will have to take place under
> the same conditions and limitations as that of the past. There is,
> then, a fundamental problem . . . (I, 291b, emphases mine).

Again, insofar as the participant subject shares in the mixed
motives to which human being is prone, his sensitivity, understanding,
judgment (and volition) will:

> suffer the same bias and fall in line with the same deviations and
> aberrations. As long as I share in them, my efforts at correction
> and selection will be just as suspect as the judgments I wish to
> eliminate. It is only when I go to the root of the matter and
> become efficaciously critical of myself that I can begin to become
> a reliable judge; and then that becoming will consist in the
> [normative] self-correcting process of learning which has already
> been described (I, 293c).[2]

Again, we shall see that the efficacious Self-criticism whereby

---

[1] It is, therefore, possible for the subject, for a community
authentically to appropriate an "inauthentic tradition," to achieve
only a "minor" authenticity (cf. MT, 80, 162).

[2] The nature of human bias will be discussed more fully in Chapter
V, Section B10.

the human subject may master his own heart, "the pull of [his] desire, the push of [his] fear and the deeper currents of passion" within him—these thieves which would rob him of the "full, untroubled and unhurried view [e.g., the genuineness] demanded by sure and balanced judgment" (I, 297b)—cannot be _fully_ recognized or achieved by him within the attitude of common sense alone.

4. The "Formal Viewpoint" of Common Sense: The "Intellectual Component"

What remains to be done in Division A of this chapter, is to analyze the "object"–pole ("field" or "formal object") of the "horizon" of common sense's "intellectual component." But, as noted, the "subject" and "object"–poles of a "horizon" are mutually determining. Thus, essential features of the "object"–pole (or "field") of this "horizon" are prefigured in outline by the "noetic" component. Thus, by proceding on the basis of the analysis of the essential structure of the "subject"–pole, essential features of the "object"–pole can be worked out. But, sections 1–3, above, have analyzed the "intellectual" component structuring the "subject"–pole of the common sense performance of the subject. And on this "basis," the "field" situating the "objects" of his "intellectual" activity can be given a five-fold account. First, this "field" selects out the relations of the things "to us." Secondly, it circumscribes the scope and relevance of human asking and answering. Thirdly, it "casts" its "objects" in a non-explanatory light. Fourthly, it places a limitation upon its subject's as well as its community's relationship to "what is." And, fifthly, there is a social and historical dimension to the specific "totalities" of "objects" to which it gives human cognition access.

First, then, Lonergan determines this "field" in terms of the potential totality of the "things" that can be "affirmed" by the subject of common sense. But these things are "situated" by their possible relations "to us," to "the concerns of man" (I, 292e), to "human apprehensions and interests" (I, 292b). They are, then, situated by their abstraction from the concerns of the scientific subject. Thus, the "field" of the subject of common sense "opens out" upon the "experiential," the "particular," the "imaginable." It "lets" the things "stand forth" in their: "individuality, their accidental determinations, their arbitrariness, their continuity" (I, 294b). It situates and prefigures its "object" as a possible:

> thing–for–us, with differences in kind defined by experiential
> conjugates, and with differences in state defined by expectations
> of the normal (I, 294b, emphasis mine).

Such experiential conjugates, by which the subject of common sense identifies and differentiates the "objects" within his "field," are grounded, precisely, in the "relatively constant" features of his everyday experience. Again, such relatively constant features of his perceptual experience as:

> visible shapes and the spectrum of colours, the volume, pitch and tone of sounds, the hot and cold, wet and dry, hard and soft, slow and swift, now and then, here and there, do not shift in meaning with the successive revisions of scientific theories; [similarly] the concrete unities that are men and animals and plants, the regularities of nature and the [spontaneous] expectations of a normal course of events [which inform his experience of the surrounding world] form a necessary and unchanged basis and context . . . [upon which his higher level common sense, and scientific discoveries and verifications supervene] (I, 296b, emphases mine).

Secondly, Lonergan determines this field in terms of its implicit "methodological" circumscription upon the scope and relevance of the further questions it permits. Under this circumscription:

> questioning ceases as soon as further inquiry would lead to no immediate, appreciable difference in the daily life of man (I, 295d).

Finally, since the circumscription of such questioning conditions the emergence of insights whose expression only incompletely abstracts from the situation of their emergence, tests of these insights are tethered:

> within the orbit of human success and failure. Still that dominance of [practical considerations and pragmatic sanctions] . . . is dictated by the object to be known . . . (I, 293b).

Still, such a circumscription does not or does not completely vitiate the "objectivity" of the learning it conditions. Thus, "(d)espite . . . [their] practicality," the subject, the community of:

> common sense is convinced that ideas work only if they are true (I, 293b, emphasis mine).

Thirdly, he determines this "field" in terms of the non-explanatory, non-technical, and largely descriptive context within which it casts the subject's as well as her community's spoken and written expressions (cf. I, 307e).

Fourthly, he determines this "field" in terms of the "section of the universe of (B)eing," the "ontological status" of the "objects" upon which it opens out. It is precisely that "section" determined by its objects' "relations to us," etc. Equivalently, it situates what "is" as what is affirmed or what is to be affirmed by the unbiased, common sense subject's:

> concrete judgments of fact, by [her] judgment on the correctness of insights into concrete situations, by [her] concrete generalizations and analogies, and by the [judgments issuing from the] collaboration of [subjects in the attitude of] common sense (I, 292c).

Fifthly, Lonergan determines this "field" in terms of the specific totality of "objects" upon which it "opens out" at any given "place" and "time." The specific totality will correspond to the specific group of questions which the subject, which the community of common sense has learned or is just learning to ask and answer. It will correspond to the specific environmental and socio-cultural situation in which her or her community's questions have arisen and query and learning have or are about to give way to rounded judgment. It will correspond to the given stage in the history of the socio-historical process by which the limitations immanent in past or present achievement are brought out, corrected, and/or transcended. Thus, specific totalities within the "field" emerge and become increasingly differentiated through and within a common sense learning process that is "with" others and set within a historical tradition, a historical vector of meaning.

But, finally, the preceding discussion concludes the "horizon" analysis of the "intellectual" component of the common sense attitude of the subject.

B. The "Practical Component"[1]

Preface

The following division of this chapter is composed of this "Preface," a brief "Introduction" and four sections. In the "Introduction," the distinctively "practical" orientation of the common sense subject is sketched. Section 1 takes up the notions of particular good and intersubjective community. These correspond to the biologically patterned, "first" level of the consciousness of the practical subject and are recalled from Chapter I of this study.[2] Section 2 begins by bringing out the relation between human practical "intelligence" and the technological, economic, and political "systems" it "grasps." It continues by taking up the notions of the good of order and civil or social community. These correspond to the practical subject's action and inter-action on the "second" or "intelligent" level of consciousness. Section 3 lays out the notions of value and

---

[1]This division within this chapter corresponds to the "positive" portions of Chapter VII of Insight but also draws, in terms that will be complemented in Chapter VII of this study, on Chapter XVIII.1. The relationship between Lonergan's title for Chapter VII and our own for this chapter division can be explained as follows. Insofar as the "structure" of the "practical" development of the common sense subject is unveiled, the focus of the discussion cannot prescind from the "structure" of the "object" of which his own as well as his community's activity is constitutive. But this additional content corresponds to "Common Sense as Object." Again, the decision to incorporate the rational component of the common sense subject's practise into this chapter has introduced questions which, on this author's judgment, Lonergan has not answered. Thus, there is nothing in Chapter X of Insight corresponding to the common sense subject's judgments of value or the "formal object" of his practise. Again, the subject of Chapter VII, of, even, Chapter X of Insight is not the, minimally, intellectually Self-appropriated and highly critical subject initiating chapter XVIII and the issue of an ethic. In settling these issues the author has found Lonergan's unpublished paper "Horizon," written in 1963, helpful. Finally, Lonergan's reflections on the notion of the "subjective" and "field" poles of the "relative" and "absolute" horizons of the subject are concisely set forth in this paper.

[2]Also cf. Chapter II, pp. 34-35 n5, above.

undifferentiated <u>cultural</u> community. These correspond to the practical subject's operations and co-operations on the "third" level of consciousness. In these three sections, then, three-fold notions of the **good** and of **community** are derived from a reflection upon the tri-fold structure of the subject's conscious, common sense <u>activity</u> in the world. Finally, <u>Section 4</u> lays bare the "field" of the <u>practise</u> of the common sense subject in a manner that reflects and parallels the reflections of Section A4, above.

Introduction: The Practical Situation of the Learning of the Common Sense Subject

As already suggested, the limits implicitly respected by the common sense subject's advancing cognition, reflect both the social situation of his "interests and apprehensions," but also the distinctively practical bearing of the activity called forth to meet it. Such limits contextualize the "intellectual" development[1] of the common sense subject by its relevance to what is to be done. Thus, the maturation of his intellectual powers is for practical intelligence, rationality, and decision. It is for establishing his ability "skillfully" to transform and integrate the situation of the "things . . . which are related to us" (I, 207a).[2] Thus, it is only because the relevant clusters of insights, the relevant powers of practical reflection and action, etc., have been "acquired," "tested," and "perfected" by a socially mediated process of trial and error, that the common sense subject develops practically. Through such a process, then, the otherwise coincidental movements of the subject's arms, hands, fingers, eyes, wrench, etc., are spontaneously integrated in accord with the requisite flexible ranges of schemes of recurrence. And through their integration, his client's car's failing carburator is restored to functioning with the addition of but a few further insights and the ensuing precision efforts, etc., etc.

---

[1] Cf. Division A of this chapter, above.

[2] The "us" in this quotation refers to the desire and labor, to the sensitive apprehension and appetition of the subject and of his community.

1. The Sensitive Consciousness, Particular Good, and Intersubjective Community of Practical Common Sense

Even as the subject of common sense is intelligent and rational, that is is able to recognize when action upon her understanding would yield no further relevant questions, so also is she incarnate and sensitive. Hence, she is at least implicitly aware of the sensitive and intersubjective attachments and interests, symbols and feelings which limit the scope of her questions and give practical orientation to her concern. Anticipating, it can be said that these sensitive and intersubjective attachments are situated by the subject's "dramatic pursuit of dignified living," of a "sustained succession of artistically transformed acquisitions and attainments" (I, 272a).[1] But with this anticipation qualifying what follows, Lonergan's analysis of the biological pattern of the consciousness of the subject must be recalled. First, in light of the **sensitive** character of the desire which limits her concern, the common sense subject will tend, spontaneously, if implicitly, to identify the good as the "object" of her desire, as "particular good," as what is intended and enjoyed on the first level of her conscious life. Again, subjects in whom such a pre-reflective, pre-intelligent "component" of the good predominates will be designated "sensate."[2] Further, whether or not such a component predominates, her consciousness will always include such a sensate component.

Secondly, in light of the **intersubjective** character of the desire which limits her concern, the common sense subject will tend, spontaneously, to identify and act upon her community with the other as a pre-reflective field of sharing particular goods and belonging

---

[1] Cf. Chapter II, pp. 34–35 n5, above.

[2] This is my term, not Lonergan's. It corresponds on the individual level to his discussion of Pitirim Sorokin's notion of "sensate culture" in, for example, Understanding and Being, p. 273b, to the "moral" development of the subject from out of an "aesthetic sphere" (UB, 288b, cf. I, 624c ff). For the reference to Sorokin see Social and Cultural Dynamics, (New York: American Book Company, 1937–1941), 4 volumes.

together. Again, communities in which such a pre-reflective component of its members' relationships predominates will be designated intersubjective. Finally, whether or not such a component predominates, her community will always include such an intersubjective dimension.[1] For example, then, in primitive fruit-gathering cultures, the community is predominantly intersubjective in form. The good sought pertains, predominantly, to the particular. The practical common sense is relatively unspecialized and undifferentiated and, therefore, distributed fairly evenly among its members. Again, it tends to grow in only minor ways, to be passed on relatively intact from generation to generation, and to go hand in hand with a relatively static social structure.

---

[1]It should be added here that if they may predominate, no human community is **only** intersubjective, no human subject is **only** sensate. Rather, if intersubjective or sensate being cannot completely exclude the intelligence and rationality of the human, they can make them subservient to their own less comprehensive goals, their less expansive limits, their unquestioning extroversion of attitude.

2. The Intelligent Consciousness, Good of Order, and Civil Community of Practical Common Sense

But, some food gatherer implicitly recognizes that the undifferentiated routines and schemes of recurrence which inform the practise of his community could be "ordered" more agreeably, less laboriously, and with wider satisfaction. His fidelity to the ensuing question of what further or differently it would be well to do, will sooner or later, and through a self-correcting process of learning, call forth the relevant practical insights and the relevant powers of reflection and action upon them.[1]

These practical insights will grasp the components of the "order," of the requisite set of "schemes," by which the exigences of the situation are met by the results in which their corresponding, rationally chosen actions issue.

And if practical criteria proximately guide the subject's disinterested negotiation of the trials, corrections, and accumulations of insight, their remote validation comes at a later date. That date is arrived, initially, when there are, say, hunters or fishers in the community, who, the requisite skills having been learned from others, routinely take time out to fashion the spears or nets to which their further educated, role-taylored action is skilled. It is arrived when their seemingly oblique efforts are, in fact, amply compensated by "the greater ease with which more game or fish is taken on an indefinite series of occasions" (I, 208a). Efforts are further compensated when, say, the specialization and co-operation of the labors of net-making and net-using subjects in the community yield better nets and better fishers to use them.

But if in order to exemplify the structure of the practically oriented intelligence of the subject, Lonergan has selected a deliberately simple example, his selection forms the basis for a series of generalizations.

---

[1]The reader has noted that the preceding analysis invokes the **three** levels of human consciousness to account for the practical subject's invention, his creativity.

Lonergan argues, _first_, that the indirectly desired objects of the practical subject's invention, e.g., his spears and nets, the "education" of his thought and action necessary to put them into effect, etc., are both primitive forms of **technology** but also "initial instances" of the economic idea of **capital formation.** He claims that the "history of man's material progress lies _essentially_ in the expansion of these ideas" through the recurrent application of the _process_ of practical intelligence which guides and controls their development.[1]

---

[1]In what follows, "S_2," for example, will be used to abbreviate the specific _situation_ of the desire and labor or work of the subject, of the given _community_ of practical common sense. "Q_3" will abbreviate the proximate, unmet issues raised by "S_2." "T_3" will abbreviate the technological innovation, the indirectly sought for object of human desire which:

a) is the "object" of the subject's, of her subgroup's _practical_ insight into S_2 and her judgment that action upon it will meet Q_3;

b) presupposes and corresponds to some requisite level to the intellectual, rational, and practical development on the part of its originator(s);

c) calls forth, among the relevant members of the community that further set of intellectual, rational, and practical skills necessary to apply T_3 to S_2 and, therefore, transform it;

d) therefore, leads to the actual meeting of Q_3. But, the meeting of Q_3 calls forth S_3, Q_4, etc. Again, S_2 is constituted, partially by its natural–environmental conditions but at least to some extent and, potentially, to a large but never complete extent by T_2, etc. But the "etc." closing the preceding two sentences signifies, respectively, that S_2 admits an indefinitely large number of future, higher determinations by the proceeding intelligent and rational action of the community. It signifies that similar _analysis_ of S_2, of any of these situations, could be extended backwards indefinitely through S_1, S_0, etc., etc. Again, the dynamic to the series is "structured" in terms of an intentional circuit which starts from an _experience_ of some S and the _issues_, Q, which it calls forth. It proceeds from there _to_ an _insight_ which grasps T of S. It proceeds from such an intelligent grasp of the situation to _judgment_ and _action_ upon T. In the best case, such action "meets" Q of S and calls forth its successor, etc. Finally, the basic scheme and its underlying structure are sufficiently flexible to admit multiple variations and expansions. Thus, only with the emergence of T_{3c} which takes up the complementary innovations of T_{3a} and T_{3b} might Q_3 be fully met. Again, developments are minor or major depending upon whether they found new epochs, new horizons of possibility in the community's technical existence, etc.

As inventions [e.g., T_2] accumulate [e.g., circulate among and are applied by the requisite members of the community to, thereby, transform their concrete situation from S_1 to S_2] they [e.g., S_2 mediated by T_2] set [further] problems [e.g., Q_3] calling for more inventions [e.g., T_3]. The new inventions complement [e.g., transcend the limitations of] the old [by squarely meeting Q_3, which action informed by T_2 in S_2 cannot, in fact, resolve. But to do this is] . . . to reveal fresh [horizons of] possibilities [e.g., T_4] and, eventually, to call forth in turn [not merely the minor deductive or homogeneous expansion of previous practical insights and the situations their applications inform, but] the succession of mechanical and technological higher viewpoints [e.g., T_5, T_6, T_7, etc.] that mark epochs in man's [e.g., the community's] material progress [e.g., S_5, S_6, S_7, etc.] (I, 208b, emphases mine).

Again, in correspondence with each successive stage of this intelligently, rationally, and communally mediated process, there is some new:

measure and structure of capital formation, that is, of things produced and arranged not because they themselves are desired but because they expedite and accelerate the process of supplying the [particular] goods and services that are wanted by consumers;

technological obsolescence of capital equipment . . . (I, 208b).

Secondly, Lonergan argues that the concrete conditions for the realization of the succession of new practical "ideas," e.g., for the realization of T_4 in S_3, of T_5 in S_4, etc., will not take place without the successively higher educations, specializations, and the consequent divisions of the labor of the community of subjects. He argues that they will not take place without the consequent "cooperation" of efforts which have been divided and become specialized. But this will involve the assignment of tasks and the spelling out and grouping of roles. It will involve the institution of their grouping on some intelligent and rational basis, one which leaves room in the concrete for further developments. Again, he argues that they will not take place without the adaptation of the sensitivity and intersubjectivity of the individual and community to: the succession of these higher educations, specializations, co-operations, and their particular institutions; the advancing technological differentiations of the community.[1]

But, thirdly, factors that remain unsystematized by the major or minor technical expansion of the community, will inevitably call forth further, proximately relevant questions of a decidedly practical but non-technical kind. And on the conscientious handling of these issues, the underlying, normative line of continuing technical invention will depend. Thus, the technical differentiation of the community abstracts from the issue of how "the balance between the production of consumer goods and capital formation" is to be settled. It abstracts from procedures which would determine "what quantities of what goods and services are to be supplied" (I, 208c). It includes no system for determining how tasks, roles, and produce are to be assigned to individuals within the community. Thus, it operates under a constantly re-iterated "limitation." It, therefore, falls to a further, distinctly practical but **economic** differentiation of the subject's, of his community's learning, of the powers of intelligence, judgment, and skill such learning calls forth, recurrently to transcend this limitation. It falls to such a further differentiation serially to discover, evaluate, and apply the relevant programs, policies, systems, e.g., E_4, E_5, E_6, etc. These systems correspond to some set of stages in the unfolding technical situation of the community, e.g., S_3, S_4, S_5, etc. And they successively integrate their successively outstanding economic demands. Again, the concrete conditions for the realization of the succession of economic innovations, e.g., for the realization of E_4 in S_3, of E_5 once S_4 has been achieved, etc., will not take place without the successively higher educations . . . of the activity of the community of subjects. It will not occur without a consequent "cooperation" of their efforts. But this will involve the assignment of new or the modification of older tasks, and the spelling out and grouping of further roles. It will involve the institution of their grouping on some intelligent and rational basis, a basis which,

---

[1]The failure of such adaptation is the failure to set the social conditions necessary for the emergence of the next successor step of the technical innovation of the community, the disturbance of the normative pace and line to the technical dynamic of the community.

minimally, is open to further improvements. Again, he argues that they will not take place without the **adaptation** of the sensitivity and intersubjectivity of the individual and community to: the **succession** of these higher educations, specializations, co-operations, and their institutions; the advancing economic differentiation of the life of the community.[1]

But, <u>fourthly</u>, factors that remain unsystematized by the major or minor <u>technical</u> and <u>economic</u> expansions of the community, will inevitably call forth further, proximately relevant <u>questions</u> of a decidedly practical but non-technical <u>and</u> non-economic kind. And on the conscientious handling of these issues, the underlying, interlocking, normative line of continuing technical <u>and</u> economic invention will depend. Thus, at the starting point of each minor or major phase in the community's technico-economic differentiation, further questions arise. These questions head for the relevant practical insights, proposals, etc. But the ideas and policies proposed by different subjects or different groups of subjects will <u>differ</u>. Given this, the problem of achieving a <u>common</u> understanding of the proposals, a <u>common</u> assent to and consent for the practical "ideas" that <u>genuinely</u> meet the demands of the social situation, recurs with the commencement of each new phase.

Again, this problem represents a constantly re-iterated limitation to technico-economic process. The distinctively **political** specialization of the common sense of the community emerges in response to the recurrence of this problem, in response to the need systematically to transcend this limitation. The subject of this specialization of common sense, then, is skilled by his capacities for persuasion, conflict resolution, and consensus formation. He has acquired a keen understanding of:

> when to push for full performance and when to compromise, when delay is wisdom and when it spells disaster, when widespread

---

[1]Substituting "E" for "T," the schema presented in footnote 1, on page 82, becomes relevant here. Again, it is <u>not</u> to be inferred that there is or <u>should</u> be a one to one correspondence between the pace and line of technical and economic innovation.

conscent must be awaited and when action must be taken in spite of opposition ($\underline{I}$, 209a).

He is further "skilled" by his practically honed ability to identify, under the specifically challenging conditions within which the community must choose, just those proposals which genuinely and rationally meet the relevant issues. He has discovered ways to transpose the general orientations but also deflect the specific stands of opposed members or groups within his community into correspondence with "his" concrete identifications. He knows how to awaken just the kinds of questions concerning the meaning of "right" living, of the living of a fully genuine human life, that in the short or long run feed, transcend, or correct these transpositions, the identifications which underly them, etc. He has learned effectively to institute, complement or sustain, and work within the "systems," the political means necessary for recurrently but flexibly securing the community's attention to and option for intelligent and rational "possibilities" of action. And he has discovered that in order to be effective these "systems" must secure legislative, judiciary, and executive functions. Thus, the institution, conservation, and improvement of higher, "political" differentiations and integrations of the life of the community is called forth by its underlying technico-economic development. Again, the realization of the called for series of political innovations, of the further series of political diferentiations and integrations of the life of the community, has conditions. Thus, the realization of political "system" P_4 within technico-economic situation S_3, of P_5 once S_4 has been instituted, etc., will not take place without the successively higher educations . . . of the activity of the community. It will not occur without a consequent "cooperation" of efforts that have become "educated," divided and specialized. But this will involve the assignment of new or the modification of older tasks, and the spelling out and grouping of further roles. It will involve the institution of their grouping on some intelligent and rational basis, a basis which, minimally, is open to further improvements. Again, it will not take place without the

adaptation of the sensitivity and intersubjectivity of the individual and community to: the **succession** of these higher educations, speciali- zations, co-operations, and their institutions; the advancing political differentiation of the life of the community.[1] Finally, the upshot of the institution of the fully practical political intelligence of the community will be some closer approximation of its underlying economic and technical expansions to their normative cycles of innovation and development.

Fifthly, the subject of common sense is implicitly aware of his own, of his community's querying, intending, and "understanding" of the "things" in their relations "to us." Again, the "things" in question could pertain to any accessible natural or human "object."[2] He is also always implicitly aware of his own, of his community's querying, intending, and "understanding" of the technical, economic, and political "possibilities"[3] revelatory of the things as they "might be." Again, he is implicitly aware of his own, of his community's action upon and realization of the practical "possibilities" affirmed to be worthwhile. What the practical subject "understands," then, is some "possibility" of a higher intelligible "ordering" of his "situation," of the actions and inter-actions, events and things which actually inform it (cf. C1, 115a).[4]

Thus, in the first proper step of the argument of this section, a

---

[1]Substituting "P" for "T," the schema presented in footnote 1, page 82, becomes relevant here, etc., etc.

[2]The point, here, again, is that the subject of common sense can query, and judge, etc., **prior** to embarking on the path of Self-querying, Self-affirmation, etc.

[3]Such querying, intending, understanding of possibilities is a function of the second level to the subject's consciousness.

[4]In Section A of this chapter, this study has frequently spoken of the "objects" of the "cognitional," common sense subject's affirmations. It should be noted, here, that, to a greater or lesser extent, these "objects" are the relevant possibilities of the technical, economic, and political situation of the subject that have already been brought about by the individual and co-operative efforts of the members of the community.

"fruit gatherer" "grasps" the "possibility" of a net or spear for his "situation," its implications for the life of his predominantly intersubjective community. In the third, the "possibility" of a higher, ongoing, economic "system" for the life of the community is grasped. In the preceding paragraph, the "possiblity" of a still higher, ongoing political "system" for that life was grasped. Such practical possibilities:

> stand [forth] as higher [intelligible] syntheses that [would or do] harmonize and maximize the satisfaction of individual desires [of individual subjects in community] ($\underline{C}_1$, 115a).

They do this by asking members of the community to learn new skills, and by grouping, re-grouping, and instituting skilled performance in an ongoing multiplicity of novel, needed ways. Furthermore, the upshot of the ongoing differentiation and coordination of the efforts of the community is the recurring flow of desired, particular goods for any member of the community who wants and needs them.

Again, in Division A of this chapter we have seen that human intelligence is a source of generalization and analogy. We have seen that its implicit "principle" is that "similars are to be similarly understood." But these facts have implications for the intelligent "practise" of the common sense subject. As intelligent and in community with others, the practical subject is at least implicitly committed to the principle that "similar" contributions to the welfare of the community are to be "similarly" rewarded. He is implicitly committed to making of himself no exception from this principle.[1] And he is commited by it to placing pre-intelligent anticipations of this principle on an intelligent and rational basis (cf. $\underline{I}$, 219b).

Sixthly, then, at a further level of development, the subject, the community of common sense subjects will tend, spontaneously, to adopt a new notion of the good. They will identify the good as the "object" of practical intelligence, as intelligible **good of order**, and,

---

[1]That similar contributions to the good of the community are to be similarly treated by its members will be regarded as the "heuristic principle" of the practical intelligence of the subject. For an explication of the notion of "heuristic principle" see Chapter V, Sections B1-3, below. Also cf. p. 396a, above.

if not initially, then ultimately as an intrinsically "dynamic" order. The good of order, then, is a "formal" intelligibility. It is only intended by raising the relevant questions, only grasped through the accumulation of the relevant practical insights, etc. It lies "beyond" the biological "horizon" of the subject and is not equivalent to the "particular goods" which its smooth operation generates and makes recur. It is, nevertheless, not "some [ideal] entity dwelling apart from . . . [the] actions and attainments [of the subject or of his community]." It is not some "unrealized ideal that ought to be but is not." It is rather something "immanent in" the actions and inter-actions of the subject and his community and, therefore, quite "concrete" and "real" (I, 212b). Specifically, it consists in:

> [the specific] intelligible pattern of relationships [immanent in a society of subjects] that condition the fulfillment of each . . . [subject's] desires by his contribution to the fullfillment of the desires [and labors] of others and, similarly, protects each from the object of his fears in the measure [that] he contributes to warding off the objects feared by others (I, 213b).[1]

Again, the good of order is not static. It possesses its own "normative line of development." This normative line actually occurs inasmuch as:

> elements of the idea of order are grasped by insight into concrete situations, are formulated in proposals, are accepted by explicit or tacit [communications and] agreements, and are put into execution [through co-operative effort] only to change the situation and give rise to still further insights (I, 596e).

Still, the good of order does place "limited restrictions" upon the practise of the subject and his community. Thus, it calls forth the **adaptation** of sensitive and intersubjective spontaneities to the demands of human practical intelligence and reasonableness.[2] And it

---

[1]Such specific intelligible patterns, of course, leave open "possibilities" of further development. Possibility, here, means what is proximately possible in light of already existing, already operative schemes. It does not refer to abstract or logical possibility (cf. H, 8i).

[2]As already noted, until such adaptation is achieved, the implementation of the concrete reasonableness of the situation proceeds

does this anew at each successive step of a prospective development.
Again, the restrictions which the good of order successively imposes
are more than adequately recompensed by the "fertility" of the
intelligent guidance of human action and interaction it affords.   Such
guidance, then, secures for the developing practise of a community of
subjects, the regular recurrence of "an otherwise unattainable
abundance of satisfactions" (I, 596d). And it secures this good on the
successively higher levels of operation and co-operation which it calls
forth.

Seventhly, the discoveries and institutions of the good of order
which human, intelligent practise effects, may cease to be merely
"incidental" additions to "the spontaneous [predominantly
intersubjective] fabric of human living . . ." (I, 213a). They may, in
fact, come to "penetrate and overwhelm" its every aspect.   Corresponding to such a situation, the subject will tend, spontaneously, to
identify his community with the other as civil or social. Such civil
or social community, then, is the "complex [and ongoing] product" of
its member's intelligent cooperation and invention.   It embraces and
harmonizes:

material techniques, economic arrangements, and political
structures. The measure of its development distinguishes primitive
[and, at the lower limit, purely intersubjective] societies from
civilizations (C1, 115e).

Again, communities in which technical, economic, and political systems
are not incidental to their subjects' relationships and, in which,
therefore, the good of order predominates, will be named civil.
Finally, whether or not it predominates, the practical subject's
community with the other will always involve such a social or civil
"component."

---

neither smoothly, "spontaneously," nor with the "mass and momentum"
afforded by human feeling, imagination, and conviction. This point is
taken up at greater length in Chapter V, Section B10, below.

3. The Rational Consciousness, Notion of Value, and Cultural Community of Pratical Common Sense

As noted, the developing insight of the "intellectual" subject of common sense reaches its term in, for example, the relevant, concrete judgments of fact. Similarly, the common sense subject's practical insight, his "grasp" of "possible" courses and systems of action: "reaches its <u>term</u> in judgments of value and in [the] choices [which take them up into deeds]" (<u>C1</u>, 115b, emphasis mine).[1] That latter term presupposes the existence of a cluster of "practical insights," e.g., I_5.[2] This cluster pertains to some socio-environmental situation, e.g., S_4. It answers to a conscientiously pursued set of <u>delibera-</u><u>tions</u>. These involve the asking, under the conditions of S_4, of the question, "What should I, what should we, as a community, do?" Again, such a question emerges on and inititates operations on the <u>second</u> level of human consciousness. On the other hand, the "value judgments" and corresponding "choices" of the common sense subject answer to his conscientious <u>evaluation</u> of the possibilities brought out by I_5. This involves his "practical reflection" upon the worth of doing, of taking up I_5 into action under the conditions of S_4. Such reflection, in turn, involves the practical subject's unbiased pursuit of the answer to the question "<u>Is it so</u> that doing I_5, under conditions signified by S_4, is really good or better than its alternatives?" The latter question occurs on the <u>third</u> level of the consciousness of the subject. Again, if it is to actually find its mark in such a truly worthwhile action or "object," there must occur a conditioned, e.g., the "prospective **value**" of action in accord with "I_5" under the circumstance of S_4. There must occur a link between the subject's

---

[1]Such judgments, of course, occur, minimally, on the third level to the consciousness of the subject.

[2]Cf. footnote 1, page 82, above. The insight-cluster, for which "I_5" stands, is a "grasp" upon some "possible" form of action. Thus, it may be "into" some technological device, some facet of an economic or political system, or some manner of living or doing in an already largely instituted social world.

prospective judgment of value and its conditions. This link is that I_5 has to be grasped in a manner that satisfies the criterion of truth, of no further relevant questions.[1]

But such a grasp occurs in the relevant act of "reflective understanding." Such a grasp heads for the relevant "judgment of value," and the relevant "decision" and "action" upon it.[2]

Again, Lonergan's account presupposes the existence of a practical subject who can or could implement the various stages and components of the preceding process. But such a subject would have to be highly developed intellectually, rationally, volitionally, and sensitively to do this. Still, at least some of the conditions and characteristics of the practise of such a subject can be specified in advance.

First, his practise will meet all the novel or familiar questions called forth by his proximate situation in the world. Again, such a situation may involve environmental as well as technical, familial, economic, and political components. The questions it raises are, therefore, likely to be extremely complex.

Secondly, such practise presupposes that its subject has excluded the interference and secured the co-operation of the sensitive and intersubjective dimensions of his conscious living. But this exclusion and cooperation are necessary if he is to actually exercise his decision for the intelligent and reasonable course of action, for action consistent with the "good of order" as a true value.

Thirdly, the practise of such a subject will respect the

---

[1] Lonergan is not sufficiently clear on this point. This author has taken his clue from discussions in Insight, pp. 707-710; cf. p. 621c. Again, the reader should recall the discussion of Section A3, above.

[2] Again, "value" can now be "defined" as the "object" of the conscientious deliberation, evaluation, and rational choice of the subject. Thus, the human subject cannot avoid asking such questions as "What is to be done?," and "Is it really worthwhile?" He cannot evade decision since not to choose is itself a choice. Hence, all human subjects always have some "notion of value" even if they do not know, do, or agree upon what is truly worthwhile in any given situation. These points will be developed in Chapter VII and Chapter V, Section B10, below.

principle of the good of order.[1] It must also respect, then, all this principle's concrete implications for his own living and that of his community. Thus, he must decide for only those particular goods consistent with the good of order in the community. He must be willing to acknowledge, conserve, correct, or complement the institutions already conditioning that good. Again, he is implicitly committed by his adherence to that principle to setting:

> the [dynamic] good of order above [the] private advantage [of himSelf or any particular subject belonging to his or any other community, etc.], . . . [to subordinating] the technology [of the community] to [its] economics, . . . [to referring its] economics to [the] social welfare, and, generally, . . . [to meting out] to every finite good both appreciation and criticism (C1, 115b).

Finally, he is implicitly committed to respecting the incarnations of this principle in the proverbs, analogies, stories, parables and concrete generalizations of the community. Thus, he would "do unto others . . . ." He would remember that what is "sauce for the goose is sauce for the gander." And he would "always be fair." Again, further insights into the concrete situation will tell the subject just when and how such maxims are applicable, just how and when they need to be complemented, augmented or ignored.

Fourthly, the practise of such a subject will reflect the same two "sources" of reflection and judgment that were set down in the cognitional context of Division A3c of this chapter. As the reader recalls, these are both proximate and "individual" and remote and "communal" in character.

Fifthly, his practise will reflect his consideration of questions with only a relatively proximate practical relevance. Thus, his action is not suited to situations in which issues are theoretical, complicated, and disputed, and/or long term and wide-ranging in consequence. Thus, the practise of such a subject will not necessarily involve his explicit achievement of a "theoretical" or "intellectually" patterned "attitude" towards the world. It will not necessarily involve his insight into insight, his Self-affirmation, or moral

---

[1]See the sixth "generalization" in Section B2, above.

"Self"-choice, etc. But, then, the practise of such a subject will accord with fully objective judgments of value insofar as it confines itself to the relatively short-run and local issues which come up in the course of his everyday living.

But the remarks of Sections B2-3, above, do not sufficiently or explicitly consider the developing sets of meanings and values which condition the agreement and cooperation of the community of subjects at each step of its social development. These meanings and values are "objects" of intelligent grasp, and reasonable affirmation and action. Thus, they correspond to operations performed on the "third" level of human consciousness. These meanings and values "carry" for the society of human subjects, its understanding of itself. They "carry" for it its affirmation of the worth, appropriateness, and significance of its way of life. Under the circumstances, they stand to the social order of the community as:

> soul to body, for any element of social order will be rejected [by the community] the moment it is widely judged inappropriate, meaningless, irrelevant, useless, just not worthwhile (C2, 102a).

They are carried, for example, by the developing "rites and symbols, [the] language and art" of the subject's community. At their level:

> meaning is felt and intuited and acted out [quasi-spontaneously]. It is like the meaning already in the [subject's] dream before the therapist interprets it, the meaning of the work of art before the critic focuses on it and relates it to other works, the endlessly nuanced and elusive and intricate meanings of everyday speech, the intersubjective meanings of smiles and frowns, speech and silence, intonation and gesture, the passionate meanings of interpersonal relations, of high deeds and great achievements, of all we admire, praise, revere, adore, and all we dislike, condemn, loathe, abominate. Such is meaning for [the] undifferentiated consciousness [of the subject and his community of common sense], and it would seem to constitute the spontaneous substance of every culture (C2, 102b, emphases mine).

But, since such meanings and values always implicitly condition the context of his social living, the practical subject will tend, spontaneously, to identify his community with the other as cultural. First, since such community with the other is uncritical, since it does not explicitly issue from a community of reflective analysis by morally and intellectually Self-appropriated subjects, it pertains to the cultural infrastructure of the community. Secondly, whether or not it predominates, still, the community of the subject will always involve such a **cultural** dimension. Thirdly, the preceding descriptions have confined themselves to the analysis of the community of the "practical" subject of common sense. For this reason they have justifiably abstracted from consideration of the cultural superstructure of the community, from the issue of critical culture and its stages. Again, such a further cultural dimension of the life of the community emerges in response to the "limitations" and "biases" inherent in common sense and its cultural infrastructure. Thus, it is best discussed in the context of the notion of dialectic (cf. Chapter V, Section B10, below).

4. The "Formal Viewpoint" of Common Sense: The Practical Component

What remains to be done in Division B of this chapter, is an analysis of the "object"-pole ("field" or "formal object") of the "horizon" of common sense's "practical component." But, as noted, the "subject" and "object"-poles of a "horizon" are correlatives. But Sections 1-3, above, have analyzed the "practical" component structuring the "subject"-pole of the subject's common sense. And on this "basis," the "field" situating the "objects" of her practise can be given a five-fold account. First, the "field" selects out those "objects" which bear upon the immediate "interests" of "man." Secondly, it qualifies the scope of the questions which mediate the deliberation and evaluation of human action and its products. Thirdly, it "casts" human practise in a non-explanatory light. Fourthly, it places a limitation upon its subject's as well as its community's relationship to what is truly "good." And, fifthly, there is a social and historical dimension to the specific "totalities" of "objects" constituted by the field and to which it gives human practise access. Again, this account complements and parallels the analysis of the "formal viewpoint" of the "intellectual component" of common sense already advanced in Section A4 of this chapter.

First, Lonergan determines this "field" in terms of the potential totality of socio-cultural "objects" which call forth and answer to the "action" of the common sense subject. But, these "objects" are, in turn, determined by their appeal to the palpable "interests" and "apprehensions" of "man." This field, then, abstracts its "object" from individual, social, historical, and environmental **implications** that are long-term and/or wide-ranging in scope, theoretical in character and/or intricate and disputed in consequence.

Secondly, he determines this "field" in terms of its implicit "methodological" circumscription upon the scope of the further deliberative and evaluative issues it admits. Thus, the "field" imposes a "pragmatic" and, therefore, relatively short-sighted criterion on the understanding and judgment of practical possibilities. But this will have an effect on which and what kind of practical

insights are instituted, on how they will be corrected, improved, etc.[1]
Thirdly, he determines this "field" in terms of the relatively
non-explanatory, a-theoretical and, in this sense, non-technical
context within which it casts the subject's actions and inter-actions,
her operations and co-operations.

Fourthly, he determines this "field" in terms of the manner in
which it situates the "good's" relationship to "man." Thus, value has
been implicitly defined as what calls forth and answers to the
subject's intelligent and rational practise. But the "field" of the
"practical" common sense of the subject only lets the "good" be
apprehended and carried out under the limited aspect of its intelligent
and reasonable "relations to us." Again, the first through the third
points, above, further indicate the "limits" which the "field" imposes
upon the human grasp, affirmation, and action upon the good.

Fifthly, Lonergan determines this "field" in terms of the
specific totality of "objects" upon which it "opens out" and which it
consititutes at any given "place" and "time." The totality will
correspond to the specific group of circumscribed competencies which
the subject has learned or is learning to manifest and discharge.[2] It
will correspond to the specific environmental and socio-cultural
situation in which her deliberations have arisen and her query,
learning, and trials, have given way to rounded practical judgment and
capability in action.[3] It will correspond to the given stage in the

---

[1]Thus, the subject of practical common sense is content to act
after having learned only enough about the institutions, values and
disvalues which inform her society and culture, about their history and
prospects and tensions, about the horizon of her practise, etc., to
make it possible for her to attend to her own affairs and perform the
tasks associated with her public duties (cf. MT, 184b).

[2]Thus, the specific character of the "field" situating the action
of the common sense subject corresponds to the stage, society and area
of her practical development.

[3]Thus, the specific character of the "field" corresponds to the
specific socio-cultural situation of the subject.

history of the socio-cultural process in which limitations immanent in the present or past situation of her practise are brought out and transcended.[1] Thus, specific potential totalities within the "field" "emerge" and become increasingly differentiated. And this emergence and differentiation correspond to a practical learning process that is "with" others and set within a historical tradition, a genetic constitution of meanings, cooperations, institutions, etc. Again, within some more widely achieved community, specific "totalities" will differ individually, socio-culturally, and historically. For this reason, although the common sense of a first century Athenian, of a contemporary Russian farmer, of the natives of the Trobriand islands, of a Japanese corporate executive, etc. is not ours, is "strange" by comparison, it is, nevertheless, accessible to us. Again, doctors, computer programmers, politicians, engineers, industrialists, workers, etc., will know about each other's different "worlds," acknowledge their existence and worth, and ascribe to each other's achievements a corresponding "deformation professionelle" (H, 2j).[2]

---

[1] Thus, the specific character of the "field" corresponds to the specific historical situation of the subject.

[2] Expanding the context of these remarks to include A1-4, it can be said that what lies within the specific "field" to the common sense subject's knowledge and action is a "known known." It comprises: "what fully engages . . . [his] attention, what . . . [he] know(s) all about, what . . . [he] comes to be able to do anything with. He may be a clumsy fellow but put him in the driver's seat in one of those enormous twelve-wheel lorries and he is completely master of any situation that can arise" (H, 2b).
But just "beyond" the central field of the subject's "known known" there lies a penumbral dimension, a "known unknown." It comprises the subject's compass of: "vague and inadequate knowledge, of minor interests, of secondary causes [of further questions he at least knows how to ask]. One will talk about it but only casually; if one talks about it at length, one will not do it; if one starts doing it, one does not stick to it" (H, 1p-q).
Again, just "beyond" the penumbra of the central field there is the "region" of the "unknown unknown," of: "what . . . [the subject] knows nothing about [it's all Greek to me; I did not understand a single word he said] and what does not possess the slightest

But, finally, the preceding discussion concludes the "horizon" analysis of the "practical" component of the attitude of common sense.

---

significance for me [I just couldn't care less]" (H, 1o; N.B. the brackets are Lonergan's or his transcriber's).

Corresponding to the "intellectual" and "practical" development of the socially and historically situated subject, there is the expansion of the "field" into its "penumbra," and the penumbra into its "region." Similarly, the penumbra can remain stationary or collapse into its field. Again, with the necessary changes made, similar analysis could be made of the development of the historically and communally situated scientific, philosophic or fully ethical subject, etc., etc.

Finally, the "known known" of the common sense (or, say, the scientific) subject at some stage of practical and/or intellectual development corresponds to the "relative horizon" of the subject. The distinction between the absolute and relative horizons of the subject, as well as the differentiations within the history of meaning of the stages which have led to their current apprehension, etc., are made from the standpoint of her "absolute horizon," or "universal viewpoint." Cf. p. 44 n, paragraph d, above.

C. Concluding Remarks

First, there is no "human" action without cognition. On the other hand, cognition tends to flow spontaneously over into action. But, then, the relatively parallel explications set forth in A1-4 and B1-4, above, must be regarded as complementary and, partially, interpenetrating. As such they bring out the integral relative "Horizon" of the common sense attitude and community of the human subject. Secondly, "common sense," e.g., the subject of the common sense attitude, "cannot explicitly formulate" the "nature," "logic," "methodology," or "horizon" of her own performance (I, 297b). These she undertakes to grasp "in . . . [her] own shrewd fashion through instances and examples, fables and lessons, paradigms and proverbs . . ." (I, 297b). Thus, the attitude of the common sense subject should not be identified with that of either the scholar, the scientist, or the critical, Self-knowing, or ethical subject. Thus, it spontaneously and necessarily involves neither the systematic, reflectively pursued achievement of insight into insight, Self-affirmation, etc., nor the engagement of such achievement critically to guide and facilitate the evaluation of what is to be done.[1] The subject of common sense, then, may be entrusted with the juror's role, with the task of reading the color of litmus paper or fixing a carburetor, etc. But the interpretation of a case in the history of law or ethics, the discovery and verification of the formula of a new compound, the discovery and affirmation of the principles of combustion, of her own conscious being, or of Being generally, etc., lie well beyond her competence (I, 420). Thus, the reflections of the preceding chapter transcend the limited "horizon" of the common sense subject they purport to explicate. They are the fruit of the subject's pursuit of an intellectually differentiated Self-knowledge. They crystallize her

---

[1] As we shall see in ensuing chapters, however, there is nothing, in principle, to prevent and much to recommend such an involvement. Cf. Chapters VI, Section 8, and VII, below.

"heuristic" appropriation of the essential structures of her, or any common sense living. And they, therefore, represent her abstraction from the local sets of meanings, values, conditions, etc., which circumscribe her own or her community's, any subject's or any community's way of life.[1] Thirdly, neither the judgments nor the rational actions of the common sense subject completely abstract from either the interestedness of her relatively immediate, sensitive concern or the particularities of her situation. Thus, she will inevitably tend, either spontaneously or when she initiates Self-reflection, _falsely_ to identify her knowing and objectivity, her and her world's Being and value, her community, with their biologically pattered counterparts outlined in Chapter I.

---

[1]Three brief points should be made here.

First, "forms" can be considered abstractly or in the manner in which they integrate their underlying manifolds. Thus, economic system can be considered in its essential terms and relations. On the other hand, such system can be studied in its actual functioning, its actual ordering of lower, unintegrated manifolds, its actual development, etc.

Secondly, building on his discovery of the tri-leveled structure of the common sense subjectivity of the subject, Lonergan has, in first approximation, specified the formal structures through which the history of the individual and his community proceed. On the other hand, such structures can be studied in their actual functioning at specific places and times in human history. Thus, we might inquire into the specific values, and the technical, economic, and political relations which functionally inform the life of a given community. We might inquire into how they have progressed and/or regressed over time, etc. And it is precisely because, considered abstractly, the basic structures remain fixed, that, considered concretely, a range of values and developments can be determined.

Finally, the invariance of the basic, tri-fold structure and, therefore of the further notions defined on its "basis," is established in Chapter VI, below.

CHAPTER IV

THE DRAMATIC PATTERN OF EXPERIENCE

ANALYSIS

In a further set of reflections,[1] Lonergan notes that there is a further dimension to the conscious, everday living of the subject which fails to correspond to either its biological, aesthetic, practical, or intellectual patterns. This dimension of his living lacks the more explicit, synthetic character of his scientifically and/or reflectively mediated living. On the other hand, it does call forth and integrate a flow of ingredient conscious acts and their contents, of percepts, memories and anticipations, images and desires, insights and judgments, decisions and actions, etc. Again, it does manifest a pre-reflective, "vital" or "organic" unity, an intelligibility that can be characterized as "artistic," as one of "orientation," "mode" or "style." Thus, it corresponds to a properly dramatic pattern or aspect of his consciousness.

First, the subject in the dramatic pattern is caught up in the ordinary performances and everyday, "practical" concerns which animate his daily living in a "world" of common sense. Thus, "within" such a world of "objects," the dramatic subject is always also elementally aware of his own living and dying, his own loving and hating, his own rejoicing and suffering, his own desiring and fearing, etc. Still, such relatively unreflected upon concern with his own Being, is neither to be confused with, nor taken as subordinate to, either the organically aligned pattern of his biological consciousness or its similarly oriented, if more differentiated, practical extension. Thus, if the desire of the subject of common sense, e.g., his hunger, etc.,

_____

[1]Cf. Insight, Chapter VI, Subsections 2.1–2.7.7.

102

manifests the underlying organic "component" of his conscious being, still it also manifests something "more," a further motivation and intelligible unity. Thus, the contents and affects, emerging into the consciousness of the dramatic subject as, for example, he seats himSelf to dine, have always already been **aesthetically** "dignified." As such, they have been "liberated" from their "biological" origins, from their "spatial and psychological" connections with "the farm, the abbatoir, the kitchen." They have always already been **artistically** transformed by: the "elaborate equipment [and manner] of the dining room" (I,187b); conversation "with those with whom . . . [one] feels at home;" communication of one's delights and frustrations, sorrows and laughter, purposes and labors, etc. (cf. I, 471b). Again, the coloured plumes of birds as well as the furs of animals are demanded, supplied, and purchased rather than a more functional but anonymous drapery. But this is because clothing must not only warm and cover the "sensible and sensing body" but also adorn, suggestively "disguise" and, thereby, dramatically heighten the presence of the incarnate, Self-expressive subject (I, 187b). Finally, she may not be able either to will or think away the suffering and the disfigurement of, say, a physically handicapping condition. Still, for the dramatic subject they are taken up into the fluorish with which she brandishes, the dexterity with which she employs, the eloquence by which she expresses herSelf through her carved, oaken cane. They are forgotten in the manifest virtuosity and delight with which she ascends a double flight of stairs as well as the sincerity but wit with which she asks "How are you this morning?" And they are transcended in the style with which she empathically embroiders her role as counselor to similarly disabled children.[1]

Secondly, then, the "first artwork" of the aesthetically

---

[1] In the derelict, the business executive consuming, in perfect isolation, "belt after belt" of liquor at a crowded bar, the housewife who has "given up," etc., we have examples of the dramatic patterning of experience on the wane. Still, a brief interpretation of its decline, breakdown, and re-gathering will be deferred until the nature of dialectical process has been discussed in Chapter V, Section B10.

liberated subject of the dramatic pattern, his first and, therefore, pre-reflective incarnation of his sensitivity to possibilities of "style," to "(the) fair, the beautiful, the admirable," etc., is "his own living" (I, 187c, emphases mine).[1] Again, the Self-constituting dramatic artistry of the aesthetically liberated subject has been granted a wide berth and is, therefore, able to "transform" the biological influences upon his consciousness with a creativity that varies with "the locality, the period, the social milieu" (I, 187c), etc. But if human consciousness "floats upon" and is, therefore, affected but not controlled by the demands of either his organism or his social-"world" situation, still, there is the inverse point. Thus, even given such latitude in free space and artistic variation, such a pattern to the subject's intelligent operations defaults upon its properly dramatic function, if it fails to integrate the underlying, neuro-organic demands upon his everyday living. Thus, if an Indian child would no more don black to attend his uncle's funeral than his counterpart at an Irish wake clothe himself in white; if a woman in Alexandria would no more eat with her left hand than her counterpart in Ohio use her fingers, still the same functions of artistic integration are being fulfilled by each of the subjects in each of their respective contexts. And underlying each of the two contexts within each pair there is a relative, transcultural constancy to the underlying demands which are being integrated and which, despite variations in the style of the integration, neither can afford to ignore.

Thirdly, the "experience" of the dramatically patterned subjectivity of the subject is never purely an individual affair. Thus, the dramatic subject is always already at least implicitly "in the presence of others" (I, 188b).[2] If the subject, then, is disturbed

---

[1] It is not surprising, then, that the scholar-subject can work back from the art of a community of subjects to some approximate understanding of the "tone of feeling," the "character," the difficult to conceptualize dramatic life of a people (cf. LE, 7 ff).

[2] Thus, the dramatic subject is always at least implicitly "doing . . . [his] little act in their [e.g., others'] presence and . . . thinking about what they think of . . . [his performance]." The two

by a guest as he lay reading, alone in his room "there is a complete
shift in the flow of [his] consciousness. [He is] . . . reacting to
the presence of someone else" (LE, 82c, emphases mine).[1] Again, even
as Monet might do twenty or more studies of a river before he was
"satisfied" with his creation, so on the basis of the requisite
"artistic and affective criteria" (I, 188c 7) does the subject advance
in his achievement of a dramatically integral Self-"constitution." And
if such advancing Self-achievement finds its greatest lower bound in
organic conditions that are not so pliant as the painter's palette,
canvas and oils, so are such specific criteria, the acts which follow
from them, largely the donation of other counselors. Thus, his
dramatic Self-development finds its inspiration, guidance, and
justification in the example and emulation, the admiration and
ridicule, the precepts and prohibitions, the praise and blame of
others. Both because "he imitates and learns from others" and because
others imitate and learn from him, the artistry ingredient in the human
drama "accumulate(s)" and advances "over the centuries" (I, 188b).[2]

But, fourthly, the artistic Self-achievement of the dramatic
subject is developmental and, therefore, temporal and historical. In
the individual, then, it is the process, stretching from infancy
through adulthood, by which the aesthetically liberated subject
successively fashions and re-fashions, from out of the maturing

---

usages of "implicitly" signify that the subject's experience frequently
slips into the dramatic pattern even when he is physically separated
from others.

[1]Lonergan's point is that something more is happening in such a
case than the subject's brute clash with "reality" or his surprise at
unequivocally frustrated expectations.

[2]In light of the point to the previous paragraph we would note
that, on the one hand: "the style that is the man is not [merely]
something individual. It belongs [in common] to the group" (LE,
10-16c, emphasis mine). On the other hand, against the background of
the recognizable style of the group, there will be "individual
variations" effected by each subject in each case. Thus, Robert was
obviously a Kennedy, yet his style, his way of doing things, was
identifiable as uniquely his own.

organic, social, and practical demands upon his conscious being, himSelf as his own first work of art, his own style and flexible system style and flexible system of everyday living. And it is, therefore, through such a process of successively higher, Self-re-integrations, that the "second nature" of the subject, that the dramatic dimension of his "role" in society becomes determinate. It is through such a process, then, that his "character" among characters,[1] in the primordial drama "which the theatre only imitates," is serially "moulded" (I, 188c) and expanded. And if through such a process, the subject comes gradually to identify with and enlarge upon his "roles," if they cease to be merely props or crutches of his personality but, by stages, become indispensable, seemingly inevitable extensions of his daily living and being, the identification process must not be conceived of naively. Thus, it does not involve the subject's looking out upon the role to be performed and then imposing it over both the refractory desires and feelings "in here" and the unassimilated movements and features "out there" (cf. I, 189a). Rather, at any fairly integrated stage of his dramatic development:

> the materials [e.g., the affects, desires, images, performance repertoires, etc.] that emerge in [his sensitive] consciousness are already [dramatically and, therefore, intelligently] patterned [at the given stage], and the pattern is already charged emotionally and conatively (I, 189a).

Again, socially and practically motivated neural demands continue to exert themselves upon the consciousness of the subject. At particular stages of his development, their specific demands for corresponding "apprehensions and objects" will be legitimate, but unassimilable by the subject's already achieved level of dramatically mediated, sensitive-performative integration. At such points, the subject of the specific dramatic integration of his existence is thrown into question. But his question brings out the limitations of his dramatic development at that time. It calls forth and orients his "other"-motivated discovery and en-actment of the "role"-possibility which transcends

---

[1]Cf. Lectures on Existentialism, p. 22 f. Again, the notion of the "character" of the subject recurs in the distinct context of Lonergan's ethical discussions of the subject (cf. UB, 282-286).

these limitations. It calls forth and anticipates his passage to a dramatically richer "future."[1] Again, the "question" into which the dramatic subject is, by stages, thrown, directs him to an understanding and an "artistic(ally)" motivated "evaluation," e.g., a judgment upon these novel, relatively un-assimilable "contents." And even if he lacks the standpoint of the hard sciences, of psychology, of philosophic reflection, etc., he would "understand" and "evaluate" them. He would do this in the depths of their incarnate, social, and practical demands upon his conscious being. He would do this under the aspect of the dramatically integrable possibilities of living to which they point. And he would do it with an eye towards the time of his minor or major re-"casting."[2] Thus, even as, for example, the trial-validated common sense insights of the subject develop, even as they:

> emerge and accumulate, so do the insights that govern the [possible, probable, and actual] imaginative projects of [the] dramatic living [of the subject "in" his "world"] (I, 188c).

Finally, if it exceeds the biological orientation of his conscious

---

[1]The emergence of such demands: (1) heralds the inadequacy but also the precariousness and contingency of the dramatic synthesis of the subject's way of living; (2) signals his need to expand but, thereby, risk the dis-integration of the pattern to his conscious being. Thus, as Lonergan notes in Insight, p. 533 n, the emergence of such demands will frequently be accompanied by his sense of "anxiety" or of the "uncanny," of "horror, loathing, dread." But, then, such inverse components of the "psychic operator" of the subject, e.g., his sense of "Mystery" (cf. I, XVII.1, interpreted in Chapter VI, Section 11, below) are revelatory of the concrete temporality of the subject. This is so because they bring out the limitation which informs his Dasein, his manner of "being-in-the-world." It reveals his commitment to effecting its next proximate but still contingent transcendence. It calls forth, in short, his need to develop, to crystalize his next proximate push into the "future."

[2]Lonergan's soon to be re-iterated point, here, is that once the re-scripting has taken place, once his minor or major venture towards a more dramatically integral living has been re-achieved, the conditions are re-set for the emergence of the further organically stimulated images and affects which the higher dramatic constitution of the subject cannot assimilate. Thus, the process is tri-fold. It involves

life, still the development of the dramatic subject can be decisively influenced by his own or others' intellectual, philosophical, or ethical reflections.[1] Still, even before ethical or intellectual considerations supervene upon the process, even before there can be:

> criticism, evaluation, or deliberation . . . the intelligence [of the subject] must collaborate [successfully with his imagination] in representing the projected course of action that is to be submitted to . . . [these higher level operations].

Thus, already in the prior, proceeding collaboration of intelligence and imagination by which the conditions for the **effective** supervention of, for example, his ethical deliberations are fulfilled, the dramatic pattern to the subject's conscious operations is in play. And if its play is effective, it is already:

> outlining how . . . [the dramatic subject] might behave before others and charging the outline with an artistic transformation of a more elementary [e.g., an organically based] aggressivity and affectivity (I, 189a, emphases mine).

But, fifthly, a relationship of "dynamic correspondence"[2] between the psychoneural and intentional "strata" of the Being of the dramatic subject is necessary if the dramatic pattern to his consciousness is to emerge, survive, and develop.[3] But such a relationship will obtain only if two immanent conditions are fulfilled.

---

the subject's sensitivity to underlying neuro–organic demands. It involves his "understanding" and "evaluation" (in an other–informed context) of their meaning and that the dramatic artistry of the subject, that the drama, generally, develops. Again, "sensitivity" in the immediately preceding sense presupposes the dramatic subject's knowledge of neither the existence of a nervous system nor of its neurophysiology, etc.

[1] If the motivation may not be either initial or ordinary, it can, nevertheless, be "decisive" (cf. I, 188c 11–13).

[2] Cf. Insight, Chapter VI, Subsection 2.6. The notion of "dynamic correspondence" will be interpreted further in Chapter VI, Section A11, below. Also cf. Chapter V, Section B9b.

[3] Thus, the actual, dramatically patterned flow of the consciousness of the subject, can be "traced" to these two "principles" or strata of the conscious Being of the dramatic subject (cf. I, 217b #(2)).

First, if they are to respond to the aesthetically liberated concerns of the dramatic artist, the gross and fine motor operations of the incarnate subject must manifest an at least initial **detachment** from the organically based conative, sensitive, and emotive states which originally "direct and release them" (**I**, 189b). Thus, if his arms, hands and fingers, his vocal cords and lungs, his eyes, tongue, mouth and lips, etc., were "locked from birth" into biological schemes of advancing, but pre-set, stimulus and response, then the "wailing and gurgling," the wiggling and nodding of the infant could never have developed into the visually, manually, and symbolically mediated activities of the mature subject's articulate speech and writing, listening and reading. Similarly, unless this condition were fulfilled, the mature dramatic actor could never have learned to respond **either** easily, quickly, and almost imperceptibly to the demands of his affectively charged, symbolically motivated personal encounters, **or** with all the nuanced expressive resources the thousand or so muscles in his face, hands, and throat make possible.

Secondly, if the underlying, neuro-organic demands upon his everyday living are to be taken up into the aesthetically satisfying artistry of his dramatic living, the subject must manifest a **pre**-conscious openness to their maturing, upwardly directed demands for sensitive representation and artistically charged, dramatic integration.[1] The contents which enter the sensitive **consciousness** of the subject are always already in some pattern, and as thus patterned, allow consciousness its dramatically integrative function. But the patterning connotes a "**principle** of selection and control [over which contents will emerge]" which, since it is effective at the **juncture** between the non-conscious and the conscious, must, at least initially, be operative "**prior** to [the] conscious [or deliberate] advertance of the [dramatic] subject" (**I**, 192b–193a, emphasis mine). Again, this **pre**-conscious function of effecting the dynamic correspondence between

---

[1]Cf. footnote 3, p. 108, above. **Proximately**, the relationship of dynamic correspondence must obtain between the principle of this sensitive openness and its underlying manifolds.

the maturing, neural-organic demands upon the subject and his conscious, intentional orientation, is "now familiar as Freud's censor." Again, when it is functioning **constructively**, the pre-conscious censorship is aligned with the authentic, dramatically oriented Self-concern, the dramatically oriented Self-questioning, the intelligence of the artistic subject.[1] As thus aligned, the censorship will select and arrange sensitive contents, i.e., memories, hopes, affects, fears, gestures, phantasies, images, dreams, etc., into patterns that answer to his properly dramatic concerns, his properly dramatic questioning. But as selected and arrayed by these questions and concerns, these materials will give rise to his affectively charged **understanding** of his "situation." Such understanding, then, is concrete insight into how it stands with the purportedly integrated but potentially starved, distorted, or unnecessarily repressed, psycho-neural demands upon his everyday living. Such understanding "heads for" their **dramatic** integration "within" their subject's "socio-practical" situation. It reflects the continuing efforts of the dramatic subject to take up the "biological" origins of his incarnate subjectivity into the aesthetic of an artistically manifested dignity. It involves his continuing efforts to learn how to achieve such dignity without violating either its implicit "artistic" criteria or the legitimate, underlying demands upon his time and living.[2] Again, ''selection is also rejection. But, if the "constructive" censorship "abstracts" from some "materials" that it might array and advance these relevant others, it is not to the end of "inhibiting" specific sets of

---

[1]The orientation of the "censorship" is **properly** in alignment with the intelligence of the dramatic subject in its grasp upon artistically integral possibilities of being in the "world." Thus, remotely, the relationship of dynamic correspondence must obtain between this principle, e.g., the dramatically oriented intelligence of the subject, and its underlying manifold.

[2]If neither this interpretive work nor the text of Insight accentuates the fact, there will also be legitimate, overriding **ethical** demands to be respected even if the dramatic subject's skill at Self-reflection has not reached the point at which he can recognize their fully immanent claim upon his conscious being and living.

neuro—organic demands. It is, rather, in order to fit its "claims" into the process by which the concrete, authentic Self—questioning of the dramatic subject "opts" for a needed stasis or growth (cf. I, 192b). It is to fit its demands into a process by which it gives itself clues for **understanding** what is essential for its dramatic stasis or development and "leaves out" what is not so relevant. Finally, the procession to the Self—"questioning" of the dramatic subject recurs at each minor or major stage of his dramatic maturation. But, then, through such a process clusters of "tested," dramatically relevant insights will coalesce into balanced "viewpoints." These will make for series of ever more integral and aesthically satisfying syntheses to his "being—in—the—world;"[1] the greater "at homeness" with his neural demands which each successive higher integration represents. Again, such "at—homeness" is continuous with his increasing social and practical situation in the "world" of common sense, will always remain to be achieved, will dovetail with the maturation, the development of these other facets, e.g., the common sense dimension, of his conscious being.

To conclude this chapter, we offer the following three points.

---

[1]The point should be made here that the dramatic subject is, minimally, not necessarily in the intellectual pattern even if the dynamic and "principles" of her development can be, e.g., have been, reflected upon from out of a philosophical expansion upon that pattern and its expanded viewpoint. In the intellectual pattern, the sensitive process of the subject, aligning itself with her higher level, formal operations, contracts to "an unruffled sequence of symbolic notations and schematic images" (I, 186a) devoid of affective content or motivation. On the other hand, in the dramatic pattern, the sensitive process of the subject will hold out for her pre—intellectually and pre—reflectively patterned Self—understanding, "images . . . tinged with affects" (I, 201a, emphasis mine; cf. I, 196b). It will not, then, exclude the dramatically charged, affective dimension of the "data," the dimension communicative of the integration of his organism, of the incarnation of her being and living in the "world." For this reason, the dramatic Self—"understanding" of the practical subject "in" society can eventuate in her advance to a new stage of vitally adapted, dramatic performance and receptivity. It can effect the re—organization, in line with her dramatic maturation, of already established, seemingly spontaneous constellations of affective and intersubjective response.

First, the preceding has intepreted Lonergan's reflections upon the dramatic pattern to the subjectivity of the subject. But they are no more the reflections of a subject "in" the dramatic pattern than earlier reflections were those of a subject in the pattern of common sense, human biology, the aesthetic, or art. Rather, they are the reflections of a subject who has pushed for and achieved a scientific, psychological, and reflectively nuanced "viewpoint" upon herSelf. They are the reflections of a subject who has learned enough about herSelf to relate her everday living to: (1) its neuro-organic conditions; (2) its artistic and aesthetic dimension and not merely to its mere practical conditions or achievements; (3) the tri-fold structure of human consciousness; (4) the notion of development.

Secondly, the above reflections render only a "first approximation" to the nature and development of the dramatic subject. Thus, the "biasing" of that development and, therefore, a second approximation to its understanding will be taken up in our section on "dialectic" in Chapter V.

Finally, for those who deem it desirable or necessary, we offer the following summary of the preceding interpretation. The dramatic pattern of the experience of the subject subtends an expanding, cumulative series of "syntheses." Through these "syntheses," the aesthetically liberated "sensitivity" and "performance" of the subject of practical/intellectual common sense, accomplishes the higher, artistic integration of the underlying, neuro-organic exigences on her conscious Being. It does so within the "role"-mediated social "theatre" of her everday living with other, similarly developing subjects. Again it does so in a theatre which successively stimulates only to transform successively such demands.[1]

---

[1]In Chapter II, above, it was pointed out that the analysis of "Mystery" and "symbol" to be carried out in Chapter VI, above, transforms understanding of the meaning and purpose of the aesthetic/ artistic pattern of the subject's experience (cf. p. 38 n1). But, so, then, do we invite the reader to reflect upon how it transforms the understanding of the dramatically re-oriented and conditioned "aesthetic-artistry" of the incarnate subject's own, everyday living. Finally, a further transformation of both issues would have resulted had it not been decided to abstract from Lonergan's treatment of the God question in both its philosophic and religious aspects.

CHAPTER V

THE INTELLECTUAL PATTERN OF THE SUBJECT'S EXPERIENCE:
THE SCIENTIFIC DIFFERENTIATION[1]

Introduction

The aesthetic "liberation" of the sensitive flow of consciousness
from its undertow of biological demands exhibits and generates a
"flexibility" in human experience, a level and "region" of "detachment"
from its vital purposiveness. This flexibility opens the flow for
patterning by the questions of the subject, by the intentionality to
know and learn which we have already analyzed in the context of the
subject's aesthetic and dramatic artistry, and his common sense. But
it also opens the sensitive stream to her consciousness for patterning
by her desire to know the "what is." But it is this which the full
dynamic to the intentionality of the subject anticipates and, at the
limit, truly grasps. Thus determined by the pure question, the
sensitivity of the scientific subject is cooperatively disposed. Thus
disposed, it releases for focal attention just those contents which may
call forth the acts of insight and reflective understanding which
settle the movement of consciousness which the question itself has
evoked.

In the theorist, intent upon a problem, even the subconscious goes
to work to yield at unexpected moments the suggestive images of

_____

[1]For purposes of contrast, an incipient determination of the
"subject"-pole of this attitude of human subjectivity was already
offered in Chapter III, Section A2, above. There it was indicated that
the scientific subject wants a "universal" understanding of the things
in their "relations to each other," that her understanding finds
expression in technical language and that it is sought, at least in its
pure form, for its own sake even if practical applications ensue.

113

clues and missing links, of patterns and perspectives that evoke the desiderated _insight_ and delighted cry, "Eureka!" In _reflection_ there arises a passionless calm (_I_, 186a, emphases mine).

Both mathematical and empirically scientific attitudes of questioning go forward in the intellectual pattern of the subject's experience. It is to the determination of the "horizons" of these two attitudes and, therefore, of their "subject"- and corresponding "object"-poles, that Divisions A and B of this chapter are, respectively, devoted.[1]

---

[1]Further clarification of the differences between the two horizons is offered in the first footnote of Chapter VI, Section 4, pp. 329-330, below.

A. The Mathematical Learning of the Subject:

Attitude and Object

Introduction

In Insight, Chapter I, Sections 2 through 3.7, Lonergan
generalizes upon the nature of the "subject"-pole of the mathematical
attitude of the subject. And he does this in the context of reflecting
upon two simple examples of what he does. The first is drawn from
elementary geometry. On its "basis," the role of the "image" in human
knowing is thematized. Distinctions are drawn between his nominal and
explanatory definitions of what he has "understood" therein. And the
character of the mathematical subject's reflection upon the "truth" of
his understanding is briefly sketched.[1] The purpose of Lonergan's
second example is to explicitly thematize the subject's intellectual
development. This is done in the context of his doing number theory.
Thus, Lonergan reflects upon the subject's deductive and homogeneous
expansion upon an initial set of definitions. He goes on to thematize
his discovery of further outstanding "elements" in the "data" which
they do not order. And he concludes by reflecting the consequent
discovery of the need for and actual achievement of a fuller
understanding of the outstanding "data" and, therefore, a higher
defining "viewpoint."[2] Again, in Insight, Chapter IX, Section 8,
Lonergan clarifies his reflections upon the process that leads from the
mathematical subject's "Is it so?"-asking to his judgment. From these
cases, the essential, tri-levelled "structure" of the mathematical
subject's learning is inferred. And it is a structure essentially
parallel to those uncovered in Chapters II-IV. Again, in Chapter IX.8,
Lonergan broaches the question of when human understanding, formalization and judgment are uniquely mathematical? Why, he continues, are

---

[1]This first example is taken up in Section A1 of this chapter,
below.

[2]This example is taken up in Section A2, below.

they sometimes relevant to and "isomorphic with" the "external" world? Implicit here is the question of the proper "field" or "object"-pole of the intentional "activity" of the subject of the mathematical attitude.[1]

Finally, in order to shed further light on one dimension of the subject's mathematical development, introduce terminology that will be needed in later sections, and clarify the issues, the raising and answering of this last set of questions is prefaced with a background analysis of the subject's implicit notions of "inverse insight" and the "empirical residue."[2]

---

[1]These issues are discharged in Section A4, below, where clarification of the nature of the mathematical subject's judgment is also offered.

[2]This background analysis is carried out in Section A3, below.

1. First Example

Attending to the image of a cartwheel, the subject would know <u>why</u> it is round.[1] By stages she develops to the point of being able to <u>affirm</u> that if the co-planar radii of a uni-centered figure are equal in length, then the given figure <u>must</u> be round, <u>must</u> be a circle. Reflecting on the intentional process which attention to the image initiates and his affirmation concludes, the subject would know what she is doing. To bring out essential, if implicit aspects of that activity, the following five of Lonergan's reflections are briefly sketched.

<u>First</u>, the subject's "Why?" intelligently questions only the "immanent ground" or "formal cause" of the roundness of the figure. Thus, it heads her for its <u>explanatory</u> definition and abstracts from considerations regarding the material, efficient or final cause of any given cartwheel.

<u>Secondly</u>, the subject's <u>nominal</u> definition of a given term relies only upon her understanding of "word usage" to determine her "object." Thus, her account of a circle as a "perfectly round plane curve" (<u>I</u>, 10f) must be superceded in explanatory contexts by a "further insight into the <u>objects</u> to which language refers" (<u>I</u>, 11d, emphasis mine), whether these be only intentional or real. Again, Lonergan notes that David Hilbert's[2] device of <u>implicit definition</u> is explanatory by its method of <u>mutually</u> and exclusively explicating a set of terms by the field of relations which they sustain. Thus, as the equality of radii is a "postulational" or analytic element in the definition of a circle, so is Hilbert's determination of the meaning of both point and line by the relationship that two and only two points define a straight line. But, then, Hilbert's definition of a point is satisfied by an ordered

---

[1] Cf. <u>Insight</u>, pp. 7–12.

[2] Cf. <u>Foundations of Geometry</u>, trans. E.J. Townsend (La Salle: Open Court, 1947).

pair of numbers and by Euclid's notion of position without magnitude, etc. His definition of a line is satisfied by a first degree linear equation, etc., etc. In general, then, two major advantages to implicit definition can be singled out: (1) its abstractness which excludes all residual descriptive and nominal elements, and all ties to the concrete; (2) its consequent applicability to any system or set of data isomorphic to it.[1]

Thirdly, Lonergan argues that the alternative that if definitions are not based on undefined terms, that they are, therefore, defined in a circle, betrays an oversight of insight. Even implicit definition only emerges in the context of an intentional process and is the expression of a prior act or set of acts of understanding. No such act or set thereof can be expressed in a single term. Hence, every "basic" insight involves a defining circle of terms and relations such that "the terms fix the relations, the relations fix the terms, and the insight fixes both" (I, 1b, emphases mine). Thus, the terms plane, radii, circumference, line, point, equality are singly necessary and jointly sufficient to express the subject's understanding of an imagined plain curve. Thus, different sets of basic insights into the relevant images or constructions, when differently grouped in different definitions underly different mathematical systems and their formulations.

Fourthly, the cartwheel image remains relatively concrete and retains the latter's indeterminacy.[2] Thus, to complete a reflective "check" on the truth of his "understanding," the subject must transcend the limitations of the imagination towards the abstractness, the

---

[1]Hilbert's notion runs on only a conceptual-linguistic plane. Lonergan's adjustments appear directly.

[2]The reader should note that "concrete" and "abstract" are themselves relatively and implicitly defined. Thus, relative to an actual cartwheel the image is abstract. Relative to the Cartesian formula for a circle, e.g., $(x_2 + x_2) = r_2$, it is not, etc.

universality of conception. That transcendence is effected in an insight which adds the intellectual supposition of points,[1] lines, circumference and equal radii to the imperfect hub, rim and unequal spokes of the image. The former terms and relations include a reference to the image but enrichen it with a conceptual component not actually but only virtually present on the level of imagination. This component is the grasp of necessary connection between the appropriately related concepts.

Fifthly, the subject's "grasp" of the necessary connection through the mediating image is "self-justifying." Thus, once the subject, upon reflection, understands that if the co-planar radii are equal, then the given figure cannot but be round, then there is simply nothing further necessary for her correct answering of her original "Why?" Again, the subject's grasp does not occur in isolation but emerges from a process. Thus, it is "solidary" with the image that clued the insight and the formulation which is its expression. Again, it is solidary with the "discovery" that no further questions remain open, that the virtually unconditioned has been grasped, and the subsequent act of judgment that is enjoined.

---

[1]Thus, a point is not a dot, possesses position without magnitude, can be conceived but not, qua point, imagined. Again, no actual circular object has exactly equal radii, etc.

2. Second Example

Confronted with a finite number of instances of "one" within the class of positive integers, the subject would have "some definition" of the class. Again, his underlying "What?"—question proceeds under the supposition of an actual multitude of instances of "one" and the acceptance of elementary notions of "one," "plus," and "equals." The desired definition for the class is ventured when the subject concludes his successive additions of "one" to "one," his consequent generation of tables for defining "two," "three," "four," with a pointed "etc., etc., etc, ..."

First, if the subject is to define the class, "there is no alternative to insight" (I, 14a, emphasis mine), and the "etc. . . ." gestures its occurrence. He has "caught on." In its absence, the operation of "+" could continue being applied to the number one or the result of any previous operation of "+," thereupon. And this could go on indefinitely without the class being defined. Once having occurred, an intelligible relation unifying, governing, and ordering the infinite manifold of the positive integers, a set larger than any and every finite set of its members, is "grasped" by the subject in a single act of understanding. Again, once having occurred, the further definition of the potentially infinite number of elements in the series is understood to be irrelevant since nothing that is **intelligible** has been omitted.

Secondly, the subject can generate an indefinitely great "deductive expansion" of his preceding definition by introducing a precising definition for equality and constructing tables for adding "two," "three," "four," "etc. . . . ." Again, the "etc. . . ." signifies that the subject has "caught on" to the "principle" of the expansion, can generate any member of the series on its basis.

Thirdly, the subject's "homogeneous expansion" of his already deductively enlarged field of definition adds new operations to that of addition and proceeds under the proviso that he extend the implications but not modify the nature of "+" (cf. I, 15d). Thus, the operation of multiplication is <u>defined</u> as the <u>addition</u> of a number to itself so many times; powers are defined in terms of "x." Again, tables of operations "inverse" to those defined above, e.g., subtraction, division, roots, respectively, are constructed on the condition that their application preserve the closure to the field of integers, e.g., that they return the results of the previous application to their "point of origin" but not beyond. The "etc. . . ." is operative in each case and signifies the subject's discovery that a positive integer is any number which follows from the use of any of the preceding operations under the conditions that have been specified.

<u>Fourthly</u>, when the subject applies the inverse operators in their "full generality" (<u>I</u>, 15e), he moves beyond the origin point of the integers to generate negative numbers, fractions and surds, and thus brings into question the application of the operators to the newly generated terms. For example, neither the new elements nor the rules for operating on them can be specified by the extant tables. Thus, a <u>further set of questions</u> calls forth the subject's inverse discovery of both the limitations of his previous viewpoint and his need to transcend those limitations and move to a "higher viewpoint."

<u>Fifthly</u>, <u>reflecting</u> upon what he has already done, the subject discovers the method of implicitly defining numbers by the <u>operations</u> that generate them, and implicitly defining these operations in terms of the <u>rules</u> which determine their use.[1] Given this discovery, a new insight emerges. This insight supervenes upon and is "into" his own mathematical operations performed according to the old rules. It grasps the <u>higher</u> set of rules which determine the new applications for the operators which fix, for instance, the elements judged anomalous from his preceding viewpoint. It results, then, in the re-definition of such notions as addition, multiplication, powers, subtraction,

---

[1]Lonergan will use the discovery that rules may define operations and operations define the numbers that issue from their application to define a "department" of mathematics. Departments of mathematics can then be related to each other according to the respectively higher or lower viewpoints they map in the series (<u>I</u>, 311b-c; cf. 312c).

division and roots (cf. I, 17a).[1] Finally, it does this without sacrificing definition for the positive integers which the lower viewpoint adequately specified.

In Lonergan's first example, the insight-mediated transition from image to definition represented a movement from the relatively concrete and imaginable to the unimaginable and conceptual. Between cartwheel and concept "there is an approximation but only an approximation" (I, 16e, emphasis mine).

> Now, the [the subject's] transition from arithmetic to elementary algebra is the same sort of thing. For an image of the cartwheel one substitutes the image of what may be named "doing arithmetic" . . . . In this large and virtual image, then, there is to be grasped [by the subject] a new set of rules governing operations . . . . In brief, they will differ from the old much as the highly exact and symmetrical circle differs from the cartwheel (I, 16e, emphases mine).

Sixthly, the subject "understands" that if he is to **develop** mathematically, he must:

> perform, over and over, the same type of **transition** . . . [that] occurred] in [his] advancing from arithmetic to elementary algebra (I, 17b, emaphsis mine).

It is only through the occurrence of these "transitions" that the limitations of his previous viewpoint, are transcended. Again, it is through the community of mathematical subjects in collaborative "transition" at various levels that the "serial" order to the

---

[1]Thus, given that "a" and "b" are any of the positive integers, a fraction will be any value resulting from operations upon them in accord with such rules as the following:

1. $\dfrac{a}{b} + \dfrac{c}{d} = \dfrac{ad + bc}{bd};$

2. $\dfrac{a}{b} - \dfrac{c}{d} = \dfrac{ad - bc}{bd};$

3. $\dfrac{a}{b} \times \dfrac{c}{d} = \dfrac{ac}{bd};$

4. $\dfrac{a}{b} - \dfrac{c}{d} = \dfrac{ad}{bc},$ etc., etc.

departments of mathematics has been generated.[1]

At each stage [and within each department] of the [collaborative] process there exist a set of rules that govern operations which result in numbers. To each stage there corresponds a symbolic image of doing arithmetic, doing algebra, doing calculus. In each successive image there is the potentiality of grasping by insight a higher set of rules that will govern the operations and by them elicit the numbers or symbols of the next stage (I, 17c, emphases mine).

Seventhly, understanding of the examples brings the subject to the further grasp that instead of:

the definition of the circle he can take any other intelligently performed act of defining . . . (I, 31b);

the transition from elementary arithmetic to elementary algebra one may review the process from Euclidean to Riemannian geometry [etc.] (I, 31b).[2]

Finally, then, the point to Lonergan's "second example," to the parallels and generalizations with which he associates it, has been to bring to the fore the operating "subject" of the mathematical attitude. It has been to bring to the fore the successive intellectual developments, the successive higher viewpoints which his intelligent operation implies. It has been to relate these developments and their corresponding "viewpoints" to an intentional circuit which proceeds on

---

[1]Thus, Lonergan notes that: "(a)ny department of mathematics can be cast in the form of a treatise by the method of logical formalization. But as Godel's theorem implies, for every set of mathematical definitions and axioms there is also a set of further questions that arise but cannot be answered on the basis of the definitions and axioms. Hence, mathematics cannot be included within a single treatise and, no matter how long one's series of treatises may be, there always will be occasion for further discoveries and further treatises" (I, 574b, emphases mine). Again, reflection on the process can yield insight into its "upper context," i.e., the unified "structure" of the intentional activity of the subject which founds and conserves the need for the further treatises (cf. I, xxxvc-xxxvib).

[2]The principles of a given geometry can be regarded as invariants under the permissible sets of transformations specified by the geometry. Thus, Lonergan, in Chapter V of Insight, notes that the sets of invariants represented, respectively, by "Euclidean, affine, projective, and topological geometries" represent "successive" higher viewpoints and, therefore, reflect the activity of the mathematical subject "in transition" (I, 147b).

three basic levels.   Thus, we have focused on the subject's "image,"
his "question-insight-formulation," and "reflection," etc.   But the
same three levels of human consciousness were in play in the first
example where their developmental implications were less clear.

3. Background

In Insight, I.4, Lonergan distinguishes between "direct" and "inverse" insights. Both arise within a prior experiential or imaginal context of conscious contents. Direct insight "grasps the point, sees the solution, comes to know the reason." Its content is some "positive intelligibility" that is "absent from our knowledge when we do not understand and added . . . inasmuch as we are understanding . . ." (I, 19d). Its conceptual expression may affirm this positive intelligibility "though it may deny [e.g., abstract from] expected empirical elements" (I, 19c, emphasis mine). Likewise, to "deny an intelligibility already reached" is to recognize questions left unanswered by the direct insight(s) which grasp(s) it. It is to recognize the need to complement or correct the direct insight(s) already arrived at. But this is not what is involved in the case of inverse insight. The latter:

> apprehends that in some fashion the point is that there is no point, or that the solution is to deny a solution, or that the reason is that the rationality of the real admits distinctions and qualifications (I, 19a, emphases mine).

Again, the conceptual formulation of an inverse insight may affirm "empirical elements only to deny an expected intelligibility" (I, 19c), even if this runs "counter to the spontaneous anticipations of intelligence" or faults not "answers but . . . questions [being asked]" (I, 19d). Thus, in a "demonstrative science," the emergence of an inverse insight is tantamount to proof:

> that a question of a given type cannot be answered. In an empirical science it is to put forward a successful hypothesis or theory that assumes that certain questions mistakenly are supposed to require an answer (I, 19d, emphases mine).

Furthermore, such insights will only come up:

> in the context of far larger developments of human thought. A statement of their content has to call upon later systems that positively exploited their negative contribution. The very success of the later systems tends to engender a routine that eliminates the [earlier] spontaneous anticipations of intelligence . . . (I, 20b).

Thus, a surd is generated when the subject follows out the inverse operation of division to its full generality. But the positive intelligibility of a rational fraction, which his question for intelligence "Why is a surd a surd?" anticipates, cannot be attained in principle. And this is so because the positive content of the insight that the number have magnitude is complemented by a negative component that "denies the possibility of applying to certain magnitudes some types of measurement . . ." (I, 20c). Similarly, the subject spontaneously anticipates the positive intelligibility of a countable multitude among the numbers between zero and one. But the infinite decimals are non-countably numerous and this was unanticipated. Lonergan adds two examples from physics. Thus, the Aristotelian anticipation of motion only in the presence of external force is denied by the principle of intertia embodied in Newton's first law. Thus, the proposals of Lorentz and Fitzgerald that the contraction of length and the dilation of time were only apparent in relation to an absolute space-time, are denied in Einstein's proposal that the mathematical expression of laws is to remain invariant, i.e., covariant, under inertial transformation.[1]

The "empirical residue" can only be "grasped" by a kind of inverse insight. To it no positive intelligibility corresponds (I, 27a). Still, it is something positive, consisting in "positive empirical data." But if it is the content of some primitive experience, prior, in the first instance to question, it is to be "denied any immanent intelligibility of its own" (I, 25c, emphases mine). But while lacking per se intelligibility, it is "connected with some higher compensating intelligibility of notable importance" (I, 26a). It is that from which the subject abstracts when he grasps what is truly important, significant, essential in the data, e.g., its "higher compensating intelligibility." The empirical, scientific

---

[1] The reader should note, then, that, in general, the subject's discovery that a given "viewpoint" in, for example, mathematics or

subject proceeds from description and classification of experiential
data to systems of laws which implicitly define the terms they relate.
But there is the "ideal goal" intended by the procession of such
explanatory systems where and when:

> all aspects of the data, except the empirical residue, will have
> their intelligible counterparts in systems of explanatory
> conjugates and ideal frequencies (I, 313b, emphases mine).

Thus, even "when a science or group of sciences reaches full
development" (I, 31a), e.g., this ideal goal of complete explanation,
the empirical residue would remain unexplained. Lonergan renders four
examples of the empirical residue: (1) particular places and times; (2)
the individual-"ity" of the individual, e.g., merely numerical
difference or manifoldness between instances; (3) non-systematic
divergence; (4) the continuum.[1] It is from the first of these four
that the intelligent subject abstracts when he grasps relationships of
invariance holding among objects of possible spatial and temporal
experience. Thus, different geometries offer:

> different intelligible orders for the differences in place and time
> that all equally presuppose and, quite correctly, none attempt to
> explain (I, 27b, emphases mine).

This residuality makes the collaboration of empirical scientists
possible since it assumes that:

> there is no discrimination against any result merely because of the
> place or merely because of the time of its origin (I, 28a).

It is from the second that intelligence abstracts when it grasps, for
instance, the "nature" of objects of possible experience. This grasp
is formulated in systems of laws by the method of implicit definition.

For if the individuality of the individual were explained, it would

---

science, fails to meet "all the relevant questions," is mediated by the
occurrence of an inverse insight. For this reason, inverse insight has
a special role in the dialectical method of the scientific subject (cf.
Section B10, below).

[1]Lonergan acknowledges that the list may not be complete, that
new, empirically residual elements may be uncovered "through the
introduction of new techniques of abstraction [in the sciences]" (I,
312c).

be meaningless to suppose that some other individual might be understood in exactly the same fashion . . . . because the individuality of the individual is not explained, it is only an exhaustive tour of inspection that can settle whether or not there exists another individual similar in all respects (I, 29b).

Thus, the technique of classical scientific generalization is possible because differences between individuals are merely residual. It is from the third of these that the intelligent subject abstracts when he grasps the ideal frequency with respect to which further differences among the actual frequencies of runs of events are merely random.[1] It is from the fourth that intelligence abstracts when it grasps the ideal limit.[2] Likewise, direct insight grasps the invariant, the universal, the ideal frequency, the limit in abstraction from their residual counterparts. Still, if they can be thought, they cannot be in separation from the latter.

---

[1]Cf. Section B4, below, on the "non-systematic."

[2]An example of this is given in Section B5, below.

4. The "Field" of Mathematical Activity

Governing the third level of human intentionality is the question for reflection "Is it so?" It triggers a mathematical process of checking whether understanding is correct? The "goal" of this checking is to:

marshall the evidence in the shape in which reflective understanding can grasp the virtually unconditioned, and so ground rational judgment. In so far as the checking reduces conclusions to premises, there is the virtually unconditioned of the form of deductive inference. In so far as the definitions and postulates coalesce into a self-justifying meaning, there is the virtually unconditioned of analytic propositions (I, 310e, emphases mine).

Thus, the general form of deductive inference, where "A" and "B" stand for propositions that have been affirmed is:

If A, then B
But A
Therefore B.

The major affirms the link between the conditioned and its conditions. The minor affirms the fulfillment of the conditions. B follows with necessity assuming the truth of the major. Analytic propositions are:

instances of the virtually conditioned in which the conditioned is linked to its conditions by syntactical rules and the conditions are fulfilled by defining terms (I, 313c).

Lonergan claims, first, that terms in their analytically defined senses are "not assertoric" and may occur in no "supposition or judgment" apart from the "affirmation of the analytic proposition" (I, 306a).

Secondly, where they do so occur, they "must be consistent with the analytic propostion . . ." (I, 305i). Thus, they are only "hypothetical."

Thirdly, analytic propositions can be "produced more or less at will and indefinitely" (I, 306c), by appropriately selecting (or stipulatively defining) rules and partial terms of meaning.

Fourthly, analytic propositions stand in "sterile isolation" (I, 306b), from the "texture of knowing" (I, 306b), unless they undergo "validation," i.e., unless their same terms in the same sense occur in "some other supposition or judgment"[1] (I, 306b, emphasis mine). It follows from this, then, that:

significant increments of knowledge are not to be obtained by mere ingenuity and, in fact, the analytic proposition, by itself, is not a significant increment of knowledge (I, 306c);

[Lonergan is] . . . in substantial agreement with the contemporary view that analytic propositions are tautologies (I, 306d).

In response to his third determination of analytic propositions, Lonergan notes that the premisses of mathematical thought are to be reached "only through the discoveries of genius and the labour of learning what genius has grasped" (I, 310f, emphases mine). In response to the fourth, there is the fact that some departments of mathematics consist of probable analytic principals, e.g., analytic propositions which have probable existential reference to the universe of real, emergent being. How, Lonergan asks, could this be if they are mere tautologies? Furthermore, prior to probable existential reference, there is:

a possible existential reference or isomorphism; before a department of mathematics can be applied, it must possess an inherent possibility of being applied. What, then, is that inherent possibility? (I, 310f-311a, emphases mine).

Thus, mathematical propositions are not merely analytic and the "problem of mathematical judgment," then, "consists in determining what else is required [besides analyticity] for such judgment" (I, 310e, emphases mine).

Lonergan claims that the answer to these questons is a function of three elements and that they are, respectively, material, formal, and actual. First, Lonergan distinguishes these elements generically. The first is the empirical residue, corresponding to the subject's experience. The second is the enriching abstraction—intelligible unities, correlations, laws—"added" to the data, corresponding to the intentional level of understanding. The third "lies in the conjunction

---

[1]Lonergan is talking about their occurrence in an analytic "principle." This is an analytic proposition whose terms and relations occur in certain or merely probable judgments of fact (I, 313c).

of the formal and material elements" (I, 311g) corresponding to the intentional act of judgment. Then, Lonergan applies this distinction of elements to the field of mathematical objects to resolve the questions raised in the preceding paragraph.

First, then, "mathematical **matter**" corresponds to the particularity of the cartwheel image in the first example, or the ununified manifold of "concrete instances of one, two, three" (I, 312b) with which the defining process began in the second. Recall the pre-supposition of:

> an indefinite multitude of instances of "one." They may be anything anyone pleases, from sheep to instances of the act of counting or ordering (I, 13e).

It is not the "thingness" of sheep, their or any other being's unity-identity-wholeness which figures in this defining process. What figures is the individuality or discreteness of any possible focus or datum in any possible field of human experience from which human intelligence must abstract to make sense. Thus, these "instances" are concrete and empirically residual in the sense that they represent the unordered manifold of discrete intentional data to-be-ordered but not actually ordered. Thus, no idea of the positive integers can emerge until, through acts of human understanding, the discrete intentional data are unified in thought. Once the idea has been grasped, there is nothing left to define. Yet the discreteness of the mathematical "data" remains unexplained even though insight has occurred and an adequate definition rendered. If the concern of the empirical researcher is to abstract from the empirical residue insofar as it bears on his specialized field of inquiry, the mathematician's is to discover possible orders unifying the total field of what any and all the empirical sciences must "leave unexplained."

Secondly, the **formal** element in mathematics corresponds to the definition of the circle in the first example, but, more properly, to the "dynamic" movement from a lower to a higher viewpoint in the second. Thus, logically, departments within mathematics are discontinuous. But "intellectually" they are related inasmuch as the "symbolic representation of operations in lower fields provides the images" through which questions for intelligence can orient consciousness towards the grasp of "the **new** rules that govern the operations in the higher field" (I, 312a, emphases mine). Wherever this transition has occurred, the higher mathematical viewpoint will order elements which from the lower viewpoint were regarded as merely residual or coincidental.

Thirdly, the **actual** element in mathematics "lies in the [serial] conjunction of the formal and material elements" (I, 311f). Cognitionally, this corresponds to the rendering of a mathematical judgment on the basis of the grasp of the virtually unconditioned. Thus, questions for reflection condition acts of "checking."

> Definitions are worked out. Postulates are added. From the definition and postulates it is shown that all the conclusions of the department can be reached by the rigorous procedures of deductive inference (I, 310d).

One's understanding of the field of mathematical data has been "validated" and ordered, and the validations occur "serially" in correspondence with successive transitions to higher viewpoints. But some mathematically validated systems function in the "upper blade" of empirical method. If empirical method anticipates complete explanation, still it requires experiential data (cf. the "Canon of Selection" (I, III.1)) and abstracts from the empirical residue.

> On the other hand . . . mathematical thought . . . begins from the empirical residue and endeavours to explore the totality of manners in which enriching abstraction can confer intelligibility upon **any** materials that resemble the empirical residue, (I, 313b, emphases mine).

Since the field from which the movement of scientific thought abstracts is the same as the one which the subject of the movement of mathematical thought takes as his data for discovering possibly relevant principles of order, the two movements are "complementary." Lonergan argues that:

> if the mathematical exploration of intelligible systems is thorough, then it is bound to include the systems of explanatory conjugates that the empirical sciences will verify in their respective domains (I, 313b).

Again, the movement of mathematical intelligence is under two constraints. First, it must traverse its series of stages while intending a "complete" account of residual, mathematically material data.

If there exist concrete instances of one, two, three, the mathematician [sequentially] explores the totality of positive integers, of real numbers, of complex numbers, of ordered sets. If there exist edges and surfaces, the mathematician works out not merely one geometry but the total series of possible geometries. If there are various fields in which it seems mathematics may be applied, the mathematician sets out to [sequentially] explore the whole of each region in which the fields occur (I, 312b, emphasis mine).

Secondly, it is limited by its material element not to:

individuals that exist, to continua that exist, to places and times that exist, to non-systematic divergences that occur . . . (I, 312c),

but to any intentional data [e.g., images, etc.] which sufficiently resemble the empirical residue. Hence, at the origin of the mathematical attitude is the intentionality of human consciousness oriented toward a complete account of all its proper data as it explores the possible intelligibility of anything which sufficiently resembles the empirical residue.

Thus, the object of the subject in the mathematical attitude is to establish serially but "generally, completely, and ideally":

the range of **possible** systems that include verifiable scientific systems as particular, fragmentary, or approximate cases (I, 314a, emphasis mine).

This is exactly equivalent to saying that the basic propositions which mathematics seeks to establish are "serially analytic principles" (I, 313c). Thus, the principles of mathematics are not merely analytic propositions since their limiting field comprises the empirical residue. Their possible existential reference results from the fact that they map out possible orders within the residue, some of which may have empirical application. Yet per se, the subject of the mathematical attitude is not concerned with or out to ascertain any matter of fact. She makes no claims concerning the actual world of experience which empirical method probes. Rather, she utilizes or constructs her own images where these resemble the empirical residue from which empirical method abstracts. In these images her intelligent queries grasp intelligible terms and relations which remain unspecified and coincidental from the perspective of human imagination. Insights coalesce and ground sets of definitions, postulates and theorems. Shortcomings of prior positions are recognized and corrected in reflection. Lower operations and symbols function as a "field" within which new understanding and conception take place. New definitions and postulates are projected and a larger field of deduction is set up and validated. The **shift** to a higher viewpoint occurs again and again. That process of shifting is cognitionally structured on three levels to which there correspond mathematically material, formal and actual elements. The greatest upper bound of the process would correspond to the subject's knowledge of the totality of possible mathematical systems. The greatest lower bound is the empirical residue by which the movement to totality is limited.[1] Human understanding is the key to the dynamism of the movement. Therefore, at the origin of the mathematical attitude is the pure intentionality of human conscious-ness, structured on the three intentional levels of experience and imagination, understanding, and judgment, oriented towards a complete account of the proper data of its field as it sequentially explores the possible intelligibility of anything that sufficiently resembles the empirical residue. And, finally, even as the mathematician may transpose her operations at some lower mathematical level into an image through which she may seek to decipher the outlines of a higher system, so the philosopher may transpose her own conscious operations of doing mathematics, ascending to higher possibly relevant viewpoints, etc., into an image through which she may be able to catch a clue to the outlines of the essential dynamic structures of her own activity, herSelf. But to have effected this transition, she must have transcended the mathematical attitude.

---

[1]Thus, the process to mathematical inquiry has upper and lower limits.

B. The Empirically Scientific Learning of the
Subject: Attitude and Object

Introduction

In Insight II.2, II.4, XV.7, and VII.5, Lonergan reflects upon the performance of the modern scientific subject. Through these reflections, he distinguishes and relates his, respectively, classical, statistical, genetic, and dialectical methods. And he prepares the ground for relating the particular "horizons" they circumscribe to their global explanatory "Horizon" of emergent probability (I, IV; cf. XV.5). In this chapter division, then, we will thematize these reflections from the point of view of the light they shed on the Being of "man." This can be done neither quickly nor easily, yet the fruits to be won justify the effort.

First, then, Lonergan's sense of the "heuristicity" of human consciousness will be introduced. Secondly, the "Notion of the Empirical" differentiating the mathematically and empirically scientific attitudes of the intellectual subject is sketched. Thirdly, the "Classical Heuristic Structure" of the scientific subject as well as the "systematic process" to which it corresponds are brought out. Fourthly, a reflection on the application of classical laws leads to the discovery of a "non-systematic" component in the data. But, "Statistical Heuristic Structure" brings the intelligibility of such processes to heel and this is the topic of a fifth subsection. The sixth and seventh subsections of this division sketch the notion of "Emergent Probability" implicit in the "complementarity" of the classical and statistical methods of the subject. Eighthly, from the viewpoint won by the preceding reflections, the notion of the "thing" is set forth and a fully explanatory "definition" of the "thing-subject," "man," is laid bare. Ninthly, the "Genetic Heuristic Structure" of the subject is set forth and its presupposition in the preceding reflections is brought out. Tenthly, the "Dialectical Method" of the subject is sketched abstractly and, then, by relating it to the expanded considerations of the issues raised in Chapters I to V, above. _Finally_, a brief conclusion to the preceding reflections is added. And this addition will involve a brief reflection on the "proximate" and "remote" criteria of truth. The proviso should be included that if the communal and historical dimensions of the human, scientific pursuit and, specifically, their corollary notion of _belief_, have been implicitly present throughout the discussion, we have abstracted from their theoretical discussion. And we have done so not because they lack importance, but only on pain of contributing further length to an already long explication.

1. Lonergan's Analysis of the Heuristic Notion and Structure of Consciousness

From ingredient acts of understanding answers issue into the flow of human consciousness. And prior to this issue are the questions which anticipate answers and the relevant insights which condition them. Such anticipation:

> may be employed systematically in the determination of answers that are yet unknown; for while the content of a future cognitional act is unknown, the general characteristics of the act [of understanding] itself not only can be known but also can supply a premise that leads to the act (I, 392a, emphases mine).

The process of antecedently determining the "general characteristics" of the human act of understanding in respect of which it grasps its contents is the process of human consciousness discovering and bringing forth into thematic awareness the structural "heuristicity" of its own conscious activity of discovery.

> "Heuristic" is from the Greek word heurisko, to find. In Greek, the ending —ikon denotes the principle. So a heuristic is a principle of discovery (UB, 74b, emphases mine).

Taking the discovery of the self as a heuristic principle as a clue, Lonergan distinguishes the heuristic notion and structure of human consciousness.

> A heuristic notion . . . is the notion of an unknown content and it is determined by anticipating the type of act [of understanding] through which the unknown would become known (I, 392a, emphases mine).

But how are the "general characteristics" of the future act of understanding which will guide the inquirer in her attempt to discover the unknown content of the act be determined in advance? Lonergan's answer is that they will be uncovered by reflecting upon and correctly grasping what is already implicitly understood about one's object when from within the intellectual-scientific attitude of experience one raises a **question** for intelligence.[1] Thus, specific heuristic notions

---

[1]There are also heuristic notions associated with questions for reflection, deliberation, salvation, etc. Here I am confining myself

are implicit in questions for intelligence of given kinds. They
represent what is implicitly pre-understood when, from within the
scientific attitude, the subject raises an intelligent question. The
following example initiates a clarification of Lonergan's intent. It
turns upon the distinction between heuristic and explanatory notions
(or concepts) and suggests that the intentional identity of the
heuristic notion of the subject forms the unifying "base" for an
indefinite but converging "series of scientific explanations."[1] Thus:

> things may not change, but man's understanding of them may develop.
> Now a change of understanding involves a change in explanatory
> conception, for the explanatory concept may be defined as an
> expression of the content of the understanding. Yet here there is
> an important distinction between heuristic and explanatory
> concepts. Fire was conceived by Aristotle as an element, by
> Lavoisier's predecessors as a manifestation of phlogiston, and by
> later chemists as a type of oxidation. But though the explanations
> differed, the object to be explained was conceived uniformly as the
> "nature of" a familiar phenomenon, and without this uniformity it
> would be incorrect to say that Aristotle had an incorrect
> explanation of what he meant and we mean by fire (I, 737c, emphases
> mine).

Lonergan offers a second example in which the series of successive
revisions of the conceptual framework for explaining the nature of free
fall is traced. Thus, historically, we have the accounts of Aristotle,
Galileo, Newton, and Einstein. But while explanatory concepts admit
revision:

> (o)ne cannot revise the heuristic notion that the nature of free
> fall is what is to be known when the free fall is correctly under-
> stood; for it is that heuristic notion that is both antecedent to
> each determinate account and, as well, subsequent to each and the
> principle of the revision of each (I, 394a, emphases mine).

In both examples, then, the heuristic notion implicit in the humanly
posed "What?"-question guides the converging series of successively
revised explanations towards its goal. Again, it is such "What?"
-asking which signals the intentional anticipation of a "nature-to-be

---

to one of the heuristic notions of consciousness.

[1]My examples are drawn from classical scientific notions of
consciousness. But modern statistical method also involves an implicit
notion, etc.

-known," the lack of or inadequate understanding of the described phenomena, and the need to press on with inquiry until, in the limit, the goal of complete explanation is achieved and the unknown nature is known. Furthermore, that initial anticipation:

> implies that there is something there to be known by understanding. It is fruitful in the measure that it leads through partial insights and further questions to an adequate grasp of the speculative or practical issue at hand (I, 541c–542a).

But since **all** human subjects inevitably raise such questions as "what?" and "why?," **all** are committed by virtue of the implicit intentionality of their own asking towards, all have an <u>implicit</u> sense of the meaning of, the "nature of . . . ." Granted this <u>implicit</u> grasp, many remain "at a loss to say what they mean [by it]." Granted an <u>explicit</u> grasp of this notion, it still remains that one "has to discover what the nature [in any given case] is . . . ." Still, the notion of nature "used properly . . . supplies the dynamic base on which <u>the whole of</u> <u>scientific knowledge</u> is erected" (<u>I</u>, 683b, emphases mine).

But what is the force of the "used properly" which opens the preceding quotation? Lonergan's implicit answer turns on a distinction between heuristic <u>notion</u> and heuristic <u>concept</u>. The former is the subject's pre-predicative pre-"understanding" of her intended "object" which she possesses in virtue of her ability to raise questions with explanatory intent. This <u>notion</u> is utterly invariant, prior to any conceptual or linguistic expression, and absolutely normative with to respect to particular inquirers. The latter is its <u>conceptual</u> expression. It can admit a measure of development. Thus, "with the discovery of the significance of measurement" (<u>I</u>, 737d) for understanding the surrounding world of nature, there was a <u>first</u> "shift" or progression in heuristic <u>concepts</u>. The shift turned classical scientific inquiry away from a "vague" anticipation of the "nature of . . ." based on the similarities of "things in relation to us" (<u>I</u>, 37g), and the merely classificatory concepts (cf. <u>I</u>, 37i) which it introduced into the data to be explained. This **first** progression turned scientific inquiry <u>towards</u> a more precise mathematical <u>expression</u> of the heuristic <u>notion</u> of nature (at least for sciences such as physics, chemistry, etc.) in terms of an "indeterminate function to be determined" (I, 737d). With this shift, empirical inquiry could avail itself of the explanatory possibilities of measurement through which scientific understanding could probe the relations of "the things in relation to each other." Thus, the relevant similarities of classical modern science transcend or leap beyond the field of thing-to-us, sensitive, imaginable, common sensical or descriptive relations. Its focus may pivot beyond audio-visual, tactile, figure-ground, or everyday similarities to grasp counted, quantified and/or measured similarities of remoteness or proximity, concomitant variation, antecedence or consequence, proportion, etc. Such similarities are the "proximate materials of insight into nature" (I, 38a). Thus, things may be:

> similar in their [measurable] proportions to one another, and such proportions may form series of [implicitly defined] relationships, such as exist between the elements in the periodic table or between the successive forms of life in the theory of evolution (I, 37h);

And the science of "mechanics studies the relations of masses, not to our senses, but to one another" (I, 78a). Again, in a **second** progressive shift, the initial development in the classical heuristic framework of inquiry from one that is basically Aristotelian to one associated with the work of Newton, Clerk-Maxwell, and Einstein, is itself retained and transcended. It has, in fact, been:

> complemented by statistical [method], and both [classical and statistical methods] may be complemented by genetic and by dialectical methods (I, 737d).

In explanation of this complementation, Lonergan notes that when contemporary scientists failed to obtain theories of a classical kind that explained all the experimental data, they changed "the ideal [of scientific explanation] itself from law and system [e.g., explanation in classical scientific form] to states and probabilities" (UB, 6c).[1] Thus, the heuristic notion of:

---

[1]Lonergan's point here is important and must not be missed: "basic" method structures even such a development. Thus, once modern classical understanding of the empirical data of science was judged to

what one is seeking in knowledge, is something that is not conceptually explicit. It becomes explicit in the [successive historical reflections upon the] pursuit of [scientific] knowledge (UB, 6b).

Thus, Lonergan is arguing that the development in heuristic conceptions, signaled by the two-fold progressive shift sketched above, represents the development of the manners in which one and the same scientific goal is pursued, e.g., for Aristotle (as well as for Newton and Einstein), the nature of the object is conceived as what would be known were it fully understood. Thus, the two-fold shift represents an "affirmation of identity not only in difference but in development" (I, 739b), implies no "ultimate multiplicity" (I, 739a) of heuristic concepts. Lonergan suggests that "behind" any such variations in heuristic concepts lies both the identity of the pre-conceptual heuristic notion and its question, and a "conceptual constant that can be formulated from a universal viewpoint" (I, 739a, emphases mine, cf. I, 564-568). He argues that the name:

"method" suggests . . . [that] these [variations in heuristic concept] are not determinations of a new goal [for scientific inquiry, but merely] determinations of a new procedure or technique for reaching the goal that already was envisaged, though hardly attained, when men referred to what was to be known by understanding as "the nature of . . . ." (I, 737d).

The heuristic structure of human consciousness guides the movement of inquiry through the a series of stages by which some "object" of experience and imagination first, calls itself into question; secondly, is inquired into so that the unknown object will become known, e.g., correctly understood; thirdly, is in fact affirmed to be known. Thus, because of the "heuristicity" of conscious structure, every unknown theme for human inquiry is always already a

---

leave too many kinds of questions unanswered, to be neither false nor entirely adequate despite manifold attempts at such understanding over long time intervals, these recognized limitations propelled a movement to fuller non-classical kinds of human understanding to complement what had already been achieved in the first development. Thus, the implicit "notions" of the statistical, genetic, and dialectical, their "transcendence" of the classical, of each other, will be discussed below.

"known unknown."[1]   Lonergan's algebraic analogy for this structure starts with a question: when after three o'clock will the minute hand meet the hour hand?

In a _first_ step, the subject names the unknown.   But this act of "letting X be the required number of minutes" outlines this unknown against the background of the number field and implicitly anticipates the discovery of a fixed pattern of determinable relations with a potential infinity of numbers.   Thus, a guiding "notion" of X has already been put into play by this naming and its underlying asking.

Secondly, she "infers the properties and relations of the unknown," usually by marking or constructing a diagram symbolizing all the known features of X. Manipulating a clock face, we note that as the minute hand moves over X minutes, the hour hand moves through X/12.

In a _third_ step, she combines these properties and relations to form an equation: X=X/12+15. Lastly, she solves for the unknown.

In this subsection, then, Lonergan's reflective revelation of the "heuristicity" of human consciousness, of the heuristic "notion" and "structure" of the subject's scientific funtioning have been brought out.   Again the important sense in which the subject's heuristic conception of her "object" mediates the development of her knowledge while being itself subject to _development_ was also "clarified."

---

[1]Corresponding to its different heuristic notions, the heuristic structure of scientific consciousness can be distinguished as classical, statistical, etc. But the latter, like their corresponding heuristic concepts, can develop.   Thus, when Lonergan recapitulates the statistical heuristic structure of scientific consciousness (on "analogy" with its classical complement), he does so _not_ with: "the hope of determining what precisely probability must be in all cases but rather with the intention of grasping the underlying anticipations that inform statistical inquiry and are to be expected gradually to mount through trial and error, through theoretical discoveries and developing techniques, to some rounded methodological position such as already is enjoyed in classical investigations. [Thus] . . . there is genesis of scientific method itself . . ." (_I_, 62c). Again, this process of methodological development is triadically structured by the recognition of an inadequate unification of sets of _data_, _understanding_ (with its preliminary rounds of trial and error), and the _affirmed_ adequacy of a rounded methodology.

2. The Notion of the Empirical

In _Insight_ II.1.1-1.2, Lonergan performs a reflective analysis of, first, the key similarities and, then, the key differences between the mathematical and scientific horizons of human inquiry. Thus, if correct, such analysis has a priori significance. This significance lies in its differentiation of _two_ distinct orientations of the subject-toward-his-"objects" within its intellectual pattern of experience. The ulterior point of the analysis, then, is to bring out the implicit notion of the empirical underlying human scientific intentionality and to answer the question "What is the character of the materials I am understanding when I am doing science?" This implicit question and its notion have a priori significance for the analysis of the subject. Thus, whenever he understands scientifically, no matter how "remote" his object is from sources in immediate perception, his understanding ultimately proceeds _from_ the experience, observation, and imaging of concrete sets of data. Thus, it is ultimately only with respect to the empirical that human scientific intentionality gathers, refutes, corrects validates and revises its manifold acts of understanding of its objects. This notion of and, hence, orientation of scientific consciousness towards the empirical underlies all five of its differentiations from the mathematical which Lonergan brings out.

Considering the similarities, we can say in advance of any actual inquiry that, first, both intentions would grasp only the immanent formal intelligibility of their respective objects and abstract from all not immediately relevant to it. Thus, consideration of the material composition, agency, and human purpose of a cartwheel are as irrelevant to grasping the implicit set of terms and relations defining its circularity as analogous considerations would be to grasping the laws which render the free fall of a canon ball intelligible. Secondly, both forms of inquiry anticipate a priori that correlations will be discovered unifying quantifiable aspects of the data. Thus, the common if implicit assumptions to which the inquiries of a Pythagoras, no less than a Galileo committed them would be that objects sustain observable and measurable relationships; that these could be mastered by "understanding;" that understanding could be so determined in exact mathematical terms as to prove isomorphic with further sets of relevant empirical data. Finally, it holds a priori that both mathematical and empirically scientific acts of understanding grasp terms and relationships that "transcend" the concrete and, hence, are only approximated to by the data of experience. Thus, just as the sum of the angles of a triangle can be established mathematically but only approximately diagrammed or imagined, so the law of falling bodies holds "only in a vacuum" and no perfect vacuum, in fact, exists.[1]

Considering the key differences, we can say in advance of any actual inquiry that, first, whereas mathematical inquiry regards images in any way resembling the empirical residue, empirical inquiry regards only images founded on what is perceptually given, e.g., tables, charts, etc., constructed from sets of descriptions and measurements. Secondly, the images of the mathematical subject will always consist in a continuum of data, e.g., smooth lines, etc. Given the inevitable discreteness of observation and experiment, the images which represent them for the empirical subject can offer no more than discontinuous, serial and unconnected sets of data for understanding. Thirdly, "in"

---

[1]Lonergan's point here is not that these laws make reference to and apply only in an ideal state of affairs. His point is that the terms and relations of the law specify the elements implicit in an abstract conceptual system. But conceptual systems abstract from the concrete components of the data and, hence, always remain, to some extent, indeterminate in relation to the fullness of concrete reality. Thus, the indeterminacy of the conceptual is correlative with the non-systematicity of the concrete. Thus, correctly to apply Galileo's law to concrete objects, further determinations would have to be added. These would include laws of air resistance, friction, and further statistical laws. Thus, Lonergan writes: "(t)he law of falling bodies is not a statement of what would happen in a perfect vacuum; it is the statement of an element in an abstract system, and the complete system can be applied to any particular case. Again, Einstein's differential equations are not statements about positions and velocities in defiance of Heisenberg's principle; they are statements of the abstractness and so invariance of classical laws. The proper answer to the old determinism is an affirmation, not of indeterminism on the same imaginative level, but of the indeterminacy of the abstract" (I, 101b, emphases mine).

such images, the mathematician may grasp relations of <u>necessity</u> or <u>impossibility</u>.

> But the [empirical inquirer's] insight into the discontinuous series of points on the graph [of the empirical data] consists in a grasp . . . simply of possibility (<u>I</u>, 34e).

Thus, short of the ideal limit of human inquiry where all the <u>relevant</u> data are in, and in accurately, alternate curves might be devisable that would account for all the relevant <u>available</u> data. Further data gathering could alone decide between the two possibilities. <u>Fourthly</u>, we can anticipate in advance the mathematical subject's serial construction of images that keep pace with the thinking his insights have triggered. Thus, he <u>thinks</u> of lines, but <u>imagines</u> fine threads (<u>I</u>, 35a). The scientist's imagination will also emit phantasms in "closest aproximation to the laws he conceives." But it is true a <u>priori</u> that his data will always:

> go their own way with their unanalyzed multiplicity and their refractoriness to measurements that are no more than approximate (<u>I</u>, 35a).

<u>Finally</u>, although the circuit of mathematical inquiry advances through a linked intentional sequence of operations toward the discovery of higher viewpoints "in" lower symbolic images, the circuit remains wholly "immanent." On the other hand, "the circuit of scientific development includes action upon <u>external</u> things . . ." (<u>I</u>, 35c, emphasis mine).

Thus, although the subject of empirical inquiry also traverses a circuit which advances through a linked set of higher viewpoints, he is always implicitly committed by his own or his associates' activities of collecting, tabulating, and search for the correct understanding of the immanent laws of these collections and tabulations of data, to the <u>transcendence</u> of the "world," to the submission of his discoveries to <u>its</u> authority, to the <u>independence</u> of its objects and relations from his pre-scientific concerns. Thus, initial insights into the data may reflect nothing more than the grasp of unverified possibility. But, controlled experimental attempts independently to verify his under-standing will uncover the fresh, overlooked or discarded empirical evidence "for the confirmation or the revision of existing views" (<u>I</u>,35c).

3. Classical Heuristic Structure

In the preceding section, the heuristic significance of the empirical as the starting point for scientific questioning of the surrounding world process was outlined. In _Insight_, Chapter II, Sections 2 and 4.4, and _Understanding and Being_, pp. 76c–83a, Lonergan presents the fruits of his reflections upon the "classical" heuristicity of human consciousness as evolved and refined into a methodical structure of human inquiry. In this section of this chapter division, the distinguishing elements of the intentional "structure" Lonergan has brought out are sketched. _First_, the heuristic notion guiding and prefiguring the classical subject's understanding of the empirical data is explicated. _Secondly_, the ways "up" and "down" of his inquiring, the distinct ways in which his heuristically guided anticipations of his "object" are "filled out," are traced.

First, the heuristic notion of the classical scientific attitude is "the nature of . . . ."[1] This notion is implicit in questions of the form "What is X?" or "Why is Y X?" Thus, prior to Galileo's discovery that free fall was a constant acceleration, he already knew:

> from the mere fact that he inquired . . . that a free fall possessed a nature, though he did not know what that nature was (_I_, 37, emphases mine).

At the root of this notion stands two corollary heuristic "principles." _In the first place_, similars are to be similarly understood. Thus, for example, the individuality of the individual is consigned to the empirical residue. This principle anticipates the content of a "universal definition" which will "be the same for all similar sets of data" (_I_, 37c), which will fit the gathered data as well as all similar cases thereof. _In the second place_, the field of relevant similarities abstracts from the relations of things **to us**. Rather, it heads for and, at the limit grasps, the relations of things to **each other** by

---

[1] The naming of the classical scientific subject's "known unknown" represents a first correspondence to the algebraist's naming of his unknown "X."

availing itself of standardized measuring contexts.[1] Thus, the classical subject advances *from* preliminary sensible classifications, through experimentally measured similarities of things to each other, to the limit at which an understanding of the explanatory terms and relations governing the interactions of these things are correctly determined and affirmed. Thus, the "nature" of the "object" of the classical subject's at first, classified and, then, measured and collated data is initially to be expressed as "the unspecified correlation to be specified. It can, alternatively, be expressed as the undetermined function to be determined" (I, 38a), the unknown law or equation to be known, the undetermined **implicit definition** to be laid down.[2]

Lonergan's point here is that given the legitimacy of the first heuristic conceptual development, that both at any given "stage" of classical scientific inquiry as well as at the "limit" where anticipation and approximation by stages has given way to a unique, accurate, and complete determination of natures, that the initially sought after correlation, function, law (or unified set thereof):

---

[1]Two points should be made here.

First, Lonergan's specification of these corollary "heuristic principles" corresponds to the algebraist's setting down of all the properties and relations, of everything he already knows about "X."

Secondly, Lonergan notes that: "the principal technique in effecting the transition from description to explanation is measurement. We move away from colors as seen, fom sounds as heard, from heat and pressure as felt. In their place, we determine the numbers named measurements. In virtue of this substitution, we are able to turn from the relations of sensible terms, which are correlative to our senses, to the relations of numbers, which are correlative to one another. Such is the fundamental significance of measurement" (I, 165a, emphases mine).

[2]Lonergan's point here stems from the fact that any mathematical equation can be expressed functionally by substracting the set of terms appearing on one side of the equation from both sides. From $z=x^2+y^2$, therefore, we can arrive at $z-x^2-y^2=0$, or in more general terms $f(x,y,z)=0$. Thus, for some determinate set of magnitudes designated by "x," "y" and "z," the value of the function is zero (cf. Pat Byrne, "Lonergan and the Foundations of Relativity Theory" in Creativity and Method, ed. Matthew Lamb (Milwaukee: Marquette University Press, 1981), p. 483 n12). Finally, on either interpretation, a set of empirically

(1) is grasped in a single insight or a unique, orderly basic set thereof;

(2) grasps the "immanent intelligibility" of its queried "object;"

(3) groups and, thereby, implicitly defines a field of primitive terms[1] and relations where the terms fix the relations, the relations fix the terms, and both terms and relations are fixed (not merely by an underlying insight or orderly set thereof) but by their relations to an open set of empirically established and/or establishable measuring contexts;

(4) specifies the "nature," or "formal cause" of its queried object precisely by relating it as what is implicitly defined by this set of terms and relations;

(5) specifies the empirical presence of its queried "object" as whatever "falls under" or "converges upon" concrete sets of measured determinations isomorphic with those that have been abstractly defined.

Thus, in response to the question "What is mass?" one may proximately reply that it will be "whatever fulfills the fundamental equations as regards masses" (LED, VI.3.4, p. 142c).

> Thus, masses might be defined as the correlatives implicit in Newton's law of inverse squares. Then, there would be a pattern of relationships constituted by the verified equation; the pattern of relationships would fix the meaning of the pair of coefficients, m_1, m_2; and the meaning so determined would be the meaning of the name, mass (I, 80c).

Subsequently, however:

> when you add on a new fundamental equation about mass, as Einstein did when he equated mass with energy, you get a new idea of mass

---

measurable terms are being implicitly defined by their relations to one another. This is the original insight organizing the discussion of the classical heuristic notion of the subject.

[1]Lonergan also refers to such terms as pure or explanatory "conjugates." They are "correlatives implicitly defined by empirically established correlations, functions, laws, theories, systems" (I, 80b). Thus, the explanatory conjugates intended by the subject of classical understanding are implicitly defined in terms of the experimentally verified relations and symbolically specifiable operations which group them.

(<u>LED</u>, VI.3.4, p. 142c).

Only at the ideal <u>limit</u> of inquiry and <u>if</u> mass is a "notion that survives in fully explanatory science" (cf. <u>I</u>, 437d) would the <u>full</u> explanatory meaning of this pure conjugate form be fixed.[1]

<u>Secondly</u>, the classical inquirer "moves in" from two intentional "angles" (cf. <u>UB</u>, 241b) upon the immanent law of "nature" he is seeking. There is, on the one hand, the "ascending" movement of consciousness, from the below of <u>data</u> "up" and, on the other, the "descending" movement from high order laws provided by the mathematician "down" <u>to</u> the unknown law in question.

Within the movement of <u>empirical</u> conscious inquiry "upwards," a series of stages can be distinguished. In the simplest case, the <u>classical</u> inquirer:[2]

(1a) is <u>oriented</u> to discover an "intelligibility" in the **data**. But, the "data" have already been pre-scientifically described on the basis of immediate, sensible similarities (cf. <u>I</u>, 38b, 63c). And the relevant intelligibility is to be expressed mathematically in terms of his **notions** of, first, the empirical, and secondly, "the nature of . . .;"

(b) <u>redescribes</u> his data field to invest it with potential "explanatory" relevance. Thus:

> **measurement** is added to observation and mere sensible similarity gives way to similarities of conjunction and separation, of proportion and concomitant variation (<u>I</u>, 64b, emphasis mine).[3]

---

[1]Thus, Lindsay and Margenau argue that Maxwell's field equations may themselves be regarded as defining the meaning of its key terms. They write that: "(i)t seems most logical to . . . treat E and H as defined by the field equations in all cases. The commoner definitions can then be looked upon as mere <u>picturizations</u>." <u>Foundations of Physics</u> (New York: Dover Publications, 1956), p. 311a.

[2]Two brief points should be inserted here. First, the key-words summarizing the steps in the process are written in bold letters. Secondly, Lonergan uses Galileo's law of falling bodies to illustrate this process in <u>LED</u>, VI.1.

[3]The classical inquirer: "measures, but he does so many times, and his accepted result is just the probable mean of actual results. He reaches a conclusion with which others agree, but the agreement

This redescription, then, involves the selection of variables that are quantifiable, measurable, and heuristically promising. The redescription is extended by, for example, **tabulating** known results and constructing a **graph** from the table. The representation of known values for measured variables on distinct axes of the graph constitutes the construction of an **"image"** or phantasm heuristically "representing" the things in their relations to each other. With his preparation of this **"phantasm"** mediating the intentionality of his question, the subject may <u>attempt</u> the further transition to the explanatory grasp of the immanent "functional relations" ($\underline{I}$, 64b) ordering the data;

(2) discovers in a "leap of constructive intelligence" ($\underline{I}$, 64f), e.g., an act of **understanding**, the "simplest" ($\underline{I}$, 90c) intelligible law which will enrich what, from the scientific viewpoint of the subject, is no more than a coincidentally and factually related set of data, tabulations, points plotted on a graph, etc., with its higher <u>intelligible</u> complement. This intentional "leap" of understanding, therefore:

> goes beyond ascertained measurements to posit a functional relation on which the relations between all appropriate subsequent measurements should converge as on a limit . . . ($\underline{I}$, 64f).

This leap is further prepared for by the use of such practical techniques as **curve fitting** and/or the use of a digital computer. Since the success of the leap is limited by: inadequately large and/or any distorted data samples, the inadequate skill and/or detachment of the inquirer, the

---

makes allowance for the intrusion of extraneous factors and it acknowledges no more than a limited number of significant decimal places. At every turn it seems apparent that <u>the</u> concern of experiment is to determine, <u>not the particular observable qualities of the particular materials with which one deals, but a theoretical correlation between definable and abstract entities</u>" ($\underline{I}$, 90b, emphases mine). Thus, classical experimentation, like the laws to which it leads, operates under a high level of "abstraction" from the fullness of the concrete.

impossibility of formalizing the meaning of "simplicity," the impossibility of <u>demonstrating</u> that a discontinuous set of measurements is satisfied by only one law, etc., therefore, in actual fact and short of the ideal limit of inquiry, the leap only yields a <u>possible</u> law of nature;

(3) will attempt to **verify** his grasp of the possible law of nature by using it to explore data in unexplored domains. This <u>attempt</u> of the inquirer, like that of his search for the "simplest" continuous function "fitting" the set of graphed data, is motivated by his <u>ulterior</u> purpose in conducting the inquiry: to discover the <u>law</u>, to grasp in one synthetic act of understanding <u>the</u> abstract system of terms and relations which <u>correctly</u> unifies <u>not</u> <u>only</u> the known cases of measured data, the actually plotted points on a graph, but <u>any</u> empirical data of the relevant kind, <u>any</u> accurately collected and plotted set of data of a similar kind. The actual attempt to verify may proceed directly, taking the form of interpolation, extrapolation, etc., or indirectly, e.g., Galileo's law of falling bodies has figured in and received indirect verification through the construction of mechanical experiments for over four hundred years. Given attempts at verification will either provide further confirmatory evidence for the given act of classical understanding or bring forth the evidence that will rule it out, specify its limits, force its revision, etc. Thus, Galileo's semi-empirical law of falling bodies[1] $S=5t^2$, grasps the simplest rule among a multiplicity of possible hypotheses covering observed values for S and t. Attempts to extrapolate from this law proved that it only holds near the surface of the earth. Further, it contains the number "5" for which no explanation is offered. From Newton's laws, on the other hand, the formula[2] $S=1/2gt^2$ can be deduced which has a

---

[1] In this equation "S" designates the height (in meters) of a body that has been freely falling for <u>t</u> seconds.

[2] In this equation "g" means the "acceleration of gravity." Mario

wider domain of application than Galileo's law, and applies "within limits" to any homogenous gravitational field of intensity "g." Again, "g" is a non–observational theoretical concept whose meaning is implicitly defined in terms of Newton's generalized theory of gravitation. But the latter represents a first instance of the classical scientific subject's transcendence of the merely empirical generalization, his achievement of a "systematic," verified understanding of physical phenomena.

Thus, the movement of inquiry upwards advances along the following path: empirical data, a "what?" or "why?" question with its heuristic notion, the use of measurement, tabulation, and graphing to construct an "image" of the data, "understanding" of the data, "verification" of the understanding. The circuit closes and opens and only closes for good when adequate understanding finds verification.

The movement of classical scientific inquiry from "above" downwards "to" the data of experience avails itself of the mathematician's verified understanding of intelligible systems of relations in pure quantitative manifolds, e.g., any manifolds which sufficiently resemble the "empirical residue," to discover empirically verifiable mathematical laws, functions, etc.[1] Thus, just as the algebraist approaches his unknown by inferring the properties and relations of "X," so, in still another context, the empirical inquirer

---

Bunge offers a clear account of this material on Galileo. He goes on to note that this second law: "could not have been obtained by induction because it contains a non–observational theoretical concept [e.g., an act of understanding is necessary to grasp this law as a whole] . . . designated by "g," which . . . makes sense [only] in a **theory** of gravitation [e.g., with its set of implicitly defined but verified terms and relations]. Considerations of simplicity are also alien to this law . . . the final word then, is given neither by induction nor by simplicity but rather by the continuity with the bulk of scientific knowledge." Scientific Research I (New York: Springer Verlag, 1967), pp. 285a, emphases mine; cf. pp. 280–290.

[1] The reason why independently generated mathematical systems should prove relevant to the determination of empirical laws has been discussed in Section A5, above, concerned with the nature of the mathematical attitude of the scientific subject.

can immediately determine certain very general features of his data by "writing down differential equations which it [e.g., the unknown function] must satisfy" (I, 38e, emphases mine).

Two kinds of further determinations guide the step downward from these extremely general determinations to the unknown law. On the one hand, paralleling the fifteen minute head start of the hour hand at three o'clock in the algebraic example, there are the empirical "boundary conditions that restrict the range of functions satisfying the differential equation" (I, 39c). On the other hand, the classical empirical inquirer has to select from the range of functions which represent particular solutions to the differential equations, the one that: fits not only the given case but all similar cases and which is consistent with the laws discovered to be already applicable in all other cases.[1] Thus, very general heuristic theorems based on a reflective understanding of human cognitive intentionality and its heuristic notions[2] guide the movement "downward." Lonergan determines them as heuristic principles of "invariance" and "equivalence."

To sketch the first, it must be recalled that because differences of place and time belong to the empirical residue, scientific discoveries are both independent of the place and time of their origin and claim truth independently of merely spatio-temporal differences of

---

[1]Thus, the ideal of system is to be respected by the classical inquirer. The ideal of systematic unification is effected: "in the logical or conceptual order. It is attained when the totality of laws is reduced to minimum sets of defined terms and postulates, so that any law can be related to any other, and any aggregate of laws can be intelligently combined and simultaneously employed" (I, 92c). Lonergan adds that the "canon of operations" (Cf. Section B7, below) forces empirical inquiry to head beyond aggregations of isolated laws towards the discovery of correlations between laws. Thus: "(t)here exists . . . a movement towards the systematic unification of classical laws and, as this unification is prompted by concrete problems, one may expect that, when all laws are known exactly and completely, there also will be known a systematic unification commensurate with world process in its concrete, historical unfolding" (I, 91d). Cf. footnote 3, pp. 149-150, above.

[2]I have in mind the notions of the empirical and, more importantly for the discussion that follows, the corollary to that of "nature" concerning the understanding of similars.

applications. Physical motion is a change in place and time. But particular places and times are always represented, and that representation in terms of points and instants is always relative to a particular origin and orientation. Hence, the application of physical laws to motions is always mediated by the particular origin and orientation of some specified kind of reference frame. But:

> . . . when a special effort is made, the mathematical expression of physical principles and laws undergoes no change in form despite changes in spatio-temporal standpoint [e.g., reference frame] and then the mathematical expression is said to be invariant under some specified group of transformations [between frames] (I, 40a, emphasis mine).[1]

Thus, the physical "nature" which is understood, the set of physical laws which is grasped, is not to be limited to the particular origin and orientation of a given reference frame of a particular kind but must be "invariant" under any relevant group of spatio-temporal transformations among frames of that kind. The canon of invariance, therefore, protects the heuristic assumption that similars are to be similarly understood. Thus, the relevant physical correlations are not to vary with but to hold independently of merely spatio-temporal differences of reference.

A second principle, that of equivalence is invoked to specify under which group of transformations invariance is to be achieved. It asserts that physical principles and laws "are the same for all observers [e.g., for all local frames of reference]" (I, 40c). This principle follows from the first heuristic development of classical scientific method, namely, that the relations of things not to us, to our sensitivity, but the relations of things to each other are to be thematized if a full explanatory viewpoint is to be achieved. Lonergan's point here is that since classical scientific laws are arrived at by abstracting from and transcending the relations of things to the observer's senses and determining the abstract laws governing

---

[1]The discerning reader may have noted Lonergan's underlying point—an "inverse" insight mediates the subject's discovery of the invariance of classical laws.

relations between the concrete measured relations of things to one another, that these laws lie "outside" the field of the things' relations to us. Thus, physical objects may not look the same from all observational standpoints, nor need they be identically represented with respect to all possible relevant frames of reference. But, even so, as equivalent they will sustain the same set of invariant physical laws "for all 'observers.'"

> It is, for example, not the appearance of colours but the general explanation in terms of wave-lengths of light that is exactly the same no matter what may be the state of the observers' eyes, the lighting by which they see, or the speed with which they may happen to be in relative motion (I, 41b, emphases mine).

Lonergan concludes his discussion of these two methodological principles of classical scientific understanding by showing their interpretative adequacy for rendering key features of Special and General Relativity Theory. Thus, while the movement of consciousness "downwards" presupposes empirical data, the notion of "nature," and sets of collated and graphed measurements, it understands its data with the help of systems of mathematical understanding that are relevant to its inquiry. Governing the choice of those systems or the functions they yield will be the principles of invariance and equivalence both of which are methodologically grounded on the analysis of the "heuristic" character of modern classical understanding. Thus, with the aid of the mathematician there is discerned a downward thrust towards a verified understanding of the data. When coupled with the, essentially, triadic movement "upwards," the analysis of the two angles from which scientific consciousness heuristically pursues its unknown law of "nature" has been completed. What the unknown "form" is in each case is to be determined by inquirers in the particular science.

Finally, it must be recalled that the entire preceding analysis is reflective in character. It is the verified fruit of a reflective inquiry into the notion and structure of one's own conscious operations insofar as these are classical in character and, therefore, represent the movement of modern classical subjectivity.

4. The Discovery of the Non–Systematic: Transition to Statistical Method

As a result of proceeding on the basis of the anticipations and assumptions described above, the subject generates scientific understanding laws, and systems of the classical type. But procedures and theories of this type are not without their limitations and these, in turn, have called forth the methodical elaboration of complementary anticipations of a statistical type. Lonergan approaches their determination in three broad steps. The first specifies the requirement of further insights into the concrete to apply classical understanding. The second specifies the construction and concrete verification of processes of two ideal types, e.g., systematic and non–systematic, depending on whether the insights which apply classical systems to them are, respectively, unified or non–unified. Thirdly, the non–systematic is described as answering specially, though not exclusively, to questions of a "statistical" kind.

First, Lonergan shifts the focus of his reflection to an intentional analysis of the classical scientific subject in the process of applying[1] his system of laws,[2] of using it to mediate his predictions to a particular case.[3] What he discovered was that the addition of further complementary insights into the particular situation was always necessary to effect the application of abstract classical laws to the case.[4] Unless they are forthcoming, the subject

---

[1] Following Lonergan, this exposition abstracts from concrete inferences that are practical in character.

[2] It is here irrelevant whether these laws were discovered and/or verified immanently by the inquirer himself, his predecessors, or contemporaries.

[3] Lonergan is referring, here, to cases that are concrete and existent although he actually begins his reflections from ideally conceived or imaged possible representations of concrete conditions.

[4] Recalling that conceptual systems are neither sensible nor imaginable and, hence, transcend the frontiers of the concrete (cf. I, 86c, 46 ff, 89b), this discovery can also be regarded as a theorem to

is unable to:[1]

(1) <u>select</u> "the relevant laws" which will enrich the case at hand with intelligibility;

(2) <u>combine</u> the selected laws so that they are applicable to the case;

(3) <u>pick out</u> which "dimensions of the situation are to be measured" to bring it under the correctly selected and combined laws, <u>substitute</u> numerical values which measuring interaction has yielded for their implicitly defined variables, <u>determine</u> the latter's "undetermined constants" (should there be any), etc. (<u>I</u>, 46c, 197de).

<u>Secondly</u>, Lonergan[2] begins by focusing on the problem of the construction of <u>ideal</u> cases (<u>I</u>, 46-53, <u>UB</u>, 83-86). They abstract from <u>concrete</u> conditions and <u>concrete</u> applications but are so constructed as to be consistent with classical laws and to satisfy sets of <u>ideally</u> specified conditions and/or phantasms. But such cases can be of <u>two</u> ideal kinds. On the one hand, the subject can construct cases that yield fully general and correct predictions of <u>everything</u> that is "going to happen along the line" (<u>UB</u>, 84c) or any similar line, that perfectly fulfill and correspond to his unified classical anticipations. Thus, from an insight into Newton's laws, the problem of how a determinate mass would move in a central field of force can be framed. One can use these laws to show that its trajectory describes a conic section. Thus, the selection and combination of Newton's law of universal gravitation and his second law of motion can be so particularized to ideally specified conditions as to construct the

---

the doctrine of the indeterminacy of the abstract.

[1]Here, all the concrete conditions necessary for the occurrence of the situation to which the subject would apply are being assumed to be actually fulfilled. Thus, "all things" are being assumed to be "equal" and all conditions are being considered ideal, "in this case" (cf. <u>I</u>, 65e).

[2]Lonergan is <u>assuming</u>, as he had in the previous paragraph, complete knowledge of classical laws.

ideally proceeding circuit of the elliptical planetary orbit.[1] Given the specification of similar ideal conditions these laws could be similarly applied to yield a similarly elliptical ideal process. But it is also possible to work out cases in which even one's hypothesized complete knowledge of classical laws does not suffice, in the general case, for the prediction of exactly what is going to happen in the next case. Such cases evade subsumption under an ideal, unified, solution and, therefore, reveal a limitation immanent in the classical heuristic structure of inquiry.

Lonergan's ideal specification of the break of a pool game represents such a case.

> The cue ball can be shot from any of an infinity of positions from the middle of the line to the left, and from an infinity of positions to the right. Further, it can travel with any of an infinity of mass velocities and it can hit the triangular configuration of balls at a variety of points. Moreover, the balls of the configuration can be grouped with many different degrees of tightness. When all of this is determined in any particular case, one can figure out exactly what is going to happen, but that would be extremely difficult . . . . not only because of the question of how tightly the balls fit together, but also because there are interferences. Balls bounce against the bands and come back, and they move at slightly different speeds. The direction of the cue ball will determine whether the balls collide or not, and whether or not they do collide determines later movements. The whole would have to be followed through step by step (UB, 85b);
>
> What would be the general solution to the problem of what happens at the break at pool? There is no general [e.g., unified] solution [e.g., a different solution is required at each step]. The problem involves an indefinite series of cases (UB, 85c, emphases mine).

Consequently, although the case is consistent with classical explanation, precisely because it admits no general solution a different selection, combination and/or particularization of classical laws would be needed to bring each case in this indefinitely long series under the initial set of classical laws. Similarly, the insights which mediate the application would be different for each case and, therefore, non-unified. Thus, Lonergan has constructed and explicated a case such that "knowledge of the laws [of the system

---

[1]Actual planetary paths can be expected to deviate non-systematically from the ideal projection.

alone, even if complete] does not enable one to predict in the general case what is going to happen" (UB, 86a).

Having clarified the distinction between these two kinds of ideal processes, Lonergan resumed his reflections upon the intentionality of the application process when its term is concretely existing cases. These acts clued the realization that both kinds of ideal or typical processes are in fact verified in concrete situations. Those which approximate[1] to those of the former type were denominated "systematic" processes; those of the latter, "non-systematic." And the criterion of whether a given concrete process is one or the other turns on whether the complementary insights needed to apply classical laws to it are unified or non-unified, whether, in effect, the situation conforms to unified, classical anticipations, or does not. It is to explicit consideration of the realm of concrete processes that this interpretation now turns.

If the insights whereby the subject selects, combines, and particularizes classical laws for application to concrete conditions are unified, the process they grasp is systematic in character. The abstract laws of his system and a "few strategically chosen particular cases" (I, 87a) grant the subject intellectual "mastery" of the process as a whole. Such a process, then, is defined as "orderly" (I, 90d). Thus, the series of events it manifests is "related in accord with the dictates of . . . a single insight or . . . [a] single set of unified [classical] insights" (I, 52b). Given such [verified] ideal cases, the subject's particularized combination of selected classical laws suffices to: (1) render in a unified perspective the process as a whole and every and/or any event within it; (2) deduce any component situation from any other "without any explicit consideration of intervening situations" (I, 47b); (3) formulate exact predictions that are regularly fulfilled (I, 48b ff, cf. I, 47b).

In such cases, "schemes of recurrence" are said to govern the unfolding sequences of proceeding events. A scheme of recurrence, then, "corresponds in the actual world to a systematic insight [in the

---

[1]By definition, the concrete may always be expected to deviate non-systematically from ideal projections.

intentional field of the subject]" (UB, 91a), to the grasp of unified, classically defined laws. In concrete cases where such schemes become operative, conditions for the events governed by the selected combinations of classical laws "coil around in a circle" (I, 118a). Such laws, when conjoined with such sets of relevant conditions, so govern the procession of the case's ingredient series of events that the fulfillment of the conditions for each event discharges the conditions for the occurrence of the next so that "other things being equal"[1] the "process goes on [repeating] indefinitely" (UB, 91a).

> Schematically, then, the scheme might be represented by the series of conditionals, If A occurs, B will occur, if B occurs, C will occur; if C occurs, . . . A will recur. Such a circular arrange-ment may involve any number of terms, the possibility of alternate routes, . . . any degree of complexity . . . . [of complementation by] defensive circles . . . (I, 118a, emphasis mine);

> . . . such schemes of recurrence are[2] many not only in number but also in kind (I, 87c, emphases mine).

Granted the ideal conception and verified existence of systematically recurring cases, and that the abstract component of

---

[1]That "other things must be equal" for the recurrence to operate and the relevantly combined laws to be applicable to the case is pre-cisely Lonergan's point. The question will become whether things, in the general case, are equalized systematically or non-systematically. Lonergan claims that unified classical predictions, e.g., the transit of Venus, lunar eclipses, etc., are "generally possible only insofar as there are schemes of recurrence [operative in nature]" (UB, 91b).

[2]Lonergan gives the example of "our planetary system." It is: "periodic [e.g., over constant time intervals it approximately but recurrently exemplifies a unified classical order]; [considered in its concreteness] it is an individual set of masses [e.g., of determinate number and magnitude, in specific relative positions" (cf. I, 102a) etc., etc.]; most of them are visible; and a relatively small number of insights [grasping the "concrete" component of the situation] makes it possible [to apply the subject's system of abstract, verified physical laws and so] to determine an indefinite sequence of [further] particu-lar cases [e.g., the "abstract" component of the situation, the order it concretely exhibits] (I, 87b). Other examples of such schemes would include the "nitrogen cycle . . ., the routines of animal life, . . . the repetitive [classical] economic rhythms of production and ex-change," (I, 118c), the Carnot cycle, that of insulin synthesis, the Krebs, glycolysis and oxidative phosphorylation cycles, (cf. Patrick Byrne's, **Insight** and the Retrieval of Nature, 1987, pp. 35 ff.), etc.

their concrete relations is governed by a unified set of classical laws, Lonergan puts a further question: does the <u>totality</u> of concrete cases form an orderly series and, therefore, exhibit the properties of systematic process (<u>I</u>, 87a, 96d)? Lonergan's reply is based on an extension of the preceding argument.

First, the indeterminacy of the abstract is recalled.

Secondly, Lonergan reaffirms that its determination is effected "in concrete instances only inasmuch as [sets of positive and negative] conditions are fulfilled" (<u>I</u>, 93d, cf. 97b) and the further insights which grasp them are added. Only under the circumstances, then, of the <u>fulfillment of these conditions</u>, do schemes of recurrence <u>emerge</u> and <u>remain</u> concretely operative. A variant formulation of this point which preserves an equivalence of meaning is that each operative scheme of recurrence:

> <u>presupposes</u> materials [e.g., concrete series of conditions] in a suitable constellation that the scheme did <u>not</u> bring about, and each <u>survives</u> only as long as extraneous disrupting factors do <u>not</u> intervene.[1] The periodicity of the planetary system does <u>not</u> account for its origin [e.g., the fulfillment of the conditions necessary for its emergence] <u>and cannot guarantee its survival</u> [e.g., the continued and/or uninterrupted fulfillment of these conditions] (<u>I</u>, 87c, emphases mine, cf. <u>I</u>, 96c).

Thus, to <u>apply</u> one's unified classical understanding to the concrete situation, a second <u>concrete</u> component of the total case must be distinguished. But this component, in fact, eludes the classical subject's grasp upon the implicitly defined laws of abstract system. Again, it is the content of a concrete insight into the total situation which is fuller "than the abstract formulation" alone (<u>I</u>, 101a);[2] <u>in fact fulfills the conditions for the case's systematicity.</u>[3]

---

[1]The point is that this presupposition and non-disruption are assuring the equality of all things.

[2]This insight, of course, mediates the application process.

[3]Continuing the example of the planetary system, Lonergan points out that: "when a non-systematic process happens to give rise to a systematic process (as in recent theories on the origin of planetary systems), then the total situation must divide into two parts of which one happens to fulfil the conditions of systematic process and the other fulfils the requirement of other things being equal" (<u>I</u>, 50f).

Thirdly, Lonergan argues that these "conditions [actually fulfilled or] to be fulfilled form a diverging series." He argues, then, that:

> in the general case the patterns of such diverging series are a non-systematic [coincidental] aggregate [process, manifold] (I, 93d, emphases mine).

This third claim was clued by Lonergan's: (1) reflections upon the operations of the subject applying his unified classical laws to the procession of events contributing the concrete conditions made recurrent by a scheme; (2) his discovery of a constant intentional feature which these operations exhibit. Thus, the subject's application of classical system to the processes conditioning the concrete component of a scheme of recurrence and, therefore, to the conditions which underly its emergence and continuation, requires, as all applications do, the addition of further complementary insights. Given this shift in the term of his application, however, these further complementary insights prove, in the general case, to be objectively incapable of being unified. This discovery, in turn, led Lonergan to the following conclusion: were the concrete conditions of the subject's application not non-systematic they would not require what in fact they do—the addition of a non-unified set of complementary insights in order to complete the process of the application of classical laws to the procession of events conditioning the orderliness of the concrete case (cf. I, 89b).[1]

So far, then, Lonergan has advanced from the discovery of an intentional constant in a shifted orientation of the subject's application process to the hypothesization of a distinction, on this basis, of a non-systematic, diverging, coincidental or "concrete" component of particular cases, particular schemes of recurrence. If Lonergan is correct, it would be such non-systematic processions of events which hold out the concrete coincidental conditions which have

---

[1]It might also be argued that if the concrete, contributing, experiential conditions of a scheme's understanding were not non-systematic, that they would not comprise that from which unified classical understanding abstracts its laws (cf. I, 89a).

become recurrent, orderly, formed, systematic. And it would be to such
systematic processes that unified sets of classical laws would be
applicable in terms of concrete insights that do, indeed, prove to be
unified.

Whether such non-systematic processes actually occur, whether the
universe exhibits non-systematicity and is to that extent a
non-systematic process cannot be decided a priori but, as with the
question of the existence of systematic processes, is to be judged on
the basis of the relevant empirical evidence (cf. I, 53a). But, in
fact, there is substantial evidence that such processes exist. A
sufficient example describes:

> the path of an oxygen molecule in a room. Its movements depend
> upon its interactions with other molecules in the air, and with
> molecules in walls, doors, windows, etc. . . . a different
> application [of classical laws]—that is, a different concrete
> insight or set of concrete insights—will be needed for each
> interaction. Nor in general can it be expected that the series of
> insights which apply the laws to the successive interactions will
> fall into a unified perspective.[1]

Each different motion of a single gas molecule is intelligibly
related to the motions of other gas molecules. However, the total
movement of a gas molecule will not be intelligibly related to the
total motion of any other gas molecule and may not be in any way
related to any part of the motion of some gas molecules. There is
no absence of intelligible patterns weaving in and out of the story
lines of a non-systematic process [such as this]. What is lacking
is a single unifying pattern for an entire non-systematic process
[such as is possible, say, for our planetary system].[2]

---

[1] I draw the example and citation from Patrick Byrne's helpful
paper "God and the Statistical Paper," Zygon, vol. 16, no. 4 (December
1981), p. 351c.

[2] Ibid, p. 352c. In several further texts I understand Lonergan
to be filling out his empirically based conclusion to the existence of
non-systematic processes. To this end, he anticipates and removes
determinist objections to his hypothesis and adduces further evidence
in its favor. In the process he relies upon the premiss that at least
some verified statistical laws truly bring out a non-classical "order"
within and, hence, presuppose the non-systematic unfolding of the
processes they understand (cf. I, 67b). In the first place, then, the
determinist's claim that the concrete pattern of diverging conditions
is orderly is: "merely a hypothesis. In the second place, it is an
extremely doubtful hypothesis, for world process as a whole seems
marked by the characteristically statistical devices of large numbers

Lonergan's third point, then, argues against the determinist's claim for the unified systematicity of the totality.[1]

> There [in fact] does not exist a single ordered sequence that embraces the totality of particular cases through which abstract system might be applied to the concrete universe (I, 87d).

On the other hand, the third point argues in favor of the classical subject's de facto **abstraction** from the diverging series of conditions which trigger and support the emergence and survival of systematically proceeding concrete cases, e.g., it is precisely because these conditions will lack any further unified intelligibility, precisely because of this relative lack of intelligibility, that they can properly form the residual intentional background from which the subject of the classical scientific heuristic structure can most simply, effectively and advantageously **abstract** in order to understand. Thus, if the classical scientific subject grasps systems of laws that would explain every case of a certain kind similarly, he treats as irrelevant the attempt to explain the single events contributed by non-systematic process and the discovery of techniques "for the orderly study of groups of such events" (I, 56d). But there are reasons for

---

and long intervals of time. Finally, while this doubtful hypothesis implies that statistical method is ultimately mistaken, there is no difficulty in framing opposite hypotheses of equal value which, if true, would imply that ultimately classical method is mistaken [and that non-systematic processes are, therefore, real]" (I, 97a). Finally, Lonergan argues that: "if the totality of classical laws provided an understanding of the concrete, statistical laws would be superfluous. But the conspicuous use of statistical techniques in world process shows that statistical laws are not superfluous in an understanding of the universe [which must, therefore, include coincidental aggregates in which statistical laws discover a non-classical order]" (I, 93c).

[1]The determinist's error stems, minimally, from a faulty intentionality analysis. The determinist "begins by overlooking the fact that a concrete inference from classical laws supposes an insight that mediates between the abstract laws and the concrete situation; and once that oversight occurs there is precluded a discovery of the difference between systematic processes and coincidental aggregates [e.g., he will, then, tend to identify the "real" with the necessity and coherence of his purely ideal conceptual model, etc.]" (I, 97c, emphases mine). The reflective uncovering of the cognitional role of human understanding, then, can have an important bearing on the resolution of philosophical issues.

this neglect of events that do not systematically recur. Thus, his attempt to deduce each and every event of a non-systematic process:

> begins by demanding more abundant and more exact information than there is to be had. It proceeds through a sequence of stages determined by the coincidences [e.g., coincidental manifolds] of a random situation. It has to postulate unlimited time to be able to assert the possibility of completing the deduction. It would end up with a result that lacks generality for, while the result would hold for an exactly similar non-systematic process, it commonly would not provide a safe basis for an approximation to the course of another non-systematic process with a slightly different basic situation. Finally, it would be preposterous to attempt to deduce the course of events for every non-systematic process. Not only would the foregoing difficulties have to be surmounted an enormous number of times but this Herculean labour would seem to be to no purpose. How could non-systematic processes be classified? How could one list in an orderly fashion the totality of situations of all non-systematic processes? Yet without such a classification and such a list, how could one identify given situations with situations contained in the extremely long deductions of the extremely large set of non-systematic processes (cf. I, 56d–57a)?

Lonergan's complex position is clarified when he argues that although "all events [in a scheme] are linked to one another by [classical] law, still the laws reveal only the abstract component in concrete relations . . . ."

> (T)he further concrete component, though mastered by insight into particular cases [insights which dictate how to select, combine, and particularize the relevant classical laws], is [always] involved in the [non-systematicity of the concrete, in the] empirical residue from which systematizing [unified classical] intelligence [always] abstracts [precisely in order to achieve a classically unified understanding]; it [the empirical residue] does not admit general treatment [e.g., any unified account] along classical lines . . . (I, 87d, emphases mine).

But if the concrete component of the total case does not in fact admit of general, unified treatment along classical lines, still each different event, part, stage, etc. of this component is in **principle** capable of classical treatment. But this claim has a condition that each of this component's dissimilar parts is [in the general case] understood in a classically dissimilar (perhaps unique) manner. In **principle**, then, and under ideal conditions, each event in such a process could be successively deduced and accounted for on a purely classical basis. But precisely because the different parts of the process would be different in their intelligibility, a different understanding and/or a different combination, selection, particulariza- tion of classical laws would be necessary to account "for each part" (I, 49c). It is not true, then, that "no attempt can be made [by the classical scientific subject] at a conceptual account of the concrete relations" supporting the orderliness of a given case. Rather, it is that:

> such a conceptual account bogs down in an unmanageable infinity of cases. It does not mean that concrete relations are never recur- rent or that accurate prediction is never possible; it means that schemes of recurrence do not fall under some overarching [unified classical] scheme, that they are merely instances [cases] in which law [in fact] triumphs over [e.g., emerges from, unifies, and is sustained by] the empirical residue, that such triumphs of law do not occur in accord with some further classical law (I, 101a).

Fourthly, upon reflection it should be clear that the conception of non-systematic processes is based on an insight that is inverse and liberating. It depends on the positive revelation that first, though they constitute a positive field for inquiry, they are, nevertheless, lacking in the unified intelligibility characteristic of systematic process, and that they are, therefore, not to be explored from out of the spontaneous heuristic anticipations underlying the classical intentionality of consciousness, from those underlying what:

> Laplace is supposed to have meant when he claimed that any situation in world history could be deduced from any other (I, 56a).

Thus, even assuming the existence of ideal conditions under which they may be studied by the classical scientific subject, e.g., full information on some given situation, complete knowledge of all the relevant laws, no restriction on the lengths of time allowed for the deduction, etc. (cf. I, 49c), non-systematic processes would not be immediately deducible in all their events without consideration of the intervening stages of the process. They would exhibit "coincidental manifolds" of events which coincide only in their spatial proximity or temporal successiveness but would lack any corresponding higher intel- ligibility of a unified classical kind. They would prove frustrating (if not ultimately resistant) to the classical intention since data on

(and, hence, intelligbile law governing) any one of their situations
will never necessarily prove equivalent to that on the whole. They
will <u>not</u> uniformly manifest either the periodicity of recurrence or
reversibility associated with systematic process; may, in certain
instances and at various levels, trigger the fulfillment of conditions
for the novel emergence and/or steady conservation of systematic
processes, schemes of recurrence, etc. (<u>I</u>, 51c–53a).[1]

   <u>Thirdly</u>, the reflections of this section have brought the subject
of the classical scientific attitude to a series of <u>inverse</u>
revelations. These include his discovery of, for example:

   (1) the <u>non</u>–systematic character of the contributing determinations
       which classical intelligence and its laws, as indeterminate,
       regard as mere empirical residue. As such, these determina-
       tions are abstracted from and, hence, left behind, unexplained,
       in the wake of classical inquiry;

   (2) the consequent pointlessness of pursuing the classical heuris-
       tic's lead of searching for a unified, classical understanding
       underlying and, therefore, explaining away non–systematic
       process;

   (3) the <u>absence</u> of any overarching, classically ordered sequence
       governing the emergence and/or conservation of systematic
       process and, therefore, of schemes of recurrence in the
       universe.

And these <u>inverse revelations</u>, to which he has been brought by the
emergence of a set of further relevant questions, do not square with
the subject's classical understanding of either the world or of
himSelf. Once revealed they have next to be accepted as data. Once
accepted, they represent the grasp of a limitation on the
comprehensiveness of classical method which human understanding must
again seek to transcend. Again, once accepted, these data represent
the source of further questions heading for the second relevant set of
heuristic procedures structuring his own scientific performance. These

------

[1]The reader may find reconsideration of footnote 1, p. 164,
helpful. Cf. <u>Insight</u>, p. 50f.

procedures would:

(1) "take their stand on the simple premise that the non-systematic cannot be systematized" (I, 89a);

(2) open and structure a non-classical way of investigating coincidental aggregates of events with "scientific generality" [e.g., the classical explanation of each single event of non-systematic process one step at a time would lack such generality (cf. I, 56d)] (I, 97b);

(3) "[contribute to the] positive advance of intelligence through the gap [e.g., the defect] in intelligibility [which, from a classical viewpoint, resides] in coincidental aggregates of events" (I, 57b). Thus, it would "turn the tables" on this defect. It would do this by defining the general characteristics of the acts of understanding which grasp a non-classical orderliness in this data and so reveal the intelligibility they grasp;

(4) be the methodological analogue of the discovery of a new higher viewpoint from which to order "irrational" data which turn up by giving inverse operations full generality in the homogeneous expansion of the positive integers (cf. I, 57b),[1] etc.

Thus, on the "subjective" side, human scientific consciousness has given itself the task of modifying, adapting, and redirecting its own fundamental levels of operation. The goal of this modification would be the delivery of generalizable, verifiable and "objective" answers to the questions provoked by the revelation of the existence of coincidental manifolds in nature. The following section of this chapter turns to a sketch of the answer that the subject of the scientific attitude has worked out to meet the relevant further questions and, thereby, transcend the limitations of his own classical viewpoint. But this answer consists in: the "statistical" heuristic structure of human inquiry.

---

[1] Since this point is applicable in the case of any ascent to a higher viewpoint, we will refrain from making it in upcoming, analogous cases.

5. Statistical Heuristic Structure

In _Insight_ II.4 and III.6, and _Understanding and Being_, pp. 83-95, Lonergan presents the fruits of his reflections upon: (1) the pattern of statistical operations of the subject of the scientific attitude, and (2) the statistical heuristicity of human consciousness as evolved and refined into a methodical structure of human inquiry.[1] Here, the distinguishing elements of the structure which Lonergan has brought out are sketched. As previously noted, this structure makes good on the _limitations_ of a purely _classical_ heuristic by guiding human intentionality towards a correct understanding of the _ideal_ laws of frequency centering the occurrence of _non_-systematically related "objects"[2] of human experience. Two aspects of this "making good" should be highlighted. First, the statistical grasp of ideal laws of frequency is _not_ to be interpreted from the false pretension of classical consciousness to ultimate explanatory exclusivity. Thus, in the general case, statistical laws are not to be regarded as:

> simply a cloak for [human] ignorance. [This is so because] (t)here is something that ca_nnot_ be done by classical laws, namely, they ca_nnot_ provide a _general_ account of what happens where some scheme of recurrence is _not_ operative [where the data of experience are merely coincident_ally_ related] (_UB_, 93a, emphases mine).

Secondly, the subject of the statistical heuristic attitude of consciousness intends and achieves a non-classically _general_ account of

---

[1]As with classical heuristic structure, Lonergan is reflecting upon the contemporary state of a historically advancing structure of subjectivity. And that state is less advanced in the statistical case. Thus, here he is even _more_ emphatic that he is _not_ clearing the "definitive foundations" _of_ statistical method but _only_ outlining an intentional structure that: "not only tackles specific problems but also _develops_ its own methods as it goes along and thereby sets up an _exigence_ for a [genetic] succession of new and better foundations" (_I_, 66c, emphases mine). This proviso must be kept in mind as ensuing sections reflect upon the even less developed contemporary states of genetic, dialectical, and other methods.

[2]Statistical method is neither concerned with nor does it offer an account of individual events, but only groups thereof.

such data.   Again, data of the relevant kind will include such aggregates of events as:

> the sequences of situations created by the mobility of molecules in a gas, the sequences of generations in which babies are born, the young marry, the old die . . .,

as well as such _humanly_ devised aggregates as "the sequences of occasions on which a coin is tossed or a die is cast [or cards are dealt]" (_I_, 53c).[1] Still, this does not imply that the movement of a die or an oxygen molecule evades the laws of mechanics or that each single throw or movement might not, in principle, be independently deduced. It says, rather, that these laws:

> are not premises in the determination of [for example] the probability of casting a "seven" [in the uncovering of this real intelligibility in the data aggregate] (_I_, 53d).

Finally, what follows proceeds through two stages.   First, the heuristic _notion_ guiding and prefiguring the scientific understanding of non–systematically proceeding aggregates of observable events is set forth. Secondly, the ways "up" and "down," respectively, of statis- tical inquiry whereby its heuristic notion is filled out are traced.

First, the statistical subject's guiding heuristic _notion_ of his unknown object is "the state of . . . ." The latter anticipates and pre–names what the statistical subject's inquiring _will_ gather when she fully and with scientific generally _understands_ the immanent "ideal frequency" unifying what, from a classical viewpoint, represents only a non–systematically proceeding manifold of events. The source of this guiding anticipation of consciousness which _intends_ but is not yet in actual possession of correct understanding is a _question_. Thus, from within the scientific attitude the subject _asks_ "Why this spread of actual frequencies?," "How often?" (_I_, 83e, 53e). This asking places

---

[1]In the latter case of games of chance, players _construct_ the non–systematicity of the processes they play. For example: "before the dice are thrown one rattles the box, before dealing the cards one shuffles them . . . [one brings it about that] there is _no_ intelligible systematic link between successive occasions" (_UB_, 92b, emphasis mine).

the <u>subject</u> already in intention beyond her description and tabulation
of relative <u>actual</u> frequencies into the proximity of the <u>ideal</u> frequency, the probability function, the statistical law which correctly
"understands" the immanent <u>state</u> of the kind of non-systematic data
field motivating her investigation. Lonergan conceptually <u>reconstructs</u>
the contemporary scientific understanding of state and its mediating
intentional counterpart, e.g., probability,[1] as follows:

> Consider a set of classes of events, P,Q,R, . . . and suppose that
> in a sequence of intervals or occasions events in each class occur
> respectively p_1, q_1, r_1 . . . p_2, q_2, r_2, . . . p_i, q_i, r_i, . . .
> times. Then the sequence of relative actual frequencies of the
> events will be the series of sets of proper fractions, p_i/n_i,
> q_i/n_i, r_i/n_i, . . . where i=1, 2, 3, . . . and in each [one of
> these case(s) $n_i = p_i + q_i + r_i + $ . . . . Now if there exists a single
> set of constant proper fractions, say p/n, q/n, . . . such that the
> differences

$$\frac{p}{n} - \frac{p_i}{n_i}, \frac{q}{n} - \frac{q_i}{n_i}, \frac{r}{n} - \frac{r_i}{n_i}, \cdot \cdot \cdot$$

> are always random,[2] then the constant proper fractions will be the

---

[1]Two points should be made here.
    <u>First</u>, the conceptualizations Lonergan is reconstructing have
been historically developed and refined from spontaneous, unformulated,
and barely mathematical sources in the life-worldly experiences of the
subject of common sense (cf. <u>I</u>, 55a).
    <u>Secondly</u>, I am using ideal frequency norm, probability and
statistical laws as rough equivalents.

[2]Two points should be added here.
    <u>First</u>, Lonergan defines <u>randomness</u> as follows: "a situation is
"random" if it is 'any whatever provided specified conditions of
[unified, for example, classical] intelligibility are not fulfilled'"
(<u>I</u>, 51a). He adds that <u>non-systematic</u> process: "results from any basic
situation provided it lacks intelligible unity from a definitive viewpoint. Therefore, the rule for constructing non-systematic processes
is to begin from any <u>random</u> basic situation" (<u>I</u>, 51a, emphasis mine).
Thus, these concepts (and other similar one's such as the coincidental,
etc., could be added) are being defined in terms of the <u>negation</u> of
conditions of "intelligibility" and "intelligible unity." But the
intelligible, for Lonergan, is what is given in a direct insight and in
answer to a question for intelligence. Hence, both randomness and
non-systematicity are being defined by Lonergan in terms of his
intentionality analysis. This would seem to be an advance over
previous efforts, e.g., those of Samuel S. Wilks in <u>Elementary</u>
<u>Statistical Analysis</u> (N.J.: Princeton University Press, 1952), in which

respective <u>probabilities</u> of the classes of events, the association
of these <u>probabilities</u> with the classes of events defines a <u>state</u>,
and the set of observed relative actual frequencies <u>is</u> a
<u>representative sample</u> of the state (<u>I</u>, 58d).

First, then, Lonergan defines the notion of probability. Then he
defines the notion of <u>state</u> as the association of classes of <u>events</u>
with the corresponding probabilities. And intentionally immanent in
these notions is the corollary heuristic "principle" that the
non–systematic "cannot deviate systematically from the systematic" (<u>I</u>,
113a), from, for example, the probability, the ideal frequency norm,
etc., with respect to which differences such as $\frac{p}{n} - \frac{p_i}{n_i}$, $\frac{q}{n} - \frac{q_i}{n_i}$, etc.
"are always random." Given this principle, it follows that:

> a notable regularity [e.g., of ideal frequency] is compatible with
> random differences of events (<u>I</u>, 63d).[1]

And what of the ideal law of frequency which enriches the human
understanding of non–systematic aggregates? As <u>abstract</u> it represents

___

it was insisted that the concept of randomness is primitive,
undefined, and the object of intuitive grasp.
    <u>Secondly</u>, if "random" is used to mean that which has no cause
(and Lonergan may occasionally if unintentionally be guilty of this
usage), then there is literally <u>nothing</u> that occurs randomly or,
equivalently, by chance. This follows from the retorsively undeniable
theorem of intentionality analysis that what is is intelligible.

[1]The <u>second</u> corollary theorem immanent in the <u>classical</u> heuristic
structure of inquiry Lonergan named the "principle of equivalence." As
said, the principle asserts that implicitly defined physical laws will
remain invariant under a group of transformations and hence, the <u>same</u>
for all "good" reference frames or observer–subjects within the <u>group</u>
if they altogether abstract from the immediate relations of the things
to the sensitive flow and correctly systematize the data as measured
and quantified (cf. <u>I</u>, 40–41). But does the same principle and proviso
adhere in applications of the statistical heuristic? Lonergan answers
in the negative. If classical laws abstract completely from the data
of experience, from (1) their particularity, (2) the continuous
manifolds in which they take place, (3) their place/time location, (4)
the frequency of their occurrence, (5) in short, the totality of their
relations to the human perceptual–motor field, the same is <u>not</u>
completely true of statistical laws. In their general form, e.g., "on
p occurrences of the occasion, P, there tend to be q occurrences of the
event, Q" (<u>I</u>, 113c), these laws include an implicit reference to the
<u>relations</u> of occurring events <u>to us</u>, to concrete manifolds of
observable events <u>occurring</u> with a given frequency and diverging only

no *actual* value (whether past, present, or future) which can be ascribed to collections of events in the aggregate. It stands "outside" the series as the ideal factor around which actual values oscillate at random. Thus, the subject of the statistical heuristic, operating at variance with the classical injunction that <u>no</u> difference is too small to be neglected, <u>presupposes</u> that differences which are merely <u>random</u> in character are to be <u>neglected</u> (cf. <u>I</u>, 55a), and abstracted from, and <u>not</u> to be explained. Furthermore, they are compatible with the existence and discovery of a non-classical lawfulness in the data. Thus, probability is:

an ideal norm that, for all its ideality, is concretely successful in the long run. <u>Chance</u> [or randomness, on the other hand] is merely the non-systematic divergence of actual frequencies from the ideal frequencies called probabilities. <u>Chance explains nothing</u>. It pertains irretrievably to the merely <u>empirical residue</u>, to the aspects of the data from which intelligence always abstracts. But probability is an intelligibility; it is, as it were, rescued from the merely empirical residue by the roundabout device in which <u>inquiring intelligence sets up the heuristic anticipations of the statistical type of investigation</u> (<u>I</u>, 114a, emphases mine).

Within the <u>ascending</u> movement of <u>empirical</u> conscious inquiry, a series of stages can be distinguished.[1] In the simplest case, the <u>statistical</u> inquirer:

(1a) orients herself by her **question** "Why these actual frequencies?" towards her distinctive "known unknown." But the latter consists in the explanatory "state of . . ." her kind of <u>data</u>,

---

non-systematically from these posited laws (cf. <u>I</u>, 2nd edition, 111a 5ff). This may have been Lonergan's point when in the <u>first</u> edition of <u>Insight</u> he claimed that statistical theories "deal only with observable events" (cf. <u>I1</u>, 98b, emphasis mine). In any event, despite noteworthy and relevant changes in the text of <u>Insight</u> on pages 98 and 111, the thrust of Lonergan's argument remains the same. It is that while statistical laws <u>may</u> or <u>do</u> manifest invariance, that nevertheless this invariance lies "outside the field of [fully] explanatory relations [e.g., the relations of things to each other]" (<u>I</u>, 111a). Hence, statistical theories "cannot be subjected to a full principle of equivalence" (<u>I</u>, 1st ed., 111a).

[1]Key intentional features of the following description of this movement are in bold print. Again, for a discussion of Lonergan's distinction between the "<u>a posteriori</u> and <u>a priori</u> cases" admitted by the calculus of probabilities, see <u>Appendix I</u>, below.

which data she _initially_ confronts as _pre_-scientifically described, understood, and affirmed. Thus, her question _sets out from_ runs of _observable_ events that "despite occasional lapses are ordinary or normal, or . . . are pronounced exceptional or abnormal though they contain a few ordinary or normal elements" (_I_, 63d, cf. _I_, 63c 7-8);

(1b) _redescribes_ her data field to invest it with potential "explanatory" relevance. This relevance she achieves by, first, borrowing for this redescription the "exact [and fully explanatory] classifications [of observable events] . . . [provided by] _classical_ science" (_I_, 64b, emphasis mine). Secondly, she employs these borrowed classifications to guide her selection of the relevant kinds of classes of events. From these classes samples will be drawn and relative actual frequencies of classically defined events will be painstakingly _counted_ and _tabulated_. Thus, an **image** or **phantasm** "representing" the originally described runs of events has been constructed. With its preparation of this phantasm mediating its intentionality, consciousness may attempt the further transition to the explanatory grasp of the immanent statistical law ordering coincidental variations of actually tabulated frequencies (cf. _I_, 64b);

(2) discovers in a "leap of constructive intelligence" (_I_, 60b) which:

   i)   is facilitated by the use of practical techniques such as curve-fitting, etc.;

  ii) leaps "beyond ascertained relative actual frequencies" (_I_, 64f);

 iii) therefore, _abstracts_ from the latter's "random oscillations" (_I_, 60b)--

the "ideal" frequency, the set of "universally valid constants" (_I_, 60b) which centers these random deviations around itself. A "leap" is necessary since as with a mathematical limit:

> a probability is a number that cannot be reached from the data of a problem without the intervention of an _insight_ . . . (J)ust as the [mathematical] limit . . . lay _beyond more terms than can be conceived, so a probability lies_

concealed within the random oscillations of relative actual frequencies (I, 60b, emphases mine).[1]

Since the leap may fall short for many reasons, e.g., a faulty classification of events, failure to pick representative samples (I, 65d), the inadequate skill and/or detachment of the inquirer, etc., therefore, in actual fact and short of the ideal limit of inquiry, the leap yields only a possible knowledge of probability. At this stage of the process of statistical inquiry, there is:

> neither the recognition of a fact nor the grasp of necessity (I, 65d);

(3) will, therefore, attempt to **verify** her grasp of the possible ideal law of frequency by using it to explore aggregates of similar data or further runs of the same data, to convert her grasp of possibility into a warranted, virtually unconditioned judgment of fact.

The ascending movement of statistical inquiry, then, advances along the following path: pre-scientifically given empirical data; the question "How frequently?" with its immanent notion put to the data; the use of measurement, tabulations, etc. to "image" the data and prepare its answering understanding; understanding of the data and the mathematical formulation thereof; verification of the understanding,

---

[1]Pat Byrne gives an example of the creative arc of insight moving from concrete data to ideal frequency: "A relative actual frequency is formed by dividing the actual number of occurrences of a specified type by the total number of occasions. For example, if it rained 127 days in a city during the year 1978, the relative actual frequency would be 127/365. Next . . . statistical investigators note that actual frequencies vary from year to year. Hence, over four years, the relative actual frequencies of rain in the city might be 133/366, 24/73, 114/365, 127/365 . . . . In the case of rain on city, 1/3 might be suggested as [i.e., is grasped in a leap beyond the actual frequencies as] the ideal frequency. The actual frequency of rain might be more or less in any given year, but the pattern of differences would be random. The succession of differences between ideal and actual ratios form a coincidental manifold, for they are ordered according to the yearly sequence but lack intelligible order" ("God and the Statistical Universe," Creativity and Method, p. 356, emphases mine). at many levels but which "closes" only when correct understanding finds verification.

etc. The movement is a "circuit" which may be traversed many times and at many levels but which "closes" only when correct understanding finds verification.

In the example Lonergan has chosen of the empirical movement of statistical questioning <u>downwards</u> from "above" <u>towards</u> the data, the inquirer avails herself of the independent mathematical discovery of operator equations.[1] Thus, just as the algebraist approaches her unknown with the name "X" and by working out the terms and relations the data of her problem contribute for understanding X, so the statistical inquirer can immediately determine certain very general features of her data by naming as unknown the "state" of her data and writing out the operator equations which satisfy his data. The eigenfunctions and eigenvalues of the operator will "serve to select [from out of his data certain] classes of events and to determine the respective probabilities of the selected cases" (<u>I</u>, 64e). Any such specification of the state of the data by way of the descending intentional route will have to satisfy the principle of invariance[2] but only a limited principle of equivalence.[3] Thus, while the <u>descending</u> movement of inquiry <u>presupposes</u> empirical data, a "notion" of the unknown state in question, sets of collated and graphed counts of actual frequencies, etc., it <u>understands</u> its data with the assistance of systems of concepts and/or equations independently discovered, formulated and verified by the mathematician in pure coincidental manifolds of events which sufficiently resemble classically residual coincidental manifolds of events. Lonergan, then, has identified a descending thrust of consciousness proceeding with the aid of the discoveries of the mathematician towards a verified understanding in

---

[1]An operator equation is a linear operator in the mathematical theory of abstract spaces. For a discussion of their application in Heisenberg's quantum mechanics see Patrick A. Heelan, <u>Quantum Mechanics and Objectivity</u> (the Hague: Martinus Nijhoff, 1965), pp. 32–33, 193.

[2]This concept is sketched in the earlier section "Classical Heuristic Structure."

[3]See footnote 1, pp. 172–173, above.

the data of experience. When coupled with the triadic ascending arc of intentionality, the analysis of the two angles from which scientific consciousness pursues the unknown state(s) of its non-systematically related data has been completed. Thus, what the unknown law of ideal frequency is in particular specialized statistical inquiries is to be determined by specialized scientific subjects implicitly using the bi-directional but uni-axied structure of statistical consciousness.

Finally, it must be recalled that the entire preceding analysis is "reflective" in character and in the service of the "Self-understanding" and intellectual "Self-appropriation" of the subject. Thus, Lonergan's aim has been to:

> encourage in readers the conscious occurrence [and understanding] of the intellectual events that make it possible to know what happens when probability is grasped (I, 59b).

Lonergan's analysis, then, is the immanently and interiorly verified fruit of a reflective inquiry which understands the notion and structure of one's own conscious operations insofar as these are, first, immediately accessible aspects of one's conscious "Self-presence" and, secondly, are statistical in character and represent the movement, the learned and self-developing accomplishment of modern statistical subjectivity.

APPENDIX I

In Understanding and Being, while defending the claim that "in the present state" the mathematical calculus of probabilities "does not seem to be entirely satisfactory" (UB, 87c), Lonergan distinguishes a priori and a posteriori cases admitted by the theory (UB, 87c, cf. I, 60c–62c). Should the subject wish to know:

> the probability or the [ideal] frequency of the number of deaths per thousand of population in a given area, there is no a priori method for determining such a frequency . . . one has to approach the problem empirically (UB, 87c, emphases mine).

In cases of this kind, probabilities have to be reached:

> a posteriori and, to reach them a statistical heuristic structure has to be [e.g., has had to have been] developed (I, 62c).

A transcendental analysis of the current state of development of this structure ensues in the body of this section. On the other hand, a priori cases also exist and should be briefly discussed. Such cases are restricted to games of chance, to humanly constructed processes in which:

> because of full knowledge of operations involved [e.g., the tossing of a fair die] one can work out a priori what the [actual] probabilities are going to be (UB, 87c).

Lonergan's analysis of a representative a priori case—that the probability of tossing heads with a fair coin is 1/2—traverses three steps.

First, accepting such determinants of a given toss as its initial position, the linear and angular momenta imparted to it by the toss, the different surfaces on which it might fall, etc., the throw of heads could have turned out tails:

> had one just turned the coin over before starting . . . . [Thus,] the possibilities divide into two equal groups (UB, 94a, cf. I, 61c).

Secondly, as discussed previously, although the tossing of a coin does not involve the suspension of the laws of mechanics, although under ideal conditions each independent step in the process might be separately deduced, intelligibility is to be excluded from the "sequence as sequence" since:

> there is no [general, unified] law governing what is going to
> happen the next time if this happens this time. This is the random
> character of the sequence . . . (UB, 94b).

Thirdly, relative actual frequencies: cannot help oscillating
about one half. For the set of possible combinations divides into two
exactly equal parts; and every sequence of actual combinations is a
random selection from the set of possible combinations. Now in a
random selection of a sequence the sequence is stripped of all order,
all regularity, all law; hence, while it can and will include runs of
"heads" and runs of "tails," it cannot possibly stick to one alternative to the exclusion of the other, and so the relative actual frequency is bound to oscillate about one-half (I, 62a, emphases mine).
The intellectual grasp of this point involves neglecting random features for the center from which they randomly scatter. And that:

> abstractive grasp of intelligibility is the insight that is
> expressed by saying that the probability of "heads" is one-half (I,
> 62b, emphasis mine).

Having exhibited the centrality of insight in the understanding of the
a priori case, Lonergan goes on to point out that:

> it is only in games of chance that there can be discerned an
> antecedent [a priori] symmetry in the set of possible combinations
> of determinants of events (I, 62c).

Thus, should there actually be any:

> systematic favoring [of one side of the coin, one can conclude
> that] one is not dealing with the probability aggregate;
> statistical methods do not provide the relevant explanation . . .
> there is [a further] systematic factor at work [to be explored
> classically] (UB, 95a).

Finally, I note, but refrain from interpreting Lonergan's
speculation that the calculus of probabilities "as it exists at the
present time" may:

> actually have the status that Euclidean geometry was supposed to
> have before other geometries were introduced (UB, 89a, cf. I1, 66).

6. Emergent Probability: Introduction

Thusfar, we have considered the human subject in the classical and statistical differentiations of the modern scientific attitude towards the surrounding world. Our exposition has brought out that in taking up this attitude, the **subject** necessarily commits himself to a series of **presuppositions**. Within the scientific posture of discovery, these include, from Sections B3 and B5, immediately above, that there are, for instance, irreducibly classical and statistical:

(1) notions;

(2) inquiries to be triadically pursued to term under their guidance;

(3) laws to be **correctly** understood when inquiry has come to term.

In Section B4, we saw that one consequence of these presuppositions is that:

(4) the insights necessary to select, combine, measure and, therefore, apply classical laws to the data, will be either unified or non-unified.

But, with the uncovering of (1)-(4), above, generic[1] and invariant[2] features of the subject-"pole" of the scientific attitude of the subject have been isolated. Again, to the scientific subject's unified or non-unified insights there corresponds the distinction within the corresponding "objective" data of, respectively:

(5) systematically and non-systematically related processions of events.

---

[1] Presuppositions are "generic" when they do not pertain to the content but only the formal characteristics of the acts of understanding [and/or intended objects] to be gathered by the modern scientific subject where he has met all the relevant questions.

[2] These presuppositions are "invariant" in that they hold for the performances [and/or objective field] of any and every subject in the modern scientific attitude towards the world. They obtain despite any or all transformations from one spatio-temporal standpoint of the subject to another; any one subject's spatio-temporal standpoint(s) to

Finally, from reflective horizonal analyses sketched in sections B3 and B5 but especially B4, and drawing together implications of (1)–(5), above, two further presuppositions of the modern subject's scientific attitude can now be explicitated. Thus, his:

(6) classical inquiries anticipate and, at the limit, uncover the proper lawfulness of systematic processes;

(7) statistical inquiries anticipate and, at the limit, uncover the proper lawfulness of non-systematic processes.

With the bringing out of presuppositions (6)–(7), generic and invariant but also isomorphic features subtending the bi-polar "horizon" of human scientific consciousness have been isolated. But Lonergan's reflective breakthrough to this presupposition of horizonal isomorphism remained incomplete. This incompleteness is evidenced in the fact that the unity of the distinct classical and statistical heuristic structures and answering "objective" fields of human consciousness has not been uncovered. Lonergan engaged this incompleteness in part in materials already explicated in Section B5 of this chapter but especially in Insight IV, VII, and XIV by undertaking further reflections upon the data of scientifically patterned human consciousness. The further questions motivating these reflections are, in what follows, sequentially reconstructed and Lonergan's answers serially explicated.

---

the spatio-temporal standpoint(s) of any other such subject; despite the choice of reference frames with respect to which transformations are performed and determined. Still, Lonergan's account of these presuppositions is only "relatively invariant" since his appeal is: "not to the structure of the human mind itself, but only to our account of that structure. Just as the natural sciences are subject to revision, so too one may expect our account of inquiring intelligence to be subjected to rearrangements, modifications, and improvements. In the measure that such changes will affect the premises of the present argument [e.g., the structure of the general empirical method of the scientific subject], in the same measure they will also affect the conclusions [i.e., a sketch of man's world as structured by, for instance, an "emergent probability" of serially "conditioned schemes of recurrence"]" (I, 117a, emphases mine). Still, what is "excluded": "is the radical revision that involves a shift in the fundamental terms and relations of the explanatory account of human knowledge underlying . . . existing . . . empirical science" (I, 335b, emphasis mine).

(I) What is the relationship between, respectively, the two-fold differentiation of both the "subjective" and "objective" poles of the subject's performance within the scientific "horizon"? Thus, on the subjective "side," what is the relationship between the classical and statistical specializations of his heuristically structured desire to know and learn? On the objective "side," what is the relationship between the systematic and non-systematic process of events which he gathers within the objective data?

Further reflections upon the global horizon of human science convinced Lonergan that this relationship was one of complementarity.[1] To bring this out we proceed in two steps. First, we will exhibit this relation, reflectively, as structuring a representative sample of parallel but, in respect of the preceding analyses, ununified elements within the classical and statistical dimensions of the scientific horizon.[2] Secondly, we will unravel and contextualize the sense of the exhibited relationships.[3]

-----

[1] Lonergan seems to use "complementarity," "complementary," "complement" in two major kinds of context. The first is to be exhibited in the following pages of this study. The second involves his specification of the character of the relationship linking the intentional levels (or acts on these levels) of experience, understanding, and judgment. Thus, human experience is "presupposed and complemented" by human intelligence, which is, in turn, "presupposed and complemented" by human reflection (cf. I, 273c–d, 486c, etc., etc.). But the relationship exhibited in the first context seems to be symmetrical, while that in the second does not. Thus, while Lonergan's other uses of these terms seem reducible to one of these two, the author is not decided whether these two major usages are reducible to each other.

[2] Each of these exhibited relationships, then, rings a variation on a single theme.

[3] The full implication of this modality of relationship, on both the subjective and objective "sides" of the "horizon" of the scientific subject, will not have developed fully until question II, below, has been met in Section B7 of this chapter.

a) The Complementarity of the Classical And Statistical "Horizons" of
   the Scientific Subject

In Section B4, above, the fact of the scientific subject's valid
application of classical laws to concrete cases and the correlative
admission that the universe exhibits regularities, that is, schemes of
recurring data was brought out.   Again, this fact was taken as the
assumed starting point for a reflective analysis of the intentionality
of the scientific subject's application process and its   field.
Lonergan argued from the classical subject's concentration of his
implicitly defined sets of terms and relations in the abstract
conceptual field to the non-systematicity of the further determinations
needed by him to apply these laws (cf. presupposition (4), above).
Thus, recurring schemes in the surrounding world were interpreted as
resulting not from the reality of classical laws alone but: "from the
combinations of such laws with suitable constellations of concrete
circumstances" (I, 131c, emphasis mine).

"Within" such recurring schemes, then, Lonergan distinguished a
"concrete component" corresponding to its non-systematically diverging
"concrete circumstances" and an "abstract" component in virtue of which
the data of circumstance recur in a fashion that is systematic,
orderly, intelligible (cf. presupposition (5)), that admits classical
understanding and application.   Far from being isolated terms of a
dyad, then, these systematic and non-systematic "components" within the
recurring data are closely linked.   They are so closely linked that
they are separately necessary but only jointly sufficient to account
for the success with which the scientific subject applies his systems
of laws to "concrete circumstances," and for the conditioned regularity
this success of application presupposes and evidences in the
surrounding world.   But, as brought out in Section B4, it is the
statistical focus of scientific consciousness which first heuristically
intends and, at the limit of inquiry, correctly grasps the intelligibility underlying non-systematically diverging processes, i.e., those
which contribute content for, concretely condition and sustain
systematic, classically definable, processes.   Thus, recurring schemes

are to be interpreted as proceeding not from the reality of classical laws alone but from the combination of such laws with those of a statistical kind. But then the scientific subject's classical and statistical modes of intending and achieving an understanding of their immanent lawfulness, far from being isolated dyads, are themselves so closely linked that they are separately necessary and only jointly sufficient completely to make sense of the recurring, schematic data. Thus, a relationship of complementarity is to be affirmed linking, respectively, the subject's opposed classical and statistical:

(1) manners of subsuming a unified field of observational data under his heuristic structures (I, IV.1.1); i.e., in the former manner he will gather therefrom a systematicaly related, orderly component, in the latter, a non-systematically related component. Though possessed of opposed[1] properties, these components link up within the unity of a recurring scheme (cf. I, 67b);

(2) manners of understanding and abstracting from the data (I, IV.1 .4); i.e., complete understanding of the linked but opposed facets of the recurring data:

> results only from the combination of the two [respectively, the classical and statistical] movements [of human consciousness in the scientific attitude], and so the two [ways in which to understand the same set of data and abstract from the irrelevant therein] are complementary (I, 110g, emphases mine).

But there is a second aspect to this complementarity. The relations in which things stand are understood abstractly by classical laws but concretely by their statistical counterparts. Thus, by the principle of equivalence, classical laws abstract from the immediate relations of things to us and so regard the systematic in abstraction from its non-systematic conditions. But statistical laws do not satisfy a complete principle of equivalence since they include implicit reference to observable events and since they regard the systematic (e.g., an

---

[1]They are "opposed" in the sense of being "contradictory alternatives of a dichotomy" (I, 105c).

ideal frequency norm) "as [merely] setting bounds to the [divergence of the] non-systematic" (I, 115a). Hence, the two ways of understanding the data do not admit formal opposition since contradiction presupposes that the same things are being grasped in the same respect. Rather, they represent linked but opposed manners in which the things can be known scientifically.[1] Lonergan went on to explicate the complementarity of the scientific subject's classical and statistical:

(3) formulations (I, IV.1.3); i.e., on the one hand, the statistically focused subject depends upon the classical formulation of
   implicitly defined and empirically established pure conjugates
   to:

   (a) define the field of events into which he is inquiring;
   (b) ensure himself that the inquiries to which he commits him-
       self possess full scientific significance, i.e., are rele-
       vant to further advances within the intentional enterprise
       of scientific and merely common sense subjectivity.

   On the other hand, the classically focused subject depends upon
   statistical formulations to determine how frequently non-
   systematically occurring conditions for, first, the emergence
   and, then, the survival of schemes of the appropriate, classically definable kind, are fulfilled (cf. I, IV.1-3);

(4) procedures (I, IV.1.2); i.e., whether the scientific subject
   has focused his energies to understand the systematic or the
   non-systematic component of the data, since his grasp is only
   upon one component within "a single complementary field," it is
   always "a step towards" (I, 106d) his understanding of the

---

[1]Two points should be noted.

First, Lonergan does not deny that both classical and statistical laws fall under the principle of invariance.

Secondly, Lonergan's comments here are consistent with and hearken back to his attempts to clarify the relationship between the respectively neo-classical general relativity theory of Einstein and the purportedly post-classical quantum mechanics of Heisenberg (cf. I, 111a, 98e, where Lonergan subtly modifies his position from the first to the second edition).

other.

> For this reason it has been possible to invoke the laws of probable errors and thereby to eliminate a non-systematic component in observations and measurements [made to validate, invalidate or apply classical laws]. In like manner, Mendel's statistical laws of macroscopic, genetic characters led to the postulation of microscopic entities named genes; to each gene was assigned, on the classical model, a single determinate effect and manifestation; genes with incompatible effects were classified as dominant and recessive; and so statistical combinations of classically conceived genes became the explanation of non-systematic macroscopic phenomena (I, 106d, emphases mine);

(5) modes of verifying his laws (I, IV.1.5); i.e., on the one hand, the classical subject's verification of the unified set of classical laws, P, presupposes that there is no systematic divergence between the data and the laws of P. But such a verification admits a non-systematic divergence that "leaves room for" and opens a field for "the discovery and verification of statistical laws" (I, 111c). On the other hand, the conjugates of the classical subject's theories hold only under the proviso that "all things are equal," that is, they are only present in non-systematically ramifying processions of events with a lawfulness that "leaves room" for the verification of statistical laws.

Finally, in a brief but extremely important section (I, IV.1.6), Lonergan discusses the complementarity of the subject's classical and statistical modes of explaining the data. It is towards the clarification of the argument of that section that I devote the next four paragraphs.

As we have indicated in considerable detail in section B4, schemes of recurrence emerge and survive, only if their conditions are fulfilled. But in the general case the conditions to be fulfilled form a diverging series and: "patterns of such diverging series are a non-systematic [coincidental] aggregate" (I, 93d).[1] Each member of such a series will be intelligibly related to the others but the total

---

[1]Cf. Insight, p. 93e ff, for a fuller formulation.

series will evade subsumption under a <u>unified</u> set of classical laws. Hence, it is <u>not</u> from the consideration of only a "few strategically chosen cases" (<u>I</u>, 87a) within the conditioning series that the emergence and/or survival of the scheme can be deduced. This would be possible only if conditions were already proceeding systematically. But in the absence of an already functioning scheme this cannot be affirmed. The classically focused subject, in explaining every case of a similar kind similarly, presupposes the systematicity of the case for study and so, for example, treats as irrelevant:

(1) the diverging series which triggers the emergence and sustains the occurrences of schemes;

(2) the attempt to explain the single events contributed by non-systematic process;

(3) the discovery of techniques for the orderly study of groups of such events, etc.

But in section B5, the statistical heuristic structure was thematized as guiding the human subject's advance toward and achievement of the correct understanding of non-systematically diverging processes. Hence, the verified grasp of statistical laws and ideal frequencies to which they contribute such data, may serve to <u>complement</u> the classical moment of explanation where it breaks off. How this could be, we follow Lonergan in a sketch through three steps of a preliminary argument to discover.

<u>First</u>, in Chapter IV, Section 1.4 of <u>Insight</u>, Lonergan enlarges upon the "explanatory" character of statistical laws.

First, he notes the general form of the statistical law. It states that, ideally, "on p occurrences of the occasion, P, there tend to be q occurrences of the event, Q" (<u>I</u>, 113c).

Secondly, he points out that given this general form, at least one instance of Q, and the theorem that there are no unconditioned events, it follows that:

the occasions on which P is probable will have <u>their</u> probability, and so there arises an indefinite regress of <u>probabilities</u> from events of the type, Q. More generally, for events of any type, X, there are corresponding, indefinite regresses of probabilities (<u>I</u>, 113c, emphases mine).

Thirdly, <u>given</u> the immediately preceding two points, Lonergan assumes that such an indefinite regression of probabilities could be correctly grasped and combined within a single intentional viewpoint (I, 113d 1-5). He also assumes that the probability of Q is low. Again, the heuristic principle underlying the statistical heuristic of the subject is that:

> the non-systematic [e.g., actual frequencies of the occurrence of, say, Q] cannot diverge systematically from the systematic [e.g., the ideal frequency norm of the statistical subject] (I, 114a, emphasis mine).[1]

Futhermore, the fulfillment of sets of conditions becomes increasingly likely as: (1) the numbers of events of the relevant kinds are increased and low probabilities are, thereby, offset; (2) intervals of time are lengthened and the rarity of the relevant kinds of occasions are, thereby, offset.[2] Finally, the supposition of long time spans and large numbers of events is not inconsistent; e.g., our universe manifests both properties and actually exists.[3]

But, then, fourthly, and finally, the occurrence of what has even a very low probability, e.g., events of type, Q, is virtually assured.

> (T)his incapacity for systematic divergence [e.g., which is characteristic of the actual frequencies of events falling under statistical law] when combined with large numbers and long time intervals of time, is [therefore] equivalent to a positive [ascensional] tendency, to an intelligible order, to an effective thrust, that is no less explanatory than the rigorous conclusions based on classical laws (I, 114a, emphases mine).

Secondly, statistical and classical explanations of a set of data can be made relevant to each other if the data are recurring

---

[1] Lonergan notes that: "Probability is . . . concretely successful in the long run. Chance is merely the non-systematic divergence of actual frequencies from the ideal . . . . Chance explains nothing. It pertains irretrievably to the empirical residue . . ." (I, 114a, emphases mine).

[2] Lonergan notes that: ". . . what is probable only once on a million occasions, is to be expected a million times on a million million occasions" (I, 113d).

[3] Lonergan notes that: ". . . the rarity of occasions is offset by long intervals of time, so that if occasions arise only once in a million years, still they arise a thousand times in a thousand million years" (I, 113d).

schematically; the notion of statistical law can be so extended that probabilities can be assigned for the occurrence of the very schemes whose underlying regularities are classically but implicitly defined. Lonergan's accomplishment of this extension can be traced in two steps. He assumes the existence of a world-situation in which sets of events of the kinds A, B, C . . . possess:

(1) respectively, the independent probabilities p, q, r . . . .

But if this is so:

(t)hen by a general rule of probability theory, the probability of the occurrence of all the events in the set will be the product, pqr, . . . of their respective probabilities (I, 120d);[1]

(2) an additional property. This property would be that:

if A were to occur, B would occur. If B were to occur, C would occur. If C were to occur, . . . A would occur . . . . if any of the events in the set were to occur, then, other things being equal, the rest of the events in the set would follow (I, 120e, emphases mine).

To affirm (2), immediately above, is equivalent to affirming that the sets of events, A, B, C, . . . satisfy "K"—a conditioned scheme of recurrence. And it is equivalent to affirming that they do so:

in a world situation in which . . . K . . . is not functioning but, in virtue of the fulfillment of the prior conditions, could begin to function (I, 120e, emphases mine).

Thus, the **probability** for the **emergence** of a recurring scheme can now be specified in the general case. It:

consists in the sum of the respective probabilities of all the events included in the scheme, and it [the scheme] arises as soon as the prior conditions for the functioning of the scheme are satisfied (I, 121c).

Having actually emerged from its underlying non-schematic manifold, a scheme tends to effect its own **survival** by so continuing to order this manifold that it re-sets and re-triggers the conditions for its own repeated recurrence. Such **survival**, then, is not a matter of necessity but only of conditions that happen to be fulfilled.

---

[1] The occurrence of this set of events in accord with this product would be what Lonergan terms "isolated" (I, 259d 7).

Just as classical laws are subject to the proviso, other things being equal, so also are the schemes constituted by combinations of [the verified] classical laws [of the scientific subject]; and [once a scheme has emerged] whether or not other things [e.g., conditions] will continue to be equal [and, therefore, whether or not the scheme will continue functioning], is a question that admits an answer only in terms of [the verified] statistical laws [of the subject]. Accordingly, the probability of the survival of a scheme is the probability of the non-occurrence of the events that would disrupt the scheme (I, 121d, emphases mine).

Thirdly, with a pattern set for the assignment of probabilities to recurring schemes, the conditions are fulfilled for subsuming them within the generalized explanatory framework of statistical lawfulness, sketched in the next to the last paragraph. Thus, Q, which stood, in that paragraph, for a kind of event, could be redefined as a kind of scheme without falsifying a single further pronouncement in the paragraph. Thus, the "incapacity for divergence" would now refer to the probabilities of emergence (and survival) for Q under given conditions. And when these conditions include indeterminately large numbers and long time intervals the emergence (and/or survival) of a scheme with even a very low probability is virtually assured. Thus, the scientific subject's statistical and classical modes of explaining the data are complementary. By the former mode of explanation, he accounts for the emergence and then the survival of schemes from and with respect to the non-schematic. By the latter, he grasps the abstract laws accounting for the regularity of the schematic which has emerged and is surviving.

To summarize, the preceding five paragraphs have sketched Lonergan's reflective revelation of the complementarity of the relationship which obtains between the scientific subject's classically and statistically focused:

(1) empirical heuristic notions (I, IV.1.1);

(2) modes of understanding and abstracting from the data (I, IV.1.4);

(3) formulations (I, IV.1.3);

(4) procedures (I, IV.1.2);

(5) modes of verifying his formulations (I, IV.1.5);

(6) modes of explaining the data (I, IV.1.6).

b) Complementarity in Context

The following three paragraphs are offered to clarify and draw out implications from what has been brought out in the preceding five paragraphs.

First, the preceding revelation of a sextet of parallel dyads structured throughout by relations of complementarity, presupposes the triadic analysis of scientific consciousness carried out in sections B3 and B5, above. In these two sections, classically and statistically focused scientific consciousness was found to share a common triadic intentional structure. Thus, the first element in the sextet pertains to the level of scientifically patterned human experience or empirical consciousness. The second, third and fourth, pertain to the scientifically patterned level of human understanding or intellectual consciousness. The fifth and sixth pertain to the scientifically patterned level of human reflection and judgment or rational consciousness. Thus, points (1)-(6), immediately above, have been relating the "horizon" analyses performed upon the subject of the scientific attitude in Sections B3 and D5, above.

Secondly, upon the further reflections recounted in this subsection, the classically and statistically focused movements of human subjectivity and the irreducible anticipations of lawfulness which their respective questions carry forward are to be understood as complementary differentiations within a single, unified movement of human scientific consciousness bent upon correctly, but completely, understanding schematized fields of data. Thus, the limitations of the irreducible analyses and results of the reflections sketched in sections B3 and B5 of this chapter, have generated the further issues which have forced the emergence of a higher vantage point from which to understand the attitude of human science. From this higher vantage point, these irreducible analyses and reflections:

(1) stand forth as abstract, impoverished, isolated facets within a broader horizon;

(2) are not annulled in their irreducibility;[1]

(3) are transcended by being grouped, by being brought together as "co-operating" members within a more comprehensive whole.

Thirdly, to take up their proper places within this higher vantage point, the presuppositions recalled at the beginning of this chapter section, although not falsified by what has transpired in this subsection, require transposition and reformulation. Thus, we would now begin the reformulation of the initial paragraphs of this section as follows.

In taking up the modern scientific attitude towards the world, the subject necessarily is committing himself to the **presuppositions** that there are irreducible but **complementary** classical and statistical:

(1a) notions (of the unknown "object");

(2a) inquiries to be triadically pursued to term under their guidance;

(3a) laws to be **correctly** understood when inquiry has come to term through its self-correcting process.

Thus, a further generic and invariant feature of the subjective "pole" of the scientific horizon has been isolated in a preliminary way and added to the results of our preceding analysis.

Transposed, presuppositions, (6)-(7), above, can be reformulated as follows:

The general empirical method[2] of the scientific subject anticipates and, at the limit, correctly uncovers the proper lawfulness underlying schemes of recurring data. It does this by combining classical laws which bring out their underlying systematicity and statistical laws which bring out the ideal frequency with which

---

[1] To affirm their reducibility, or to suppress one or the other alternative, is to yield, at the limits, to mechanist determinism (cf. I, IV.3.2) or indeterminism (I, IV.3.4).

[2] By "general empirical method" the author does not mean the "generalized empirical" or "transcendental method" which Lonergan equates with "basic" method in philosophy (cf. I, 72d, 243d, 423-428).

actual schemes of the given type are emergent in and then survive under non-systematically ramifying sets of specifiable conditions (6a-7a). Thus, further generic and invariant but <u>isomorphic</u> features subtending the unified horizon of human scientific consciousness have been isolated in a preliminary way and added to the results of our preceding analysis.

7. Emergent Probability: Conclusion

Section B6 of this chapter has brought out the subject's exercise of complementary, heuristically linked triads of intentional activity. It has shown that the contemporary subject's engagement of the scientific attitude presupposes and commits her to such activity.[1] Again, it is this fact which has forced her to differentiate and group classical and statistical functions so as to overcome the limitations of their isolated operation. It is this fact which has compelled her to form a "general empirical method" applicable to any "objective" field of specialized research. Finally, Lonergan's point is that unless the preceding conclusions are drawn, the subject has not remained true to the exigence for complete understanding of the data immanent in the pure desire to know. But with these results of the preceding section of this chapter recalled, the questions of this section can be posed.

(II) First, given the preceding, is there a radical or major sense in which the subject's exercise of the complementary differentiations of her scientific attitude is dynamic and has a determinate orientation and structure? What is that sense, that dynamism, that structure? The use of "radical" and "major" is designed to put a special twist on the question. These terms direct us to ask whether, with respect to the known convergence of scientific inquiry upon the intelligibility immanent in particular fields of data, there is any intelligibility to the dynamic by which, through successive inquiries, her own successive viewpoints [and their fields] are structured? Secondly, we have seen that:

> knowing and known, if they are not an identity, at least stand in some correspondence and, as the known is reached only through knowing, structural features of the one are bound to be reflected in the other (I, 115b).[2]

---

[1]Cf. presuppositions (1a)-(3a) at the end of the last section.

[2]We have presupposed this in our definition of horizon. Cf. presuppositions 6-7 and 6a-7a in the preceding section of this chapter.

But, then, what are the implications of an affirmative, correct, and reflectively grounded answer to the preceding question for correctly understanding the immanent intelligibility of surrounding world process as a whole? To what conception of surrounding "world" process, then, does the scientific subject's commitment to and necessary presupposition of "general empirical method" commit her?

The answer to the **first** question will be approached in three brief steps. First, the radical dynamic of the general empirical method of the subject will be brought out from texts in Chapters III and V of Insight. Then, the complementary role of statistical method, operative in but, unattended to in the preceding account will be added. Finally, the role of insight in structuring the intentionality of the process will be stressed. The **second** question will be answered in two steps. First the notion of a "conditioned series" of schemes of recurrence will be brought out. Then, the notion of "emergent probability" will be explicated.

First, an initial approximation to an answer to what the major dynamism of the subject of general empirical method is, can be constructed by splicing together incomplete reflections from I, III.3 and V.4.1 and attending, in particular, to the "third case," to the third item of quotation below.[1]

> But the advance of science . . . is a circuit, from data to inquiry, from inquiry to insight, from insight to the formulation of premises [e.g., classical laws] and the deduction of their implications . . . (I, 166b, emphases mine);
>
> [these implications comprise] premises and rules for the guidance of human activity upon sensible objects. Such activity, in its turn, brings about sensible change to bring to light fresh data, raise new questions, stimulate further insights and so . . . (I, 74d, emphases mine) . . .
>
> generate the revision or confirmation of existing laws and in due course the discovery of new laws (I, 74d, emphases mine);
>
> [the first through third cases cited immediately above] force upon

---

[1]In what follows, commentary on Lonergan's claim is limited to the bracketed material. Again, the material is broken up by the concept to be conveyed and not merely by page and paragraph numbers and letters.

scientific consciousness [an awareness of] the inadequacies of [e.g., the limitations of] existing theories, to provide the evidence for their revisions and, in the limit [cf. I, 166b 12], when minor corrections no longer are capable of meeting the issue [e.g., the further unanswered questions], to demand the radical [e.g., major] transformation of concepts and postulates [to "generate the new set of insights" (I, 166b 12)] that is named a higher viewpoint (I, 76b, emphases mine);

[such a higher viewpoint or] basic revision, then, is a **leap**. At a stroke it is a grasp of the insufficiency of both the old laws and of the old standards. Finally, by the same verification, it establishes that both the new laws and the new standards satisfy the data (I, 166b, emphases mine).[1]

But the return to the data for verification re-opens the circuit. This will "in due course" bring about "the discovery of new laws" expressing a still higher viewpoint therein, etc. To summarize, the "third case" expresses the major, tri-levelled dynamism implicit in the scientific subject's presupposition of general empirical method. It describes the intentionality of the subject oriented, spontaneously, by her further questions, to the discovery and verification of the series of higher viewpoints on the data which successively unify and relate what is successively ununified and unrelated therein on each successively preceding "level." Thus, within the intentional continuity of the circuit, there can be distinguished science's:

(1) starting phase: experimentation yields a new set of intellectually patterned data. It is this data which:

   (a) is gathered by implementing the closed system of verified
       concepts generated by prior turns of the circuit;[2]

   (b) remains unaccounted for on its basis;

   (c) triggers a round of further questions;

---

[1]Data pertain to the first, inquiry, insight, and formulation, etc. to the second, and verification to the third level of human consciousness.

[2]This is true except at the greatest lower bound of human, scientific inquiry.

(2) middle phase: inquiry yields to the subject's spring of insight upon a higher circle of terms and relations. This higher set of terms and relations:

    (a) overcomes the limitations of its predecessors, by:

    (b) ordering what they leave coincidental,

    (c) without annulling their continued validity within restricted fields of data;

(3) end phase: critical reflection yields to the judgment that the new system truly accounts for all the relevant data, answers all the relevant questions germane to phase (1). But material operation on the basis of these laws eventually surfaces the further set of recalcitrant data which repositions the subject in a "higher" starting phase.

The preceding reflection, therefore, evidences the general empirical method of the subject as:

(1) radically dynamic; i.e., it is not complete when it has achieved the unity of closed system at some or any level;

(2) directed; i.e., it is oriented towards the overcoming of the limitations of prior levels of theory by transcending them to a "higher viewpoint;"

(3) determinately directed; i.e., it is oriented through series of successively higher viewpoints and, hence, in the "direction" of successively ascending levels of system;

(4) dynamically structured; i.e., it is guided by the successively experiential, intelligent, and critical phases within its circuit.

Finally, the truth of points (1)-(4), which we have reflectively evidenced, rests:

> not on the present state of the empirical sciences, but on the fundamental properties of insight. Insight is into imaginative representations. Insights accumulate into viewpoints. Images that represent viewpoints lead to insights that accumulate into higher viewpoints. This transition can be repeated [e.g., on successively "higher" levels] (I, 440d, emphases mine).

In a second approximation to an answer to the first question, the complementary place and role of the "statistical" heuristic of the scientific subject within the major dynamic (implicit in the preceding reflections) must be brought out.[1] Thus, in a later reflection, Lonergan points out that although direct insight into the data expresses itself in abstract classical laws:

> this abstractness is an indeterminacy that leaves room for the inverse insights [that underlie the] grasp of statistical laws; the compatibility of classical and statistical laws leaves room for the coincidental manifolds that provide the potency for the higher forms [and the discovery of higher systems of classical law] (I, 440d, emphases mine).

But the compatibility of classical and statistical laws also leaves room for changes of state governing systematic processes. In such cases:

> the same classical laws obtain, but statistical laws undergo modification. Nor are such changes of state without their significance, for they provide in the long run for the occurrence of emergent trends that begin from one set of classical laws and end with the verifiability of another [e.g., a "higher" set] (I, 449c, emphases mine).

Thus, the statistical heuristic structure of inquiry and reflection may determine that oscillations of actual frequencies (whether of events or schemes of events) have ceased to be random and are oscillating around new ideal norms. And, in the "third case," these determinations call forth the complementary questions which will anticipate, grasp, and at the limit, verify the operation of higher classical lawfulness in the data (cf. I, 54b).

Finally, this reflective account of the subject[2] ascending intentionally through successively higher viewpoints completely to

---

[1] Lonergan's own viewpoint in Insight keeps moving. He handles questions as and in the successive contexts in which they come up. His ideal is not logical, contextless, completeness. In the passages quoted in the preceding paragraph, it was simply unnecessary and unimportant to complicate issues by inserting the statistical complement to the major dynamic. Still, the interested reader should see Insight, p. 74c.

[2] Let "B" stand for "the subject . . . ascending through successively higher viewpoints . . . ."

understand the data of sucessively higher levels shares the <u>invariant</u> and <u>generic</u> character both of (1) general empirical method,[1] and (2) of the scientific subject's necessary <u>presupposition</u> of propositions (1a)-(3a) brought out in Section B6, above. This is so because the method and the presuppositions:

> [regard] <u>not</u> an imaginative synthesis of outer events [or any particular theoretical unification thereof] . . . but the <u>**inner**</u> <u>ground that is generative of **successive** imaginative syntheses and</u> <u>systematic unifications.</u> Such syntheses and unifications can rise and fall in endless succession <u>without altering a single element in</u> <u>the fundamental properties of **insight**,</u> for those fundamental properties are the <u>principle whence the</u> endless succession would <u>spring</u> (<u>I</u>, 441b, emphases mine);

> [rest] simply and solely upon the <u>dynamic</u> structure of inquiring intelligence (<u>I</u>, 116b, emphasis mine);

> [have] exploited the <u>basic and permanent factors that will hold</u> <u>their ground</u> in [the] subsequent modifications and improvements [of existing imaginative syntheses and scientific theories] (<u>I</u>, 441b, emphases mine).

On the basis of the first question of this subsection, then, the analysis of (A) begun in the last subsection has been deepened to bring out (B) as its consequence. Again, (A) in this further, reflective, light appears as the dynamic, determinately directed structure and "premiss" of the scientific subject's proper operation. Again, since "an account of insight <u>is</u> an account of method . . ." (<u>I</u>, 270), it is not surprising that in the course of reflectively analyzing the structure of the latter, attention should be refocused on the centrality and reality of the former. Finally, to supply a brief transition to, and context for, the abbreviated argument of the succeeding paragraphs, the following argument sketch is offered:

(1) higher viewpoints:

    (a) arise from and make orderly the coincidental occurrence of data in <u>recurring schemes</u>;

    (b) are complemented by the statistical laws governing the

---

[1]Let "A" stand for the "invariant and generic character of the general empirical method of the subject . . . ."

emergence and survival of these higher, classically defined, schemes;

(2) granting (1), classical and statistical laws can be combined to form schemes of recurrence;

(3) as statistical laws change, the concrete conditions are set for the grasp of a higher viewpoint in the data, e.g., the laws of the new schemes signaled by the changes of state;

(4) (B) follows from (A), yielding a succession of higher viewpoints;

(5) but the structures necessary to know what is are revelatory of the structure of what is;

(6) therefore, a "notion" of surrounding world process can be constructed:

(a) which shares the invariance and generic character of (A) and which anticipates, on the intentional model of (B):

(b) a "conditioned series" or a succession of higher and higher order schemes, emerging and surviving according to successive schedules of probability;

(c) to be named "emergent probability."

Secondly, in Insight IV.2, Lonergan worked out a heuristic notion of the immanent intelligibility structuring world process as a whole. This notion he denominated "emergent probability." And he so fashioned its conception that it runs parallel to the directed dynamism implicit in the complementary classical and statistical heuristic structures, to the general empirical method presupposed by the modern scientific subject's inquiry and reflection. Thus, he saw his conception as flowing, proximately, from:

(1) the conception of classically defined schemes of recurrence possessing **probabilities** of emergence and survival;

(2) the notion of a conditioned series of schemes of recurrence.

Since the former concept was handled in the preceding subsection, it is to a brief explication of the latter that we now turn in preparation for the discussion of the notion of emergent probability.

Lonergan specifies that a set of schemes, P, Q, R, . . . forms a conditioned series:

if all prior members of the series must be functioning actually for
any later member to become a concrete possibility. Then, the
scheme, P, can function though neither Q nor R exists; the scheme,
Q, can function, though R does not yet exist; but Q cannot function
unless P is already functioning; and R cannot function unless Q is
already functioning (I, 118d–119a).

Lonergan illustrates these relationships concretely by working
backwards in time from an actually verified, contemporary member of
such a series. The member he selects is the carnivorous dietary scheme
of animal life on earth.

All carnivorous animals cannot live off other carnivorous animals.
Hence, a carnivorous, dietary scheme supposes another herbivorous,
dietary scheme but, inversely, there could be herbivorous animals
without any carnivorous animals. Again, plants cannot in general
live off animals; the scheme of their nourishment involves chemical
processes; and that scheme can function apart from the existence of
any animals. Finally, chemical cycles are not independent of
physical laws yet, inversely, the laws of physics can be combined
into schemes of recurrence that are independent of chemical
processes (I, 119b, emphases mine).

Lonergan adds a further element of precision to the preceding
account by distinguishing between seriations of schemes that are:

(1) possible; these constitute the totality of seriations that can
be constructed by the subject on the basis of the classical
laws operative in the universe in abstraction from the concrete
conditions, e.g., numbers, distributions, time–intervals of
events, etc., under which they are realized. The possible
seriation, then, suffers from the "indeterminacy of the
abstract." In ranging over:

the process of any universe with [classical] laws similar
to our own (I, 120b, emphasis mine),

it, thereby, fails to differentiate from among these
possibilities the more and less probable and actual seriations
determinable, respectively, by statistical laws and measuring
techniques or unmediated observation;

(2) probable; with respect to any stage in the world process
(including the contemporary) there is the range of more and
less probable future seriations with which the movement of

world–history _realizes_ the merely _possible_ seriations of schemes envisaged classically.

> Still, if [the statistical subject's _probable_ seriation of the situation]. . . is not as abstract as the possible seriation, none the less, it is **ideal** (I, 120b, emphasis mine).

Thus, it includes: "all that _would_ occur without systematic divergence from the probabilities" (I, 119e, emphasis mine);

(3) _actual_; this the subject contacts by moving in intention:

> _beyond_ the field of all laws, classical _and_ statistical, and entering the field of _observation_, in which alone non–systematic divergences from probability are determinate [and evidence for the pronouncement of concrete judgments of fact is available] (I, 120b, emphases mine).

Unlike the more and less cumulatively ramifying branches of, respectively, the possible and probable seriations of schemes, the actual seriation is unique. It comprises all:

> of the schemes that actually were, are, or will be functioning in our universe along with precise specifications of their places, their durations, and their relations to one another (I, 119d).

Thus, working retrospectively along the unique track of conditioned series which world–historical process has laid down and now sustains, the subject may raise further, less concrete questions and, at the limit, reconstruct the possibilities and probabilities of emergence and survival of series of schemes which, at each point, have actually been realized. On the other hand, working prospectively from the data on past and present possibilities, probabilities and realizations, the scientific subject may project the successive future possibilities and probabilities. These will/may become the unknowns to be arrived at by later inquirers when they seek to reconstruct the probabilities from which past or present realizations have diverged non–systematically.

We have seen that when the prior conditions for the functioning of a scheme are realized, the probability that the scheme will begin to function _leaps_ from the product to the sum of the respective probabilities of its member events. But when a _set_ of schemes is conditioned serially, then the actual functioning of earlier schemes in the series sequentially fulfills the conditions for the possibility of the functioning of the next. This makes the probability for the emergence of each successive scheme jump from a product to a sum of proper fractions:

> But, what is probable, sooner or later occurs. When it occurs, a probability of emergence is replaced by a probability of survival; and as long as the scheme survives, it is in its turn fulfilling conditions for the possibility of still later schemes in the series (I, 122a, emphases mine).

The general notion of Emergent Probability, then:

> results from the combination of the conditioned series of [classically definable] schemes with their respective probabilities of emergence and survival (I, 122b);

> [is a further determination of the scientific subject's necessary presupposition of] the complementarity of classical and of statistical investigations [e.g., of general empirical method] . . . from the viewpoint of what is to be known [by its implementation] (I, 115b, emphases mine);

> is [equivalent to the notion of] the successive realization in accord with successive schedules of probability of a conditioned series of [classically definable] schemes of recurrence (I, 125b–126c, emphases mine).

Furthermore, Lonergan argues that when this heuristic notion is worked out in general terms, it possesses "remarkable potentialities for explanation" (I, 122b, emphasis mine). Thus, by expanding this notion, the subject of general empirical method will be able to construct a generic, explanatory framework. It will be adequate to account for any level of schematic development (or, as we shall see, regression) within any empirical universe which manifests schemes of recurrence that are ordinally related. Thus, surrounding world–process, conceived under the heuristic assumption of emergent probability, will manifest the following linked characteristics:

(1) spatial concentrations; but later schemes only become concretely possible where their earlier, conditioning antecedents have already been realized. Thus, however widespread the number of places in which the world's most

elementary schemes have been realized, there will be a progressive _constriction_ in the volumes of space in which later schemes can _emerge_.

> (I)t follows that, since the latest schemes in the series[1] have the greatest number of conditions to be fulfilled, their occurrence will be limited to a relatively small number of places (_I_, 122c);

(2) _absolute numbers_; because the emergence of the world's latest schemes always has the greatest number of serially conditioning schemes as their antecedents, they have the _lowest_ probability of emergence. Although this is true:

> low probabilities [for the emergence of the latest schemes] are _offset_ by large numbers of occasions, so that what is probable only once on a million occasions, is to be expected a million times on a million million occasions (_I_, 113d);

> . . . the lower the probability of the last schemes of the conditioned series, the greater must be the initial absolute numbers in which elementary schemes can be realized. In brief, the size of the universe is inversely proportionate to the probability of its ultimate schemes of recurrence (_I_, 123a);[2]

(3) _time intervals_; despite the world's large absolute numbers and the initial widespread functioning of schemes, the narrowing spatial volume for the emergence of later schemes progressively narrows the "basis" for further development. The rarefied character of the base is:

> offset by long intervals of time, so that if occasions arise only once in a million years, still they arise a thousand times in a thousand million years (_I_, 113d);[3]

---

[1] The reader is invited to consider, as one such latest, humanly "actualized" scheme, the general empirical method of human science.

[2] On emergent probability, then, the _reason why_ numbers have to be large is _so that_ highly developed, highly integrated schemes would emerge despite low probabilities; e.g., a "vertical" finality is operative in world process as in the subject's cognitional ascent within it.

[3] On emergent probability, then, the _reason why_ time–intervals must be long is so that highly developed schemes would emerge despite constrictions in spatial volumes, etc., etc., etc.

(4) the natural or artificial selection of scheme; schemes are selected for according to their respective probabilities of emergence and survival;

(5) stable and unstable series of schemes; e.g., the earlier schemes in the series of the former kind would have high probabilities of emergence and survival. Earlier schemes of the latter kind, have low probabilities of emergence and survival;

(6) development; schemes whose probability of survival is low but whose probability of emergence has been determined to be high would:

> readily surrender materials to give later schemes the opportunity to emerge;

> readily be available to fulfill the conditions for the functioning of later schemes (I, 124a).

Such schemes would condition the emergence of further, "higher" schemes;

(7) the openness of world process; e.g., the probable realization of possibilities is neither deterministic nor blind, i.e., in-deterministic;

(8) increasing systematicity of world process; the later the scheme realized in the series, the greater the systematization to which it subjects underlying manifolds;[1]

(9) the assuredness of increasing systematicity. But this follows from (2)-(3) above;

(10) the significance of the initial world situation; at all stages, world process is the probable realization of possibilities. But these are limited by the still latent possibilities "contained" in the initial situation and the probabilities it assigns;

---

[1]Cf. the second quotation on page 188 of Section B6 of this chapter, above. Also see Insight, 113d.

(11) break-downs; no scheme has more than a probability of survival. And a breakdown at the earlier stages of an existing series collapses its train of successors. Again, the fact of a break down holds out some probable possibility of its "reversal;"[1]

(12) blind-alleys; schemes with a high probability of survival tend to block the emergence of further schemes with in an ongoing series;

(13) distributions; the later a scheme in a series, the narrower its distribution. The narrower the distribution the more (3) must be invoked to guarantee the emergence of later schemes. The greater the probabilities of blind alleys and breakdowns the more (2) must be invoked to guarantee emergence of later schemes.

But the preceding are properties and characteristics of the world order in which we actually dwell.[2] Hence, as conceived, emergent probability would, in fact, seem to be a uniquely probable explanatory notion, since it alone, among all cosmological competitors, comprehends (1)–(13), above. Furthermore, the foregoing linked properties of surrounding world process are:

(1) generic; the notion appeals to the complementarity of classical and statistical laws, their combination in both schemes and conditioned series thereof. It does this without specifying any determinate content for these laws, their combinations, etc.:

> (a) specific account [of emergent probability] would have to draw upon the contents of the empirical sciences. It would have to appeal, not to classical and statistical laws in general, but to the precise laws that can be empirically

---

[1]Cf. Section B10 of this chapter. It takes up the heuristic notion of "reversal" in the explanatory context of a discussion of a "dialectical method."

[2]The reader would do well to keep in mind the "intentional corre-lates" of these characteristics of surrounding world process; e.g., the increasingly "higher viewpoints" to which the scientific and/or mathematical subject aspires and ascends from the base of general empirical method.

established (I, 116b, emphases mine);[1]

(2) relatively invariant;[2] e.g., they rest upon the dynamic premiss and necessary presupposition of the general empirical method of the modern scientific subject, "the invariant forms governing scientific investigation" (I, 116c). It follows that the foregoing design and characteristics of surrounding world process:

> cannot be upset by any amount of scientific work in the determination of classical or statistical laws (I, 128b);

> enjoy the invariance of the premise which we . . . [have] invoked (I, 116c);

(3) fall within the limits of possible human experience; (1)-(13), above, are implicit in the heuristic notion of emergent probability. But emergent probability is the heuristic notion of—the general empirical method of scientific subjectivity which heuristically structures the open "horizon" of human experience.

Finally, Lonergan has heuristically conceived the structure of the "world" of modern scientific subjectivity. He has done so in a

---

[1]Lonergan makes this point clearly when discussing the metaphysical analogue of emergent probability. He calls this notion "finality." Thus, his affirmation of the world hypothesis of emergent probability, like that of finality: "rests not simply on an a priori parallel [between the structure of our knowing and the known] but on that parallel as supported by vast ranges of fact. For our knowing might be much as it is, though the universe were otherwise inert, static, finished, complete, or dynamic but undirected . . . . But the fact is that this universe is . . . the effectively probable realization of its own possibilities" (I, 450a, emphases mine). Again, the notion of finality cannot be clarifed in full until the genetic and dialectical methods of the subject have been sketched.

[2]Two points should be made here.
First, in Chapter VIII, Lonergan lays down a "sequential postulate" to extend the notion of emergent probability to things. What he says of that postulate is also true, as far as it goes, of the notion of emergent probability. The notion is: "methodological; it is not some hypothesis of empirical science but rather an assumption that can generate an almost endless stream of hypotheses; it is not a scientific theory that can be verified or refuted, for it is too general to be tested in that [straightforward] fashion; it is an

manner which is adequate to house, which keeps in "dynamic correspondence" with, and which takes as its "transcendental clue," the restless
dynamic of the general empirical method of concrete, scientific
"Humanity."[1] The sketch will be further filled out in Section B8.
Here we can do no more than re-transpose presuppositions (6a)-(7a),
which we have formulated at the end of Section B6. In their next
context they read as follows.

The general empirical method of the scientific subject anticipates
and, at the limit, correctly gathers the proper lawfulness of a
universe of emergent probability (6b-7b). Thus, further generic
and invariant but isomorphic features subtending the dynamically
unified horizon of scientific consciousness have been isolated in a
preliminary way and added to our preceding attempts. . . .

-----

approach, a heuristic assumption, that can be worked out in an enormous
number of manners and that can be tested empirically only through such
specific determinations and applications" (I, 261a). Precisely because
it is a heuristic notion, then, the critically grounded affirmation of
emergent probability: "leaves to those competent in specialized
departments the task of working out precise statements on the unfolding
of generalized emergent probability" (I, 262a).

Secondly, see footnote 2 on pages 180-181 of Section B6 of this
chapter, for the sense of the qualifier "relatively."

[1]The point to the "house" metaphor is that a universe of emergent
probability is cognate with and fitting for the subject of generalized
empirical method. A mechanistic, determinist universe is not.

8. "Man" and "Thing"

Introduction

In Insight, Chapter VIII, Section 1, Lonergan recalls his
affirmation[1] of the complementarity of:

    I. the scientific subject's classical and statistical notions,
        insights, . . . explanations, etc., their correlation with the
        complementary systematic and non-systematic dimensions of
        world-process;

   II. the pre-scientific subject's "initial specification" for these
        correlative complements in terms of, on the one hand, his use
        of "experiential conjugates" and, on the other, his "common
        sense expectations" (I, 253b #1) of "ordinary and exceptional,
        normal and abnormal runs of [everyday] events" (I, 63c,
        emphases mine, cf. I, 245c).[2]

But the complements referred to in both I and II, above, pertain to
some more or less high "abstractive" viewpoint upon the data, i.e.,
both equally abstract from an "integrative" viewpoint thereupon.[3] But
it is only "from" the latter viewpoint that a potential totality of
sensory-motor "profiles" can be grasped and affirmed as aspects of some
one thing, that is, in their intelligible unity. Again, unless such an
integrative "viewpoint" is reflected upon and its sources laid bare:

    (1) the explication of the thing as an "intelligible unity" will

---

[1]Cf. Section B6 of this division, above.

[2]Lonergan thematizes the complementary, pre-scientific analogues
of the scientific subject's classical and statistical initiatives at
Insight, p. 294b 28.   For expository reasons he mentions only the
pre-scientific "classical" analogue of his empirical method in VIII.1,
245b 4-6.

[3]In this section, we will be careful to distinguish the
"abstractive" and "integrative." The point to the distinction will
emerge in what follows.

contract toward the more spontaneous and palpable notion of "body" as "already–out–there–now;"[1]

(2) the demonstrative "this" will be left without any <u>intelligible</u> reference. Thus, it will be unable, consequently, to constitute the "link between [both the descriptive <u>and</u> scientific] concepts [figuring in the subject's judgments] and the <u>data</u> [manifold] as [only empirically] individual" (<u>I</u>, 436a). It is left, literally, "pointless;"[2]

(3) the proceeding reflective inquiry will be distorted, i.e., will be unable correctly to resolve such issues as the relation between the common sense and scientific "horizons" of the subject, the <u>unity</u> to his multi–patterned, multi–levelled performances in general, etc.

Lonergan initiates his overcoming of the limited, "abstractive" perspective to the preceding reflections by recalling a fact. When the scientific subject suitably verifies and affirms an implicitly defined set of explanatory conjugates, say C_j, the proper focus of his insight and the evidence for his claim is the concrete data. But, then:

in the same data there will [always already] be [by virtue of the preceding affirmation] evidence for [the subject's further grasp and affirmation of] some <u>thing</u> that is to be [e.g., that has, in fact, just been] differentiated by the conjugates [e.g., C_j] verified in the same data (<u>I</u>, 259c, emphasis mine).

Lonergan makes an <u>exactly</u> equivalent point within the later, more fully metaphysical context of Chapter XV of <u>Insight</u>. There he argues that:

the heuristic structure that leads [the subject] to knowledge of conjugate forms [e.g., C_j] <u>necessitates</u> [e.g., presupposes] another

---

[1]As the reader recalls, these notions were analyzed in the course of reflections on the biological pattern of human subjectivity, cf. Chapter I, above.

[2]Thus, even as the subject's "What?" intends the "nature of . . ." so it heuristically <u>presupposes</u> a "this." And by "this" is here meant an **intelligibly** differentiable <u>one of</u> which he asks and to which he attributes the fruit of his <u>verified</u> inquiry. And such a claim, Lonergan notes, is not merely extraordinary, but <u>undeniable</u> on the sole supposition that we be inquirers (cf. presupposition #8, below).

structure that leads [him] to <u>knowledge</u> of [the] central [e.g., substantial] forms [of things]. For one reaches explanatory conjugates [e.g., C_j] by <u>considering data as similar to other data</u>;

but the data, which are similar, also are <u>concrete and individual</u>; and as concrete and individual, they are <u>understood [and affirmed]</u> inasmuch as one grasps [and verifies] in them [the existence of] a concrete and intelligible <u>unity</u>, <u>identity</u>, <u>whole</u> (<u>I</u>, 435c, emphases mine);[1]

<u>properties <u>and</u> things</u> are what is to be <u>known</u> by [the subject's] <u>understanding</u> [and affirmation of] the <u>same data</u> by <u>different</u> but <u>complementary</u> procedures (<u>I</u>, 485c, emphases mine).

But, first, the argument is <u>from</u> the subject's heuristic intending and verified grasp of pattern in the data <u>to</u> his necessarily presupposed grasp and, at least, implicit affirmation of the thus patterned "thing." Secondly, parallel arguments can be constructed from non-classically scientific and/or, less trenchantly and reliably, common sense considerations.[2] And, thirdly, no more is being affirmed at this point of the argument than:

(1) the <u>fact</u> of the subject's intelligent "grasp" and reasonable affirmation of things;

(2) the <u>notion</u> of the thing implicit in such insights and judgments;

(3) the, as yet, unexplicated sense of the thing as an intelligible, unity-identity-whole; the heuristically intended content of this notion;

(4) the <u>inevitability</u> of the subject's affirmation of (1)-(3), above, given, minimally his engagement in the scientific and/or common sense attitudes toward the surrounding world;

(5) the subject's necessary presupposition of (1)-(4), immediately above, given the engagement of his intentional consciousness in

---

[1]The point is that one is, therefore, grasping and affirming the "object" of one's implicit notion of the thing. Again, for some measure of further clarification see <u>UB</u>, 7c-d and 9c.

[2]Thus, for example, the subject's affirmation of ideal frequency norms presupposes that there are things whose existence and acts are subject to relevant actual frequencies of occurrence. For a similar argument from purely common sense considerations see <u>Insight</u>, 246b 7-9.

these "attitudes." But, then, continuing our numbering from Section B7, (1)-(4), immediately above, will be denominated **presupposition #8** of the intelligence and reasonableness of the subject (cf. <u>I</u>, 259c).

Finally, in what follows, those aspects of the notion of the thing are taken up which bear either remotely or proximately on the subject's search for a fully integral Self-knowledge. <u>First</u>, then, a set of further reflections will lend the notion precision and relate it to the tri-fold "structure" of human consciousness. <u>Secondly</u>, consideration of its role as the focal point of intersection for the common sense and scientific operations of the subject will bring out the <u>complementarity</u> of the "horizons" these opposed operations imply. <u>Thirdly</u>, it will bring out the <u>explanatory</u> notions of genus and species by which the "things" are to be interpreted.   <u>Finally</u>, the new Lonerganian explanatory framework will be briefly compared with its Porphyrian ancestor. Its "grounds" will be clarified. And, then, the locus of <u>human being</u> within it will be determined. Again, underlying these tasks is the thesis that the eighth chapter of <u>Insight</u> evidences the subject's desire to understand <u>himSelf</u> authentically both in the **unity** of his conscious acts, and also the universe of emergent probability within which he finds, understands, affirms and enacts himSelf.

a) The Notion of the Thing

Lonergan notes that the heuristic "notion" of the thing is "grounded in" (I, 246b) the subject's **insight** into "a concrete and intelligible unity, identity, whole" (I, 435c). He points out that such an insight emerges upon his consideration of the data: "in their concrete individuality and in the totality of their aspects" (I, 246b; UB, 126a, 125c, etc.). Such a "unity, identity, whole" as:

> differentiated by experiential conjugates and common-sense expecta-tions . . . is a thing for us, a thing as described. As differen-tiated by explanatory conjugates and scientifically determined probabilities, it is a thing itself, a thing as explained (I, 253b #1, emphases mine).

Thus, the subject's warranted grasp of the thing presupposes his effective intentional "leap":[1]

(1) **from** apprehension of an empirically distinct manifold of data in its "concrete individuality," e.g., a "totality" of spatial-ly and/or temporally conjoint aspects, "profiles," qualities, etc., which is "this-here" "object" of sensitive and/or practi-cal concern (cf. I, 246b);

(2) **to** a grasp of the "essential" oneness of the manifold.[2] Implicit in the insight which the leap involves is the sub-ject's grasp of:

(a) the "unity" of his "object":

to which belongs every aspect of every datum within the

---

[1]The implicit question underlying the following exposition, is "What am I doing when I am knowing a thing as thing?" What is the "thing-notion" implicit in knowing anything?

[2]Lonergan's point here is that knowledge of the things is not possible unless there occurs "insight" into the unity of the thing. Thus, the subject's "insight into insight" is the key to her overcoming the confusion between "thing" and "body," between an intelligible unity "in" the data and a numerically distinct composite of elements. It is, therefore, also key to the Self-discovery that she is not an empirical center of "power and Self-satisfaction" (I, 254 n) already "in here," but an intelligent, developing unity, the subject of operations on, minimally, three integrated levels. Cf. I, 67d; UB, 128a 12–15.

unity ($\underline{I}$, 246b, emphases mine);[1]

(b) the "identity" of his "object," its self-sameness under successive, multi- or uni-levelled variations in its properties, relations, and/or the probabilities which govern their seriation, etc.;[2]

(c) his object as a "whole." A whole:

has parts. The whole is related to each of the parts and each of the parts is related to the other parts and to the whole ($\underline{C}$1, 222b).

Excluding the sense of wholeness as some "conventional" or "arbitrary" collection, there is its sense as a "highly organized product of nature or art." But such a whole's:

set of internal relations is of greatest significance. Each part is what it is in virtue of its functional relations to other parts; there is no part that is not determined by the exigences of other parts; and the whole possesses a certain inevitability in its unity, so that the removal of any part would be ridiculous ($\overline{\underline{C}1}$, 222c, emphases

---

[1]Three brief points should be made here.

First, the subject's notion of the thing always, therefore, involves the "grasp" of a "unity" to which a manifold of acts, profiles, variations, etc. belong.

Secondly, within the field of his Self-presence, the subject must always already have an at least implicit notion of himSelf as experiencing; asking "Why?" about what "he," e.g., the same "one," experiences; reflecting upon what "he," e.g., the same acting "one," has understood.

Finally, the reader has perhaps noticed the fully reflective character of these considerations.

[2]Two points should be made here.

First, the subject's implicit notion of the thing involves the "grasp" of a principle of **"continuity"** through change. Thus, things are extended in space and permanent in time only inasmuch as spatially and temporally distinct data (e.g., profiles, acts, properties, etc.) "pertain to the same unity" ($\underline{I}$, 246c). Things are: "subject to change, inasmuch as there is some difference between the aggregate of data on the same unity at another instant" ($\underline{I}$, 246c).

Secondly, within the field of his conscious Self-presence, the subject always has an at least implicit notion of himSelf as continuous with his waking and sleeping, his loving and hating, his losing and gaining "inches," his learning and failing to learn, his shifts in conscious pattern, his advancing age, etc.

mine);[1]

(d) the "intelligibility" of his unified, "whole" "object" (I, 272g). The intelligibility:

    i) is evidenced in the _pattern_ to the inter-actions it sustains in relation to the sensitivity of the subject and other unities;

    ii) calls forth the pre-scientific and scientifically

---

[1] Three points should be made here.

First, the schematic functioning of some schemes fulfills conditions for their becoming "parts" of higher intelligible unities. Thus, subatomic particles _can_ be "parts" of atoms. Atoms can be "parts" of molecules, molecules "parts" of cells, cells "parts" of plants, etc. (I, 249b–250a). But such parts are _not_ "things within things" (cf. I, VIII.4). Such an affirmation would abstract from that aspect of the "whole" which "cannot be accounted for on the lower viewpoint" (I, 258d). It would abstract from an aspect which is "lost" unless its parts are grasped as "brought together" from out of the highest possible conjugate level of differentiation that they sustain. Thus, if there is evidence for a higher set of conjugates in the data, there cannot be evidence for wholes, for _things_ of a lower _kind_ in the same data. Finally, in "Cognitional Structure" (cf. C1, pp. 221-239), Lonergan thematizes that special case in which the _parts_ of the given whole are themselves _activities_: "as in a song, a dance, a chorus, a symphony, a drama. Such a whole is _dynamic materially_. But dynamism may _not_ be restricted to the parts. The whole itself may be self-assembling, self-constituting; then it is _formally dynamic_. It is a _dynamic structure_" (C1, 222d, emphases mine). An example of such a dynamic structure would be the _Self_-assembling of conscious acts on empirical, intelligent, and rational levels of consciousness by the responsible deliberations of the human subject. Thus, within the field of his conscious _Self_-presence, there is the subject's always at least implicitly operative notion of himSelf as such a formally dynamic "whole."

Secondly, the subject's notion of the thing involves his grasp of an _autonomous_ "center" to a field of inter-acting parts, aspects, etc. It involves the lawful relation of these parts within one or more schemes of recurrence. It involves the _completeness_ of this center relative to the conditions that must be _fulfilled if it_ is to exist. It involves its capacity to act on its own within its schemes and under the relevant conditions.

Finally, in, for example, "The Mediation of Christ in Prayer" (Lonergan, _Method_, vol. 2, no. 1 (March, 1984), pp. 1-20) Lonergan distinguishes "material" wholes, e.g., a watchcase; "functional wholes," e.g., a watch; "Self-transforming" wholes, e.g., a multi-cellular plant, and "self-constituting" wholes, e.g., human subjects in their formal dynamism.

specialized "What?"–and "How often?"–asking of the subject;[1]

    iii) is to be "known" in the full differentiation of the "thing itself" only when all the relevant questions of the fully scientific subject have been correctly answered;[2]

(3) from reflection upon the evidence of the data manifold in question to, in the relevant case, his affirmation of his grasp upon his "object" as indeed a "unity–identity–whole." Thus, if the formulation of his grasp is rarely as explicit as that set forth in (2), immediately above, still it:

> is itself verifiable; for the ancient list of four elements, earth, water, fire, air, has been rejected and the new list of the periodic table has been established on the ground of hypothesis and verification; [still] both the

---

[1] In correspondence with these two questions, the subject's thing–notion anticipates the possession of a nature and a state. Thus, within the field of his conscious Self-presence there is the subject's always at least implicitly operative notion of his own intelligence, reasonableness and responsibility, the normal and abnormal, or changing runs within which he meets or fails to meet their exigences.

[2] Two important points must be made here.

First, gathering from footnotes 1 and 2 on page 214, footnote 1 on page 215, and footnote 1, immediately above, all that is implicit in the subject's notion of the thing within its world of emergent probability, we get:
    1. a principle of unity "underlying" attributes;
    2. a principle of continuity in change;
    3. an autonomous center of activity;
    4. that which is intelligible, has a nature, etc.
But if Lonergan's reflections have cast these notes into an analogous and transposed sense and context, still they remain the classical "properties" which Thomistic philosophy has assigned to (first) "substance."

Secondly, this notion of the thing, is presupposed by the the "What?"– and "How often?"–asking of the general empirical method of the subject. But his general method underlies the achievement and will bring forth the transcendence of the specific scientific theories associated with "our time." Still, since the notion of the thing is a presupposition of that method, even a major transcendence of past scientific achievement could not invalidate this notion without defaulting upon the heuristic structure to its own transcendence. Thus, this notion, unlike modern scientific theories, is not only to be associated with "our time."

old list and the new are lists of kinds of <u>things</u> (<u>I</u>, 248b, emphases mine).[1]

But, then, the explication of the subject's implicit thing-notion represents a further "specialization" of the basic cognitional "structure" to human consciousness. This structure, the reader recalls, has been "outlined" in terms of the three levels of presentations, intelligence, and reflection" (cf. points (1)-(3), immediately above) and already "exemplified by the classical and statistical phases of empirical method . . ." (<u>I</u>, 282c), by the dynamic to his common sense learning, etc. Thus, the "insight" by which the subject grasps the unity-identity-whole in the data is analogous in its integrative context, to that through which he grasps a higher, abstractive viewpoint in a coincidental "data" manifold. And it is no less in need of a critical moment of reflection before judgment is warranted. Finally, the following summary and concluding remarks can be made concerning the subject's always already at least implicit notion of the thing.

<u>First</u>, it rests upon the fundamental properties of human intentionality, i.e., insight's grasp upon the "unity" of the manifold, rationality's affirmation of what is immanently grasped.

<u>Secondly</u>, it does <u>not</u> depend upon, for example, the state of contemporary scientific knowledge of the world. It is <u>presupposed</u> by his heuristic intending and warranted grasp upon explanatory (and/or experiential) conjugates.

<u>Thirdly</u>, it figures, by virtue of the first two remarks, immediately above, to stand its ground as basically and relatively

---

[1] Recapping, the notion of an intelligible unity-identity-whole is always implicit in the subject's "understanding" of a thing if his understanding has been correctly affirmed. But in Chapter XV.2, Lonergan denominates the "metaphysical equivalent" of such a true affirmation, such a correct understanding, <u>central</u> **form**. He denominates the "metaphysical equivalent" for its <u>empirically</u> residual individuality <u>central</u> **potency**. He denominates the metaphysical equivalent for what is affirmed, <u>central</u> act. "Central," is used to differentiate these elements from their "conjugate" counterparts. Cf. Chapter VI, Section 8, below.

basically and relatively invariant despite the expansions, contractions, distortions to the global or specialized movement of human cognition, refinements in the description of its nature, etc.

Fourthly, it is, therefore, opposed to the biological subject's no less spontaneous notion of "body." Again, it can be used to criticize and correct the common sense or scientific subject's engagement of the latter notion once its fully critical "grounds" have been laid bare.

b) Corollaries to the Basic Notion

Two corollaries to the preceding characterizations of the subject's implicit notion of the thing must now be added.

First, this notion constitutes the common integrative point of reference <u>at</u> which the insights, terms, formulations, criteria, judgments, etc. of the subject in her "common sense" <u>and</u> "scientific attitudes" towards the world meet, overlap, etc. It, therefore, <u>brings</u> these two <u>attitudes</u> of the subject as well as the horizons they outline into interaction. It lets them be of relevance to and, therefore, have a bearing upon, one another. In so doing, it fulfills a necessary condition: "for the continuity [i.e., for the development "in difference" but with commensurability] of scientific thought . . ." (<u>I</u>, 247c). It does this since the <u>scientific</u> subject:

> <u>needs</u> the notion of [that which—] . . . has as its properties both experiential <u>and</u> explanatory conjugates, . . . by its identity demands a coherent <u>explanation</u> or <u>set of explanations</u> that is verifiable in the easily ascertainable data of the thing as described (<u>I</u>, 247c–248a, emphases mine).

This need is evidenced by the subject when her minor theoretical revisions do <u>not</u> meet the further relevant questions called forth by the data and she is forced to advance to a successor system or series thereof to do so. While such systems need to be discovered and verified in the "data" rendered descriptively:

> they <u>cannot</u> be discovered and verified in <u>any</u> data whatever; <u>neither can they</u> be discovered and verified in the data which they themselves select, for then a number of incompatible systems would be equally verifiable <u>for each would satisfy equally</u> well the data it selected. Accordingly, scientific thought **needs**, not only explanatory systems, but also <u>descriptions that determine the data which explanations must satisfy</u> (<u>I</u>, 247c).

Thus, <u>without</u> her notion of the thing which both her descriptions <u>and</u> explanations must satisfy, the scientific subject's intentional convergence upon the conceptual system which renders fully intelligible the data–as–described would be <u>meaningless</u>. But such convergence is rather the presupposition and indirectly but factually evidenced consequence of her conscious intentional dynamic. And as both ingredient within, and as the <u>integrative</u> intentional focus for, that dynamic, the subject's notion of the thing shares in its generic and invariant character. In this capacity, then, it represents the <u>intentional ground</u> for the real **complementarity** of the relationship between the distinct common sense and scientific attitudes of the subject. But its role as such a "ground" admits the following, six-fold characterization.

First, then, it "grounds" the complementarity of the **criteria** that structure these two attitudes of human knowing. Thus, it is the "fundamental difference":

> in the criterion of the relevance of [the] further questions [of the subject] that marks the great divide between a common sense and a scientific attitude [to the things]. Because he aims at [their] ultimate explanation, the scientist has to keep asking "Why?" [of them], until ultimate explanation is reached . . . . the layman aims at knowing [the same] <u>things</u> as related to us, as entering into the domain of human concerns . . . (<u>I</u>, 295c, emphases mine).

Thus, the questions which the common sense subject poses of the things cease as soon as:

> further inquiry would lead [her] to [answers that make] no immediate appreciable difference in the daily life of man (<u>I</u>, 295c, emphases mine);

> [she reaches] the virtually unconditioned to pronounce true judgments of concrete fact and to discern correct insights into [the] concrete situations [of things]. Without those basic judgments [on the things], science has no starting-point [or end point] . . . (<u>I</u>, 296a).

Secondly, the notion of the thing "grounds" the complementarity of the **insights** that underly the, respectively, common sense and scientific attitudes of human knowing. Thus, the "intelligibility" of the <u>things</u>:

> that science <u>grasps</u> comprehensively <u>is</u> the intelligibility of the concrete [e.g., of the <u>same</u> things] <u>with</u> which common sense deals effectively (<u>I</u>, 297c-298a, emphases mine).

Thirdly, it "grounds" the complementarity of the **terms** which the common sense and scientific subjects, respectively, "predicate" of the things. But predicates of the former kind bring out the elemental regularities and transitions of shape and color, of sound and movement, of scent, touch and taste, of juxtaposition and succession, extension

and duration, size and shape, etc. But precisely because they attach
to the things of the subject's everyday world, these predicates:

    do not shift in meaning with [e.g., in explicit dependence upon]
    the successive revisions of [her] scientific theories (I, 296b).

And because they do not so shift, they constitute the explanatory
foothold and test-point upon the interactions of the things themselves
by which the scientific subject can, respectively, advance towards the
system or series of systems of explanatory terms which will explain
them and apply the provisional explanatory predicates whose mismatch
with them will fuel her further advance.

    Fourthly, it "grounds" the complementarity of the linguistic
frameworks within which the common sense and scientific subjects,
respectively, express their incipient or actual knowledge of things.
Given such a ground, then, the subject can: (1) characterize the same
"object" as "at rest," e.g., at the place where "the sun rises and
sets," and "in motion," e.g., within an approximately elliptical orbit
with the sun at one of its foci (cf. I, 295a-b); (2) credit the former
characterization as evidence for the latter, the latter as explanation
for the former. In this way, then, science:

    advances through the interaction of increasingly accurate
    descriptions and ever more satisfactory explanations of the same
    objects. Unless the objects are the same, there is no relation
    between the description and the explanation and so no reason why
    explanation should modify description or description should modify
    explanation. But the only object that is the same is the concrete
    and intelligible unity, identity, whole [of which the subject
    always already has a notion] . . . (I, 436a, emphases mine).

    Fifthly, it "grounds" the complementarity of the judgments made
by the respective subjects of common sense and science about their
"objects." Thus, the judgments of the common sense subject posit the
similarities and differences, the usual and unusual patterns of
recurrence, etc., inherent in the immediately sensible and practical
bearing of the things in their relations "to us." But even as
essential for the genesis and application of her scientific knowledge,
the contents of such judgments are empirically residual from the full
explanatory viewpoint of the scientific subject. From the latter

viewpoint, the subject affirms (or _intends_ the affirmation of) the _same_ real things in their relations to each other; in the classical and statistical forms or stages of lawfulness they sustain; in the possibly non-countably great multiplicities with which they sustain these relations and are ranged over by these laws.

Sixthly, it "grounds" the complementarity of the **horizons** of the, respectively, common sense and scientific attitudes of human consciousness. The former horizon is in play when the subject's basic tri-fold set of intentional operations is so patterned that within the coincidentally related data the _relations_ of the _things_ "to us" are always already called forth for consideration in advance. But, then, for this very reason, the common sense "horizon":

(a) stands "open" on the "subject"-side to the re-orientation of pattern which would conform it to the general empirical method of the _scientific_ subject;

(b) stands "open" on the "object"-side to the objective relations of the things "to each other." This latter field of relations, a field which opens out intentionally beyond the realm of the immediate data, **includes** the relations of the things "to us" _within itself_. But it includes these relations not as "sensed or described but **explained**" (_I_, 514c, emphases mine);[1]

(c) stands to the bi-polar horizon of human _scientific_ subjectivity in the relationship of lower to higher viewpoint, image to the insight which systematizes it and, therefore, in the

---

[1] The modern subject intends the "complex transition" from: "the latent to the evident, . . . the vague to the definite, . . . the implicit to the explicit, . . . the naked fact to the scientific elaboration, . . . [a common sense to an explanatory grasp upon the things]" (Lonergan, "The _Gratia Operans_ Dissertation: Preface and Introduction," _Method_, vol. 3, no. 2, p. 20a). Still, the common sense horizon remains essential, minimally, for fitting the explanatory relations of the things into the intersubjective, social, and perceptual-motor network of their relations to embodied human subjects. It remains essential, minimally, then, for the discovery and application of their laws.

metaphysical order, the relationship of potency to first act.[1]
Thus, the common sense and scientific horizons are fixed by the
distinct ways in which the same basic set of intentional operations are
oriented and patterned within two distinct attitudes of human
subjectivity. Still it must be insisted that these orientations or
attitudes of the subject comprise:

> functionally related parts [and, hence, fix functionally related
> horizons] within a single knowledge of a single world [e.g., of
> emergent probability]. . . . To regard them as rivals or
> competitors [out to negate, repress, or annul each other's pursuit
> of their own kinds of knowledge of the things] is a mistake, for
> essentially they are **partners** . . . (I, 297c-298a, emphases mine).

Thus, it is:

> (o)ne and the same universe of being [e.g., one and the same
> "world" whose things are] sensed, described, understand and
> affirmed [e.g., whose things show forth within the common sense
> horizon as sensed and described and the scientific horizon as
> understood, affirmed and explained] (I, 514b).[2]

Finally, it is through the dynamic and cooperative interaction of these
two "horizons" that the subject's knowledge of the things develops. So
also is it through their practical complementarity that the community

---

[1]Grasp of the meaning of any of these three relationships in the
full sense Lonergan intended, requires the appropriate "insight into
insight."

[2]Three brief points should be made here.
First, "universe" or "world," when it is used as the former's
equivalent, is a heuristic notion for Lonergan. It anticipates the
totality of all actual or possible objects of human investigation
consistent with the notion of emergent probability.
Secondly, the relata specified in the first through the third
points, immediately above, pertain to the second level of human
consciousness. Their application presupposes a first even as it
implies the third level cited in the fifth and reflectively
appropriated in the sixth point.
Finally, the complementary common sense and scientific differentiations of the tri-fold consciousness of the subject could be said to
open out upon complementary "section(s)" within the "universe of
[emergent] **being**" (I, 292c, emphasis mine). And, the determination of
the color of things as a wave of light, their sounding as a longitudi-
nal wave in the air, their heat as a form of energy defined by the
first law of thermodynamics, a style of living by its subject's need to
avoid anxiety, etc., represent, presuppose the subject's openness to,
her ability to "zig-zag" between these two "sections."

of subjects generates and improves:

> applied science and technology, that [it] adds inventions to scientific discoveries, that [it] supplements inventions with organizations, know-how and specialized skills (I, 298a).

Secondly, if much time has been spent explicating Lonergan's analysis of the subject's always already presupposed notion of the thing, still, the analysis abstracts from, not only the specific nature of the thing in question but also any, indeed, every particular thing. But once the notion has been reflectively grasped, the subject can revert from such "general considerations" to both "things of determinate kinds," e.g., humans, rabbits, etc., but also the "particular," e.g., this man, this rabbit. Reflecting on the latter case, Lonergan points out that the particular to which the subject reverts may stand forth:

(a) "here and now" within the compass of her immediate perceptual-motor relations with the world;

(b) "outside" the proximity of the field of such relations. Then, her observation will require "other things," e.g., a measuring instrument (I, 250a 18) and a spatio-temporal frame of reference (I, 249b) to "extend" her perceptual-motor grasp upon the world and locate and, therefore, describe the object with respect to the origin and orientation of that extension;

(c) against the horizon of the fully explanatory attitude of the scientific subject which: "deals with the things, not as related to our senses, but as related to one another" (I, 249a).

But the appearance of the things within the human perceptual-motor field is transcended:

> as long as one considers things themselves, things as explained, things as related to one another, things as equivalent for all observers inasmuch as one prescinds from all observers (I, 249a, emphases mine).

But the appearances are in "potency" to the intentional transcendence by which the subject intelligently grasps their unity. Again, the ontological ground of the individuality of the thing is to be attributed to the "prime matter" or "central potency" which:

stands [ontologically] to the intelligible unity or [central] form of the thing <u>as data stand to insight</u> (<u>I</u>, 249a, emphases mine).[1]

---

[1]Again the central act grounding the existence of the thing stands to its intelligible unity as insight stands to judgment. Cf. footnote 1, p. 217, above.

c) The Notion of Genus as Explanatory

On the basis of the discussions of the preceding chapter-sections of this study, we affirm that _implicit_ in his _achievement_ of the modern scientific attitude towards the surrounding world is the subject's:

(1) grasp upon a set of conjugate forms, C_i, implicitly defined by their empirically established correlations;

(2) combination of these correlations to yield the actually functioning ranges of schemes of recurrence, S_i. These schemes:

(a) are themselves subject to the complementary determination of the statistical laws, F_i, in respect of their _emergence_ and _survival_ under determinate conditions;

(b) make systematic the occurrence of the events or acts, E_i, which, without S_i would occur non-systematically;

(c) will so function as to make possible and, to some extent probable:

a non-systematic occurrence of [the] events, E_{ij} . . . (I, 259d),

that _would_ only occur regularly were conjugates, C_j, and schemes, S_j, to have actually _emerged_ in the data.

But granting (1)-(2), above, and the soundness of "presupposition 8" laid down in the introduction to this section, then:

(3) _if_ the subject has _correctly_ affirmed the existence of C_i, and also, possibly, F_i, then, **there exist the things, T_i.**[1] But if the things, T_i, exist, then:

(a) the occurrence of their acts, E_i, is made systematic by S_i and F_i;

(b) they admit the occurrence of E_{ij} as a possibility, with some degree of probability, F_j,[2] but in such a way that E_j

---

[1]Cf. presupposition #8 brought out in the Introduction to this section. Here, Lonergan refers to it as the "logical postulate" of the notion of the thing ($\underline{I}$, 259c).

[2]E_{ij} is, _ex hypothesi_, _possible_ since none of its members "exceeds the capacity of T_i" ($\underline{I}$, 259d). But what is possible has some probability of occurrence however small. Hence, the probability of E_{ij}

would occur regularly <u>only if</u> there existed "things of a higher order" ($\underline{I}$, 259d), e.g., T_j, differentiated by, C_j, etc., etc. But given large enough numbers of, T_i, and long enough time intervals, <u>some</u> <u>non</u>-systematic occurrence of E_j is inevitable, is assured given F_j.[1]

But from heuristic principles uncovered by tracing the notion of <u>emergent probability</u>, it follows that:

(4) given the non-systematic occurrence of E_{ij}, there <u>will</u> **emerge**:

conjugates, C_j, of a higher order to make the recurrence of the aggregates systematic [e.g., to effect S_j] ($\underline{I}$, 260a).[2]

But with the emergence of C_j and S_j to systematize the recurrence of E_{ij}, there follows, again by presupposition #8:

the existence of <u>things</u>, T_j, of the <u>higher order</u> ($\underline{I}$, 260a, emphases mine).

But since the occurrence of E_j is regular and unexplained by C_i, the scientific subject has:

the evidence that is necessary and sufficient to <u>affirm</u> the existence of another set of conjugates, C_j, <u>defining another **genus** of things</u>, T_j . . . [and functioning through the higher set of schemes, S_j] ($\underline{I}$, 438c, emphases mine).

---

of T_i occurring will equal the product of the respective probabilities of its member events. Lonergan calls this the "probability" postulate of the subject's notions of the thing and emergent probability.

[1]For the reader's convenience we offer the following table:
1. "C_i"---verified set of implicitly defined conjugate forms;
2. "S_i"---the set of schemes whose functioning "C_i" explains;
3. "F_i"---statistical laws governing the emergence and survival of "S_i" under relevant conditions;
4. "E_i"---events or acts associated with "S_i," etc.;
5. "T_i"---"things" whose schematized ("S_i") action ("E_i") is defined by "C_i" (and "F_i");
6. "E_{ij}"---includes that set of acts of T_i whose non-systematic occurrence is linked to S_i but not explained by "C_i," i.e., this set requires the higher integration of C_j if the occurrence of its members is to be systematic.

Finally, when "i" appears singly, the given forms, schemes, etc. pertain to the same level of intelligibility within the universe of emergent probability.

[2]Lonergan calls this the "evolutionary" postulate of the subject's heuristic notions of--the thing and emergent probability. Cf. $\underline{I}$, 126b, #4, and subsection B7, above, and the ninth property it associates with the notion of emergent probability.

Thus, to things of the explanatory genus, T_j, the subject will properly attribute explanatory conjugates from C_i, and C_j. But, all conjugates of types C_i and C_j, respectively:

> are defined by their [respective] relations to one another . . . . Then, since C_i and C_j' differ [in this way], there will be two different systems of terms and relations [which are both applicable to T_i]; as the basic terms and relations [of each system] differ, all logically derived terms and relations [within each system] will differ, so that by logical operations alone there is no transition from one system [applicable to, Tj, e.g., C_i] to the other [e.g., C_j] (I, 255b, emphases mine);

(5) the foregoing realization of the concrete "possibility" of emergence can recur.[1] Thus, just as E_{ij} was empirically residual, a merely coincidental manifold with respect to C_i, etc. but in potency to higher ordering by the C_j and S_j of T_j, so T_j will admit E_{jk} that is empirically residual with respect to C_j, etc., but in potency to higher ordering by C_{jk} of T_k.

> (A)ccordingly, there can be a series of genera, T_i, T_j, T_k, . . . (I, 438d, emphasis mine).[2]

Thus, in this broadened context, the re-invocation of the heuristically grounded possibility of recurring emergence affirms the further possibilities not only of a matching

---

[1]Lonergan refers to this as the "sequential postulate" of the subject's heuristic notions of the thing and emergent probability. It: "adds an affirmation of the possibility of applying the other three postulates over and over so that one could begin from the simplest things [e.g., hydrogen atoms] and proceed to the most complex [e.g., human life, etc.]" (I, 260d, emphases mine).

[2]In things of a higher genus, therefore, there can be distinguished lower conjugate potencies, forms, and acts. Thus, biological, chemical and physical laws are attributable to multicellular plants. But from this it does not follow that there can be distinguished lower (or higher) things within things. Again, this is so because "a thing is the concrete and intelligible unity of concrete and individual data; the same data from different viewpoints can provide the evidence for different conjugate forms; but the same data under the totality of their aspects cannot be the data for different things (I, 438a–439a, emphases mine).

conditioned series of recurring schemes, e.g., S_i, S_j, S_k, . . ., etc. but also of:

> things . . . realized cumulatively in accord with successive schedules of probabilities [e.g., in accordance with the notion of emergent probability] (I, 260d, emphasis mine).

But upon this extension of the notion of emergent probability to the things there follows the corollary extension of this notion's full explanatory significance to the regard of:

> the differentiation, numbers, distributions, development, survival, disintegration, of things as well as schemes of recurrence (I, 261c, emphasis mine).

But to say that of T_i, C_i is properly said, that of T_j, C_i and C_j, are properly said, of T_k, C_i, C_j and C_k, are properly said, etc., is to say that:

(6) corresponding to the successive genera of things, T_i, T_j, T_k . . . ., there will be distinct but autonomous sciences. This can be brought out, assuming (1)-(5), above, in three brief steps. First, C_i, C_j, C_k . . . ., figuring in the above-cited attributions to the things, represent the contents intended but, only at the limit, correctly and completely grasped by the subject of general empirical method. Secondly, from the concluding quotation in #5, above, it is clear that C_i, C_j, C_k . . . ., are not, without the introduction of further empirical premisses, related through the supervention of the **logical** operations of the subject upon their respective fields of conjugates and laws.[1] Thus, thirdly, the subject's notion of distinct, autonomous, independent genera of things reflects his heuristic anticipation that some intelligible and rationally affirmed explorations of the things will be logically unrelated. But if the possibility of the logically independent genera of things has been brought out by a reflection upon what is implicit in the subject's achievement of the general empirical

---

[1] From this it follows that neither T_i's relations to T_j, nor T_j's relation to T_k . . . ., is one of simple class inclusion.

method, so the <u>fact</u> of their independence is "compatible with,"
is, in fact, <u>demanded</u> by the division of "the sciences as they
[in fact, currently] exist" (<u>I</u>, 257d).[1] Thus, the laws of the
contemporary science of:

> physics [which implicitly define C_p] hold for subatomic
> elements [e.g., the members of the genus designated as T_p];
> the laws of physics <u>and</u> chemistry [e.g., C_p, C_c] hold for
> <u>chemical</u> elements and compounds [T_c]; the laws of physics,
> chemistry <u>and</u> biology [e.g., C_p, C_c, C_o] hold for <u>plants</u>
> [T_o]; the laws of physics, chemistry, biology, and
> sensitive psychology [e.g., C_p, C_c, C_o, C_z] hold for
> animals [T_z]; the laws of physics, chemistry, biology,
> sensitive psychology <u>and</u> rational psychology [e.g., C_p, C_c,
> C_o, C_z, C_r] hold for <u>humans</u> [T_r] (<u>I</u>, 255c, emphases mine).

On each successive level, then: "one is confronted with an
entirely <u>new</u> set of <u>basic</u> concepts and laws" (<u>I</u>, 255c, emphases
mine); the things display a certain level of systematic
activity that is regarded as "a mere pattern of happy
coincidences" (<u>I</u>, 256b) on the basis of these basic concepts
and laws; this unaccounted for systematicity motivates the
subject's further questions, his grasp upon and positing of the
basic higher laws to the next autonomous science of the things,
etc.[2] But, then, the successively higher, relatively

---

[1]So, Lonergan will note, is it demanded if we credit the
"immemorial convictions of common sense" (<u>I</u>, 441d).

[2]Thus, to judge by the achieved level of the modern sciences, the
coincidental at:
1. the subatomic level is the "regular <u>behaviour</u> of atoms," e.g.,
   E_{pc} of T_c;
2. the chemical level is the "<u>metabolism</u> and division of
   cells," e.g., E_{co} of T_o;
3. biological level is the "<u>behaviour</u> of animals," e.g., E_{oz} of
   T_z;
4. sensitive level is the "<u>operations</u> of mathematicians and
   scientists," e.g., E_{zr} of T_r (<u>I</u>, 256, emphases mine).
The reader should note that it is by the study of the "kinds" of
<u>behaviours</u> that a thing exhibits that the scientific subject knows <u>what
it is and</u>, therefore, to which genus (and species) it properly <u>belongs</u>.
But this is but a further exemplification of the scholastic maxim
"agere sequitur esse"--to know what a thing is, you must thematize what
it does!! Thus, the subject studies his "nature" as human by reflecting upon the dynamics to his schematically recurring <u>conscious</u> <u>acts</u>.

autonomous systems, the successively higher explanatory genera to the things:

(7) correspond to the successive stages through which the major dynamic of empirical method passes if it is to account scientifically for all the relevant outstanding data.[1] Thus, the successive departments of the science of the modern subject are, in fact, related neither by the unsupplemented logical performance of the subject, nor as points of distinct logical application for a reductive mathesis universalis. They are related because:

(a) the laws which link C_i of any of the proximately and relatively prior systems in the series:

yield images [e.g., of E_{ij}, the manifold of acts attaching to T_i which are merely coincidental in respect of C_i] in which [question motivated] insight grasps clues to laws of the higher order [e.g., which link C_j to make the occurrence of E_j of T_j systematic] ($\underline{I}$,[j] 256c, emphases mine);

(b) the laws linking C_j will yield images of E_{jk} which bring out the manifold of acts (attaching, in fact, to T_k) which are merely coincidental with respect to C_j. And in these images "insight grasps clues . . .," etc., etc., etc.

In this fashion, the Bohr model of the atom is an image that is based on subatomic physics which leads to insights into the nature of atoms. Again, the chemistry of the cell can yield an image of catalytic process in which insight can grasp biological laws. Again, an image of the eye, optic nerve, and cerebrum can lead to insights that grasp properties of the psychic event, seeing . . . . Finally, it is with respect to sensed and imagined objects that the higher level of inquiry, insight, reflection, and judgment [which have presided over the warranted discovery of the preceding laws and the trans-logical transitions from one set thereof to the next] function ($\underline{I}$, 256c–257a, emphases mine).

(c) there exists:

    i) a higher viewpoint:

---

[1]Argument for this clue ensues directly.

when images of lower level operations [e.g., E_{ij} of . .
.] yield insight into the laws governing higher level
operations [e.g., C_j governing E_j of T_j] ($\underline{I}$, 439c,
emphases mine);

ii) a succession of higher viewpoints when:

each ["viewpoint"] is expressed in its own system of
correlations and implicitly defined conjugates; and
each successive system makes systematic what otherwise
would be merely coincidental on the preceding
viewpoint [without interfering "with the autonomy of
the lower [viewpoint]" ($\underline{I}$, 256b)] ($\underline{I}$, 268b).

(d) they sustain, as evidenced in (7b), such a relationship of

successive higher viewpoints as set forth in (7c) ii),

immediately above. Thus, "it is because new insights

intervene" that the higher sciences are: "essentially

different from the lower" ($\underline{I}$, 257b).

And just as in our reflection on the activity of the mathematical
subject we saw that the image of "doing arithmetic" leads to the
insights that ground algebra:

so images based on the lower [empirical] science lead to insights
that ground elements of the higher science ($\underline{I}$, 257b)![1]

Thus, ours is a universe in which both the classical-statistical and
complementary common-sense movements of human consciousness are
relevant to knowing. It is a universe in which the notion heuristically underlying that which they know is that of the thing. In such a
universe the notion of higher viewpoint seems to be the only way:

of intelligibly relating the generically distinct properties of the
same thing without violating the autonomy of the sciences ($\underline{I}$, 485);

in which logically unrelated sciences [of the things] can be
unified ($\underline{I}$, 440c).

Thus, Lonergan claims that his account of explanatory genera is

_____

[1]Cf. Section A, above, in which the mathematical attitude and
horizon of the scientific subject has been explicated to recall the
evidence for the claim being made. That claim is that the higher
viewpoint structure common to the empirical and mathematical sciences
is, in fact, implicit in the general, triadically structured method of
the subject of the modern intellectual attitude to the world. Thus,
the intentional structure of human consciousness is in fact invariant
with respect to these sets of sciences!

"uniquely probable"[1] since it "meets the issue of distinct but autonomous sciences" "fairly and squarely," and since:

> there are no available alternative views [that meet all of the relevant issues, e.g., mechanist–determinism has already been ruled out, cf. Sections B4–5, above] (I, 441b).

Moreover, in this case as in that of the theory of emergent probability, "this probability is of a higher order" (I, 441b, emphases mine). And the fact of this higher order probability rests:

> not on the present state of the empirical sciences but on the fundamental properties of insight [e.g., which mediate the subject's major dynamic through successive higher viewpoints] (I, 440d, emphases mine);

> [on] the basic and permanent [intentional] factors that will hold their ground in subsequent modifications and [even radical] improvements [in the sciences] (I, 441b).

Hence, the notion of the successive genera of things, which is intentionally grounded on the higher viewpoint structure of human intelligence, can be expected to stand fast even at the ideal limit of inquiry where the things are "completely" explained (I, 440b). Thus, propositions #s (1)–(7), above, the theory of explanatory genera/ species no less than that of emergent probability now extended to the generically and specifically differentiated things, share in the invariant and generic character of the general empirical method of the human subject. And this method, as said, represents the highly sophisticated differentiation of the intentional fact that:

> data are to be understood, that understanding grasps concrete unities, systematic relations, and non-systematic probabilities of existence and occurrence . . .;

> inquiry moves in a determinate direction . . . this direction implies an emergent probability [but also a generic/specific differentiation] of things and [their] schemes (I, 261c–262a, emphases mine).

---

[1]Probability is not meant here in a statistical sense.

d) The Notion of Species as Explanatory[1]

In _Insight_, Chapter VIII, Section 6, Lonergan focuses on the differentiation of _kinds_, e.g., of species, _within_ some explanatory genus.[2] In this context, he offers the precision that:

> any lower _species_ of things, T_i, with their conjugates, C_i, and their schemes, S_i, admit(s) a _series_ of coincidental aggregates of events, say E_{ijm}, E_{ijn}, E_{ijo}, . . ., which stand in correspondence with a series of conjugates, C_{jm}, C_{jn}, C_{jo},[3] . . ., of a _higher genus_ of things, Tj (_I_, 262c, emphases mine).

Lonergan gives and serially arranges a number of examples to make his point. To exhibit more economically the structure to Lonergan's series of examples and to bring out the direct relationship between a more advanced place in the series and the greater degree of freedom from the limitations of underlying _and_ surrounding manifolds, we begin by laying down the following four sets of heuristically specifiable, implicitly defined terms:

---

[1]Since the arguments in behalf of Lonergan's theory of explanatory species run parallel to those used to buttress the theory of explanatory genera, they are omitted from this subsection.

[2]As we have seen, Lonergan uses "E" to stand for the given events or acts corresponding to some species of things "T," differentiated by "C," etc. Further, he adds an extra subscript, e.g., E_{ijn} to stand for the non-systematic occurrence of _specifically_ different acts of T_i which require _specifically_ different higher integration _within_ the higher genus T_j. The point is a simple one and, if the reader may need to review it, he should allow neither it nor the conventions which follow it to distract him.

[3]Thus, S_i admits _not_ just _one_ coincidental aggregate but a series, say, "x" thereof, ranging over m, n, o, . . ., etc. All of the latter will be explained by different combinations of the laws of the higher system, which laws implicitly define C_j and, hence, belong to the same genus. And within the higher system there will be a corresponding series, say X_1, of grouped sets of conjugates. These sets will range over, stand in correspondence with, and order, respectively, the lower sets of aggregates m, n, o, . . ., etc.

$$3. \quad T_j\text{----}C_{jy}\text{----}S_{jy}\text{------}E_{ijy};$$
$$2b. \quad T_j\text{----}C_{jx}\text{----}S_{jx}\text{------}E_{ijx};$$
$$2a. \quad T_j\text{----}C_{jx}\text{----}S_{jx}\text{------}E_{ijy};$$
$$1. \quad T_i\text{----}C_i\text{----}S_i\text{------}E_{ijx}. \quad _1$$

First, let "i" in #1 range over, respectively, the things (e.g., T_i), conjugates (e.g., C_i), schemes (e.g., S_i) (and acts (e.g., E_i)) reached by <u>subatomic physics</u>. And let "E_{ijx}" stand for:

a <u>sequence</u> of aggregates [e.g., x] of subatomic events [e.g., acts associated with T_i, differentiated by C_i], where each aggregate is merely coincidental from the viewpoint of subatomic laws and schemes (<u>I</u>, 262d).

But upon symbolic <u>images</u> of E_{ijx}, <u>insights</u> emerge cluing the <u>verified</u> grasp of C_j, etc., pertaining to the higher viewpoint of **chemistry**. In #2a, "C_{jx}" signifies the <u>series</u> of relationships implicitly defining the conjugates which constitute the periodic table of elements. These relationships differentiate the element-things which fall under it, systematize the occurrence of E_{ijx} through the <u>series</u> of schemes S_{jx}, provides the <u>background</u> against which the occurrence of the aggregates of the chemical elements, E_{ijy}, stand forth as merely coincidentally related. In #3, "C_{jy}" signifies the series of relationships implicitly defining the conjugates which constitute the laws of chemical <u>compounds</u>, differentiate the compound-things which fall under them, systematize the occurrence of E_{ijx}, etc.

Secondly, let "i" in #1 now range over, respectively, the things, conjugates, schemes (and acts) reached by <u>chemistry</u>. And let "E_{ijx}" stand for:

[a sequence of] agregates [e.g., x] of chemical processes [e.g., acts associated with T_i, differentiated by C_i], where each aggregate is merely coincidental from the chemical viewpoint (<u>I</u>, 262e).

But upon symbolic <u>images</u> of E_{ijx}, <u>insights</u> supervene cluing the <u>verified</u> grasp of C_j, etc., pertaining to the higher viewpoint of **biology**. In #2a, "C_{jx}" signifies the <u>series</u> of relationships

---

[1] As expected, T, C, S, and E stand for, respectively, things, conjugates, schemes of recurrence and acts or events of a kind to be specified by the appropriate use of subscripts, etc., etc.

implicitly defining the conjugates which constitute the laws of uni-
cellular life. These relationships differentiate the kinds of cell-
things which fall under them, systematize the occurrence of E_{ijx}
through the series of schemes S_{jx}, provide the <u>background</u> against which
the occurrence of the new and larger aggregates of cells E_{ijy} stand
forth as coincidentally related, etc. In #3, "C_{jy}" signifies the
series of relationships implicitly defining the conjugates which constitute the laws of multicellular life-forms, e.g., of plant life,
differentiate the kinds of plants which fall under them, systematize
the occurrence of E_{ijy} through the series of schemes S_{jy}, etc., etc.[1]

Thirdly, let "i" in #1 now range over, respectively, the things,
conjugates, schemes and acts reached by <u>biology</u>. And let "E_{ijx}" stand
for a sequence of neuro-organic acts [e.g., acts associated with the
<u>neural</u> specialization of T_i differentiated by C_j] where each aggregate
is merely coincidental from the viewpoint of biological laws and
schemes. But upon symbolic <u>images</u> E_{ijx}, <u>insights</u> supervene cluing the
<u>verified</u> grasp of C_j, etc., pertaining to the higher viewpoint of
zoology or **sensitive psychology**. In #2b, there is specified the <u>series</u>
of relationships implicitly defining C_{jx}. These serial relationships:

(a) constitute the species specific sets of laws, higher integrations of sensitively conscious stimuli and response which make
systematic through their operation:

merely coincidental aggregates of neural events, E_{ijx} (<u>I</u>,
263c).

Thus, these <u>serially higher</u> systematizations of E_{ijx}, are
exploitations of possibilities which E_{ijx} held out with their
emergence but T_i neglected. They <u>are</u> the opening upon the
emergent world in various forms--<u>through</u> various flexible

---

[1]Lonergan points out that "minor changes" in underlying and/or
environmental aggregates: "yield <u>variations within the species</u>; major
changes that are surmounted successfully yield new types of solution
and so <u>new species</u>. The existence of a <u>series</u> of such <u>major</u> changes is
the biological content of the sequential postulate of generalized
<u>emergent probability</u> [according to which solutions "take into account
and . . . rise upon previous solutions"] . . ." (<u>I</u>, 263b, emphases
mine).

circles of instinctively based and/or triggered schemes of sensitive recurrence, S_{jx}, and <u>in accord with</u> their successive schedules of probability—of the <u>horizon of sensitive animal</u> **<u>consciousness</u>**. As we have already seen, taken generically, consciousness in this "pattern" is <u>for the sake of</u> the more efficient translation and prosecution, representation and integration of the demands of lower level <u>organic</u> manifolds (cf. Chapter I, above). Finally, and in general terms, the field will genetically group acts of sensing, desiring, imagining, fearing, feeling, remembering, moving, anticipating, etc. The grouping will result in such movement sequences as pursuing a predator, moving towards the sunlight, mating, moving with the herd, securing one's territory, etc. Finally, it is through such acts and their law—governed trains that the animal relates to and integrates not only the demands of his lower level organic manifolds but also the outer circumstances, the environment, the habitat into which it is born;

(b) <u>differentiate</u> the series of distinct animal species where:

> specific differences are differences of **sensibility**; and [consequently] it is in <u>differences of sensibility that are to be found the basis for differences of organic structure</u> . . . (<u>I</u>, 265b–266a, emphases mine);

Fourthly, let "i" in #1 now range over, respectively, the things, conjugates, schemes and acts reached by the science of <u>zoology</u>. And let "E_{ijx}" stand for a sequence of aggregates (e.g., x) of conscious acts (e.g., acts associated with T_i differentiated by C_i) where each aggregate is merely coincidental from the viewpoint of the laws of sensitive psychology (e.g., fully motivated and warranted acts of human discovery, etc.).[1] But upon symbolic <u>images</u> of E_{ijx}, e.g., the discovery by—Einstein of a neo-classical physics, Mendeleev of the periodic table of elements, Watson and Creek of the structure of the DNA Molecule, Kohler of the figure/ground structure of human perception, Archimedes of the principles of hydrostatics, Euclid and Riemann of, it

---

[1] Thus, "j" ranges over such acts.

turns out, alternate geometries of things, the founding fathers of con-
stitutional principles for a republican governmental form; of oneself
doing and advancing in empirical science, mathematics, and the exercise
of practical/dramatic rationality, etc., insights supervene. But these
insights clue the [soon to be more formally] verified[1] grasp of C_{jx},
etc., pertaining to the higher viewpoint of human **rational psychology,
philosophical anthropology.** Thus, in #2b, the "j" in T_j ranges over
the class of human subjects. C_{jx} signifies the series of relationships
implicitly defining the systems and sub-systems of conjugates which
comprise the human arts and sciences, differentiate the things which
fall under them, systematize the occurrence of E_{ijx} (e.g., of relevant
series of insights) through the series of schemes S_{jx} (e.g., the
specially requisite methods and skills of these particular arts and
sciences), provides the background against which the occurrence of the
aggregates of religious acts, E_{ijy} or E_{jk} stand forth as merely coincidentally related. But the series of relationships C_{jx} ranging over all
the species of things is constituted by the "inquiry and insight, reflection and judgment, deliberation and choice" (I, 266b) of the human
subject, by this basic, formally dynamic intentional structure her acts
exemplify.[2] And acts of such kinds are no more than coincidentally
occurring or related from the zoological viewpoint. Finally, S_{jx}
stands for all the combinations and/or specializations of these laws
which schematize, habituate, skill the subject's flow of conscious
operations—to a given task, within a given field of being, from out of
any of the relevant patterns, differentiations, etc., of human
consciousness.

Fifthly, the relationship which serially obtains between, for

---

[1]The formal verification of the point will take place with the
Self-affirmation of the knower in Chapter VI.

[2]Thus, in the fourth place, the subject's discovery pertains to
the pattern of her own conscious acts of discovery, etc. or those which
she has reactivated by repeating the discoveries of others through the
use of this structure; a further level of dynamic lawfulness to be
uncovered within the movement of emergent world process by and within
the conscious subject who has emerged from it.

example, E_{ijx} of which the subject forms an image and C_{jx} which is the object of the subject's rationally affirmed grasp admits two isomorphic if familiar characterizations. As should be clear from the examples, on the "subjective" side of the scientific horizon, this relationship is fixed **reflectively** by the serial succession of higher viewpoints achieved and/or to be achieved by the scientific subject—in response to the further relevant questions that recur on the successive levels of her inquiry.   On the "objective side," it is fixed by the serial succession of more systematic "solutions," e.g., explanatory genera and species, called forth according to the emergent probability of world process in response to the re—emergence of the coincidental on successive levels.[1]

Sixthly, the chemical compounds display a "**first** degree of **freedom**" from the subatomic weights and numbers by which the relationships ordering the elements within the periodic table are completely determined.   Thus, the properties of salt can neither be reduced to nor generated by merely mixing the periodically and subatomically fixed properties of sodium, chlorine, etc.

A "**second** degree" of such freedom is exhibited by the multicel-lular plant. The laws by which it systematizes its underlying cellular aggregates represent:

an idea that [by stages] unfolds in the process of growth . . . (I, 264b, emphases mine).

They represent a principle, now, of "immanent control" by the plant over the "aggregates of aggregates" it successively determines.

A "**third** degree" of such freedom is present in animal life. Acts which reflect neural development but remain coincidentally related by the immanently unfolding laws of plant speciation are taken up, devel-oped and successively systematized by the animal organism according to laws of psychic stimulus and response.   Such laws:

---

[1]It should be recalled that such "solutions" worked out by the objective process of emergent probability are: "the sort of thing that insight hits upon and not the sort that result . . . from accumulated, observable differences" (I, 265a, emphases mine).

(a) "immanently" organize the duration and direction of the organism's open field of sensitive consciousness;

(b) flexibly but effectively **confine** the organism to prosecuting and meeting more or less determinate organically based dynamisms under, essentially, environmentally pre-set conditions. Thus, the activity of the animal organism is:

> [in varying degrees] . . . limited but not controlled by underlying materials and outer circumstances (I, 266a, emphases mine).

A "**fourth** degree" of such freedom is evidenced in the life of the human subject. Thus, through her own immanently initiated and executed deliberations, the human subject opts for a specialized method, enforces its norms in pursuit of the truth. She inquires only to grasp the universal apart from sensitively apprehended particulars, the limit apart from the continuum, the invariant apart from particular places and times, etc. And she affirms the immanence of what she has abstractly grasped in the things and relations of the surrounding world. Thus, the human subject is able to:

(a) abstract completely from underlying, empirically residual manifolds in pursuit of understanding, truth, value, etc.;[1]

(b) determine, legislate for her own actions, e.g., even if she is not free from the limitations of her neuro-organism and situation she is free from confinement by or specific necessitation according to their recurring demands.[2]

Thus, a non-classical shift in the integrative emphases of the things is evident as one moves from the subatomic through to the human realm. The shift is away from integrative confinement by initial, lower level

---

[1]This is possible for the human scientific subject because the "higher system" to her intelligent and rational operations: "develops not in a material manifold but in the psychic representation [e.g., the images, phantasms, tables, graphs, diagrams, etc.] of material manifolds" (I, 469b, emphases mine).

[2]Because the subject as "higher system" is a "legislative function," and both discovers but also makes the laws of human community, because she can and, sometimes, does do so intelligently and reasonably, ethics as science is possible (cf. I, 617c f; Chapter VII, below).

materials. Again, the continued contributions of these manifolds are needed if the higher, unconfined integrative possibilities generated at the apex of a conditioned series of things and schemes are to be realized and not break down. And the human "thing-subject," as one such realized possibility, as thus supported by conditioned series of natural and human (i.e., social, cultural, educational, linguistic, etc.) schemes, evidences the shift in the fourth degree in, for example, her capacity to wonder, to **learn** about and to **know** the surrounding world. She especially evidences this shift by her ability to reflect upon, understand, and know herSelf, her knowing, her place and function within the world towards the knowledge of which she is oriented, etc. Similarly, even as multicellular plants and animals pre-consciously systematize aggregates of cells which they themselves have initially assembled, so, at the apex of the line of human development, the incarnate subject is able to control and develop herSelf and also to participate in the founding, conservation, correction, and improvement of her community, her world. And she is able to do this Self-consciously and in the name of her own Self-development.

e) Framing the Framer: the Locus of Human Being within the Old and New Typologies of the Real

By the Porphyrean process of logical division, a summum genus, e.g., being or substance, is broken down into a series of dichotomous subclasses. The division of these subclasses into mutually exclusive and jointly exhaustive species within the given genus proceeds according to their member's possession or non-possession of the relevant differentia. Division continues until infimae species— simplest classes of the genus divisible only into the individuals comprising their membership—are reached. Conversely, the process of logical classification starts from the arrangement of infimae species and continues to group the latter until that highest class is reached to which all of the original classes belong. Allied to the pre-modern scientific context set by Aristotelian science, these processes yield the familiar tree of classification associated with Porphyry's name. Thus, for example, substantial being is divided into living and non-living. Living being divides into animal and vegetative. Animal being divides into rational and animal. Human being, then, is:

(1) the rational animal;

(2) therefore, signified:

    (a) as a whole but indeterminately by its possession of sensitivity, desire, self-motion, etc. But these are processes it shares with all of its fellows of the genus animal;

    (b) in part but determinately by the rationality which specifically differentiates and perfects his animal being or sensitive "nature."

The Lonerganian transposition of the earlier scheme, on the other hand, sets a modified framework for the generic and specific similarities and differences of the things within an ultimately trans-generic and trans-formal horizon of being.[1] Furthermore, it represents the

---

[1] If Aristotle's concept of being is already "in advance" of Porphyry's, e.g., for Aristotle being is not a genus, cf. Posterior

transcendence of the limitations of earlier approaches. Thus, it transcends the purely _logical_ Porphyrean solution to the problems of the division and classification of things; the purely _descriptive_ horizon of Aristotelian science within which the specific solutions to these problems had been worked out. Again, it transcends the mechanist-determinist abandonment of a framework for the real generic and specific similarities and differences of the things. It abandons it in favor of the three-fold reduction of: things to material bodies in motion; explanatory conjugates to those of physics (and/or chemistry); explanation to that of the classical type. On the other hand, as explicated, Lonergan's neo-modern "framework":

(1) involves the assignment of a _thing_ to a given genus and/or species. It is so assigned when the validated classical laws of the appropriate kind are _verified_ in its statistically recurring acts and under the statistically occurring conditions for its existence;

(2) involves the premiss that:

the _conjugates_ [but _not_ the things] of the lower order [e.g., genus] exist in the things of the higher genus. . .,

since it is a fact that:

the laws of the lower order are _verified in_ the [acts of the things of the] higher genus . . .(_I_, 258d, emphases mine);

(3) stands its generic and specific determinations for the things in isomorphic correspondence with the successively higher and cumulatively advancing scientific viewpoints. Again, by these viewpoints the scientific subject successively overcomes the renascent _issue_ of the coincidentality of the occurrence of the acts of the things on successive levels and on successive sub-levels within them;

(4) orders the possible ways in which the scientific subject can _predicate_ of a given thing. Again, he predicates the

---

Analytics, 2.7 (9214). Still, the ultimate meaning of being for Aristotle is no more than form, cf. _I_, 366c ff.

methodologically grounded, implicitly defined and empirically warranted sets of theoretical conjugates, the "first intentions" implicit in a given relatively higher or lower viewpoint and/or can meaningfully relate these predications to each other;[1]

(5) is, therefore, heuristic in character. As such it reflects his discovery as "transcendental clue" for the working out of this framework the implicit intentional structure of his own scientific performance, e.g., the restless major dynamic for higher viewpoints of general empirical method;

(6) admits for stratified arrangement the cumulative, progressing and, hence, variable contents turned up and reorganized on multiple levels by his execution of this dynamic;

(7) therefore, shares the relative invariance and generic character of:

(a) this "basic method" of the subject,[2] cf. presuppositions (1a)–(3a), and especially (3a) of section B6 of this chapter division, above;

(b) the notion of the emergent probability of surrounding world process:

i) also "modelled" on presupposition (3a) set forth in Section B6 of this chapter; cf. presuppositions (6b)–(7b) of Section B7, above;

ii) for whose successive intelligible strata of schematized things it provides the subject with a matching conceptual framework of commensurate determination;

(8) remains, then, in its general "second intentional" outline, as a relatively fixed frame of reference which minor and/or major revisions and/or re-organizations in its contents, e.g., the

---

[1]Explanatory conjugates, e.g., first intentions, can be classified according to the way in which they attach to reality. Thus, "genus," "species," "difference," etc., e.g., terms of "second intention," do not refer directly to reality, but constitute reflectively grounded headings under which to range terms of first intention.

[2]This is corollary to (5), above. Thus, as with the underlying

closed explanatory systems of the subject, <u>cannot</u> upset;

(9) already fixes in advance human being's place in relation to the otherwise variable and re-organizable contents within this fixed framework. This place in the framework which <u>cannot</u> be overthrown by such variations and reorganizations always already lies <u>at</u> that point <u>at</u> which, for instance:

(a) the advancing empirical sciences are[1] <u>generated</u>;

(b) conscious Self-presence gives way[2] to a <u>reflection</u> on such generation and the discovery of the intentional laws according to which the generation is effected and improved;

(c) reflection on these laws yields[3] to a world-view of emergent probability and the implicit framework of genera and species within which the contents of such a world-view are generated and serially ordered;

(d) the question of the place and full nature of the subject of such generation and reflection within such a framework arises;[4]

(e) the proximately highest of the serially related contents generated <u>through</u> the <u>empirical</u> application of the <u>laws of human intentionality</u> (cf. "b" above), leaves open just those coincidental manifolds of events which are[5] ordered

---

structure of human consciousness on whose pattern it is based, revisions in our description of the general genus-species framework will affect <u>nothing but our formulations</u>. Thus, our improving descriptions of the notion of higher viewpoint, for example, do not affect its reality, that of the scheme of higher genera and species, or that of the dynamic structure of human consciousness on which the preceding are based. Similarly the scheme does <u>not</u> predetermine the nature of the empirical contents it orders.

[1] . . . or could be . . . .

[2] . . . or could give way . . . .

[3] . . . or could yield . . . .

[4] . . . or could arise . . . .

[5] . . . or could be . . . .

within surrounding world process by operations in accord with those intentional laws;[1]

(f) the "intelligible" action of a world of emergent probability becomes[2] "**intelligent.**"[3]

Now let us add a minor precision to Lonergan's explication of this framework. Thus, let the "**pure**" or "**differentiating**" form or nature of the things of some genus T_j be indicated by the conjugates and laws of the highest proximate order, C_j, which are predicable of T_j. Then the nature or essence of T_j in the "**full**" sense, will take in the conjugates and laws of the pure form. But it will also "take in" **all** or all the **relevant** regressively lower systems of manifolds which serially both condition and sustain the operation of T_j according to C_j and whose operation in T_j only ultimately receive their generically commensurate "pure" integration with the emergence of C_j.[4] But let "T_r" range over the members of the explanatory genus comprising the totality of human subjects. Let "R_m" stand for the conjugate forms implicitly defined by the laws of the pure form of human being. Thus, the classical function:

$$\text{I.} \quad T_r = f(R_m),$$

differentiates human being in its pure form. Heuristic definitions of the nature of the human subject in, alternatively, the **fullest** sense and, less fully, as subject to **development**, and, finally, as subject to **conscious** development are signified, respectively, by the following three classical functions:

---

[1] Lonergan's point then, briefly, is that such a framework cannot be affirmed without thereby affirming human being's unique place and nature within it.

[2] . . . or has the potentiality to become . . . .

[3] Given the current ordering and state of the sciences, this possibility opened with the emergence of manifolds at a zoological level.

[4] My precision concerning the pure and full form or nature of T_x would approximate to the ancient distinction between the formal cause and the "to ti en einai" of the thing, on the one hand, and its essence or quiddity, on the other. The latter includes the "common matter" of T_x but abstracts from its "individual matter."

$$\text{II.} \quad T_r = f(P_i, C_j, B_k, Z_e, R_m);$$
$$\text{III.} \quad T_r = f(B_k, Z_e, R_m);$$
$$\text{IV.} \quad T_r = f(Z_e, R_m);[1]$$

In these definitions:

(1) the capital letters within the parentheses represent the relevant level of implicitly defined conjugate form, e.g., P=physical, C=chemical, B=biological, Z=sensitive, L=supernatural, etc. Thus, at "any stage of his development" a human being is, minimally:

> an individual existing unity differentiated by physical, chemical, organic, psychic and intellectual conjugates (I, 470b);[2]

(2) the subscripts range over the relevant conjugates at that level. Thus, C_1 might stand for the chemical element hydrogen. Z_6 and L_5 might stand, then, for, respectively, the forms of sensitive affection and religious love appropriate to some level of human development;

(3) the commas, read from left to right represent, alternatively, the coincidental sets of lower order conjugate acts in potency

---

[1] What has been said here is not completely accurate since the higher dimension to the religious love of the conscious, developing subject has been omitted. "Definitions" V, VI, VII, below, serially clear these inaccuracies. Again, note that the integral subject as, respectively, developing, and developing consciously corresponds to definitions VI and VII.

$$\text{V.} \quad T_r = f(P_i, C_j, B_k, Z_e, R_m, L_t);$$
$$\text{VI.} \quad T_r = f(B_k, Z_e, R_m, L_t);$$
$$\text{VII.} \quad T_r = f(Z_e, R_m, L_t).$$

Definitions I-IV are retained, despite their inadequacies, because they respect the limits of philosophy. Still a fully integral perspective, an adequate "science" of human Being is not possible unless the added dimension is taken up. Finally, for the idea underlying definition V and, therefore, this section, I am thoroughly indebted to the extraordinary work of Philip McShane. For a somewhat different treatment of the issues involved, the reader is advised to consider the "Epilogue" to his The Wealth of Self and the Wealth of Nations.

[2] In Chapter XX of Insight, Lonergan adds the level of supernatural conjugates, e.g., L_t, to his account. In any event, a

to and, in fact, integrated by the presence of higher forms or
the symbolic imaging of these lower acts in which the subject
has grasped a higher viewpoint;

(4) "R" represents the level of conjugate form implicitly defined
by the intentional laws of human consciousness;

(5) "m" ranges over the kinds of intentional operations performed
by the human subject, e.g., acts of inquiry, understanding,
reflection, affirmation, evaluation, decision, etc. When
affixed to "R" of T_r, it signifies these kinds of conscious
operations as:

(a) implicitly defined by: the intentional relations they
sustain within the integrative, self-assembling, and pure
conscious movement of the subject towards knowledge and
decision; the subject's pure desire to know (and love),
etc. Key in fixing the order and level of these relationships, in orienting and grouping operations towards their
proper and successively higher terms, are the expressions
of this intention in the "What?," "Is it so?," and "Is it
worthwhile?"-asking of the subject;[1]

(b) therefore, ordering at a higher level, coincidental
elements within Z_e of T_r, e.g., the dynamic system of the
subject's sensitive operations--acts of relating figure and
ground, of imagining, desiring, laboring, etc.;

(c) therefore, a contributory source, but also judge, evaluator
and implementer of meanings in the surrounding world, etc.;

(d) therefore, capable of being turned by the subject to the
further tasks of reflection, of Self-knowlege and, hence,

---

single human action can, therefore: "involve a series of components,
physical, chemical, organic, neural, psychic and intellectual, and the
several components occur in accord with the laws and realized schemes
of their appropriate levels" (I, 470a).

[1]Lonergan contends that such questions are "operators" of human
intentional development, one's pure desire to know and decide.

the formulation both of the meanings affirmed in definition I,[1] but also, with the help of non-reflective, auxiliary premises supplied by empirical inquiry and satisfying the implicit intentional laws of R_m in definition I, those affirmed in II and III.

Finally, then, it should be pointed out that the full definition of human being rendered within the context of Lonergan's neo-classical typology:

(1) is <u>not</u> based upon the older descriptive and logical division of animal being into two species—man being one;

(2) nevertheless safeguards the human difference, the "**fourth** degree" of the transcendence of the free human subject over confining determination by lower level manifolds. Thus, human being:

    (a) comprises a distinct explanatory genus differentiated by the pure form of Rm;

    (b) is, therefore, that being in whom the highest level of integration is neither a static nor a dynamic system but:

a variable <u>manifold</u> of dynamic systems. For the successive systems that express the <u>development</u> of human understanding are systems that regard [not primarily the experiential field of the subject, but rather] the universe of being in all its departments (<u>I</u>, 508b, emphases mine).

Hence, by R_m, human being is "coincident with [all] species" within the universe of emergent Being;[2]

(3) clarifies by ruling out the possible naturalist confusion that human being is merely one species of animal being;

---

[1] Such reflection is possible because the subject, in intending <u>any</u> object, is always already <u>implicitly</u> aware of herSelf <u>and</u> the character of the act she is performing. Cf. point (9b) above and <u>I</u>, Chapter Sections XI.1–XI.1.4.

[2] In our earlier formulation of human being under the convention of C_{ix}, the "C_i" is equivalent to R_m while the " " ranges over the universe of being in all its department and species. Thus, it represents the specialization of the basic method of the scientific subject along a potentially infinite number of relatively autonomous, developing, special lines.

(4) reinforces by re-conceiving the point to the Porphyrean inclusion of human being within the genus animal. Thus, the fact that "B_k" and "Z_e" are attributable to "T_r" indicates that one and the same subject of R_m shares in both the sensitive-intersubjective and organic dimensions of animal life.[1] Furthermore, for the human subject to deny this point would be for her to deny her existence within such patterns of experience as, for example, the practical, the dramatic, but especially, the biological within which, for example, the "sensitive" dimensions of her nature can or do figure importantly. It would be for him to deny the "preconscious and subconscious influences upon consciousness" (I, 442a), etc. And it would be to deny the findings of such empirical human sciences as human physiology, anatomy, neurology, endocrinology and the various branches of psychology which study human emotional, perceptual-motor and intersubjective development.[2] Finally, the fact that the inquiry, reflection and deliberation of the subject always already need sensitivity for their functioning, are always already therefore conjoined with the dynamic sensitive and intersubjective functions of human experience,[3] opens for further reflection the **tension** at that point within the subject's consciousness at which the Self-**transcending** character, the disinterestedness and detachment of the former meet the tendency towards self-interestedness and self-attachment, the self-**limiting** character of the latter;[4]

---

[1] Cf. definitions III and II, above.

[2] The reader should note that such empirical sciences proceed as specialized applications of the laws implicitly defining R_m. Hence, they presuppose the fourth degree of human freedom. Thus none of their findings could undercut its premiss without destroying themselves!

[3] The latter flow, it is recalled, is similarly connected with its organic base.

[4] The reader may recall that from within the biological pattern, the subject is bound to conceive of herself as a center of "self-satisfaction and power," cf. Chapter I, pp. 29-30, above.

(5) involves two components. On the one hand there is the pure component signified by R_m. As has been and will continue to be more fully brought forth, conceptual <u>revisions</u> of this signification affect nothing but the ways in which the implicitly defined conjugates at this level are objectified, can be no more than minor in character (cf. <u>MT</u>, 19a). On the other hand, the further component of the definition, signified by P_i through Z_e, represents the <u>application</u> of the series of explanatory systems representing the leading contemporary efforts of the scientific community to <u>know</u> the reality <u>of</u> the being properly differentiated by R_m, by its capacity, for example, to know and learn, to know themselves, etc. But both <u>these</u> specific **further** components as well as the <u>specific</u> order in which they are arrayed are subject to minor and/or major revision as the sciences which generate and relate them advance toward an ideal term. Still, underlying such advance there remains the <u>basic empirical method</u> of the subject signified by the relatively <u>invariant</u> pure component. Thus, there is both a probable <u>and</u> a certain component to the definition of human being in the full sense. Furthermore, in the case of this definition, the probability of the one component counts as further evidence for the certainty of the other since one ca<u>nnot</u> be uncertain of the principles which make the revision of probable judgments possible. Finally, it should be noted that if the <u>specific</u> serial ordering of P_i through Z_e is <u>not</u> invariant, still it:

(a) accounts for all the data contributed by the modern empirical sciences;

(b) would survive even major revisions on any of its extant levels, e.g., a breakthrough in chemistry need not upset that science's ordering in the scheme;[1]

---

[1]Could we be sure in advance that major revisions would not upset the <u>specific</u> ordering of these levels, the further component of the

(c) would seem to be a highly stable, because resilient concrete framework for scientific collaboration in general and
for the contributory study of human being in particular;

(6) "revives" in a new but recognizable guise and within a context
adequate to house the most advanced results and developments of
modern science, art, politics, etc., the classical and
renaissance notions of "Man" as reality in microcosm, as
bringing together, as sharing **both** in his being and
intentionality in all the kinds and levels of being within
surrounding world process.[1]

---

definition could be regarded as specifically fixed in its heuristic
character, as subject to no more than minor variation although major
variations might occur but only within them.

[1]Cf. Giovanni Pico Della Mirandola, Oratio de Hominis Dignitate,
trans. Elizabeth L. Forbes (Lexington, Kentucky: Anvil Press, 1953).

Summary

This section has explicated the following points by Lonergan:

(1) if the subject of general empirical method heuristically intends the data as intelligible, then she <u>necessarily</u> also intends the data as <u>one</u> (cf. the introductory Subsection above);

(2) implicit in her grasp and affirmation of the oneness of the data is its sense as an intelligible unity–identity–whole within the world of emergent probability (cf. Subsection a, above);

(3) the things stand out against complementary common sense and scientific horizons which reflect the answers to the questions of the subject of, respectively, the common sense and scientific attitudes to the world (cf. Subsection b, above);

(4) the framework for the generic and specific determination of the <u>things</u> reflects the higher viewpoint structure implicit in the major dynamic of the human scientific subject (cf. Subsections c and d, above);

(5) the subject can place herSelf within the invariant framework she has worked out for the "things." As a "substance–subject" she will share in the determinations of things at all levels but forever uniquely occupy that point of **transition** and/or **shift** in the world of emergent probability where the intelligible becomes intelligent, where a fourth degree of freedom from underlying and environmental determination becomes manifest (cf. Subsection e, above).

9. Genetic Heuristic Structure[1]

Introduction

In Insight Chapter XV, Section 7, Lonergan turns to an analysis of the specific heuristic notion and "structure" implicit in the study of development and to an analysis of the "genetic" method of the scientific subject. Again, since it follows the ontological reflections of Chapters XII and XIV of Insight, the context of the analysis is distinctly metaphysical. And since this study will defer full consideration of the grounds of such a context until the next chapter, this may cause difficulty for the reader. First, the subject's discovery and metaphysical recounting of the "development" of the "things" is sketched. Secondly, the heuristic "notion" and corollary "principles" of development are brought out. Again, it is inferred that the primary "clue" for their discovery was the intellectual development of the subject in general. It is inferred that the primary "instance" of the principles uncovered is the intellectual development of the subject. Thirdly, the ways "up" and "down" animating the two-fold structure of developmental inquiries are brought out. Finally, we here add that the notion of development, as well as those of "the nature of . . ." and the "state of . . ." are both consistent with, and are further interior differentiations within that of emergent probability.[2]

---

[1]Patrick Byrne has provided an excellent introduction to the issues we have attempted to address in this section in "The Question of Development: The Rise of the Methodological Approach in the Thought of Bernard Lonergan" (M.A. thesis, Boston College, 1972).

[2]The further point to this section is to contribute some of the determinations necessary to render intelligible Lonergan's account of the "Laws of [Integral] Human Development" (I, XV.7.4). Still, analysis of those laws has been judged to be out of place here. It will be taken up in Chapter VII.

a) Discovery of the Heuristic Notion

In _Insight_ XV.7[1] Lonergan reflects upon a further situation of the scientific subject. It is a situation in which:

(1) he has grasped and correctly affirmed: the <u>oneness</u> of the data in the totality of their concrete aspects; the classical <u>lawfulness</u> to the unity of its acts; the differentiation of the unity by the relevant classical laws;

(2) he has, thereby, implicitly committed himself to the existence of a <u>thing</u> of certain kind, e.g., T_o. But to have done so, is to have committed himSelf to the <u>central</u>:

  (a) <u>act</u> whose existence he affirms;

  (b) <u>form</u> whose intelligible unity his affirmation grasps;

  (c) <u>potency</u> from whose empirically residual individuality his affirmed grasp abstracts;

(3) the classical laws which have allowed him to <u>differentiate</u> the <u>per se</u> unity of T_o at its <u>inception</u> are:

  (a) <u>not</u> those which he grasps and correctly verifies either at its end state or in those intervening between the latter and its inception;

  (b) <u>not</u> sufficient for such differentiation either at its end state <u>or</u> in those intervening between the latter and its inception;

(4) each <u>successive</u> set of classical laws by which the subject differentiates T_o represents a fuller, more comprehensive, effective and differentiated set than its predecessor. But this implies that the possibilities held out by the initial manifolds of T_o are being integrated by stages. It implies that the "limitations" they place upon its successive integrations are being met and, therefore, by stages, <u>transcended</u>. But, then, T_o is being brought to fully differentiated term;

(5) he has, thereby, implicitly committed himself, ontologically,

---

[1]Cf. _Insight_, p. 461c ff.

if minimally, to the affirmation of the ascending **series** of sets of conjugate:

(a) acts whose respective and successively higher forms of orderliness he affirms of T_o;

(b) forms whose respective and successively higher forms of classical lawfulness he grasps in T_o's successively higher fields of activity;

(c) potencies whose successively renascent coincidental act manifolds, the successively higher forms to the orderly activity of T_o turn to their own advantage;

(6) he has realized and confirmed that the procession to the operation-level of T_o from the first set, through intermediary sets, to its last, terminal set of proper laws, is "regular" and, therefore, "has" a **higher** intelligibility of its own. But this intelligibility is not[1] assimilable to that of:

(a) classical law, i.e., "there are no classical laws about changes of classical laws;"

(b) statistical law, i.e., the procession is "not an indifferent choice between a set of alternative [classically specifiable] processes [with different probabilities of occurrence] . . ." (I, 482a, emphases mine);

(7) from the higher and fuller genetic viewpoint won by him in (6), the subject's critical grasp upon:

(a) the incompleteness of the initial classical integration of T_o's act-manifold in the series, implicitly commits him to its potential intelligibility, i.e., to the affirmation of conjugate **potency**, etc.;

(b) the completeness of the terminal integration of T_o's act-manifold in the series, implicitly commits him to its actual intelligibility, the affirmation of conjugate **act**, etc.;

---

[1] The reader should note that an inverse insight mediates the scientific subject's transition to the discovery of genetic intelligibility, of genetic method.

(c) the intelligibility of the <u>procession</u> of the stages to T_o's act-manifold <u>from</u> the initial, <u>to</u> the terminal stage of its integration commits him to:

    i) the quasi-**formal** <u>genetic</u> intelligibility of the procession;

    ii) the affirmation of the conjugate quasi-"**formality**" of the series of "operators" governing T_o. These operators lawfully replace the "limitation" or the <u>in</u>completeness of the initial integration of T_o's activity with those which are <u>successively</u> <u>less</u> incomplete. Again, they do this until the fullness of its terminal integration and mature mode of functioning is reached;

(d) (a)-(c), above, implicitly commit him to the affirmation of the "horizontal" finality <u>of</u> T_o, i.e., to **the** end or limiting term that results from "what" it is, i.e., from: "what follows . . . [from that determination] and what it may exact;"[1]

(e) (a)-(d), above, implicitly commit him to the affirmation of the ontological <u>limitation</u> of T_o to just that level of <u>essential</u> being circumscribed (dynamically yet) in advance by its initial act manifold, by the conjugate <u>potency</u> of T_o;

(8) he realizes and confirms that:

(a) a "vertical shift" has taken place at the point of the terminal integration to T_o;

(b) the shift:

    i) reflects the emergence of "different initial [coincidental] manifolds" of a terminally integrated T_o under a changed context of conditions;

    ii) involves the transposition of the thing into a higher

---

[1] Lonergan, "Mission and Spirit," <u>A Third Collection</u>, ed. Frederick Crowe (New York: Paulist Press and London: Geoffrey Chapman, 1985), p. 24c. Future references to "Mission and Spirit" are abbreviated by <u>MS</u>.

level of generic and/or specifically determinate form, e.g., T_z;

(c) there has been, is, an "effective probability" of T_z and, therefore, of (8a) given: "large numbers of instances [of T_o] and . . . long periods of time" ($\underline{I}$, 455a);

(d) the shift is properly interpreted as T_z's "vertical" **transcendence** of the limitations ingredient in T_o's full development, as the vertical "dynamic" of a lower level of integrated development for a higher and more effective order;

(9) his realization and confirmation, set forth in (8), implicitly commit him to:

(a) the relative incompleteness of the terminal integration of T_o's dynamic. Thus, in light of the newly emergent and unassimilable manifolds referred to in (8b), subheading i), above, the subject is committed to affirming the terminal integration of T_o as conjugate **potency**;

(b) the relative completeness of the terminal integration of T_z's dynamic. Thus, in light of its ability to order the manifolds unassimilable by T_o, the subject is committed to affirming the terminal integration of T_z as conjugate **act**;

(c) the quasi-**formal** genetic intelligibility of the "vertical" procession of the thing's activity from the incompleteness of its initial to the relative completeness of its successor dynamic. Thus, the subject-inquirer is implicitly committed to the "**formal**" intelligibility of the "operator(s)" of this transition. But this is to commit him to the affirmation of conjugate "**formality**." In this way, then, he is also committed to the "vertical" finality of the thing in question. This finality is to a term "higher" than its initial, horizontal or proportionate end. Again, in this case, it involves the "participative" subordination of the thing's lower to its higher dynamic integration and the term thereof (cf. $\underline{MS}$, 24d). But with this the genetic inquirer is returned on a higher level back to, approximately, (5), above, and implicitly (1), etc, etc., etc.[1]

(10) he is, thus:

<u>forced</u> to recognize the fact of a **third** type of process [e.g., one which is developmental and which has a kind of intelligibility all its own] to be investigated by a third, **genetic** method (<u>I</u>, 482a, emphases mine).[2]

---

[1]The "subordination" referred to in (9c) <u>could</u> be of an instrumental rather than a participative kind.

[2]See <u>Appendix I</u>, at the end of this section.

b) The General Heuristic Notion of Development

First, the genetic subject's guiding heuristic <u>notion</u> of her unknown "object" is "the (operator(s)[1] governing the) development of . . . of T_x." The latter notion:

I. is <u>implicit</u> in the scientific subject's further <u>question</u> of the "Why?" of development;

II. anticipates and pre-names what her further questions <u>will</u> gather when she fully and with scientific generality <u>understands</u> the higher dynamic intelligibility within the otherwise coincidentally related integration-series to the activity of T_x. Thus, the operator <u>abstracts</u> from random variations in the route and/or time-frame of the development of things of the kind;

III. engages her heuristic <u>principle</u> that significantly **dissimilar** individuals are to be understood by: "subsuming their respective histories under <u>common</u> [i.e., similar] genetic principles" (<u>I</u>, 479a, emphases mine).

Lonergan proceeds to argue that once metaphysically unpacked and, in light of the interpreted facts gathered in Subsection a), above, that there are <u>seven</u> principles to which the genetic subject's "understanding" of her developing "object" commits her. Thus, there is the principle of:

(1) **emergence**, i.e., the otherwise merely coincidental manifolds of

---

[1]The reader should note that (1)-(9), of Subsection a), above, comprises a reflectively grounded argument in behalf of the adequacy of potency, form and act categories to "cover," to "explain" any process of this third, genetic, kind. If this study has correctly outlined how we are knowing <u>when</u> we are knowing a developing "object," then the basic clues have already been laid in for rendering this object in metaphysical categories of this kind. Thus, Lonergan's use of metaphysical categories to determine the subject's heuristic notion of development will be treated without excessive further ado (cf. <u>I</u>, 451c, 479a 15 ff). Finally, we would note but not develop the point that the "limitation-transcendence" distinction is as "analogous" in character as that between "potency-act." Thus, both are "supple" enough to apply in cases of "horizontal" as well as "vertical" finality, etc.

the lower conjugate acts of T_x:

> invite [i.e., call forth] the higher integration effected by higher conjugate forms (<u>I</u>, 451d).

Thus, for example, and "prototypically" (cf. <u>I</u>, 481c), the relevant "image" for the inquiring scientific subject is a coincidental manifold. Again, her correct "understanding" "intelligently relates" the components of the image <u>beyond</u> the reach of the imaginal. But the image, in calling forth the relevant questions and inquiries, makes the emergence of correct "understanding" effectively probable. But in this case, what is effectively probable will become actual given sufficient time and sufficiently large numbers of (collaborating), intellectually genuine human inquirers;[1]

(2) <u>correspondence</u>, i.e., the otherwise merely coincidental manifolds of the underlying acts of T_x which differ significantly:

> require <u>different</u> [higher] integrations (<u>I</u>, 451e, emphasis mine).

Thus, the scientific subject's accurate gathering of significantly different manifolds of experimental data requires her discovery and verification of different theories to explain them.[2] When such differing manifolds are successive (e.g., M1, M2), the theory (e.g., F1) integrating the predecessor manifold (M1) and by whose use the successor manifold (M2) was uncovered is forced out. In effect, then, it is eliminated by the presence of the significantly different successor manifold (M2)

---

[1] Lonergan's analysis of the proper orientation of the subject's genetic query will be explained under heading "c," below, entitled "The Ways 'Down' and 'Up' of Genetic Inquiry."

[2] Again, the differing stimulation manifolds of the auditory and optical specializations of his nervous system call forth the subject's distinct conscious acts of hearing and seeing, etc. Further, within <u>limits</u>, the <u>same</u> higher integration <u>will</u> systematize differing lower manifolds. Thus, one and the same carbon atom can, and at different times, does in fact have electrons at different energy levels <u>without</u> becoming different in kind.

which the predecessor system (F1) can<u>not</u> integrate;[1]

(3) **finality**, i.e., the underlying manifold is:

> an upwardly but indeterminately directed dynamism toward ever fuller realization [e.g., integration] of being. Any actual realization [of the underlying manifold] will pertain to some determinate genus and species, but this very determinacy is **limitation** and every limitation is to [i.e., vertical] finality a barrier to be **transcended** (<u>I</u>, 452b).[2]

In this context, Lonergan goes on to distinguish "static" and "dynamic" higher integrations. **Both** are <u>products</u> of "finality" in the sense of emergent probability. But within limits, the dynamically, "Self-integrating" **thing**:

(a) fulfills the conditions for its <u>own</u> finality **once** certain external conditions are contributed and fulfilled. Again, these conditions are functions of the proximate members of the conditioned scheme-series set forth by emergent probability;

(b) immanently generates, sustains, replaces its <u>own</u> higher systems from within itself, "for" itself, and according to a principle of "inner" and "upward" directedness to term;

(c) has, therefore, <u>interiorized</u> the "finality" of what on lower levels is a merely "externally" advancing proces;

(d) effects the "interiorization" of emergent process with ever greater degrees of **freedom** from lower level determination.

---

[1]Thus, if the reader would have examples, any in Subsections c) or d) of Section B8, entitled <u>Man and Thing</u>, will suffice. In these subsections, a higher genus or species of things emerges under conditions of a lower. But while development is in accordance with the principles of emergence and correspondence, <u>not</u> all cases falling under them are instances of the (horizontal) devel<u>opm</u>ent of a thing.

[2]Paralleling the finality of surrounding world process on the "side" of human subjectivity, is the finality of human intentional consciousness. This has already been traced in detail in Sections B6-7, above, on "Emergent Probability."

To drive these points home, Lonergan suggests that a **dynamical-ly** Self-integrative system[1] can always be thematized under two aspects. As "**integrator**," such a system orders its underlying manifolds schematically according to stage specific classical conjugates. As "**operator**," such a system so orders its underlying manifolds as to <u>prompt</u> just **the** underlying instability, un-equalize just the relevant conditions that will:

(a) eliminate or replace its existing but now incomplete integration (e.g., the system <u>itself</u> as integrator) according to the principle of correspondence (cf. principle (2), immediately above). It will do this:

(b) <u>in order that</u> a more "definitely differentiated" higher integration can assert itself according to the principle of emergence (cf. principle (1), immediately above). It will do this:

(c) according to the age and/or circumstance of the system.

When a system is **static**, on the other hand, although it is a <u>product</u> of the vertical finality of world process, it:

> <u>dominates</u> the lower manifold with complete success [i.e., <u>manitains</u> "all things" as "equal"] and thereby brings about a notable imperviousness to change (<u>I</u>, 452c, emphasis mine).

Objectively speaking, then, there is <u>not</u> a different law of gravitation, atoms, molecules, electric charges, etc., for each successive age (cf. <u>I</u>, 460b) or place. Finally, **stable** static systems such as the inert gases:

> lock coincidental manifolds of subatomic events in remarkably permanent routines (<u>I</u>, 452c);

withold the conditions which finality might develop. **Unstable** static systems, on the other hand, may "enter into" higher

---

[1] We are, here, preparing to make Lonergan's distinction between dynamic and static higher systems to an underlying manifold.

level static or dynamic systems. Yet carbon, for example, no matter how easily and extensively it enters into compounds:[1]

> never gives rise to a developing series of instances of carbon of that weight and number (I, 481a);

(4) **development**, i.e., where the higher integration of T_x as **"operator"** repeatedly and successively transforms itself as **"integrator."** Here, the underlying manifolds of T_x are systematized according to an "intelligibly linked" sequence of dynamic higher integrations (cf. principle (3), immediately above). Within such a developmental sequence, the initial manifolds of T_x are:

> systematized and modified by a [e.g., by the operator of the] higher integration so as to call forth a second;[2] the second leads to a third; the third to a fourth; and so on, until the "possibilities" of development [for Tx] along a given line are exhausted [i.e., have reached a limit] and the relative stability of maturity is reached (I, 452d, emphases mine).

Thus, for example, human sensitivity and imagination contribute the underlying manifolds for human intellectual development. In accord with the principle of emergence, the subject's **insights** supervene upon this manifold:

> to unify and correlate [its] elements . . ., ground the formulation of such unifications and correlations in concepts, thoughts, suppositions, considerations, defini-tions, postulates, hypotheses, theories, and through such conceptual constructions, or their deductive expansions, or their concrete implementation, to give rise sooner or later to further questions [etc., etc.] (I, 469a).

The "conceptual construction," then, corresponds to the formulated higher system of the subject as **"integrator"** of his "intellectual" development at some determinate stage of learn-ing. But with the integrator galvanizing his relations with the data, the subject:

---

[1] E.g., graphite, charcoal, methane, diamond, etc.

[2] This will occur through the principles of limitation and transcendence.

(a) brings forth refractory data;

(b) thereby makes relevant things "unequal;"

(c) thereby brings out, effects the _incompleteness_ of the formulated system as integrator;

(d) has, thus, initiated the process of _eliminating_ the integrator system according to the principle of correspondence;

(e) has, thus, begun to raise the further relevant questions which anticipate and set the limiting conditions for the _replacement_ of the integrator according to the principle of emergence.

But (d) signals and (e) effects the transition of the **intentional** system of the subject _from_ integrator _to_ **operator**. They constitute it as a dynamic higher system with an inherent "finality" and an "exceptional principle of control" [i.e., the grasp of the intelligible as well as the virtually unconditioned!] (_I_, 469b).[1] But the further questions of the subject will:

> lead to _further_ insights only to raise still _further_ questions. So insights accumulate into viewpoints [i.e., conceptually crystallized _integrators_ of the data manifold], and lower viewpoints lead [by further superventions of the higher intentional system as operator] to [still] higher viewpoints. Such is the [dynamic, interactive] circle of the **development** of [human] understanding, and it occurs in the different departments of logic, mathematics, common sense, and philosophy, according to differences in the route of the circle (_I_, 469a, emphases mine);

(5) **increasing explanatory differentiation**; i.e., the development of T_x will advance _from_ generic and relatively _unrefined_ stages of initial integration **in the direction of** increasingly

---

[1] In other words, the human subject's "capacity" for "understanding" and for "critical reflection, for grasping the virtually unconditioned . . ." are the proper "criteria" of the intentionality of her consciousness (_I_, 469b). And depending on the given case, it is precisely the further questions of the subject which propel the minor or major dynamic of her inquiry, of her community, cf. Section B7, above. Again, the following quotation in the text describes the "major" dynamic of the subject.

systematic integrations of increasingly specialized operations.
It will advance, then, _from_ generic potentiality _to_ specific
act. Thus, if the capacity of the human subject for intellectual development has its "roots" in her native desire to know,
it is only brought to act in the succession of increasingly
differentiated and integrated capacities of the subject for
understanding, evaluating the evidence, deliberating, etc.,
etc. It is only brought to act through her variously differentiated and highly refined and developed common sense, scientific, reflective, and religious attitudes towards the world.
Thus, the Aristotelian, Galilean, Newtonian, and Einsteinian
accounts represent successively higher realizations of the
intellectual and reflective capacities of the scientific subject, i.e., successively more highly integrated, nuanced Self-
differentiations of her pure desire. And these successively
higher Self-differentiations are manifest in her successively
higher capacities to prounounce truly upon the nature of free
fall and to determine actual values under determinate conditions. Similarly, for example, the consciousness of the common
sense subject can be regarded as "undifferentiated" in respect
of its scientific complement, that of the scientific subject
"differentiated" in respect of its common sense complement.
Again, the consciousness of the scientific subject can be
regarded as "undifferentiated" with respect to its philosophic
complement, etc.;[1]

(6) **minor flexibility**; i.e., given that the initial underlying
manifold of T_x, in evoking its initial integration, thereby
"determines" its terminal counterpart, still:

> (i)n virtue of this determination the course of development
> can yield to circumstances and so follow _any_ of a set of
> alternative linked sequences [in coming to term] (_I_, 453b,
> emphases mine).

---

[1]Similarly, the study of the chromosome structure of the
fertilized human ovum or the histodifferentiation of ecto-, endo-, and
mesodermic layers in the gastrula several days later, do not bring out
"differences that are comparable to the later differences in [mature
human] functioning" (_I_, 453a).

Thus, Lonergan argues that:

> the same science can be taught successfully in accord with different methods, and the same discovery can be made in different manners (I, 453b).

Along the latter lines, D.J. Struik has argued that the revolutionary discovery of the infinitesimal calculus was independently made by Newton and Leibniz through the use of differing approaches that were, respectively, arithmetical and geometrical.[1] Again, to teach metaphysics:

> one may begin from knowing, arrive at [a notion of] objectivity, work out the metaphysics of objects and of knowing, and then repeat the whole account of knowing in metaphysical terms (UB, 220b, emphases mine).

On the other hand:

> one can begin with the metaphysics of the object, proceed to the metaphysical structure of the knower and to the metaphysics of knowing, and move on to complement the metaphysics of knowing with the further psychological determinations that can be had from consciousness (UB, 220c, emphases mine);

In each of the two cases, the inquirer:

> will be completing the same circle, except that one will be starting at a different point. One can begin from what is prior quoad nos, what is first for us, or one can begin from what is prior quoad se, what is first in reality. As long as one completes the circle, the same thing will be said, but it will be said at different points along the line (UB, 220c);[2]

(7) **major flexibility**; i.e., the emergence of new coincidental combinations to the initial, underlying manifolds of T_x,

---

[1] Cf. D.J. Struik, A Concise History of Mathematics, 3rd ed. (New York: Dover Publishing, Inc., 1967), pp. 110c, 113b.

[2] A further example would be the subject's achievement of psychic health whether by "untutored spontaneity" or "the ministrations of the psychiatrist" (I, 453b). Again, if this case is to be distinguished from its dialectical counterpart, the proviso must be added that the subject of the relevant ministrations has not suffered a "breakdown" (cf. Subsection c), below).

"provide the materials for" ($\underline{I}$, 449), make its development "capable of": "a shift or modification of . . . [its] ultimate objective" ($\underline{I}$, 453c); further scientific systematization by a higher species and/or genus; the **transcendence** of the "limitations" of essence associated with the flexible pursuit of its prior, generically and specifically set end(s). In accord with this principle, then, T_x is capable of adapting ($\underline{I}$, 455a)[1] itself to new or enlarged sets of external conditions, to the cumulative changes effected in these conditions by newly emerged developing systems (cf. $\underline{I}$, 455a). And this can happen even through a sequence of major "upward" shifts akin to the series of higher viewpoints which mark human intellectual development in all its forms. Thus, in human cognitional activity, the major flexibility of finality:

> appears in the manner in which inquirers, often enough, begin from one problem only to find themselves by the logic of issues forced to engage in the solution of another ($\underline{I}$, 453c-454a).

Lonergan's claim, then, is that the fact of the subject's study of developing processes always already presupposes in advance the use of categories and laws which approximate to the preceding. And he claims that this is so because the latter are implicit in the intentional-structural components which render the study of development intelligible. Still, the "principle illustration" and, perhaps, also, the "prototype" of this notion is "human intelligence" ($\underline{I}$, 458b) itself. Again, this has been confirmed, not only by the brief illustrations given above, but by the reflectively evidenced fact of the advance of human intelligence presented throughout the preceding sections and chapters of this study. Whether it has been in the case of the intellectual or practical attitudes of his common sense, the dramatic pattern of his everyday life, the mathematical and/or scientific pattern to his query, etc., we have found that an:

---

[1] The minor flexibility of development, then: "exhibits potency as ground of limitation. But potency is also the ground of [vertical] finality . . . [of a "major" flexibility towards a higher and fuller realization of being]" ($\underline{I}$, 454b).

otherwise coincidental manifold of data or images is integrated by
insights; the effort to formulate systematically what is grasped by
insight or, alternatively, the effort to act upon it gives rise to
further questions, directs attention to further data, leads to the
emergence of further insights, and so the cycle of [the intentional
Self-] development [of the subject] begins another turn. For if
one gives free rein to the detached and disinterested desire to
know, further questions keep arising. Insights accumulate into
viewpoints, and lower viewpoints yield to higher viewpoints (I,
458b).

And as we have brought out:

if images serially related to facts form the basis [of the
"movement"], the development is mathematical;

if data in their bearing on human living determine the circle,
there develops common sense; if data in their relations to one
another are one's concern, there develops empirical science;
finally, if [we attend] . . . to the circuit of development itself
and to the structure of what can be known of proportionate being,
the development is philosophic (I, 458, emphases mine).

In each of these areas, then, as well as in those of organic and
psychic growth, there is operative:

a flexible [i.e., a minor and/or major], linked sequence of dynamic
and increasingly differentiated higher integrations [of the
subject's, of his community's capacities, i.e., for organic,
psychic, intellectual and/or reflective performance. These higher
integrations] . . . meet the tension of successively transformed
underlying manifolds [which prove refractory to the already
achieved integrations and this] through successive applications of
the principles of correspondence [i.e., the subject allows the
further questions to surface] and emergence [i.e., the subject
continues his inquiry until the relevant insights, the relevant
viewpoint ordering the refractory data emerge(s)] (I, 458b,
emphasis mine).

c) The Ways "Up" and "Down" of the Genetic Inquiry

Within the ascending movement of the genetic, conscious inquiry of the subject, a series of stages can be distinguished. In the simplest case, the genetic inquirer:[1]

I. (1a) works back, possibly by way of a specifiable series of determinate steps, from his **experience** of the distinctive, actually occurring acts of T_x. He works from such an experience to a technical **description** of a "flexible circle of schemes of recurrence," the flexible "capacities for performance" which determine its acts at the given **stage** of development;

(1b) brings forth **images**, **phantasms** of T_x. These symbolize the manifolds of acts underlying those described technically in (1a), insofar as they are ordered by the laws of the next, proximately lower science(s);

(2a) advances by the structure of the classical heuristic of inquiry to the discovery and verification of the semantically linked theoretical **conjugates** which:

i) explain the regularities that have only been technically described in (1a), above.

He explains them precisely as lying "beyond" the reach of the laws relevant to the imaged, lower level processes of T_x and by advancing laws from which the **distinctive** acts of T_x deviate only at random;

ii) open for possible construction by the subject the total set of flexible circles of schemes of recurrence which mediate the distinctive concrete acts of T_x;

iii) thereby constitute the higher system as "**integrator**" of T_x at the given stage of its developing activity;

(2b) advances by the structure of the statistical heuristic of

---

[1]The following is a generalization of the genetic method Lonergan triply exhibits in Chapter XV, Subsections 7.2–7.3

inquiry to the discovery that conjugate acts verified in T_x are <u>not</u> recurring with the same frequencies. Thus, he discovers that the divergences from these frequencies have, furthermore, become systematic. But this makes possible and effectively probable that the activity of T_x satisfies a new, i.e., a higher, set of **classical** laws. But this <u>re</u>-opens the classical portion of the circuit of this preliminary inquiry, returning the scientific subject to (1a), etc., etc., etc.;

(2c) repeatedly moves through the circuit set forth between (1a) and (2b), above, until the totality of the higher systems of T_x as <u>integrators</u> of its development have been arranged sequentially according to the genetic principles of finality and development set forth in Subsection b), above. Further, the subject:

    i) <u>compares</u> the successive integrators, their scheme-mediated acts, etc.;

    ii) contrasts "normal and abnormal" successions in the instances of T_x he studies, etc., etc.

In this way, the genetic subject has so re-constructed the materials laid out in (1a)-(1b), immediately above, as to invest them with full <u>explanatory</u> **relevance** vis-a-vis the <u>question</u> of the development of T_x. Again, he has, thus, assembled "the data on the operator(s)" (<u>I</u>, 466b) of T_x, which operator (or series thereof) has been the remote if implicit "object" of his inquiry from the start;

II. (1a) orients <u>himself</u> explicitly by the **question** "What is the development of T_x?" But by this question and its implicit heuristic notion and corollary principles the subject intends his "known unknown" object—the **"operator"** (or series thereof) which **orders** the assembled data from the higher viewpoint of <u>genesis</u>;

(2b) discovers the "operator(s)" of T_x in a <u>leap</u> of constructive intelligence which:

    i) sublates the unexplained fact of the relationship between the higher systems of T_x as **integrators** of its activity;

    ii) abstracts from the minor flexibility of the relations between and random oscillations within the higher system it orders;

   iii) is complemented by a statistical investigation which distinguishes those changes in underlying manifolds generated by the operator of T_x and those contributed externally by the <u>context</u> of T_x;

    iv) provides the backdrop against which the changes of state could be verified which signal the emergence of, minimally, a new terminal set of classical laws in T_x; the major flexibility and vertical finality of the operator of the development of T_x; the need for the further inquiry of the subject necessary to specify its character;

III. (1a) recognizing that the intentional <u>leap</u> of II.(2b) may fall short for many reasons, also acknowledges that in actual fact and short of the ideal limit to the inquiry, that it yields only a **possible** **understanding** of the operator(s) of the development of T_x;

  (2b) will, therefore, raise the further question of truth. Thus, he will attempt to **verify** his grasp upon the immanent operator(s) of T_x by using it to study the activity of further instances of the kind. Thus, he would convert his grasp of "possibility" into a warranted, virtually unconditioned factual judgment. The attempt to verify the possibility may, however:

> not only confirm it but also give rise to further questions. The further questions will lead to [the] further insights and so to [the] still further questions [of the genetic subject]. In this fashion, . . . [the subject's] <u>understanding of</u> <u>the operator begins to be an</u> <u>instance of higher system on the move in the development of</u> <u>scientific knowledge of development</u> (<u>I</u>, 467b, emphases mine).

Finally, then, the movement to the genetic inquiry of the subject passes through two phases. Thus, a circuit of classical <u>and</u> statistical investigations turns upon the experiential data of T_x until the relevant explanatory **data** are assembled. Upon such data, there supervenes the question for **intelligence of** the genetic subject, which question terminates in the discovery and formulation of the operator of T_x. Finally, the question for **reflection** by the subject turns on the surfacing of the relevant evidence and closes in the responsible utterance of a probable judgment. And the tri-levelled, dynamic operational structure of the genetic heuristic of the subject, therefore, runs parallel to its classical and statistical counterparts. Thus, the subject of genetic method must "work out" structures which will function in relation to the notion of development much as that of measurement has functioned in relation to the classical subject's use of differential equations. These structures would allow him to apply and distinguish components within, to work "down" from the general and abstract notion and principles of development. Such structures, furthermore, would have to be worked out differently to meet the specific exigences of study in botany, zoology, anthropology, etc. Again, it is to this latter end that Lonergan has set forth specific "'Laws' of Human Development."[1]

Finally, in Insight, Chapter XV, Section 7.1, Lonergan notes, importantly, that whereas measuring and curve-fitting are basic procedures in chemistry and physics, that an "intelligent" rather than "servile" adaptation of their techniques to the study of organic, animal, and/or human development should start from the recognition of their increasing loss of "efficacy" and "significance" in and as one ascends through these areas (I, 463b). Thus, in the preceding fields, the subject's use of measuring techniques loses its:

(1) significance because:

within limits, [the higher integration is] independent of the exact quantities of the lower manifold it systematizes. Moreover, the higher the integration, the greater the [e.g., its] independence of lower quantities [altogether], so that the meaning of one's dreams is not a function of one's weight, and one's ability in mathematics does not vary with one's height (I, 463b, emphases mine).

---

[1] As noted, these laws are taken up in Chapter VII, below.

(2) <u>efficacy</u> because the general notion of development is <u>not</u> mathematical, is not akin to the differential equation whose boundary conditions are to be quantitatively specified.

APPENDIX I

It is extremely important that the reader note that in the metaphysical order of essence, conjugate potency plays a dual role in Lonergan's framework. Thus, it is, simultaneously, the ground of:

1. the "Limitation" of the conjugate form of the thing to just its given level and manner of systematization, e.g., S_7. As such, it:

   (a) imposes conditions, makes demands upon, i.e., circumscribes the limits for the system(s) of conjugate form that it will receive and continue to sustain;

   (b) effectively prevents the emergence of the systems or eventually excludes those which have already emerged but which do not adquately accomplish its higher integration;

2. the "Transcendence" by the thing of that level of orderliness e.g., S_7, it has already achieved for some higher level, e.g., S_8, which does effectively integrate manifolds still outstanding with S_7.

Furthermore, conjugate potency is this ground in at least two distinguishable respects. Thus, where T_x is developing, it represents the ground of the horizontal transcendence by the thing of the "limitations" interior to its earlier stages, cf. (7a)-(7e), above, but especially (7d) and (7e). As noted emergent probability is the intelligibility interior to surrounding world process. Generically it has sway over non-developing as well as developing things. Thus, it is the ground of the vertical transcendence by things of specific kinds over the "limitations" inherent in some lower level to their generic and/or specific functioning. And this will occur according to the effectively probable possibilities. Here, the reader should consider (8a)-(8d), above; the analysis of "emergent probability" in Section B7 of this chapter division; the determinately directed, dynamically structured unfolding it represents; the successive "interactions" of conjugate potencies, forms, and acts which, from the vantage point of this chapter, can be said to be constitutive of its process on successively higher levels of world process.

Again, "prime" potency, which Lonergan speculates might correspond to **energy** (I, 443b–444d; cf. I, 510a), would denote (1) the greatest lower bound to the vertical finality of emergent being; (2) the principle of universal "limitation" underpinning its procession. It would represent the purely coincidentally manifold limiting the lowest genus of things within world process. It would be the latent and virtual source of the totality of potentialities that are realized on each successive level of the transcendence to the process. Thus, the existence of potency "explains" and is at the root of, the immanent **"tension** of opposites" (I, 450b) with which the universe is riven. Thus, it is the **tension** between "limitation and transcendence" which is successively **transposed** by emergent process. It is transposed into developing, consciously developing, and then, in the human, to intelligently, rationally and rationally Self–conciously developing **Being**.

Finally, the relationship between limitation and transcendence is alternatively rendered on the level of developing things by the distinction between their "higher system" as, respectively, integrator and operator (cf. the "law of finality," described in Subsection b), heading (3) of this section). Thus, for example, in human being, sensitivity is simultaneously the ground of the higher system of the subject as conceptual "integrator," but also the source of the further questions that transform it into an "operator."

10. The Dialectical Method of the Subject

Introduction

What follows proceeds in three steps. <u>First</u>, the "notion" and proper "subject matter" of the "dialectical method" of the subject are brought out in an incipient fashion. This is done by reflecting on the "limitations" of genetic method and explicating the context which has spawned its emergence. <u>Secondly</u>, we will interpret Chapter VII, Section 5 of <u>Insight</u>, Lonergan's single longest <u>theoretical</u> explication of the notion of dialectic in that work. His account is framed abstractly so that it will be rife with general implications and possibilities of application. Still, its very abstractness distances the reader from its roots. These lie in a "further" achievement in "Self"-knowledge and from further appropriation of the structure of both his intentional process and the "products" which result from its application, etc. To reduce that distance, these roots will be laid bare first, by specifying a set of conventions and, then, by employing them to interpret a paradigmatic instance of dialectical process as abstractly conceived.[1] These roots will be further clarified as the preceding analysis is exemplified in a set of three, isomorphically structured cases. <u>Thirdly</u>, a series of further questions will be raised on the basis of the last of the cases in which dialectical process is exemplified, that of "philosophic" process itself. These further questions will pertain to: (1) the "grounds" of dialectical method; (2) the "critical" Self-understanding and, therefore, the critical "viewpoint" on human process which it presupposes and implies; (3) the relationship of dialectic to both the larger dynamic of emergent probability and also the potency-form-act structure of

---

[1]This instance is <u>not</u> Lonergan's. But this author believes that it, or some similar, if probably more complex, example was at the center of his reflections. Again, the example should be conceived in light of the reflections on human intellectual development set forth in Section B9, above, and Chapter VII, below.

proportionate Being.[1]

---

[1]After concluding summary reflections on the notion of dialectic (I, 244b-244), Lonergan "hopes" that "a fuller study of . . . [the human mind] will provide us with further general elements relevant to determining a far more nuanced yet general critical [i.e., dialectically "based"] viewpoint" (I, 244b). His hope enters in because dialectical method exists at a relatively early, if well-founded stage of its development. And the reader should not expect much more precision than Lonergan's discussion can bear; even the level of precision achieved in determining genetic method. Finally, for want of time and space the situation of Lonergan's notion of dialectic in the history of philosophy and, therefore, the question of a genetic procession and/or a dialectic of dialectics, will not be taken up.

a) Discovery of the Heuristic Notion

The subject of genetic method has hypothesized and verified the operator(s) "W_o" in key instances and at key stages of the development of "T_r." And "W_o" would seem to render intelligible T_r's procession from the relative incompleteness of some early stage to the schematic, classically specifiable integration of its acts, e.g., SR_1, C_1, A_1,[1] to the relative completeness of some further stage, e.g., SR_{10}, C_{10}, A_{10}. He is considering "h," a representative, exemplary sample of T_r at some stage 6 of its development. As expected, he discovers that at this stage, members of "h" are functioning under the newly emergent conditions, S_7. Again, and as also expected, the functioning of members of "h" at this stage: has successfully integrated S_6 through A_6 in correspondence with SR_6; has, thereby, contributed to the emergence and survival of S_7; cannot integrate the exigences, the coincidental elements ingredient in S_7, without advancing to the higher mode of functioning signified by SR_7, C_7, A_7. Finally, as exemplary, members of "h" have manifested relatively "normal" patterns of development up to stage 6, and this under "normal" sets of successively transposed conditions.

But, first (1),[2] contrary to what his genetic investigations, performed under ideal conditions, have led him to expect, and even controlling for minor flexibilities, the expected development to stage 7 is not forthcoming. This **distortion** of the genesis of members of "h" may consist in their convergence towards a static, inertial system.

---

[1]"SR" specifies the flexible set of schemes of recurrence verifible in T_r's functioning. "C" will stand for the set of classical laws which renders that functioning intelligible. "A" stands for some set of activities of T_r. The subscript signifies the stage of T_r's development relative to which "SR," "C," "A" can be properly attributed to T_r.

[2]The following five points are being numbered to admit simple reference in Subsection e) of this section, below.

It may consist in a $\underline{variance}$ or $\underline{regression}$ of their schematic functioning, that is $\mathbf{not}$ directly intelligible given the "operator" of T_r's "development." But in $\underline{none}$ of these distinct cases does the functioning of members of "h" $\underline{mature}$ to the higher schematic level at which S_7's exigences are integrated and the conditions for their $\underline{next}$ stage of development are called forth, etc.

$\underline{Secondly}$ (2), failing to meet S_7 with SR_7, C_7, A_7, etc., one of two things tends to be verified in members of "h." On the one hand, their failure to develop may continue and lead to the "verification" of a $\mathbf{destructive}$ breakdown in functioning. But, then, the individual, e.g., T_r "at" C_6, does not survive the situation of S_7. On the other hand, failure and the $\underline{survival}$ of a breakdown may call forth a structural change in the functioning of the individual. It may lead to the "verification" of its consequent, and so to the eventual achievement of the higher system(s), etc. Given the occurrence of such a $\mathbf{constructive}$ breakdown, then, the individual resumes the $\underline{dynamic}$ verifiable in its earlier history and consistent with "W_o."

$\underline{Thirdly}$ (3), reflecting on and generalizing from the preceding data, the subject realizes that on both of the preceding alternatives (i.e., whether by a "destructive" or "constructive" breakdown) the individual's functioning "at" SR_6-C_6 and "short of" SR_7-C_7 is "removed." T_r's $\underline{variance}$ from and $\underline{tension}$ with the operator(s) guiding its development has conditioned the destructive "removal" or "reversal" of T_r's functioning at C_6. There is, then, a $\underline{further}$ "intelligibility" to the latter process that is $\underline{neither}$ classical, statistical, $\underline{nor}$ genetic. This has methodological implications, since it forces him (in order to do justice to the "data") to transcend the "horizon" of development, of genetic method in the strict sense. Again, indirect, empirical evidence for his generalizations is forthcoming when his newly informed anticipations are validated in other samples of T_r at the same and/or other stages of their development.

But, $\underline{fourthly}$ (4), the preceding three discussions determine the application context and give incipient determination to the subject's "notion" of "dialectical process." Thus, this notion is implicit in his "Why?" in the face of a further, non-genetic "intelligibility" in the data, where the "data" "ought" to have manifested a dynamic system.[1]

Fifthly (5), the so-far undisclosed context of the inquiries reflected upon in the preceding "reflections," has been the scientific subject's study of **human being**. Its context was emergent probability. Its principle anticipation was of human "development." Its "data" was the "distortion" of that development and the "tensions" which that distortion sets up. And the "intelligibility" uncovered was that of the "'reversal'/removal" of that distortion. Again, that context ranges over any particular human subject, any particular community of human subjects, any particular "social world" founded and conserved by the inter-actions of individual subjects in community.[2]

---

[1]The point here is that an inverse insight mediates the subject's discovery that there is a further, non-genetic intelligibility in the data. It mediates his discovery that there are further heuristic anticipations which inform his search for its "nature" (cf. I, 30b).

[2]Again, it is through an inverse insight that the subject grasps that where there "ought" to be sets of intelligent and rational actions, social relationships, social institutions, etc., there is not. For a complex introduction to a complex point, the reader might consult and bear in mind Insight, p. 628a.

b) The Dialectic of the Scientific Subject—Conventions in the Context of a Paradigm Case[1]

Consider, say, a physical scientist's discovery of a higher viewpoint, e.g., C_6.[2] This is to affirm C_6 as integrating the otherwise coincidentally related data-manifold, S_6. Again, let us refer to the scientifically differentiated intelligence, reasonableness (and willingness) of the subject as one "principle," B, operative in the process of his discovery and verification of C_6 in S_6. And let us refer to the instrumentally extended "sensitivity" by which he has gathered the data, e.g., S_6, which C_6 orders and to which it applies as co-"principle," A, in the same process.

But, first, then, dialectic involves some "aggregate of events of a determinate character" (I, 217b #1). But in the above case, such an aggregate comprises S6 as made determinate by the verification and application of C_6.

Secondly, there is a dialectical process only if the aggregate of events, i.e., their explanation by C_6, can be "traced back" and accounted for in terms of their relations to "either or both of two principles" (I, 217b #2). But the explanation of S_6 by C_6 originates from the subject's sensitive representation of "external" data and the subject's exercise of intelligence and reasonableness. It therefore originates from the self-correcting "interplay" of principles A and B, above.

---

[1] The major context of the following discussion is set by Insight, VII.5. There Lonergan analyzes the notion of dialectic under four headings. Still, it has seemed to this author that he is making two distinct points under the fourth heading. Thus, the second of the two will be brought out under a fifth heading and set forth in terms of Lonergan's own precision on p. 233b. Finally, the background of the discussion is set by Insight, pp. 242b–244c.

[2] "Logic" contributes to the scientific pursuit, over time, by clarifying, working out the implications of, and formalizing the expression of C_6. It is: "the effort of knowledge to attain the coherence and organization proper to any stage of its development [e.g., C_6]" (I, 276e).

Thirdly, dialectical process is a function of principles which are "opposed yet bound together" (I, 217b #3), and this in more than one sense.

First, then, A and B are "linked" together. As such, they are distinct, autonomous, but related. As "distinct," the sensitivity and intelligence of the subject instance differentiable strata within the global "horizon" of emergent probability. As "autonomous" they are only adequately explicable in terms of mutually exclusive systems of closed, implicitly defined conjugate forms. As "related" the "higher" principle, B, finds its coincidental manifolds on the preceding level and the "lower" principle, A, "supplies" the coincidentally related "data" for the higher principle (cf. I, 618c). Again, the two principles are related as patterning to materials patterned, as system to materials systematized, as "integrator" and its "integrated" elements.

Secondly, the two "principles" are "opposed" and that in at least two senses. Thus, precisely because they are linked together, the higher principle as integrator, C_6, "abstracts from" what is merely empirically residual in S_6 and "constructs" (thereby, "repressing") what is genuinely irrelevant on the lower level. Even the "perfection" of the "higher integration's" abstraction cannot "eliminate" the integrated, S6. They are opposed, again, since A and B possess the contrary properties of, respectively, self-centered personal and/or intersubjective "interest" and the "dis"-interested inquiry and reflection presupposed by the grasp of the virtually unconditioned, the knowledge of truth.[1]

Fourthly, dialectical process involves "principles" that are "modified by the changes that successively result from them" (I, 217b #4, emphases mine). Thus, the functioning of B, i.e., the subject's discovery and application of C_6 in S_6, involves changes in the

---

[1]Lonergan will refer to such an opposition as "dialectical," to the "dialectical opposition" between the sensitivity and intelligence, e.g., the pure desire, of the subject, his community (cf. I, 422b). Again, these properties are not contraries in a merely logical sense.

subject's gathering of underlying data-manifolds, i.e., the uncovering of the further set of data, S_7, which are coincidentally related from the viewpoint of <u>both</u> C_5 and C_6. But, the further manifold uncovered in A calls forth the recurrence of B's transition **from** integrator **to** operator. This is equivalent to the <u>subject's</u> raising of the next set of further relevant questions which "head" his inquiry for the higher viewpoint signified by C_7. Thus, the "harmonious working out of [the] opposed principles [e.g., A and B]" introduces successive sets of higher determinations "into" the initially gathered aggregate of events. Again, it brings an "ideal line" of pure progress into the <u>subject's</u> knowledge <u>of</u> the data. But, in the above case, the structure of dialectical process coincides with the dynamic system thematized by the <u>genetic</u> theorist's study of human intellectual development.[1]

But, <u>fifthly</u>, if dialectical process rests on the concrete unity of opposed "principles":

> the <u>dominance</u> of either principle [e.g., A] results in a distortion [of the proper "interplay" between A and B and, therefore, of the normative line of, in this case, intellectual development which should be its resultant.[2] Again,] . . . the distortion both <u>weakens</u> the dominance [of A] and <u>strengthens</u> the opposed principle

---

[1]Three points should be made here.

<u>First</u>, in this case, then, <u>dynamic</u> system is to be regarded as a subset or degenerate case of <u>dialectical</u> process in the **"full"** sense. Thus, what Ron McKinney <u>refers</u> to as the "dialectic of sublation" is equivalent to dynamic system. What he refers to as the "dialectic of complementarity" is equivalent to the proper "interplay" or "harmonious working together" of linked but opposed principles. Again, the "dialectic of sublation" is a consequence of the "dialectic of complementarity." Cf. his "The Role of Dialectic in the Thought of Bernard Lonergan" (Ph. D. dissertation, Fordham University, 1980), pp. 28-59.

<u>Secondly</u>, and conversely, when dialectical process involves a "reversal," when it is dialectical in what <u>we</u> will refer to this "full" sense, it manifests a "developmental" character of a <u>not</u> strictly speaking "genetic" kind (cf. <u>I</u>, 422b).

<u>Thirdly, in the above senses</u>, dynamic system is "dialectical" and "dialectical" process is developmental. Again, the hermeneutical "retrieval" of a content which has fallen into obscurity, been "lost," would be developmental in one or the other of the two preceding senses.

[2]Thus, according to McKinney, a "distorted dialectic" is the consequence of the dominance of "either" principle (Ibid. 28-48). As said, such a dialectic can involve the cessation, aberration or, perhaps, in the worst case, the regression of the anticipated instance

[B] to restore an equilibrium [and the consequent development of, in this case, the scientific subject] . . . . Indeed the essential logic of the <u>distorted</u> dialectic is a <u>reversal</u>. ($\underline{I}$, 233b, emphases mine).^{1}

The dominance exists when further manifolds have been gathered, e.g., S_7, which <u>want</u> higher integration. For then the subject <u>allows</u> his already achieved <u>sensitive</u> attachment to the "object" understood and verified at C_6 to **prevent** the emergence of the further relevant questions they raise and, therefore, his transition, through B, from **integrator** to operator, etc. But, then, if C_6 <u>cannot</u> meet the exigences of S_7, it will, eventually break down. B has entered, under the

---

of development. Again, it would seem that on this present account a "distorted dialectic" would also be the consequence of the contrary case in which B dominates A, etc. But, then, two "contrary" cases would represent "dialectically opposed" forms of dominance; distorted dialectical processes, etc.   This author leaves open the question of whether and/or how Lonergan's <u>Insight</u> broaches these issues, as well as that of, say, "dialectically opposed 'counter-positions'" in philosophy, etc. (cf. Chapter I, pp. 20–21 n3, above). Finally, the "counter-positions" are defined in Chapter VI, Section 6, below, and alluded to in Subsection e) of this section.

^{1}Three brief comments are required here.

<u>First</u>, the "logic" to the <u>reversal</u> is non–formal in character and presupposes the <u>fact</u> that the "orientations" of, respectively, the intelligence and sensitivity/intersubjectivity of the subject, are linked but opposed. Still, the language of the logical "negation of a negation" can interpret the dialectic if it is transposed into a performative context ($\underline{I}$, 543a, etc.). In the general case, then, and assuming this transposition, the starting point of the dialectic is the "subject's" failure or refusal to "negate" her sensitive "negation" of (interference with) the dynamic to her intelligence and reasonableness. The consequence of this failure or refusal is the introduction of a series of further "tensions" into the action, social interactions, social institutions, etc., of the subject.

<u>Secondly</u>, the claim that the <u>proper</u> or <u>full</u> "intelligibility" of the dominance relation, of the "distorted dialectic" it engages, is its "reversal" and a consequent <u>recovery</u> of development, will be regarded as Lonergan's "fifth principle" of dialectical process (cf. $\underline{I}$, 217b #1–#4). Again, dialectical process in the "inclusive" sense will manifest <u>either</u> the reversal <u>or</u> the destructive removal set forth in the introduction, above.

<u>Finally</u>, McKinney identifies the full or proper process of "reversal" with a "dialectic of contradiction" in the above, non–formal sense.

pressure of A's interference, into "contradiction"[1] with the "norms" inherent in his inquiry (i.e., in his determination that there are "no further relevant questions" in his pursuit and affirmation of the "truth"). Thus, he has entered into variance with himself, with his own pure desire and the immanent criteria his desire engages. But over time and further trials, the negative consequences of C_6's failure to integrate S_7 become increasingly evident. B's variance with the normative exigences of the subject's own inquiry and rational reflection become more palpable and intolerable. And if they do not result in the destructive breakdown, in the mere removal of C_6, they head for the "reversal" of B's variance with its own "nature" and, through this, the resumption of the dialectical pursuit which "heads for" and, eventually, achieves C_7, etc.[2]

Finally, there is a structural isomorphism between the _five_ "principles of dialectic" which Lonergan avows, the preceding case by which they were exemplified and, minimally, the following three cases. To bring out that further isomorphism, to the demonstration of the fertility of the dialectic's five heuristic principles we must now turn.

---

[1]Again, the "contradiction" is not merely formal.

[2]Thus, in the context of a reflection on the "most general aspects" of cognitional process, Lonergan notes that: "(d)ialectic . . . rests on the [constructive] break—down of efforts to attain coherence and organization at a given stage [of intellectual development [e.g., C_6] and consists in bringing to birth a new stage [e.g., C_7] in which logic again will endeavour to attain coherence and organization" (_I_, 276e; alternative interpretation of the preceding could be constructed on the basis of points two and, especially, three on p. 284 n1, above). Again, it is clear from the context of the above quotation, that the cited breakdown of efforts, the maieutic which leads to the recovery of _development_ is, in fact, communal and historical in character.

c) The Dialectic of the Dramatic Subject—Analysis[1]

Consider the dramatic subject's discovery of a higher, aesthetically "satisfying" way, e.g., C_6, of "artistically" bringing together
the underlying (otherwise coincidentally related) neuro—organic demands, e.g., S_6, upon her conscious being "in" the socio—cultural
world. Again, let us refer to the "censorship" determining the "sensitivity" of the subject as one "principle," e.g., B, operative in the
constitution of the sensitive flow to her conscious life. And let us
refer to the "neuro—organic demand functions" whose contents (e.g., S_6)
C_6 "artistically" integrates, as co—"principle," A, in the process.[2]

First, then, the "contents and affects emerging into [the dramatically patterned] consciousness [of the subject]" represent the
requisite aggregate of events. But in the given case, such an aggregate comprises S_6 as made determinate by the "dramatically informed
synthesis" of C_6 (cf. I, 189a).

Secondly, these "contents and affects," their integration by C_6,
can be traced back to the functioning of A and B, and therefore, to the

---

[1] The context of the ensuing analysis is set, not only by the
immediately preceding reflections, but those of Chapter IV, above,
upon the dramatic patterning of the subject's experience. Furthermore,
there is a further reference back to the aesthetic pattern analyzed in
Chapter II, above, which must go uncommented upon here.

[2] If this case turns out to be isomorphic in structure to the
preceding, it is more complicated. Thus, a first complication is that
principle A is non-conscious. It is further complicated since the
censorship, if it is properly to integrate the underlying neural
demands upon her sensitivity, must do so in a manner that aligns
itself, proximately, with the exigences of the dramatic "liberation" of
the subject's experience and, remotely, with those of human intelligence and reasonableness in general. Finally, a condition of
dialectical process for Lonergan is that at least one of its two
co—principles, e.g., A or B, pertains to human **consciousness**. Thus,
Lonergan's notion of dialectic is: "a restricted and differentiated
tool; it is relevant to human knowledge and to human activities that
depend upon [or unconsciously and/or sensitively condition] knowledge;
. . . and it has no relevance to purely **natural** [e.g., non—conscious]
process" (I, 422b, emphases mine).

relevant "neuro-organic demand functions" and the "constructive" censorship. The censor is "constructive" if its imaginal, affective, and symbolic integrations of neural demands allow "contents" to "surface" into consciousness which are relevant to the subject's intelligent and reasonable performance, generally and, in particular, to her intelligent, dramatically charged performance at C_6 (the processes of development to which both of the preceding commit her efforts).

Thirdly, the neural demand functions and constructive censorship are related as:

> patterned and patterning; they are opposed inasmuch as the censorship not only constructs [e.g., selects and arrays relevant elements] but also represses [those which are not relevant to her dignified pursuit of dramatic living, etc.] . . . (I, 217b).

They are opposed, further, since if the constructive censorship selects and arrays contents by their pertinence to her higher level, disinterested functions, the neurally mediated demands are themselves functions of the immediate, biological purposiveness of the organism.

Fourthly, the functioning of the dramatically, intentionally aligned constructive censorship, B, calls forth changes in the underlying demand functions, A, and the manifolds they gather, S_7. And these changes will evoke a modified higher integration, C_7, and, ultimately, a higher level to her artistically charged, dramatic functioning. Again, they will do this by effecting B's transition from integrator to operator, etc.

Fifthly, the neuro-organic orientation of the subject's being dominates the censorship when there are further manifolds, e.g., S_7, which "want" higher integration beyond C_6. The censor allows the organism's assimilation to the immediate "objects" attained through C_6 to interfere with its bringing above the threshold of consciousness its situation at S_7. This allowance by the censor coincides with the subject's higher level "flight from dramatic Self-knowledge" and action. The subject's assimilation to C_6, therefore, is allowed to interfere with her transition from higher system as "integrator," e.g., T_r as C_6, to "operator," e.g., T_r as headed for C_7. But such an allowance represents the formation of a "scotosis," a "blind-spot" in the censorship (cf. I, 191b ff). The scotosis will systematically "inhibit" demands for "images," e.g., dream symbols, phantasies, etc., that would condition the subject's unwanted "understanding" of herSelf, her unwanted revelation of herSelf to herSelf. Again, it will systematically dissociate affects from their real "objects" to give them initially safe, non-"Self"-revelatory ones. Following suit will be the psychic "division" of a persona and ego and, the formation of, respectively, their inverse shadow and anima functions. And when, for example, the subject's dreaming is no longer able to vent adequately the first neglected and now destructively "repressed" demands, they will, eventually and increasingly assert themselves in the subject's conscious living. They will begin, thereby, to "demand" a higher, dramatic "integration" of the subject's living and being. Thus, they will interrupt her sleep, disturb her ability to discharge smoothly high level intellectual and deliberative functions, invade her consciousness with the anxiety, pathological guilt, compulsions, phobias, para-praxes, etc., associated with the psycho-neuroses.

Thus, over time the subject's, e.g., C_6's, failure to integrate S_7 becomes increasingly evident by the "distortions" it introduces into her daily "living." B's variance with its own integrative function within the psyche becomes increasingly manifest. B's variance with the higher order orientation of intelligence and reasonableness, with her anticipated growth in dramatic artistry becomes plain. Again, if the subject's flight from dramatic Self-knowledge does not result in her total, destructive breakdown, the process can be "reversed." But the reversal will, probably, be mediated by the context of the analytic situation in which the therapist's reconstruction of the unwanted Self-revelation will be "resisted," and the underlying, dissociated demands it represents will be "transferred" onto the person of the analyst. In that context, the analyst must ally the subject's intelligence and reasonableness to her own search for the "truth," and so help the subject discover and responsibly assimilate her secret desire gone "underground." This happens in the context of "inquiry into" her own affectively charged dream images, childhood memories, gestures, omissions, etc., i.e., contents which surface in the "drama" of the analysis.[1] Finally, the analyst is functioning as the "agent" of the "dialectic of the dramatic subject," of the intelligible "possibility" which the latter's bias holds out for "reversal." But this function is only itself "possible" because the biased subject's Self-concealment as well as the correlative distortion of her "censorship," is at variance with the dynamic structure of her own, as well as her analyst's, intelligence and reasonableness. And it is such a variance which the analyst, if she is herSelf free of scotoma, etc., can help the patient to "discover" and "correct." But this is to the end of the subject's recovery of the dynamic to her "own" dramatic living "in" the "world" with others, with all the consequences this has for the other dimensions, the other patterns of her living and being.[2]

---

[1]The dramatic subject is not per se also in the intellectual pattern even if the pattern to her dramatic living can be or has been reflectively and intellectually mediated. Thus, unlike her "intellectual" counterpart, the dramatic subject's insights, reflections, and judgments: do not occur in a pattern which excludes the flow of (dramatically charged) emotions, affects, associations and phantasies, etc.; remain in close "proximity" to her sensitive life, etc. For these reasons, the subject's dramatic Self-understanding, mediated by analytic reflection upon her dream symbols, phantasies, daily life, etc., can result in the only seemingly spontaneous re-organization of sensitive attitudes, apprehensions and affects, etc. Again, they can result in her advance to a new, "higher" stage of dramatic development.

[2]Lonergan's reflection on the institution and reversal of the dramatic bias of the subject represents one of his most complex analyses. I have only attempted to bring out its main lines and relate it to the issue of dialectical process. I have also abstracted from the issue of the relationship between the dialectics, i.e., between the dialectics of the dramatic subject and her community, of the aesthetic and scientific subjects within community, etc., etc. (cf. I, 218b).

d) The Dialectic of the Practical Subject of Common Sense—Analysis[1]

Consider the practical subject's discovery and rational option for some higher technical, economic or political viewpoint, e.g., C_6. This rational option for C_6 integrates the otherwise coincidentally related data-manifold of S_6. Again, let us refer to the intelligent, reasonable (and willing) subject "in" community as one "principle," e.g., B, operative in the process which institutes C_6 in S_6. And let us refer to the desire and labor of the individual subject, but also the intersubjective community in which he is always already spontaneously engaged as co-"principle," e.g., A, in the process.

But, first, then, the relevant aggregate of determinate events comprises S_6 as made determinate by C_6, i.e., the "socially" determined situation of the community "at" C_6.

Secondly, the social situation of the community at C_6, can be "traced back to":

the two principles of human intersubjectivity [e.g., A] and practical common sense [e.g., B] (I, 217c);

and to the Self-correcting "interplay" of A and B.

Thirdly, the two principles are "bound together":

for the spontaneous, intersubjective individual strives to understand and wants to behave intelligently; and inversely, [practical] intelligence would have nothing to put in order were there not the desires and fears, labours and satisfactions of individuals (I, 217c–218a).

Again, these two "principles" are "opposed." Thus, to each subject:

his own desires [and labours, joys and sorrows], precisely because they are his own, possess an insistence [and "reality"] that the desires [and labours . . .] of others can never have for him (I, 215a).

Further, if "the bonds of intersubjective community make the experience of each [subject] resonate to the experience of others" (I, 215a), still they have only limited (i.e., non-universal) scope and

---

[1]The context of the following discussion is set by Chapter III, Division B, above, and its analysis of the practical, common sense subject.

retain the attachment and exclusivity of sensitive spontaneity. On the other hand, as <u>intelligent</u>, the subject cannot but "devise **general** solutions and **general** rules." He cannot "enjoy peace of mind" unless his solution meets <u>all</u> the relevant further questions posed by the demands of the "good of order;"[1] i.e., unless:

> he subsumes his own feelings and actions under the <u>general</u> rules he regards as intelligent. Yet feeling and spontaneous action have their home in the intersubjective group and it is only with an effort and then in only favoured times that the intersubjective groups fit harmoniously within the larger patterns of social order (<u>I</u>, 215c-216a, emphases mine).

<u>Fourthly</u>, these linked but opposed principles are modified by the changes that result from them, since:

> the <u>development</u> of common sense [intelligence, e.g., $C_4 > C_5 > C_6$, etc.] consists in the further questions and insights that arise from the situations produced by previous operations of practical common sense [e.g., $S_3 > S_4 > S_5$, etc.]; and the alternations of social tranquility and social crisis mark successive stages in the <u>adaptation</u> [and/or non-"adaptation"] of human spontaneity and sensibility [and intersubjectivity, e.g., A] to the demands of developing intelligence [e.g., B] (<u>I</u>, 218a).

<u>Fifthly</u>, the sensitive and/or intersubjective orientation of the subject's (and of his community's) being <u>dominates</u> his (and his community's) practical common sense when there are <u>further</u> coincidental elements in his situation, e.g., S_7, which "want" integration <u>beyond</u> C_6. The subject (and his community) <u>allows</u> his (its already achieved sensitive and/or intersubjective) "adaptation" to the "orders" understood and instituted at C_6 to <u>prevent</u> the emergence of the further relevant questions they raise and, therefore, his transition through B, <u>from</u> integrator <u>to</u> operator, etc. But, since C_6 cannot meet the exigences set up by S_7, there is introduced into the situation a distortion which anticipates <u>either</u> its constructive "reversal," (the re-institution of the dynamic to the good of order, e.g., $C_7 > C_8 > C_9$, etc.) <u>or</u> the merely destructive removal of C_6. Again, with slight variations, these general, heuristic anticipations can be further determined in three

---

[1] The reader should note that such a solution may not, in the given society, coincide with the good of order as instituted, e.g., C_6 in S_6 (cf. <u>I</u>, 610b 10 ff).

manners relative to three kinds of "practical" contexts.

First, the "egoist" (the "individually biased" subject) is motivated by his sensitively attached "concern" for the "object" of his own
palpable, immediate, and potentially, exclusive interest. Again, this
motivation signifies his explicit or "implicit" refusal to accept the
demands which intelligence and reasonableness (the dynamic good of
order) make upon his freedom.[1] If he proceeds "intelligently," it is
to "size up" the social order by uncovering its weak points and loop-
holes, and to "discover" possible ways of benefiting himSelf without
contributing (or contributing equitably) to the welfare of others.[2]
Thus, the sensitive motivation of the subject is allowed to rule out of
court the criterion of "further relevant questioning" which would have
revealed his course of action and his habitual inclination to act, to
be short-sighted, Self-interested, and at variance with the relative
generality of the solutions worked out and imposed by practical intelligence. Such a course of action is inconsistent with the "common"
good of order of his community and at variance with the intelligence of
the dynamic, historical process by which the underlying demands of the
community as a whole are met. Again, his egoism is "opposed" not only
by the dynamic exigences of his own intelligent and rational "nature"
but by those stemming from his limited, "intersubjective" community of
"interest" with the local "other." Finally, then, it is by these two
forms of opposition to his bias, that the egoism of the individually
biased subject will, sooner or later, be either "reversed" or destructively removed.

Secondly, the bias of a merely dominant "group" in the community
is similarly motivated. Consistent with such a motivation, the further

---

[1] As was noted in Chapter III, part two, above, this principle
underlies the possibility of a truly common good of order. Again, if
the subject's acts are at variance with this principle they are also at
variance with his intelligent and reasonable choice.

[2] For the subject to do this is for him to except himself from the
"heuristic principle" of his own intelligence as practically oriented,
etc. Cf. Chapter III, p. 88 n1, above.

relevant "**questions**" which would reveal to its members that the original "usefulness" which swept them into a position of "power" in the community (e.g., their recommendation and institution of C_6 to meet S_6, etc.) has come to an end, since C_6 has called forth S_7. The benefits they receive from the community now far exceed their contributions. They are gaining at the expense of the community's other contributing groups, etc., whose relevant further questions **are not pursued** and **are systematically excluded from consideration**. As dominant, such groups will use the power which they retain to block the emergence of, communal conscent to and/or implementation of practical "ideas" (e.g., C_7) which genuinely meet the transformed, underlying conditions (e.g., S_7). In so doing, however, they argue against their own retention of power.

But, there are consequences to the exclusion of C_7. Thus, S_7 is not enriched with the needed higher "intelligibility" of C_7. The conditions for securing the "common good" of the community under a new set of initial conditions are not fulfilled. The succession of intelligent and reasonable "corrections" and "complements" that would have supervened upon the introduction of C_7 in S_7 are prevented from going into effect and, thereby, integrating S_7 on successively higher levels. But, then, the situation becomes, not only, increasingly less intelligible (increasingly a "surd") but also increasingly insistent, as the exigences which C_7 would meet go unanswered or answered in a distorted fashion. Thus, the increasingly distorted situation draws the community's attention to itself. In such a context, a "schism" develops between the dominant but uncreative "ruling" group(s) in the community and those depressed, frustrated, but creative groups which have or have begun to champion C_7. But as recognized problems continue and expand unresolved, the community must eventually turn to the ideas of the intelligent but depressed group(s) or face extinction. Thus, the institution of C_7 takes place either through the removal and replacement of the old group by its depressed counterpart(s), or through the winning over of the dominant group to the new idea. Again, the emergence of S_8 is called forth by the institution of C_7. And if the next "new" idea does not, in fact, meet the further questions raised by S_8, then, in the very best case, the dialectic continues to turn until C_8 does emerge and is instituted. But C_8 calls forth S_9. And S_9 is, again, in "potency" to the rekindling of the dialectic if and when the previously creative, executor group(s) of C_8 turn(s) dominant. Finally, then, the "group biasing" of the process of common sense generates the **"shorter cycle of decline"** in which nations go to war, revolution wracks the state, and lags afflict the institution and correction of reasonable projects and policies constitutive of the dynamic, common good of order.

Thirdly, in Sections B3-4 of Chapter III, above, we pointed out that even if the common sense subject along with his community, is intelligent and reasonable, still he, nevertheless, labors under a "limited" viewpoint. Thus, from this viewpoint, the possible, practical ideas he would institute, are screened and evaluated in terms of:[1]

(1) their proximity to the concerns, desires and fears, apprehensions and interests "of man;"[2]

(2) their abstraction from individual, social, historical, and environmental implications that are long-term and/or wide-ranging in scope, theoretical in character or complex and disputed in consequence;[3]

(3) criteria that are "pragmatic" and, therefore, relatively short-sighted;[4]

(4) [their relevance to a relatively] non-explanatory and non-technical context.[5]

Again, it was pointed out that such screening and evaluation involve neither his:

---

[1]The following five points refer back to our interpretations of the limited viewpoint of common sense and elaborate upon reflections set forth in Chapter III, above.

[2]Cf. Chapter III, pp. 73a-74a, 96b, above.

[3]Ibid.

[4]Cf. Chapter III, pp. 74b, 96c-97a, above.

[5]Cf. Chapter III, pp. 74c, 97b, above.

(5) systematic, reflectively pursued achievement of insight into

> insight, Self-affirmation, the viewpoint of emergent
> probability on human [and/or natural] affairs, etc., . . .
> [nor] his engagement of such achievement critically to
> guide and facilitate his evaluation of what he, what his
> community, should do.[1]

Thus, if the subject (the community of common sense) is, in principle, equal to the task of overcoming individual and group bias, then for precisely the preceding reasons—reasons which go to the essence of the attitude of human common sense performance—they fall victim to a further "general" bias of common sense. But, the source, then, of this bias lies in the subject's conviction that the "horizon" of common sense is cognitionally, ontologically, but also practically "total and basic." Thus, the common sense subject will tend to regard a fully "rational account" of "what is to be done" as "empty theorizing." He will consider such pursuits as the "scientific" study of the dynamic of human or natural history, as well as the philosophic "sciences," etc., **irrelevant** to the understanding and guidance of human "practise." Again, he will not regard such attitudes as "limitations" to be transcended.

But the actual exclusion of "theory" from the field of human history, community, and action, when coupled with the shorter cycle of decline fosters a **"longer cycle"** of deterioration. Thus, at the "ideal" limit of such a regression, and through a series of actual or possible transformations (cf. I, 230d-233a), the implicit, "common sense" conviction that theory must be excluded from practise to make practise "possible," turns into and brings to political power the viewpoint of "totalitarian practicality." But the subject (the community) of the latter viewpoint has made the "discovery" that in a world in which "interest," desire and fear, technical control and security, etc., are the original motivations, force is the only ultimate "unifying" or "binding" principle which can brake the otherwise inevitable "war of all against all." From this politically effective "viewpoint": no political or "theoretical" appeal to "human rights," to universal

---

[1]Cf. Chapter III, pp. 75b, 97c-98a, above.

"principles of justice," to the intelligent and rational exigences constitutive of human "nature," community, and history can be anything
more than naive;

> every type of intellectual independence, whether personal, cultur-
> al, scientific, philosophic, or religious, has no better basis than
> non-conscious myth (I, 231b, emphases mine);

> theory [e.g., natural science, "scientific" history, normative sci-
> ence, philosophy, etc.] is reduced to the status of a myth that
> lingers on to represent the frustrated aspirations of detached and
> disinterested intelligence (I, 232a);

> (r)eality is the economic development, the military equipment, and
> the political dominance of the all-inclusive State (I, 232a);

> [legitimate] means [to preserve such dominance] include not merely
> every technique of indoctrination and propaganda, . . . [but] every
> device for breaking down the moral conscience and exploiting the
> secret affects of civilized man, but also the terrorism of a polit-
> ical police, of prisons and torture, of concentration camps, . . .
> and of total war (I, 232a).

But nations not "tempted" to use the totalitarian's methods by
their "ambitions or their needs," "will be subjected to . . . [this
temptation] by their fears of danger and by their insistence on self-
protection" (I, 232b). And with such a viewpoint mediating the political decisions of nation states within the world community, one cannot
but anticipate the eventual:

> catalytic trifle that will reveal to a surprised world the end of a
> once brilliant day (I,210a);

> great crises that [will] end [with the world, the longer cycle] in
> complete disintegration and decay (I, 233a).

There will come the "destructive" **removal** of the (bearers of the) viewpoint of common sense "practicality" which spawned and sustained the
world-community's decline. On the other hand, Lonergan argues that:

> there is a convergence of evidence for the assertion that the long-
> er cycle is to be met [e.g., its decline **"reversed"**], not by any
> idea or set of ideas on the level of technology, economics, or pol-
> itics, but only by the attainment of a higher viewpoint in man's
> understanding and making of man (I, 233a, emphases mine).

But there are **pre-conditions** of the implementation of such a higher viewpoint.[1]

In the first place, human being and community fall within the dynamic of emergent probability insofar as their <u>insights</u> and <u>decisions</u> remain:

> probable [e.g., <u>classically</u> specifiable] realizations of concrete possibilities, and inasmuch as earlier insights and decisions determine <u>later</u> possiblities and probabilities of insight and decision [on a higher level] (<u>I</u>, 227a, emphases mine).

But with the emergence of human being and community within history, the process of emergent probability took a new <u>course</u>, and this in two respects:

> . . . in the **first** place, <u>insight</u> is an anticipation of possible [i.e., <u>classically</u> definable] schemes and <u>decisions</u> bring about the concrete conditions of [i.e., shift probabilities in the direction of] their functioning instead of waiting for such conditions to happen; moreover the greater man's development, the greater his dominion over circumstances and so the greater his capacity to realize possible schemes by deciding to realize their conditions (<u>I</u>, 227a, emphases mine; cf. <u>I</u>, xiid 6-7, 227a 30-35).

But, as noted, the new course of "insight-mediated" decision is faced with the prospect of its own annihilation by the effects of the conjoint group and general biases of common sense.

> But there is also a **second** and profounder difference. For man can <u>discover</u> emergent probability [cf. Subsections B6 and B7, above]; he can work out the manner in which **prior** insights and decisions [which fall under emergent probability, therefore,] <u>determine</u> the possibilities and probabilities of **later** insights and decisions [i.e., higher practical viewpoints of common sense]; he can <u>guide</u> his **present** decisions in the light of their influence on **future** insights and decisions; finally, this <u>control</u> of the emergent probability of the future can be exercised . . . by mankind in its consciousness of its <u>responsbility to the future of mankind</u> (<u>I</u>, 227a, emphases mine).

But, in the second place, to exercise such a responsibility to the "future," the <u>history</u> which has determined contemporary possibilities and probabilities will have to be methodically studied. And since man's being is being in the world, the notion of the emergent probability of "world process" can be extended to embrace the historical <u>study</u>

---

[1] It has been towards the determination of such a viewpoint and for such a purpose that this work, in its entirety, has been labouring.

of "human process." Such an extension would bring to the study of human being and history a "scientific" viewpoint, which is not only genetic but also dialectical.[1] It would be open, therefore, to the potential "totality" of genetically and dialectically <u>related</u> viewpoints,[2] (i.e., the totality of relative and absolute "horizons," etc.) which inform the probability and possibility of human knowledge, action, community, etc. Finally, it would be used to study the "past" of human being and socio-cultural community to the **end** of human Being's becoming for itself "the executor of the emergent probability of [the "future" of] human affairs" (<u>I</u>, 227a).

In the third place, if the practical, unbiased subject is to discover and institute the intelligibility of emergent process in his concrete situation, he will need the **"liberty"** to do so.

In the fourth place, a new, philosophically grounded **"critical science of man"** will be necessary. Such a science will take the "data" of human consciousness as its starting point. On the "basis" of the reflective analysis of that data, it will distinguish, define, and relate two major intentional "orientations."

On the one hand, then, it will bring out the "normative exigences" for intelligence, reasonableness, and responsibility immanent within human conscious Being. Again, it will clarify the nature of the human "genuineness" which repects these exigences. Finally, it will go on to exhibit the "subjective" development and "objective" progress which respect for these exigences generates and conditions.

On the other hand, it will bring out the nature of the "biological extroversion" (cf. Chapter I, above) into which mature human consciousness tends to lapse. Again, it will clarify the nature of the "inauthenticity" which conditions the flight from Self-knowledge and

---

[1] The relation between the intelligibility which the dialectically differentiatied subject brings out and the dynamic to emergent probability will be taken up in the next to the last paragraph of this section.

[2] The condition of such a "heuristic" openess to the historically advancing-regressing totality of human "meaning" is the potentially "universal viewpoint" of human subjectivity (cf. <u>I</u>, XVII.3.2).

Self-appropriation. But such an extroversion of attitude is contrary to and, therefore, interferes with the recognition, appropriation, and implementation of the "normative exigences." But such a flight inevitably generates inertia, aberration and the inverse succession of successively lower integrations characteristic of personal or communal decline.[1]

Such a normative, reflective science would, then, foster the personal discovery that: "(i)nquiry and insight are facts that underlie

---

[1]Lonergan's initial point, here, is that upon reflection, the subject cannot ultimately, avoid advertance to, understanding of, and assent to two "facts" about her intentional life.

The first is that "insights accumulate," that she, therefore, develops "intellectually" in mathematics, empirical science, common sense, etc.

The second point is: "the dialectical [e.g., the distorted] unfolding of . . . [her] own desire to know [and learn when it is] in conflict with other [e.g., sensitive] desires [and the consequent incompleteness or distortion of her "intellectual" development]" (I, 429b). But what accounts for the first fact is the subject's fidelity to the tri-fold structure of her intentional operations. What accounts for the second is her sensitively motivated violation of that structure. But such a violation involves her consequent engagement of an attitude of unquestioning, biological extroversion toward the "world" and her flight from or refusal of understanding, etc. (cf. I, xid-e, xxviii #1). But the consequence of the subject's reflective appropriation of the linked but opposed orientations into which her intentionality can slip, is also, simultaneously her achievement of a "critical" perspective. "From" such a perspective, she can account for the progress and/or distortion of: (1) her cognition and the decisions which extend it into action; (2) the knowledge and action of any subject at any level of development; (3) the "products" of her, of any subject's knowledge and action, etc. (xiic 4-6). The perspective is heuristic in character since it: (1) allows the subject to anticipate the structure and consequences of divergent attitudes to her, any subject's or any community's cognition, objectivity, etc.; (2) is "empty" until it is applied to the "data" relevant to the given cognitional, socio-cultural, and/or institutional processes, etc.; (3) answers to the subject's "Why?" in the face of the relevant advancing or regressing situation.

Finally, such an explanatory, potentially comprehensive "perspective" is necessary if human science, e.g., sociology, economics, political science, cultural hermeneutics, anthropology, etc. is to be "critical" and "normative," and, therefore, capable of criticizing and guiding history and not merely of reporting or reacting to it.

[the development] of mathematics, empirical science, and common sense" (I, 234b). Inversely, it would bring out the fact that the "refusal of insight":

> accounts for individual and group egoism, for the psychoneuroses, and for the ruin of nations and civilizations (I, 234b).

Thus, the "needed higher viewpoint" in human science turns on:

> the [reflective] discovery, the logical expansion and the recognition of the principle that <u>intelligence</u> contains its own immanent <u>norms</u> and that these norms are equipped with sanctions which man does not have to invent or impose (I, 234b, emphases mine).

Such a critical science, then, will presuppose and involve a reflectively mediated viewpoint upon one's own, as well as one's community's, being in history. But, then, it will foster:

> the **intelligent** emergent probability that arises in the measure that man succeeds in **understanding himself and in implementing that understanding** (I, 236a; cf. I, 690a).

In the fifth place, it is the function of the "cultural superstructure" of a community to let such a reflectively mediated viewpoint "speak" to the human "heart" as well as to the "mind."[1] Such culture, as well as the community which fosters it, transcends:

> [the geographical] frontiers of states and the epochs of history. It is Cosmopolis, not as an unrealized political ideal, but as a longstanding, non-political, cultural fact. It is the field of communication and influence of artists, scientists and philosophers. It is the bar of enlightened opinion to which naked power can be driven to submit. It is the tribunal of human history that may expose successful charlatans and may restore to honor the prophets stoned by their contemporaries (Lonergan, "The Role of the Catholic University in the Modern World," C1, 115f).[2]

---

[1]Cosmopolis, then, which is one aspect of this superstructure, confronts: "problems of which men are aware; it invites the vast potentialities and pent-up energies of our time to contribute to their solution by developing an art and a literature, a theatre and a broadcasting, a journalism and a history, a school and a university, a personal depth and a public opinion, that through appreciation and criticism give men of common sense the opportunity and help they need and desire to correct the general bias of their common sense" (I, 241b).

[2]Thus, besides the culture of the infrastructure, besides: "the meaning and value immediately intuited, felt, spoken, acted out, there

Its "business" would be to "break the vicious circle of an illusion," namely that:

> men will not venture on ideas that they grant to be correct, because they hold that such ideas will not work unless sustained by desires or fears; and, inversely, men hold that such ideas will not work, because they will not venture on them and so have no empirical evidence that such ideas can work and would work (I, 239b).

In this connection, then, human Cosmopolitan culture must accomplish an ongoing, dialectical "critique of human history" (I, 240a), of the series of "refusals to understand"[1] which pervade the opinions of the day and which motivate the sources to which they, in turn, can be traced back. Again, such critique is needed if pitfalls and/or their repetition are to be recognized and avoided and if there is to be the inverse "intelligent direction [by the community of human subjects] of [the] history [they are, in fact, making]" (I, 240a).

But, finally, the preceding six points represent Lonergan's initial, incomplete, hypothesized prescriptions for accomplishing and sustaining the "Reversal" which would restore the dynamic to human history in the face of the conjunction of the general and group biases.

---

is to any advanced culture a superstructure. To art and literature there are added criticism. To artisans and craftsmen there are added inventors and technicians. To common sense there is added science. To the proverbs of wise men there are added the reflections of philosophers. Industry and commerce are complicated by economics, togetherness by sociology, the state by political theory, the law by jurisprudence, man's body by medicine and his mind by psychiatry, schools by educational theories, and religions by theologies. Besides the meanings and values immanent in everyday living there is an enormous [superstructural] process in which meanings are elaborated and values are discerned in a far more reflective, deliberate, critical fashion" ("Belief: Today's Issue," C2, 91d).

[1]Two points should be made here.

First, if the "refusal to understand" can be "implicit," it is never fully unconscious. Thus, in Chapter XVIII of Insight, Lonergan notes that: "as the scotosis of the dramatic subject, so the moral impotence [e.g., the individual but also the group and general biases] of the essentially free subject is [e.g., are] neither grasped with perfect clarity [by him and/or his group] nor is it [e.g., are they] totally unconscious" (I, 627b, emphases mine).

Secondly, the lower and higher forms of "culture" which engage such critique can be distinguished. The "lower" regard the common sense horizon of a people or group but they lack "controls over

But the accomplishment of that Reversal turns on the fostering of the conditions which would shift schedules of probability in favor of the socio-historical subject's affective, intellectual and volitional Self-appropriation.[1]

---

meaning" and so easily indulge "in magic and myth" (<u>MT</u>, 28c). The "higher" cultivate "reflexive techniques that operate on mediate [common sense] operations themselves in an effort to safeguard meaning" (<u>MT</u>, 28c). Within the higher cultures those that are classical and modern can be distinguished by the character of these reflexive techniques. Thus, classical cultures think of control as "a universal fixed for all time" (<u>MT</u>, 29a). Modern cultures think of their highest order controls as 1) the fruit of the Self-appropriation of the human subject and, therefore, as minimally liable to a minor dynamic; 2) mediating major development on the social and cultural levels. Again, lower and higher technological, economic, and political forms might also be conceived along these lines and as paralleling the stages of culture.

[1]Cf. Chapters VI and VII, and the General Conclusion, below.

e) The Dialectic of the Philosophic Subject[1]—Analysis

Consider the philosopher's grasp as virtually unconditioned of a "higher" viewpoint, e.g., C_6, pertaining to her own cognition, objectivity, her notion of "Being," etc. Suppose that her affirmation of C_6 integrates what, from the perspective of "cognitional theory" C_5, stands forth as merely coincidentally related "data of consciousness," e.g., S_6. Again, let us refer to the intelligence, reasonableness (and responsibility) of the subject as one "principle," e.g., B, operative in her reflection, discovery and "verification" of C_6 in S_6. And let us refer to the subject's own presence "to" herSelf in the act of knowing, the presence to herSelf "by" which S_6, e.g., the "data" of her own consciousness, are present to her as ordered by C_6, as co-"principle," e.g., A, in the same process of Self-reflection.[2]

First, then, the relevant aggregate of determinate events is the subject's consciousness "of" her own cognitional performance, i.e., S_6 as made determinate by her antecedent "verification" and "application" of C_6.

Secondly, the subject's consciousness of herSelf at S_6, its explanation in terms of C_6, can be "traced back" and accounted for in terms of principles B, i.e., the reflectively turned intelligence and reasonableness of the subject, and A, i.e., the Self-"consciousness" of the subject.

Thirdly, A and B are "linked together" since without A there is no "data of consciousness" for the subject to reflect upon and understand and, therefore, neither any "Self"-understanding to be affirmed,

---

[1]To simplify what follows, the historical and communal dimensions of the constitution of philosophic meaning are abstracted from but in no way either denied or ignored. Rather they will be brought in, to some extent, in Chapter VI (cf. I, 389b). Further, the reader should be able to make the necessary changes to expand the discussion along these complex lines (cf. I, XIV.4, XII.7, XVI.5, XVII.3, etc.).

[2]Lonergan thematizes and reflects upon the Self-presence of the subject in Understanding and Being, pp. 15a–18c. The question of the nature of human "consciousness" is taken up briefly in Appendix II of Chapter VI.

nor any Self-affirmation to be deliberately implemented. Again, without B there is no pursuit or achievement of Self-understanding, Self-affirmation, Self-implementation. Again, the principles are "opposed" since they possess such "contrary" respective "properties" as attachment and disinterstedness, etc.

Fourthly, and in the least complicated case, the subject's deliberate implementation of the cognitional theory which she has affirmed of herSelf will lead to a modification of her cognitional and volitional performance. But this will lead to the uncovering of the further, coincidentally related "data of consciousness," e.g., S_7, which cannot be explicated on C_6. Thus, S_7, will call forth the subject's further efforts to understand herSelf, the transition of the higher system of the subject's intelligence and reasonableness from integrator to operator, etc. But when such an inquiry gives way to the revision of her affirmed Self-understanding and its implementation sets, it the stage for the emergence of S_8, etc., etc.[1]

Fifthly, the subject's "sensitive" attachment to the Self-understanding implicit in C_6 may interfere with the emergence of S_7, with the operative further labor of Self-pursuit it calls forth. Again, such interference will constitute at least part of the ambiguous "data" to be explored in the course of her already distorted Self-reflection. Thus, in the worst case, the subject will not merely sustain C_6 in the face of S_7, but also distort her account of C_6 to accord with the results of her reflections upon her own sensitive process as cognitional. The result of this distorted Self-pursuit, of distorted Self-"consciousness" is some variant on the "counter-positions" on human "knowing, Being, objectivity, intersubjectivity, value," etc. But, these were explicated in the course of our initial chapter's account of the

---

[1]Such a philosophic process is possible even if, for example, the structure of C_6 were relatively invariant. Still it would instance only the "minor" finality of human intentionality (cf. I, xxvia 10-12). Again, notice that the process is highly concrete, e.g., a philosopher faced with the prospect of modifying, in a second case, an avowedly inadequate, e.g., a "counter-positional" account of his own intentional process—one which he learned at college, held, taught, lived out and defended for 25 years. Under certain circumstances such a prospect would no doubt fill him with dread, anxiety, etc. (cf. I, 533 n).

biologically patterned subjectivity of the sensitive subject. Again, in the following chapter of this work, these counter-positions will be found to stand in radical "opposition" to their corresponding "positions." But the "positions" claim to do no more than explicate the Self-knowledge of the subject "in" the world in a manner consistent with, minimally, the tri-fold "structure" of human attentiveness, intelligence, and reasonableness. Again, affirmation and Self-"implementation" of the claims that knowing is "taking a look," that objectivity is equivalent to an attitude of sensitive "extroversion" towards what is "out there," etc., would, strictly speaking, exclude any essential role for the subject's "questions" for intelligence, reasonableness, and deliberation. It would exclude "insight" into the data of sense or consciousness, and her reflective "understanding" of what has been grasped. Finally, it would exclude formulation and judgment of what is understood, etc. But we have seen that the exclusion or distorted institution of these dimensions of human intentional performance introduces the element of dominance into the fifth step of dialectical process. Again, at the limit, it structures the viewpoint of "totalitartian practicality." And the point is that the counter-positions in philosophy, by reflectively mediating and systematizing the institution of that distortion, would vindicate that "viewpoint," and justify what is really the subject's failed or refused Self-pursuit, Self-"knowledge" and "deliberate" Self-enactment.

Again, in a second approximation, the term "counter-position" must be extended from the context of such reflectively mediated affirmations and motivations to **any** conscious activity by the subject which even implicity commits him to such an intentional orientation.[1] On this extended usage of the term, the subjects of examples one to three, above, were at least implicitly "in" counter-positions in step five.

In a further, second approximation, the term "position" must be extended from the reflectively affirmed and implemented attitude of the

_____

[1]This point is contestable, but there is evidence for it. Cf. UB, 229b, 287c–288a, etc.

philosopher, to any activity of the subject which is "genuine" and, therefore, commits him to an attitude of intelligence, reasonableness, responsibility. Thus, the subjects of examples one to three, above, were "in" the "positions" insofar as their performance (1) fell under steps one to four of dialectical process and (2) was subsequent to the "reversal" if it took place. Again, as conceived above, the "counter-positions" in either their reflectively appropriated or pre-reflected forms, "head for their own "reversal" or removal. This is so because the subject's implicit or explicit affirmation or action upon the counter-positions sets them at "internal" and/or "external" "tension" with demands of intelligence and reasonableness.

Still, what is the nature of that variance in its pure form? Are there critical grounds for the affirmation that the counter-positions set up such variances, such tensions and head, in the essential case, for their own "reversal"? And are such "grounds" related to the al-ready mentioned "higher viewpoint on man" which meets the longer cycle of decline, the general bias of common sense in human history? Again, if the transcendental grounds of the dialectical method of the subject can be established, then a "critical viewpoint" on oneself, the other, the totality of human process, the products which stem from it, etc., will have been won. In such a case, then, the general "form," the heu-ristic, anticipatory notion of dialectical process, will have itself been traced back to its "roots" in some essential feature of intention-al process and thus vindicated normatively and not merely empirically.[1]

Let us assume that, in general, there is some such vindication for the "dialectical viewpoint" upon her being and that of her communi-ty in history. But, then the notion of dialectic will have to be ex-panded. Thus expanded, it will include the strategies and techniques which foster: (1) Self-knowledge, authenticity and the unravelling of

---

[1]In Insight XVIII, p. 632c, Lonergan contends that some such empirical evidence is available in the fourth, fifth, and sixth volumes of Arnold Toynbee's A Study of History (New York and London: Oxford University Press, 1933–1962).

their "negations;" (2) the "reversal" of the counter-positions in all
their forms and the "development" of the positions; 3) the recovery of
the dynamic to the intelligent emergent probability of human affairs.[1]

Again, the notion of emergent probability has heuristically conceived the "order" of the totality of world process by working "from"
the anticipations immanent in the intelligent and reasonable procedures
of the contemporary, scientifically differentiated subject. But, then,
in light of the preceding discussions, that "order" must be so construed as to include intelligibilities of a "higher," distinctly"
dialectical" kind, intelligibilities which are not only to be known,
but also to be brought about by a fourth method to his scientifically
mediated performance. Thus, through cogent persuasion, the leadership
of a large corporation might become convinced of the material "inconsistency" between, on the one hand, its monopolistic designs, multi-
national purposes and local political initiatives and, on the other,
what would be intelligent and rational economic policy. But if "real"
reform were to result from that persuasion, then the "dialectic of
human history" has been methodically served. And were such a persuasion accomplished by subjects who had appropriated the full critical
viewpoint of their own intentionality and construed the situation
historically in that light, then the dialectic has been served and

---

[1]Two points should be made here.

First, such techniques will represent specializations of the
method of eliciting from the other her blind-spots, her failures or
refusals to understand (cf. I, 559a). Such a method is not "exercised
after the fashion of a steam-roller . . . but through [bringing out and
heightening] a mounting dialectical tension that makes absurdity ever
more evidently absurd . . ." (I, 526b).

Secondly, there is a general methodological point. Thus, all
other things being equal, one may legitimately argue from the decline
of the good of order to the inauthenticity of the subject(s) involved
and from the prospering of the good of order to the authenticity of the
subject or her community. On the other hand, one may argue, conversely, from the inauthenticity of the subject to the gradual distortion of
the given situation and from the genuineness of the subject or her community to the prospering of the dynamic good of order. In the former
case the argument is in the order of discovery. In the latter, the
order of explanation.

taken up in the fullest possible sense. Again, the subject's discovery of dialectical method, of the correlative "dialectical structure" of human world process represents the "reversal" of her failure or refusal "critically" to understand and "implement" her own and/or her community's being in history. Again, her discovery exemplifies the dialectical structure she has "uncovered."

Finally, if human being falls within the dynamic of emergent probability, then the dialectical intelligibility of its process ought to manifest the potency, form, act categories characteristic of proportionate Being in general and it ought, therefore, to be isomorphic with the "experience," "understanding," "judgment" structure of human intentional process. Again, as said, human "development" takes place "on," minimally, the organic, sensitive, intellectual-rational, and moral levels. It initiates and sustains the development of human society, culture, science, art, philosophy, etc. But, "genetic" method is relevant to understanding, say, human intellectual or moral development. And the latter's intelligibility consists: (1) potentially in the incompleteness of form and/or content of its earlier stages of development; (2) formally in the sequence of "operators" that would replace "generic incompleteness with specific perfection," i.e., in the human context, the operator will coincide with the "wonder" with which we associate further relevant questions; (3) actually, in the attainment of that perfection, i.e., in the human context, this will be that higher level of intellectual and/or moral functioning.

But "dialectical" method is similarly relevant to understanding and/or implementing human process. The latter's intelligibility consists: (1) potentially in the failures/refusals of either the subject, her community, or the institutions/skills grounded thereupon, etc., to be consistently intelligent, reasonable, and responsible;[1] (2) formally in the "the inner and outer tensions by which such failures and refusals bring about either the choice of their own reversal or the

---

[1]But, in the general case, this corresponds to the "data" of the dialectical subject. Cf. (1) in the "Introduction" of this chapter section.

elimination of those that obstinately refuse the reversal;"[1] (3) _act-_
ually in the consequent "removal" of the failures and refusals, the
fruits to which they had given birth.[2]

---

[1]But, in the general case, this corresponds to the "understanding" of the dialectical subject. Cf. (3) in the "Introduction" of this
chapter section. Again, the "tension" referred to here can be merely
spontaneous and non-conscious _or_ reflectively, methodically, and strategically brought out and exploited.

[2]But, in the general case, this corresponds to the verified
understanding, to the judgment or rational action of the dialectical
subject. Cf. (2) in the "Introduction" of this chapter section. The
reader should note that (3) is already implicit but unreflected upon in
(2).

C. Concluding Remarks

In conclusion, we would make four general points.

First, this chapter has reconstructed Lonergan's reflections upon the scientific pattern of human subjectivity in the contemporary stage of its development. Thus, after specifying the "horizon" of the mathematical subject, its similarities and differences from its empirically scientific counterpart were interpreted. Then, the "subject"-pole of the latter horizon was determined to be a "general empirical method." That method was specified, initially, in terms of the complementary classical and statistical heuristic structures of the subject. It was specified subsequently in a more differentiated but equivalent fashion in terms of the four-fold battery of empirical methods. On the basis of these analyses, the "object"-pole of the "horizon" of the empirical, scientific subject was determined to be that of an "emergent probability." And the latter notion was expanded to include things, their genera and species, as well as schemes of recurrence, etc. Again, since the empirically methodic subject corresponding to the "subject"-pole of the previous reflections, is herSelf only a late and lately educated emergent <u>within</u> surrounding world process, the "Horizon" of contemporary science may be <u>equated</u> with that of "Emergent Probability." Granted this, the nature of human Being can be defined heuristically in terms of the generic and specific differentiations this horizon admits. Thus, human consciousness and the attitudes and patterns which it engages, etc., fall within the dynamic of emergent process. As such, their subject is, properly a "'thing'-subject." It is <u>differentiable</u> by intelligence, reasonableness, and responsibility. It admits <u>full</u> definition in terms of an interlocking sextet of layers of explanatory conjugates, etc. Again, the development as well as the dialectic of the scientific, dramatic, practical, or philosophic subject (and/or of her community) must be construed as consequents, as interior, intelligent differentiations within the larger intelligibility of the process of emergent probability, generally. They must themselves be interpreted, therefore, as possible themes for study in terms of the four-fold battery of scientific methods, specifically. Thus, genetic and dialectical methods as well as the notion of emergent probability may be employed to understand the social development of a given individual or community. And this could be so even in the case in which the individual (or her community) has not developed beyond the limits of common sense and, therefore, lacks the ability immediately to fathom or to apply the fruits of these methods or their implicit notions.

Secondly, by starting from the five-fold determination of the "formal viewpoint" of the subject of common sense (cf. Chapter III, Sections A4 and B4, above), and making the necessary changes, the "formal viewpoint" and, ultimately, the "horizon" of human science can be further defined. Thus, the latter field, can be specified in terms of:

(1) its intended situation of the potential totality of the things affirmed by their relations to **each other**;

(2) its explicit methodological openness to **all** of the further relevant questions, etc.;

(3) the fully **explanatory**, and non-descriptive context within which it intends to cast its "objects;"

(4) that "section" within the universe of Being affirmed or to be affirmed by the intelligent and reasonable judgments of the unbiased subject of classical, statistical, genetic, or dialectical methods;

(5) the specific totality of "objects" upon which these methods "open out" at any given "place" and "time." The specific totality will correspond to the specific groups of questions which the scientific subject has learned or is learning to ask and answer and the specific sets of kinds instruments necessary to raise or apply them. These groups of questions will reflect some stage in the development of scientific knowledge. Thus, specific totalities within the "field" emerge and become increasingly differentiated through a self-correcting process that is "with" others and set within a historical tradition, a historical vector of meaning.

Thirdly, if it was earlier noted that her judgments are merely probable, a brief reflection on the empirically scientific subject's criterion for pronouncing such judgments must be included in the conclusion of the remarks of this chapter.

First, then, the "proximate" criterion of her judgments of fact is her "reflective grasp of the [virtually] unconditioned." And because the "content" of such judgments is unconditioned "it is independent of the judging subject" (I, 549d; cf. Chapter VI, Section 5, below, and the notion of "absolute objectivity").

But, secondly, in the concrete, the subject's reflective understanding is:

> itself conditioned by the occurrence of other cognitional acts; and while the content of the judgment is grasped as unconditioned, still the content either demands or rests on the contents of experiences, insights, and other judgments for its full clarification. The concrete inevitability of a context of other acts and a context of other contents is what necessitates the addition of a **remote** to a proximate criterion of truth (I, 550b, emphasis mine).

This remote criterion Lonergan identifies as:

> the proper unfolding of the detached and disinterested desire to know. In negative terms it is the **absence of interference from other desires that inhibit or reinforce and in either case distort the guidance given by the pure desire** (I, 550c, emphases mine).

Thus, even as the subject can learn to grasp that all the relevant questions are answered, that her content, therefore, "coincides" with the virtually unconditioned, so is she, in fact, able to grasp when it is "closing in upon" the virtually unconditioned through successive approximations. But such judgments as well as their underlying process of Self-correction and approximation, characterize the subject's performance throughout the four-fold unity of her scientific method.

Finally, the preceding discussion in its entirety, is written from the attitude of a **reflection** upon the already highly differentiated scientific performance of the subject. Further, at each crucial point, it either discovers or expands upon the discovery that human science represents a specific _further_ differentiation upon the tri-leveled structure of human intentional consciousness. But the achievement of such an attitude, transcends the attitude of mere natural science which it analyzes. Again, such an achievement opens the possibility of the subject's reflectively and critically mediated performance.[1] Finally, it presupposes and implies the explicit, reflective turning of the subject's scientifically differentiated intelligence and reasonableness to knowing **herSelf**.[2]

---

[1]Cf. Chapter VII, below.

[2]Cf. The "grounding" of such a "turning" effected in Chapter VI, below.

THE INTELLECTUAL PATTERN OF EXPERIENCE:

THE PHILOSOPHICAL DIFFERENTIATION—

FROM SELF-UNDERSTANDING TO METAPHYSICALLY

MEDIATED SELF-KNOWLEDGE

Introduction

In the preceding chapter, this study has interpreted Lonergan's reflective turn towards the scientifically patterned performance of the subject. It has brought out the global explanatory context to which such performance has compelled him to advance. And it has interpreted this turn and the context it achieves as the harvest of his search for a critically grounded and authentic Self-understanding. But the question advancing this search can, on the one hand, become an issue for the genuine, if still pre-reflective, subject simply because he would know and Self-consciously appropriate the nature of his own conscious being. It may and usually does, on the other hand, actually become an issue under different circumstances.

Thus, the consciousness of the adult was confined for the time of infancy to a world of immediacy. Still, the variable, differentiated consciousness of the mature subject can be decisively shifted away from its meaning-mediated scientific world. And this shift can be towards the undifferentiated "horizon" by which it was in infancy bound. Such a shift displaces the "horizon" in terms of which "objects" are given to the subject. And it simultaneously displaces the "horizon" through which he becomes present to or gains a sense of himSelf.

Thus, it is possible to thematize a first "downward" shift out of the scientific attitude and its community into that of "common sense." In it, the subject's presence to himSelf will be re-focused by the role

identifications, the skill and practical wisdom repertoires, the dramatic motifs, etc., which center his sensitively or intelligently motivated insertion in a "world" mediated by common sense meanings. In a
second "downward" shift, his presence to himSelf could be focused by
the quasi—instinctive, sensori—motor routines which orient his insertion in a "world" of "bodies" which are "already—out—there." Thus, he
will be present to himSelf as the em—"bodied" center of power, Self-
satisfaction, and perception which, in Chapter I, has been identified
with the extroverted, biological subject.

But against the latter background, the cognitional Self-presence
of the subject can only stand forth as a cold and insipid abstraction
to which, perhaps, a naive and impractical past was once given over.
Again, it might present itself as the theme for the counter—dialectical
efforts of the so—disposed cultural representatives of the community.[1]
Still, there is an intentionality operative. It runs counter to these
shifts, the counter—dialectics they might involve, the sense of bewilderment, disorientation, and purposelessness they would suppress in the
face of the **question** of the meaning of one's own Being. This intentionality, then, is equivalent to the pure desire to know, learn, and
act responsibly. It is the latter which bears the infant from the
"world of immediacy" **towards** the local and then expanding common sense
meanings and activities of his group. It is the latter which carries
the young adult **towards** the meaning—mediated scientific "world," and
then into the patterns of recurring Self-transcendence which makes the
dynamic to this intentionality effective.

But his presence to himSelf in his recurring Self-transcendence
will bring out and deepen his awareness of the integrity of the intentionally structured center of his cognitional performance. It will
bring out and deepen its unassimilability to the forms of Self-presence
and/or Self-"understanding" corresponding to his biological and/or

---

[1]The negative side of the counter—dialectic, then, would join
artists, human "scientists," literary critics, politicians, philosophers, etc., in the effort to "de-construct," to "put out of play" the
scientific attitude of the subject in its full significance. Its positive side would involve their bringing to the fore and implementing

sensitively attached modes of insertion within the surrounding "world." But the latter awareness may crystalize in the inverse revelation and affirmation that the Self which one thought one "knew" one, literally, does not. Then, the stage is set from within a dialectical perspective for the explicit raising and critical pursuit of the question "What exactly does it mean to be human?" The adult human subject, then, can withdraw into the biological pattern. Still, a feline can neither raise nor answer either the above question or those which cut across, for example, the patterns of his common sense and scientific development. Thus, there is a surplus of essential meaning over the biological implicit in the engagement of these patterns which mediates and implies the subject's differentiated being. And it is for this reason that this study has been gathering Lonergan's reflective revelation of the tri-levelled cognitional "structure" which, minimally, underlies them both.[1] With respect to the full scientific differentiation of that basic structure, Lonergan has effected a series of expansions upon an initial set of reflections. Thus, reflecting upon the second level of his scientifically patterned performance, Lonergan has singled out, drawn implication from, and affirmed, not only the fact but also the various modalities to the occurrence of human understanding. Thus, he has, first, differentiated, analyzed, and related a set of four heuristic notions, structures, and their corresponding "objective" processes. Secondly, he has articulated and specified the "grounds" of the notion of the "thing." Thirdly, he has worked out, analyzed, and set out the implications of the notion of "emergent probability." Fourthly, Lonergan has not only worked out and analyzed these notions, but affirmed their "relative invariance." But this is tantamount to a "minor" Self-affirmation. Fifthly, he has transposed the already accomplished

---

some variant upon the Self-interpretation informing the biological horizon of the subject or its common sense extension. The intended upshot of the two-sided effort? The communal shift and displacement of the Self-understanding of the community, of its members, of the actions that would follow from it.

[1] The reader should again note that this pursuit pertains to the second level of human consciousness.

reflections upon the consciousness of the human subject into the heuristic, but global explanatory perspective upon world-process which these notions make possible.

First, then, reflecting upon the performance of the scientific subject, Lonergan discovered the occurrence of direct and inverse insights in both the static and dynamic data contexts of their emergence. He allowed this discovery to structure a set of parallel, four-fold divisions. Thus, he worked out the four basic heuristic notions the respective occurrences of these insights fulfill. He went on to work out the four kinds of data process which the preceding division implies. Finally, corresponding to the four parallel lines of pre-understanding and data process, he worked out a four-fold differentiation of the basic, tri-levelled cognitional structure of the scientific subject.[1] Thus, the scientific subject's:

> anticipation of a constant system to be discovered [e.g., of a direct insight in a static context] grounds [e.g., establishes the data-conditions for his use of] classical method; . . . [his] anticipation of an intelligibly related sequence of systems [e.g., of direct insight in a dynamic context] grounds [e.g., establishes the data-conditions for his use of] genetic method; . . . [his] anticipation that the data will not conform to system [e.g., of inverse insight in a static context] grounds [e.g., establishes the conditions for his use of] statistical method; and . . . [his] anticipation that the successive stages of changing system will not be directly intelligible [e.g., of inverse insight in a dynamic context] grounds [e.g., establishes the data-conditions for use of] dialectical method (I, 485b, emphases mine).

But, any static data context must either "conform or not conform to system." Again, successive sets of data which do so conform "must be either related or not related in a directly intelligible manner" (I, 485d). Any set of data, therefore, must either so conform or not, be or not be so related. It must, then, either sustain or fail to sustain the relations characteristic of either systematic or dynamic processes. Thus, any set of data he will confront will sustain at least one of the heuristic anticipations underlying the four-fold differentiation of the

---

[1]Our interpretation of these four, relatively parallel lines of analysis is set forth in Chapter V, Sections B3, 5, 9, and 10.

basic method of the subject. Thus, the statistical subject gathers direct insights into the ideal frequencies of non-systematic process from which his limited classical viewpoint abstracts. The genetic subject gathers direct insights into the linked operators of dynamic system from which his limited classical and statistical viewpoints separately abstract. The dialectical subject gathers direct insights into the actual or possible forms or strategies for reversal from which his limited genetic viewpoint abstracts. Thus, the mode of understand-ing associated with each successive method of the subject represents his transcendence of the "limitations" inherent in its predecessor. But, then, the four, method-mediated modes of his understanding, taken together:

> are relevant to any field of data; they do not dictate what data must be; they are able to cope with data no matter what they may prove to be (I, 485b, emphases mine).

Secondly, in the course of further reflections, Lonergan discov-ered the occurrence of the "further and distinct type of understanding" by which the subject "grasps unities, identities, wholes."[1] He discov-ered that without such acts of understanding, the scientific subject can neither discover, verify, nor apply the "general systems and struc-tures" upon which the four-fold understanding of his methodologically guided performance terminates. Finally, he allowed these discoveries to structure his heuristic account of the subject's notion of a thing. But since such general systems and structures "are concerned with the properties of things," Lonergan has drawn the remarkable conclusion that always and everywhere:

> properties and things are what is to be known by [the subject's] understanding [of] the same data by different but complementary procedures (I, 485b, emphases mine).

Thirdly, Lonergan discovered the "complementarity" of the in-sights underlying his inevitable use of both classical and statistical methods to completely understand any field of data. He used this discovery to structure the heuristic notion of the "emergent probabili-ty" of the order of events he understands.[2] He used it to frame the

---

[1] Cf. Chapter VIII, Section B8, above.

[2] Cf. Chapter V, Sections B6-7, above.

heuristic notion of the "higher viewpoint" structure of his inquiring.[1]
Again, he employed it to outline the genera-species structure upon
which the "distinct and autonomous" sciences of modern scientific inquiry converge.[2] Finally, he used it to set forth "a generalized emergent probability for both things and events [e.g., for both things and
the properties thereof] . . ." (I, 485d-486a, emphases mine).[3]

But, fourthly, Lonergan argues from the universal relevance,
inevitable use, relative completeness and invariance of the structurally linked notions recalled in the preceding three paragraphs, to justify the "minor" Self-affirmation of the subject. His claim is that,
collectively, these notions represent and outline in advance, the
structural possibilities inherent in any of the scientific subject's
efforts at or achievements in understanding. Thus, they determine the
possible formal components of the objective "field" of the scientific
subject's "horizon." Finally, then, his claim is that they do this
irrespective of the character, subject matter, place or time of the
data in question.[4]

Fifthly, Lonergan allows the relatively invariant anticipations
recalled and affirmed in the preceding four paragraphs, to structure
the conception and implementation of a non-reductionistic, global,
explanatory context of surrounding world-process. He shows that this
context is adequate to integrate the results of the modern specializations of the scientific pursuit.[5] Again, he has allowed these anticipations to structure the transposition of his reflectively gathered

---

[1]Cf. Chapter V, Section B7, above.

[2]Cf. Chapter V, Section B8, Subsections c-e.

[3]Cf. Chapter V, Section B8, Subsections c-e.

[4]On our understanding of Lonergan, then, there is a "minor" Self-
affirmation involved in the subject's discovery and affirmation of the
relatively invariant forms of "understanding" to which his scientific
knowing of anything commits him. The "major" Self-affirmation of the
subject is accomplished and explicated in the ensuing paragraphs of
this chapter.

[5]Cf. Chapter V, especially Sections 6-7, and 8c-e.

Self-interpretation as an incarnate but polymorphically structured openness towards the world, of the full subjective pole of his common sense and scientific horizons, into the latter, minimally, six-tiered explanatory context.[1] He has allowed it to structure his understanding of his incarnate but intentional insertion within the world as conditional upon the fulfillment of lower, stratified, but non-consciously operative factors.

Lonergan has affirmed, then, a quadrate of notions penetrating his four-fold differentiation of methods; the notions of the thing, emergent probability, explanatory genera and species; a generalized "framework" for understanding himSelf, etc. And he has affirmed that they represent the unavoidable consequence of the fact of his scientific performance. But the question of whether he is a knower and not merely of what it means for him to know remains to be asked.[2] Again, such a question must be answered in the affirmative if the preceding affirmations are to find their adequate grounds and their ultimate "basis" in the Being of the subject. Thus, the subject's pursuit of critically grounded Self-understanding has led him by stages and inevitably to his raising of the questions "Am I a knower?" And it is to the answering of this question and to the discovery, in the context of all that has preceded, of what the content to such an answering entails that this study must now turn.

Lonergan resolves to determine whether the subject actually makes particular judgments which are, in fact, correct. In Chapter XI of Insight, he approaches an answer by raising a relevant question for reflection, pursuing it to the point of the grasp of the virtually unconditioned, and, finally, "making one." But the question Lonergan selects to approach his answer, asks whether the cognitional Self-understanding, won by reflecting on the the issue of what the subject's, what his own humanness means, is so. And, as it will turn out, the answer to the question "Am I a knower?" will not only be existentially

---

[1]Cf. Chapter V, Section 8e.

[2]The reader should note that this question arises on the third level of human consciousness. Again, it heads for the "major" Self-affirmation of the subject brought out in Sections 1-3, below.

crucial. It will also be central to the subject's reflective recognition, affirmation, and unfolding of his at least implicitly operative notions of Being, objectivity, metaphysics, value, "Mystery," himSelf. In Section 3 of this chapter, then, we explicate Lonergan's rendering of the "'Self'-affirmation" of the subject. In Sections 1 and 2, we set forth, respectively, its "conditioned" and its "conditions." Then, Lonergan's successive "expansions" upon the fact of Self-affirmation are interpreted in a set of eight further sections. In Sections 4 and 5, the subject's implicit notions of "Being" and "objectivity" are brought out. In Section 6 the "positions" and "counter-positions" implicit in his cognition as well as his notions of Being and objectivity, are clarified. In Section 7, the "notion" of a critically grounded metaphysics is laid out. In Section 8, a method for filling in this notion is first specified and, then, implemented. In Sections 9 and 10, the implications of, respectively, Being's "intelligibility" and human Being's metaphysical nature and "Spiritual" intelligibility are brought out. Finally, in Section 11, the relevance and nature of the subject's symbolic forms, the sense of "Mystery" which they imply and presuppose, are taken up in the context of the issues raised in Sections 1 to 10.

A. Outline and Analysis of the Project

1. "Conditioned" of the Self-Affirmation of the Subject

In the introductory section to Chapter XI of Insight, Lonergan sets forth the conditioned or the derived content of his prospective Self-affirmation. It consists in the proposition "I am a knower."[1]

2. "Conditions" of the Self-Affirmation of the Subject

In the same section, Lonergan goes on to specify the set of Self-referential conditions of this proposition. They are to be fulfilled by the subject's reflection upon the data field of his own consciousness.[2] Again, these conditions warrant his claim to the title set forth in the conditioned. But "I am a knower" just in case "I am a concrete and intelligible unity-identity-whole" implicitly defined and, hence, differentiated by, minimally, a tri-levelled intentional dynamic. This dynamic comprises constituent conscious acts of:

A. sensing, perceiving, imagining, etc. These will be referred to, in brief, as acts of "experiencing;"[3]

B. "what?" or "why?"-asking, etc., inquiry, understanding, formulating, etc. These will be referred to, in brief, as acts of "intelligent grasp;"

C. "is it so?" or "is it?"-questioning, etc., reflecting, grasping the unconditioned, judging, etc. These will be referred to, in brief, as acts of "reasonable affirmation" and "denial."[4]

---

[1] Cf. Insight, p. 319d.

[2] Ibid. Since all the relevant conditions for this affirmation fall within the subject's actual experiential province, the prospective judgment would be "immanently generated" (cf. I, 705b, 706a; cf. 704d).

[3] The subject's capacity to perform acts on this level presupposes his incarnation. This presupposition neither explains that incarnation nor vitiates the fact that incarnate "things" of the kind under consideration are, in fact, minimally differentiated by their performance of acts described by conditions A through C of this section.

[4] Three brief points must be made here.

3. Self-Affirmation—Breakthrough

In Insight, Chapter XI.1-.2, Lonergan takes up the issue of whether the reflectively accessible conditions of his Self-affirmation, conditions set forth in Section 2, above, are, in fact, fulfilled.

But, first, "anyone who [simply] asks such a question is merely by virtue of his performance rationally conscious" (I, 328b, emphases mine).

Secondly, the "I" of the subject unifying the tri-levelled manifold to his intentional acts "has a rudimentary meaning [and, therefore, evidence] from consciousness" (I, 328b, emphases mine), would "have to be postulated" did it not (I, 325b).[2]

Thirdly, each human subject can only ask of and answer for himSelf the question whether he sees, hears and imagines. Each can only answer for himSelf whether he asks "What?" or "Why?" in the presence of the relevant experiential data. Each can only ask for himSelf whether he reflects and grasps the virtually unconditioned "if not in other cases, then [at least in] this one."

But the fact of the [subject's] asking and the possibility of . . . [his] answering are themselves the sufficient reason for . . .

First, the "link" which compels the affirmation of the conditioned "just in case" the conditions are fulfilled consists in the fact that by knowing is meant no more than the performance of the operations whose reflective elaboration this study has been recounting. Thus, the ground of the link is the truth of an analytic proposition (cf. I, X.7).

Secondly, conditions A through C, above, "implicitly define" and, hence, "differentiate" the activity of the human subject as distinctively human. Cf. Chapter V, Section B8e, above. The details of this fact of implicit definition are systematically worked out in Appendix I at the end of this chapter.

Finally, we will have occasion to refer to the conditions A through C, specified in Section 2, above, in several of the ensuing contexts.

[2]Cf. presupposition #8, in the Introduction to Chapter V, Section B8, above. Also cf. Chapter V, subsection B8a and, especially, its footnotes for reflective determination of the "I" of the subject's intentional operations.

[his] affirmative answer [to the above question] (I, 328b).[1]

Fourthly, because it posits a conditioned whose conditions happen, in fact, to be fulfilled, the subject's cognitional Self-affirmation represents not a necessary but a contingent or contingently necessary claim. But because the subject is indeed a knower in the above defined sense, it is a fact that he makes judgments of fact.

But, fifthly, "if any judgment of fact" is made by the subject, "there must as well occur its conditions [e.g., the unfolding of the unity of his consciousness on the three complementary levels of act set forth in Section 2]" (I, 338b, emphasis mine). Thus, the retortion that insofar as he denies being a knower, he will have had to have fulfilled the conditions for the very claim whose negation he has posited, reduces him, performatively, to either Self-contradiction or silence. The subject who would attempt to undercut, replace, or transcend the point to his judgment of Self-affirmation constructs for himSelf a similarly untenable position. Thus, the further questions of such a subject would lead him to readvert to the immediately accessible data-field of his own consciousness. They would lead him to discover and formulate the terms and relations of a further manner of Self-understanding irreducible to the one set forth above. And reflecting on whether its conditions are fulfilled, he will be led to affirm or deny it. But, then, the process by which he would revise and re-assert his understanding of himSelf will always, therefore, presuppose the very tri-fold structured unity of consciousness which conditions his being a knower in the above defined sense.

Thus, the subject's efforts to undercut, replace, or transcend the latter sense of himSelf must always "contradict" his own intentional performance. They will always defeat themselves. They will always strengthen the evidence for his original claim. Again, the relativist who would assimilate the modality of the cognitional subject's Self-affirmation to that of the always in principle revisible, probable

---

[1] The condition of the subject's asking and answering as well as his reflection is the fact of his consciousness. The notion of the consciousness "of" the subject is taken up in Appendix II of this chapter.

judgments of the scientific subject also contradicts himself performatively. Thus, "every other known becomes known" through the tri-levelled cognitional performance of the subject. But, then, actually to call that performance into question is to throw into question the presupposition of one's own questioning (cf. I, 330c 9–10). It is to impugn the very intentional process which both underlies his knowing of any and every other known and which also conditions the revision of any and every other one of his empirical claims.

Thus, his engagement of the scientific attitude commits the subject, to a potentially infinite process of Self–correction and, hence, revision in his empirical judgments. But such a process, is "grounded" in, and is to be explained by reference to the unrevisable intentional fact that he is a knower in the defined sense. Thus, "revision cannot [therefore] revise its own presuppositions" (I, 336a) without turning "(s)elf–destructive" (I, 330c). And it is only subsequent to his reflective inquiry into, understanding of, and appropriation of this fact that the relativist has the proper grounds for knowing it.

Finally, the point to the preceding three arguments has been to advance the status of the subject's cognitional Self–affirmation from that of a conditional to a "performative" necessity. It has been to bring out its inherent unrevisability and certainty. And it has been to clarify its difference from the merely probable, scientific and common sense affirmations of the subject.[1]

Sixthly, Lonergan is not arguing that the content of the subject's Self–affirmation is immune to the "possibility of . . . minor revision." He is not arguing against revisions that leave the "basic lines" of his incipient Self–knowledge intact but:

> attain a greater exactitude and a greater fullness of [reflective] detail . . . . What is excluded is the radical revision [of the cognitional subject's rationally affirmed Self–understanding. What is excluded is one] that involves [a major] shift in the fundamental terms and relations of the explanatory account of the human knowledge underlying [the] existing common sense, mathematics and empirical science [of the subject] (I, 335b, emphases mine).

---

[1]The content of the subject's Self–affirmation, then, is an "analytic principle" (cf. I, 306e ff).

Thus, the subject's ascent to a higher viewpoint in, say, physics[1] presupposes, can only go forward within "the framework of [the empirically conditioned][2] inquiry[3] and reflection"[4] whose "basic lines" have already been sketched and affirmed. Still, his reflective discovery and critical affirmation of the invariant "basic lines" of his own intentional dynamic is simultaneously his realization that there could not be: "any possible higher viewpoint" which: "goes beyond that [basic] framework itself, and replaces [his data-conditioned] intelligent inquiry and critical reflection by some surrogate" (I, 394a).

But, seventhly, the defining conditions of the subject's Self-affirmation are expressed in and presupposed by points A through C in Section 2, above. They capture the invariant structure to the triadic cycle repeatedly initiated, concluded, and re-initiated by the subject's data-motivated questions for intelligence and reflection, by the operators of the subject's cognitional development. But under its dynamic aspect, this triadically structured cycle is identical to the pure desire of the subject to know.[5] And if this is true, then the subject's cognitional Self-affirmation is identical to his Self-affirmation of his desire in its purity. It is the incipient fruit of the turn of the subject's desire towards Self-knowledge. Thus, the pure desire of the subject is simultaneously:

> a constituent element both of [the Self that does] the affirming [in his Self-affirmation] and of the Self that is affirmed [therein] (I, 374b).

---

[1]This phrase could be reformulated in the terms of Thomas Kuhn as follows: "Thus, the subject's initiation of a revolutionary phase in the history of normal, physical scientific development . . . ."

[2]Cf. condition A, specified in Section 2, above.

[3]Cf. condition B, specified in Section 2, above.

[4]Cf. condition C, specified in Section 2, above.

[5]Lonergan speaks, not only of the pure desire (cf. I, 532c), but also and, by implication, the genuineness (cf. I, 624b) of the subject as the operator of his cognitional, his full intentional development.

Thus, under the aspect of its "finality," the subject's reflectively grounded cognitional Self-affirmation is the Self-affirmation of his desire to know.

Eighthly, and finally, this Self-affirmation represents the subject's **departure** from and **negation** of the naive, pre-reflective, or merely descriptive forms of Self-understanding implicit in, for example, his sensitive and/or common sense attitudes towards the surrounding world.[1] It represents his **breakthrough** into a critically grounded if still incipient Self-knowledge.[2]

---

[1]In Insight, I.1, Lonergan uses the image of Archimedes' solution to King Hiero's problem of the votive crown to set down five determinations of the insight that informed his discovery. Insight, then, is said to "come as a release to the tension of inquiry," to "come suddenly and unexpectedly," etc. But if these determinations mark off in broad but useful terms the general field of Lonergan's reflections, they are "merely" descriptive in character.

[2]Appendix III, below, briefly compares aspects of Lonergan's "argument" as set forth in Section 3, above, and Kant's attempts to "deduce" his table of the categories of the understanding.

4. The Notion of Being—Encirclement

In _Insight_, Chapter XII, Lonergan brings out the notion of Being implicit in the subject's always already operative but now critically affirmed pure desire to know. The essence of his reflections can be reduced to the following three steps. _First_, then, it involves an explication of the incarnate subject's pure desire. _Secondly_, it includes the identification of the "term" or the total and basic "horizon" of her desire with Being. _Thirdly_, it involves the identification of the subject's pure desire under its _heuristic_ aspect with her notion of Being.[1]

---

[1]_First_, it must be pointed out that the subject's Self-affirmation represents, minimally, her discovery, appropriation, and grounding of the basic, tri-fold structure which, in its general outlines, commonly informs, for instance, the common sense, mathematical, and scientific patterns of her advancing performance. Still, if we regard her Self-affirmation under the aspect of its ontological and objective and not merely its performative significance for the subject, then the issue becomes more difficult. Thus, the performance of the mathematical subject in the intellectual pattern only intends and, to some extent reaches possible or intentional "entities." On the other hand, if the performance of the common sense subject truly "reaches" the things, she knows them not as they are in themselves, but only in their relations to and bearing upon her everyday purposes and concerns. Thus, it is only the intellectual subject of the scientific pattern, taking her start from the data of sense or consciousness, who intends and, to some extent, actually and objectively knows the things themselves, the things in their relations to each other. Thus, under the aspect of its full ontological and objective significance, the Self-affirmation of the subject both presupposes and implies the intellectually patterned performance and experience of the scientific subject. And it was for this reason that Lonergan was at such great pains in _Insight_ to articulate a scientific "Canon of Selection" (_I_, 71b-74b). It was why he insisted on bringing out the "Dissimilarities" of mathematical and scientific insights (cf. _I_, 34c-35c, the "Empirical Notion" of the subject discussed in Chapter II, above), etc., etc. Still, if this correctly represents the intent of Lonergan's position in _Insight_, he is not always so clear. Thus, for example, the locution of _Insight_, p. 385b 9-11, may prove confusing to the reader since the mathematical subject is in the intellectual pattern (cf. _I_, 186a 2-4) but does not know real Being, etc., etc. To avoid confusion, then, let us introduce the notion of experiential "motivation." Thus, the intellectually patterned performance of the subject will be so motivated when it "takes its start from" and "finds it fulfilling conditions in" the concrete data of _sense_ or

First, then, the pure desire of the subject can be identified with the primordial "wonder," the primordial question which "Aristotle described as the beginning of all science and philosophy" (I, 356c). It is the desire whose internal differentiation has resulted in the specialized departments and intelligent inquirers of the modern sciences and arts. But it is her pure desire which underpins and penetrates the experiential component of the subject's (duly specialized) intentionality, thus promoting it to a fully "human" level. Thus, only insofar as the subject is "wondering about the data, trying to understand them," that her "experience ceases to be merely experienced" (UB, 186a). Only then is it withdrawn from the biologically patterned circuit of her sensitive living to become the possible spring for her inquiry and the object of her eventual insight. And it is the same desire, dipping even below the threshold of her thematic conscious life, which, under the appropriate conditions, screens and "selects the data for the [relevant] insight [of the subject]" (I, 356c). Similarly, it is through the dynamic manifested in the verbal utterance of, for instance, her "What?" and "Why?" that the subject transcends the data in pursuit of its formally intelligible content. And it is through it that she discerns whether this content has been adequately uncovered and formulated. Thus, this dynamic effects the subject's transcendence of the data as well as her advance beyond insight into the phantasm to the abstract and, then, the concrete universal which formulates it.[1] Again, this dynamic effects the subject's self-correcting advance towards and ultimate grasp of what is. And

---

consciousness. Furthermore, in "Insight Revisited," Lonergan modifies the possibly misleading formulations of Insight along lines I have been indicating (C2, 274b). Finally, this study would argue that when the subject of mathematics or common sense meets the relevant exigences of her proof or situation, that she is normatively and absolutely objective in an analogous sense even if her performance only takes its start from an image or symbolism in the first case, and is not intellectually patterned in the second, even if it only reaches possible Being in the first case and Being in its relations to us in the second.

[1]For clarification of the difference between the abstract and concrete universal, between the, respectively, formal and total processes of abstraction through which they are reached, see Understanding and Being, pp. 206–7, 186–7, 204a, 209b.

precisely as doing so, the subject's desire <u>underpins</u> and <u>penetrates</u> the **conceptual** component of her advancing cognition.

Similarly, it is through the dynamic manifested in the verbal utterance of, for instance, her "Is it so?" and "Is it?" that the subject heuristically transcends the conditioned concept of her intelligence in pursuit of the virtually <u>unconditioned</u>. It is through it that she engages the criterion by which she will discern whether the experiential conditions for her positing of the conditioned are, in fact, fulfilled. Thus, this dynamic effects the subject's transcendence of the concept as the mere object of thought. Again, it effects her advance from its intelligent grasp to the critical affirmation and, hence, positing of its unconditioned content. And precisely as doing so, the subject's desire <u>underpins</u> and <u>penetrates</u> the **rational** component of her advancing cognition.

Finally, even if a "complete increment [of the subject's] knowing occurs only in [such a rational] judgment" (I, 350a), <u>further</u> questions arise. And it is through the dynamic manifested in the verbal utterance of her further relevant questions for intelligence <u>and</u> reflection that the subject <u>transcends</u> **any** particular and, hence, partial increment to her advancing cognition. It is only through this dynamic that she reaches the relatively closed and "complete context(s) of correct judgments" (I, 348c) which define her ability correctly to ask and to answer the relevant, empirically motivated questions in particular fields of knowledge. It is only through this dynamic that she <u>tran-scends</u>, at least in intention, **any** given <u>limited</u> context to her achievement. Thus, further reflection on the same dynamic will compel her recognition that at any point in her cognitional development there is an infinitely great multitude of relevant, similarly motivated questions which remain for her to ask but which she cannot yet ask since she has not yet sufficiently developed intentionally. Again, she may never develop to the point of <u>being able to</u> or <u>wanting</u> to raise such questions even were she able to do so. But even if it always outstrips the level of her intentional development, the pure desire remains **un-restricted**. Thus, the subject can pose to herSelf the question of whether there might not be some "object" which she does not merely <u>in fact</u> not know, but which she **could** not know. Is there an intrinsically unknowable "object." But the fact that she can always raise: "a question about existence with regard to what lies beyond . . . any finite limit [to her actual knowing] . . ." (UB, 181a), both presupposes and implies that she is always already "beyond" any such finite limit which she might or could achieve.

Furthermore, for the subject actually to affirm what lies beyond her desire commits her to a further, performative Self-contradiction. It commits her to: "knowing that the unknowable [e.g., the inherently unintelligible] is" (I, 352c, emphases mine). But the subject can never know this without thereby posing its relationship to and, thereby, establishing its presence within the intentional ambit of her pure desire. She cannot do this, then, without thereby acknowledging its intelligibility in some respect. Thus, merely by the fact that the subject has doubts, she raises questions about her intentional "bounds," which:

> prove(s) that . . . [her pure desire] is [in fact] unrestricted. [For should she] . . . ask whether X might not lie beyond [the] range [of her pure desire], the fact that . . . [she] ask(s) proves that X lies within its range. Or else, if the question is meaningless, incoherent, illegitimate, then X turns out to be the mere nothing that results from aberration in [her] cognitional process (I, 352d, emphases mine).

Thus, the "radical **capacity**" that is the subject's pure desire: "is unrestricted— . . . [and its] **object is everything about everything**" (UB, 181a, emphases mine).

Secondly, the name for the correlative "object" toward which her unrestricted desire "heads" and which is "de se est illimitatum," is Being.[1] But in affirming the identification of her knowing and her knowing of Being, the subject does "not really [have] a free choice." In the first place, should she deny this identification, she "is knowing nothing" (UB, 198c) and thus performatively undercutting the ground for the truth of even her own denial. In the second place, the subject's reflective analysis of her desire-laden cognition of the data, show that she can never completely avoid locutions which performatively

---

[1]Lonergan cites Thomistic parallels to his procedure in Sum. Theol., I, q. 79, a.2; C. Gent., II, 98 (cf. I, 370b).

evidence at least two implicit recognitions. One is that what her questions for intelligence intend by going beyond the data, i.e., "what is." The other is what her ensuing questions for relection intend, that is, what she would actually attain through her grasp and affirmation of the relevant virtually unconditioned, i.e., "that which is." But, in the third place, the subject's actual "attainment of the unconditioned" in her true, data-motivated and, intellectually or intellectually and reflectively patterned judgments reveals that at some point Being has, in fact, been reached, its realm "entered" (cf. I, 378e 11-12). Thus, the subject of such patterns is, in fact, "content" to:

> restrict [herSelf] . . . provisionally, to ask one question at a time, to prescind from other questions while working towards the solution of the issue in hand. From such prescinding, which [heuristically] anticipates [the subject's] negative comparative judgments . . ., there follow restricted inquiries, restricted acts of understanding and conceiving, reflection on such conceptions, and [her] judgments about particular beings and particular domains of (B)eing (I, 642f, emphases mine).

Again, Being in its **distributive** sense[1] can be defined heuristically as the "object" of such judgments. But, in the fourth place, such knowing only knows "something about something." Thus, it represents only an increment which is barely more than an infinitesimal within the potentially unrestricted scope of cognitional process. It represents "a knowing of being" that is not yet "knowing (B)eing" (I, 354b). In its **collective** sense then, Being corresponds to the pure desire of the incarnate subject in its un-restricted sway. Again, it gathers the "horizon" of **whatever** is.[2] Thus, Being may be defined

---

[1]The reader should note that the following two heuristic definitions of Being take their meaning from the achieved reflective attitude of the subject, specify what she would grasp and affirm were she to know Being in its gathering. She should also realize that if: the sources of her meaning are data and images, ideas and concepts, judgments, her pure desire, etc.; her acts of meaning are formal, e.g., acts of defining, full, e.g., acts of reflecting and judging, and instrumental, e.g., acts of expression, etc.; her terms of meaning are the contents corresponding to these acts, then since the ultimate, all-inclusive term of her cognition is Being, then so is the subject's notion of Being (now reflectively appropriated) the "core" of all the "meaning" of the subject, of any human subject.

[2]The reader has, perhaps, noted that the "whatever" in this

heuristically as:

> the ulterior, known unknown objective of the process to the Self-transcendence of the subject. The process takes its start by opening itself to and finding its conditions in the experiential data. It continues to unfold itself on the basis of that start until all and every relevant, meaningful question for intelligence and reflection which this start calls forth and enjoins has been answered. It continues to unfold itself until all the exigences of her pure desire which these questions manifest have been met.[1]

Again, let us start by premissing and, thereby, assuming the "experiential" starting point through which her pure, a priori desire takes its start and is reduced to act. Then, Being can be more briefly defined as:

> the unknown that [the subject's] questioning intends to know, that [her correct] answers partially reveal, that [her further questioning presses on to know more fully (S, 12a) . . . [and that is only known completely when she has reached] the complete set of answers to the complete set of questions (I, 350b);

> the objective [e.g., the correlate] of the [subject's] pure desire to know [e.g., of the totality of her experientially motivated questions] (I, 348b);

> (1) all that is known, and
> (2) all that remains to be known [by the subject] (I, 350b);

> what is to be known by the totality of true judgments (I, 350b);

> whatever is to be known by [the] intelligent grasp and reasonable affirmation [of the subject] (I, 371a, emphasis mine);

> the whole of what [the] intelligence [of the subject] anticipates . . . (I, 372b, emphasis mine), etc.[2]

From these definitions it follows that in addition to being "all inclusive," Being is:

> completely concrete and concretely universal. It is completely concrete; over and above the (B)eing of anything, there is nothing

---

"definition" is vague, that depending upon how it is interpreted, Being will be construed in its distributive or collective sense.

[1]This is our rendering of Lonergan's heuristic notion of Being. It claims to offer a minor clarification of Lonergan's notion by casting it in light of the notion of "experiential motivation."

[2]The point is that although the intent of these "definitions" is relatively plain, they do not begin with an explicit mention of their "experiential motivation."

more to that thing. It is completely universal; apart from the realm of (B)eing, there is simply nothing (I, 350d, emphases mine).

Again, as noted, Lonergan's definition of Being is heuristic in character and, therefore, of:

> the **second order**. Other definitions [determined, for example, by authentic human inquirers in particular sciences, arts, etc.] determine what [actually] is meant [by Being in their particular, respective fields]. But this definition is more remote for it assigns, not what is meant by (B)eing, but how . . . [the] meaning [of (B)eing] is to be determined. It asserts that if . . . [she] wish(es) to know, then . . . [she] wish(es) to know (B)eing; but it does not settle whether . . . [she] know(s) or what . . . [she] know(s), whether . . . [her] wish will be fulfilled or what . . . [she] will know when it is fulfilled (I, 350c, emphases mine).

Finally, to deny any of the above definitions or their corollary, the subject would have to deny at least one of the following: that she is a knower; or the structure of her knowing in its unfolding; or the fact (and/or the unrestricted scope) of her pure desire. But, she cannot do this without performatively contradicting herSelf.

Thirdly, this study has noted examples of Lonergan's use of the transcendental method of determining the general characteristics of a content by reflecting upon the character of the intentional act(s) through which it is or would be given.[1] In this section, we have started from the subject's reflective discovery of the unrestricted character of her desire to know. The move from there was to name and determine the characteristics of the (always already unachieved but intended) "object" of this desire. But, then, his method here is the same and has been used to the same purpose. Thus, Lonergan has been focusing attention on the pure desire under the heuristic aspect of its anticipation of answers to the potential totality of questions which, in its purity, it only raises. And in doing this, he has been implicitly laying bare the subject's always already at least implicitly operative notion of Being. But this notion is equivalent to the notion of the ". . . is" which the dynamic to her questions always already presupposes, employs, and anticipates. It is equivalent to the ". . . is" which it can neither, therefore, deny nor destroy, revise, limit,

---

[1]Consider, for example, our discussions of the four heuristic notions of the scientific subject, the notion of the thing, etc.

transcend, or ground on or from any more primordial or exalted basis.[1]
Thus, in tandem with the pure desire and sensitive starting point of
her intentional life, the subject's always already at least implicitly
operative notion of Being, simultaneously underpins, penetrates, and
transcends each and every limited instance of the "Being" which she
knows or is to know. It outlines and circumscribes in advance a
"Region" within which and with reference to which, whatever is may be
said to be. Thus, since all human subjects inevitably understand and
reflect, since in so doing they necessarily evidence their desire and
its sensitive starting point, the notion of Being is all-pervasive. It
is common to each and every one of them. It is always already spontaneously operative in their conscious lives whether or not they know it.
Being, then, is "latent and operative prior to" any of the subject's
everyday or philosophic reflections, to any concept she might have
formed of it or taken over second hand from the reflections of others.
It is determined by the always already potentially infinite scope to
her "intelligent grasp and reasonable affirmation . . . ." And it is:

> a notion that **cannot** be controverted [by her]; it is assumed in all
> [of her] inquiry and reflection, in all [of her] thought and doubt;
> its acknowledgement is [already] implicit in . . . [her] break-
> through [into incipient Self-knowledge]; and since . . . [this
> notion heuristically] embraces all views [e.g., each and every one
> of the actual, probable, or possible (common sense and) scientific
> viewpoints of the subject] and their objects, its acknowledgement
> [by her] is an **encirclement** (I, 522a, emphases mine).

This encirclement is the subject's reflective staking out and settlement upon what Being can mean. It is her **negation** of, and **departure**
from every and any one of its naive, pre-reflective or merely descriptive senses, e.g., Being grasped and affirmed as already-out-there-now,
as, therefore, an entity, subsistent form, phenomenon, noumenon, etc.[2]

---

[1] Lonergan, it must be noted, makes the interpretive point that
"while . . . [Aquinas] did **not** distinguish explicitly between the . . .
notion of Being and the . . . concept of Being [cf. the paragraph in
the body of this study preceding the last], still he was remarkably
aware of the implications of that distinction" (I, 369c, emphasis
mine). He buttresses his point by setting down five of these in the
five succeeding paragraphs.

[2] Thus, each of the historically constituted meanings of Being

Finally, since the subject's cognitional Self-affirmation can represent her Self-knowledge only inasmuch as "knowing (B)eing . . . [has been] seen to be affirming it . . ." (I, 386a, emphases mine), this settlement is, simultaneously her **departure** from and **exclusion** of every and any naive, pre-reflective, or merely descriptive sense, etc. of what it in fact means for **her** to Be.[1] It is her implicit acknowledgement that the "field" of Being must range over the incarnate subject of the intentional operations by which its meaning was fixed. It is her acknowledgement of the total and basic character, the pure "horizonal" character of the "subject" and "object" embracing "Expanse" it defines.[2]

---

signalled by the preceding string of designations distorts, is in conflict with, the heuristic sense of Being intended by, corresponding to, and, with some frequency reached, by the intellectually converted subject's experientially motivated inquiry and judgment.

[1]This settlement, then, excludes, for example, the primacy of the biological Self-interpretation of the subject in fixing the meaning of Being.

[2]At this moment within the proceeding reflections, the subject implicitly realizes that she always has been within Being, that any level of achieved Self-knowledge which falls short of this affirmation is less than true to itself, to herself. Explicit realization and affirmation must wait for Sections 5-6, below.

5. The Notion of Objectivity

In Chapter XIII of _Insight_, Lonergan lays out the partial and principal notions of objectivity latent in the noetic _performance_ of the, by now, cognitionally and, implicitly, ontologically Self–affirmed subject.

First, then, there is the partial notion of **experiential** objectivity which is provided by the _given_ presupposed by his questions for intelligence and reflection.

> This is _very_ relevant to objectivity, because besides the _given_ there is the merely _imagined_. [The subject does] . . . not have control over the given; [but he can] _imagine_ . . . pretty well what [he] . . . please(s). If this process were simply a matter of understanding what [he] . . . imagine(d), [he] . . . would . . . [never] make mistakes. Insight is _infallible_ with respect to what [he] . . . is imagining. However, what [he] . . . is imagining may not be the same as what there is to be sensed, what can be sensed, what is given. Insight is _per se_ infallible and _per accidens_ makes mistakes. It is infallible because it is insight into what [the subject] . . . imagine(s), and it is _per accidens_ mistaken insofar as what [he] . . . imagine(s) may be very different from what is seen or heard or tasted or smelled or felt (_UB_, 215c–216a).[1]

Experiential objectivity, then, is the _given_ as opposed to what is produced _ad libitum_, what is produced at will. It is the given "from which [the subject] . . . abstract(s) and which [he] . . . adds on to an abstract essence,"] that will "_fulfill conditions_ for the virtually unconditioned [when the latter has ontological import]" (_UB_, 216b, emphases mine).

Secondly, there is the partial notion of **normative** objectivity which arises when "the exigences of [the subject's] . . . intelligence and reasonableness are met" (_C2_, 275a, emphasis mine), when he gives himSelf over completely to the immanent "norms" of his pure desire, the process of Self–development it conditions, the avoidance of all obscurantism (cf. _I_, 380c) it implies.

> [In other words] inquiry, the demand for intelligibility, the demand for the unconditioned, are [_a priori_] norms immanent within [the subject's] . . . cognitional process . . . . Insofar as [he]

---

[1]Cf. _Insight_, p. 407 n, _Verbum_, pp. 175b–176a. Furthermore, Lonergan's _proviso_ should also be kept in mind when the data in question are the data of one's own consciousness.

is meeting those requirements, [he] . . . is <u>objective</u> [in this normative sense]. Insofar as [his] . . . desires or fears or any other factor in [his] . . . makeup are interfering with [his] . . . execution of this process according to its own immanent norms, [his] . . . judgments will be merely <u>subjective</u> (U<u>B</u>, 215a, emphases mine).

But besides his <u>spontaneous</u> correspondence to the immanent, <u>a priori</u> operators, norms, procedures of his mind, there is the subject's reflection upon, formulation and affirmation of their inner exigences. Thus, there can be an "objectification" of these procedures in such principles as those of:

identity, contradiction,[1] sufficient reason and, more fully, in logics and methods. Now these objectifications [and, hence, the demands they make upon the subject's objectivity] are <u>historically</u> conditioned. They can be incomplete or erroneous, and they can be corrected, revised, developed. Consequently, they have to be [repeatedly] scrutinized, checked, verified. But the process . . . [by which the] verification [of these norms advances] appeals . . . to the data of [the subject's] consciousness [pertinent to his] . . . . asking and answering [of experientially motivated] questions (C<u>2</u>, 126c–127a, emphases mine).

<u>Thirdly</u>, there is the partial notion of **absolute** <u>objectivity</u> which "comes [reflectively] to the fore" when the subject makes a true, experientially motivated judgment, when he, thereby:

distinguish(es) sharply between what [he] . . . feel(s), what [he] . . . imagine(s), what [he] . . . think(s), what seems to be so and, on the other hand, what <u>is</u> so (<u>S</u>, 14a, emphasis mine).

Thus, the absolute aspect of objectivity:

[withdraws the content posited by the subject] from relativity to the subject that utters it, the place in which he utters it, the time at which he utters it (<u>I</u>, 378b);

[posits the] "(i)t is" [which] stands for the fulfillment of the [experientially motivated] virtually unconditioned . . .(U<u>B</u>, 212a);

constitutes the entry of . . . [the] knowing [e.g., the cognitional process of the subject] into the realm of (B)eing . . . (<u>I</u>, 378e);

[makes the content posited in that entry, makes "what <u>is</u>"] accessible not only to <u>the</u> knower that utters it but also to **any** other knower (<u>I</u>, 378c, emphases mine);

---

[1]Cf. <u>Insight</u>, p. 381b.

moves [the subject] beyond [his] subjectivity by the mere fact that
. . . [he] reaches the unconditioned. [He] . . . steps into an <u>ab-
solute realm</u>, ... (I)n that realm . . . [the subject] find(s)
not only objects but . . . [himSelf] (<u>UB</u>, 213c, emphases mine).[1]

Thus, if an appropriate virtually unconditioned is:

represented by the syllogism, If X, then Y; but X; therefore Y,
then the major becomes knows through <u>normative</u> objectivity, the
minor becomes known through <u>experiential objectivity</u>, and the virtually unconditioned becomes known [e.g., absolute objectivity is
achieved] when the conclusion is drawn (<u>C</u>2, 275a, emphases mine).

But the major set down in Section 2, above, has become known through
the normative objectivity of the subject's <u>reflective</u> inquiry. The
minor has become known through the experiential objectivity of his
reversion to the data of his own <u>consciousness</u>. The virtually unconditioned became known when he drew the conclusion "<u>Sum</u>!" Thus, the
subject's Self-affirmation is "objective" in an absolute sense. And he
<u>explicitly knows himSelf in</u> the absolute realm of **Being** which his <u>Self</u>-
affirmation reaches "<u>as</u> posited absolutely" (<u>UB</u>, 214a, emphases mine).

<u>Fourthly</u>, the subject's **principal** <u>notion of objectivity</u> is im-
plicit in relevant patterns to his positive and negative comparative
judgments. As such it answers to the philosopher's pseudo-problem of
knowing the "external" world, of establishing a "bridge" between the
consciousness of the subject "in here" and the object "out there now."
On his principal notion, then, an "object" may be designated by any "A,
B, C, D, . . .":

where, in turn, A, B, C, D, . . . are <u>defined</u> by the correctness
[e.g., the absolute objectivity] of . . . [the subject's] set of
[experientially motivated] judgments:
   A is; B is; C is; D is;......
   A is neither B nor C nor D...
   B is neither C nor D nor.....
   C is neither D nor..........(<u>I</u>, 375c).

Thus, if "A" is a knower and properly affirms "B," e.g., a typewriter,
then "B is." And if "A affirms <u>himself</u> as a knower" in the sense

---

[1]Lonergan notes that interpretations of Being or of absolute
objectivity: "in terms of space and time are mere intrusions of the
imagination . . . the unconditioned, as such, says nothing about space
or time" (<u>I</u>, 379e).

explicated in Sections 1 to 3, above, and augmented in Section 4, then "A is" and the "object" whose Being he has posited is a "subject." From here, the explication of the "bare essentials" of the subject's principal notion of objectivity is reflectively concluded:

> if . . . [he] add(s) to the judgments already discussed, viz., I am a knower [e.g., A is], This is a typewriter [e.g., B is], the further judgment that I am not this typewriter [e.g., A and B are, in fact, "within" Being, but A is not, in fact, B] (I, 376a, emphases mine).

Thus, there is objectivity in this reflectively elaborated and precise principal sense "if there are [in fact] distinct beings, some of which know themselves and know others" (I, 377a, emphasis mine). There is objectivity in this sense if the subject spontaneously "heads for" Being in his cognition and if, within that realm, there is to be acknowledged and reflectively elaborated a distinction between "subjects" and "objects."[1]

Finally, then, the four-fold differentiation to his preceding, reflectively purified notion of objectivity, represents the subject's departure from and negation of any naive, pre-reflective or merely descriptive model of objectivity. It is, then, his implicit negation of any such model which is based on:

> the unquestioning orientation of extroverted biological consciousness . . . (I, 385a, emphases mine).

---

[1]On the basis of similar considerations, Lonergan works out a non-Platonic notion of truth as correspondence (cf. I, 552c).

6. Positions/Counter-Positions—Confinement

In Chapter XIV of Insight, Lonergan takes up the **conclusions** to his preceding three reflections. On the one hand, these conclusions have pointed to adequate, performatively "grounded" notions of the subject's knowing, of Being and of objectivity. Their "premiss" has been their consistency with the tri-fold process by which they are affirmed. On the other hand, these conclusions have signified the "linked but opposed" notions which they **negate** and, therefore, force the subject to **depart**. Again, he takes up these conclusions as **foundational** for the philosophic dialogue of the subject, for the socio-historical process of philosophy which his dialogue engages. Thus, Lonergan now stipulates that his formulation will represent a **"basic position"** or **"thesis"** in philosophy if it is consistent with the fact, the critically performative necessity, and the immediate implications of his **Self**-affirmation.

Thus, a formulation is a "basic position" if its subject:

becomes known when . . . [he] affirms [him**Self**] intelligently and reasonably . . .;

[affirms] the real . . . [to be] the concrete universe of (B)eing . . .;

[regards] objectivity . . . as a consequence of intelligent inquiry and critical reflection . . . .

On the other hand, it will represent a "basic **counter**-position" or "**anti**-thesis" in philosophy if it is materially **in**consistent with the fact, the critically performative necessity, and immediate implications of his **Self**-affirmation. A formualtion is a "basic counter-position" if its subject:

becomes known [to him**Self** in some] . . . prior "existential" state;

[affirms] the real . . . [to be] a subdivision of the "already out there now;"

[regards] objectivity . . . as . . . a property of vital anticipation, extroversion, and satisfaction (I, 388a, emphases mine).

It is a counter-position, then, if its subject, thereby:

[performatively] contradicts one or more of the basic positions (I, 388b, emphasis mine).[1]

But first it must be noted that the formulation, clarification, and affirmation of the antithetically "positional" and "counter-positional" formulations of the subject have taken as their respective fields of data the mutually exclusive "intellectual" and "biological" patterns to his experience.

First, then, it is incorrect to assert either that these positional and counter-positional formulations are purely logical alternatives "of which one is simply true and the other . . . utterly false," or that the ground of the opposition is merely formal. Rather, these formulations, if performatively exclusive, are both, within their proper limits correct. The ground of their opposition, far from being "merely" formal, is the conscious and, therefore, heightened "unity-in-tension that is man" (I, 385b, emphases mine). It is the linked but factually opposed "sensitive" and "intellectual" spontaneities whose interaction is both constitutive of the "polymorphism" of human consciousness and, when properly understood, explicative of its decline and development.[2]

Secondly, the reflective analysis, formulation and affirmation of his biologically truncated subjectivity exceed the capabilities of subjectivity so patterned. Again, the subject of the biological pattern is unable to account himSelf of the conditions of his own claims to Self-knowledge. Thus, his performance and his formulation of the basic issues cannot be accounted philosophically "foundational."

---

[1] Let us define the basic set of philosophic propositions as those which formulate the subject's answers to the following set of questions. What is it to know? What is reality? What is objectivity? What does it mean to be human? These basic propositions are "positions if they are expressions of [the] intelligent and rational consciousness [of the subject] as oriented to the universe of (B)eing." They are "counter-positions if they are expressions which are contradictory to the expressions of [the] intelligent and rational consciousness [of the subject] as oriented to the universe of (B)eing" (UB, 229b).

[2] The reader should note the discussion, in Chapter VII, below, of the law of "Limitation and Transcendence" in human development. She should also recall the discussion of dialectic in Chapter V, Sections B10, above.

Rather, they are to be regarded as **antithetical** to any such performance and account.

Thirdly, as already noted, the intellectual pattern to the experience of the subject is "supposed and expressed" by Lonergan's reflective account of the basic positions. But no subject is either born into this pattern, reaches it "with ease," or remains in it "permanently." And even if his critical affirmation of the positions is proof against the confusions of the moment:

> when some other pattern is dominant, then the self of . . . [the subject's] self-affirmation seems quite different from . . . [his] actual self, the universe of being seems as unreal as Plato's noetic heaven, and objectivity spontaneously becomes a matter of [his] meeting persons and dealing with things that are "really out there" (I, 385b, emphasis mine).

Fourthly, it has only been by way of the preceding, long and difficult train of reflections upon his own Self-development and the traditions of science and philosophy which have fostered it, that Lonergan has been able to issue the preceding three points. It is only through them that he has been able to lay bare their basic antitheses adequately. It is only by way of them that he has been able to exhibit the proper "grounds" for securing their basic options.

But, finally, it is difficult and requires a lengthy study to reach and maintain the **critical** perspective invoked by the positions. Again, there is given the unity-in-tension with which the conscious being of the subject is marked. It is not, therefore, surprising that the unquestioning orientation of the subject's biologically patterned experience should survive in his dramatic and practical living. It is not surprising that it should plague his scientific pursuits and his philosophic reflections. It is not surprising that its survival should bias and/or confuse the process to his advancing Self-transcendence. It is unsurprising that the biasing and confusion of his own development should go so widely and frequently unrecognized and uncriticized.[1]

Secondly, the thoughtful subject may reflect further upon the

---

[1] Cf. Chapter V, Section B10, below, etc.

"position"-"counter-position" antithesis. He may realize that his affirmation of the counter-position on knowing intends the introduction
of a distortion, a "truncation" into the "three-fold" structure of
human consciousness. He may realize that his equation of reality and
the "already-out-there" represents his "deserting" of "the (B)eing that
can be intelligently grasped and reasonably affirmed [through the exercise of that structure]" (I, 484b, emphases mine), etc. He may realize
that his statement of counter-positions cannot "be both completely
coherent and either intelligent or reasonable" (I, 522a). He may come
to the fuller realization that the basic positions, therefore,
formulate the proper and basic **limits** of his own intentional life. But
at the term of such a series of reflections, he has uncovered the
"grounds" for affirming his enriching "**confinement**" to the exigences of
the "basic postions" (I, 484b, 521c). And he has discovered that this
confinement ranges over his "formulation of the results of common
sense, of science, and of metaphysics" (I, 523a), his performance in
all but the biological patterns of experience.

Thirdly, by implicit analogy of similars,[1] the intentional life
of any human subject, of any being subject to empirical, intelligent,
and rational consciousness, must be, not only similarly "**confined**" to
the basic positions but also at least similarly open to the **breakthrough** and **encirclement** by which they would be appropriated. Thus, as
already noted, the content affirmed in the subject's reflectively
grounded conclusion to his own confinement, is exemplary. It ranges
over the totality of human subjects who could agree with or dispute,
who could affirm or deny what is being claimed. But, then, his breakthrough, his ensuing discovery of the encirclement and confinement
"ground" the subject's "critical" Self-knowledge.[2]

---

[1]Any analogy of similars is grounded in the heuristic principle
of the classical scientific subject that similars are to be similarly
understood. It has been implicitly invoked throughout this study
whenever the trans-individual, generic implications of his Self-reflections have been drawn.

[2]The reader is again asked to recall the analyses carried out in
Chapter V, Section B10, above.

Fourthly, Lonergan makes the interpretive and methodologically grounded assumption that the metaphysical, ethical, "natural" theological, and other pronouncements of the philosophic subject represent successive **"expansions"** upon the unassailable, positional "basis" of his intentional life. Again, this warranted assumption must be properly construed. It must be construed in the context of the above-cited "analogy of similars." It must be construed in the context of the subject's critically circumscribed affirmation of his "confinement" to the positions. It must be construed in the context of the subject's already accomplished appropriation of the "intentional basis" of his own subjectivity. In this context, then, this "basis" represents a "fixed point of unity" in human, conscious Being. It is "relatively invariant" with respect to particular human subjects, their societies and cultures, their particular places and times. It is relatively invariant with respect to their particular stages of development, the genuineness or "bias" of their achievements, etc. Again, this fixed point of unity involves a basic, invariant set of "dialectical oppositions" in addition to a set of "positions." Operating from this fixed point, the subject can, for instance, engage and interpret performative theses and antitheses, positions and counter-positons within the work of any human thinker. He can, thereby, evaluate, and critique the implicit or explicit philosophic pronouncements of any human subject. He can work out in advance the outlines of fundamental divergences in philosophic method and content and use these outlines to guide his study and criticism of the historically proceeding manifold to the reflections of thinkers. Again, he can determine the "heuristic structure" implicit in his participation in the socio-historic dialectic of philosophic reflection. But this invariant, critically grounded heuristic:

> admits determination through the principle that positions invite development and counter-positions invite reversal (I, 387c, emphasis mine).[1]

---

[1]Two points should be made here.

First, the reader should note that the subject's application of this heuristic will involve his use of both direct and inverse insights

Thus, a contemporary philosopher may correctly identify the Self-affirmation of Descartes' "Cogito, ergo sum" as a position. Still, the
absence of a desired "clarity and precision" in its formulation and
context will force him to raise:

such further questions as What is the self? What is thinking?
What is being? What are the relations between them (I, 389a)?

And the subject's attempts at answering these questions will head him
towards the "further development" (I, 389a) of the **position**. On the
other hand, the contemporary thinker may have correctly identified
Descartes' "affirmation of the res extensa" with a **counter**-position.
Again his identification presupposes that a "thing" is only a "unity-
identity-whole" in the data and not "the 'already out there now real'
stripped of its secondary qualities . . ." (I, 413b). Again, it is
only the former notion which is consistent with the human subject's
intelligent grasp and reasonable affirmation. Thus, the contemporary
subject's "inverse" grasp upon this performative Self-contradiction,
heads him towards its "**reversal**."[1]

(cf. I, 387b).
    Secondly, the precept "develop positions and reverse counter-
positions" represents a further expansion upon the subject's Self-
affirmation, shares its trans-cultural invariance. But, then, it
explicitly "**grounds**," for instance, the "**dialectical method**" of the
subject set forth in Chapter V, B10, above, has explicit relevance in
the scientific, dramatic, practical, and philosophic contexts which are
there discussed. Again, in its full, reflectively mediated form, the
dialectical method of the subject will stand at the heart of the normative science of **ethics** (cf. I, XVIII.1.4).

[1]Three points should be added here.
    First, the dialectical heuristic of the philosophic subject has
its grounds in the subject's reflective embrace by the basic positions,
by their normative exclusion of their counters.
    Secondly, the structure of the philosophic dialectic is isomor-
phic with that implemented in non-philosophic contexts.
    Thirdly, in the face of the performative Self-contradiction of
the subject, the dialectic forces him to make the questions of his
knowing, being, objectivity, and humanness into topics, to engage in
the inevitabilities which structure their answering.

7. The Nature of Metaphysics

Let us recall several of the "universal principles" of human cognition implicit in the Self-affirmation of the subject. These include the pure desire of the subject. They include the tri-fold structure and objectivity of the proper unfolding of this desire. They include the notion of Being implicit in this desire. They include the relative invariance of such notions, etc., etc. Again, in Insight, XIV.2, Lonergan is claiming that such principles also "ground" the construction of a universal, relatively invariant **metaphysics**.[1] He argues this by showing that they are the principles:

A. according to which all experientially motivated human knowledge emerges;[2]

B. by which the questions to which the various field differentiations of human knowing progressively answer;[3]

C. by which positions and counter-positions are distinguished and, therefore, the former are advanced and the latter reversed;[4]

D. which include in themselves the "order," the "key-stone" (I, 391a) "that binds the other [surviving, and/or still or newly emerging] departments [of human knowing] into a single

---

[1]The key to the "construction" has already been found. Briefly, it lies in the fact that Being is what one knows when one knows objectively. Thus, metaphysics is the objective "science" of the Being which is known, when one knows objectively. But, then, (classsical) metaphysics is only "second" philosophy for Lonergan because it wants critical grounds.

[2]Thus, the subject grasps and affirms these principles and the explicit metaphysics they anticipate, as **underlying every** field of his or of any human knowing.

[3]Thus, the subject grasps and affirms them and the explicit metaphysics they anticipate, as **penetrating every** field of his or of any human knowing.

[4]Thus, the subject grasps and affirms them and the explicit metaphysics they anticipate as in the process of **transforming** the advancing field manifold of his or of any human knowing.

intelligible whole" ($\underline{I}$, 392b).[1]

But if this is so, then the same can be said for the metaphysics anticipated and "grounded" in these principles.

Thus, in its _first_ stage, the metaphysics of the subject is
"**latent**." As such it is virtually equivalent to these principles, to:

> the dynamic unity of [the] empirical, intellectual, and rational
> consciousness [of the subject, of **any** human subject insofar] as [it
> is pre-reflectively] underlying, penetrating, transforming, and
> unifying the other deparments of knowledge ($\underline{I}$, 392c, emphasis
> mine).

In a _second_ stage, the latent metaphysics _of_ the human subject
becomes "**problematic**." This occurs against the background of the bias
to the common sense of his community. It occurs against the background
of a proliferating, unintegrated panoply of scientific fields and specializations. It involves the confusion of and conflict between inter-
preters of these phenomena. It involves the actual context of philosophic "disarray" into which the distinction between positions and
counter-positions has fallen. It implies the subject's advancing alienation from him$\underline{Self}$, etc. Thus, the need for and anticipation of an
explicit metaphysics is "called forth," is gradually "evoked" by the
bewilderment and confusion felt in its absence.

In its _third_ stage of development, metaphysics becomes "**explicit**." As such, it stands forth as the permanent aspiration of and comes
"primarily" to those subjects prepared for it by the _reflection_-mediat-
ed "process to $\underline{Self}$-knowledge" which this study has, in turn, taken up
(cf. $\underline{I}$, 397c 1-2). Thus, within the socio-historical genesis of meaning and value, metaphysics emerges **explicitly** when the cognitionally
Self-affirmed subject of the preceding reflections, become intelligently and rationally present to him$\underline{Self}$ in the dialectical oppositions, in
the invariant "principles" of his intentional life, methodically $\underline{ex}$-
$\underline{tends}$ the leading edge of his Self-knowledge and reflective development. The subject extends this heuristic "edge":

---

[1]Thus, the subject grasps and affirms them and the explicit metaphysics they anticipate, as always already **integrative** of or, at least
in the $\underline{process}$ of **integrating**, the advancing manifold of fields of his
or of any human knowing.

[to effect] conception, affirmation, and implementation of the integral heuristic structure of proportionate (B)eing (I, 391d).[1]

Finally, to conclude this section, seven characteristics of such a metaphysics will be determined. First, it would be "heuristic" in character. Secondly, it would be "indifferent" to the issue of whether complete scientific understanding of the totality will ever be achieved. Thirdly, it would be "accessible" to the subject's contemporary reflections. Fourthly, it would prove to be "relatively invariant." Fifthly, it would be "progressive" in character. Sixthly, it would "refer" to Being in at least two, distinct, senses. Seventhly, it would represent a further dimension of the subject's personal, intellectual development.

First, then, as thus constituted, such a metaphysics would be heuristic in character. As such, it would outline in advance and, thus, anticipate:

the general structure of proportionate being as **explained** (I, 524b, emphasis mine);

what would be known by affirming a complete **explanation** of experience (I, 483b, emphasis mine).

Again, it would do this while leaving to the efforts of particular inquirers and the vagaries of history the acquisition of the verified contents it would work into coherence and unity.[2]

---

[1]If we have introduced the notion of experiential motivation to define Being in general, Lonergan defines proportionate Being as that which is not only to be "understood and affirmed": "but also to be experienced. So proportionate Being may be defined as whatever is to be known by human experience, intelligent grasp, and reasonable affirmation" (I, 391c, emphasis mine). First, he introduces the notion because it simplifies matters enormously by allowing him to prescind from the question of the possibility of the subject's "knowing what lies beyond the limits of human experience." Secondly, it should be noted that the objective correlate of the notion of the experiential motivation of the subject's intelligence is not necessarily proportionate being and that it admits the possibility of the subject's openness to transcendent Being as, at least, a possibility.

[2]Thus, Lonergan will argue that metaphysics is related to the "contents" of the science and common sense of the subject neither as a premiss to a conclusion nor a cause to an effect, but as: "a generating, transforming, and unifying principle . . . [to] the materials that

Secondly, such a metaphysics would be <u>indifferent</u> to the issue of whether complete scientific explanation is ever <u>actually</u> achieved. Still, it would be **un**compromising in its insistence that "here and now" the concrete subject of science and common sense:

> reject all obscurantism and so accept in all its implications the <u>effort for</u> complete explanation [implicit in the dynamic to his <u>pure desire</u> and its notion of Being] (<u>I</u>, 483c, emphases mine).

But since its construction "here and now" by the cognitionally Self-affirmed subject both presupposes and implies these attitudes of rejection and acceptance, the "value" of metaphysics is that of the "correct order and perspective" within which it casts and into which it liberates the "present knowledge and present inquiry [of the subject]" (<u>I</u>, 483c).

<u>Thirdly</u>, such a metaphysics, would be **accessible** to the subject in advance of any possible achievement of complete explanation. This is so, since its basic structures would be isomorphic with the order immanent in the <u>dynamics</u> of <u>all</u> [human] knowledge whether past, present or future (<u>I</u>, 483c, emphases mine). It is so since the order to his advancing knowledge has been grasped, affirmed, and shown to be invariant. It is so since the dynamic structures necessary to know Being must also correspond to the "structures" of Being on pain of retorsive Self-contradiction.

<u>Fourthly</u>, such a metaphysics would be **relatively invariant** and, therefore, immune to **revolutionary** change. This is so precisely because it represents the objective correspondant of the relatively invariant structures of human cognition (cf. <u>I</u>, 393e).

<u>Fifthly</u>, such a metaphysics would be **progressive**. Thus, it <u>is</u> subject to the <u>minor</u> dynamic of human intelligence. This is so insofar

---

it generates, transforms, and unifies" (<u>I</u>, 393d). But if the sciences of nature and of man: "can derive from metaphysics as a technique a common yet systematically and critically differentiated object [e.g., a pre-understanding of a systematically related set of differences within the proportionate object of their inquiry], so, inversely, metaphysics derives from the sciences the content and enrichment that actual activity brings to a dynamic structure" (<u>I</u>, 509b).

as it draws upon the discovery of new methods, of new fundamental differentiations of its basic, tri-fold, cognitional structure, of further emergent components within the minor Self-affirmation of the subject, to augment its heuristic outline of the structure of proportionate Being (cf. I, 392d–393a).

Sixthly, such a metaphysiscs would be "**referred**" to Being in two senses. Thus, on the one hand, it would be "explicitly" and "primarily" referred to Being in its explanatory sense. In this sense it is that which is intended and, by stages, affirmed by the subject of the empirical, scientific attitude. On the other hand, it would be "implicitly" and "secondarily" referred to Being in its descriptive sense. In this sense it is that which is intended, grasped, and affirmed by the subject of the common sense. Thus, if descriptive relations are included within metaphysics, they are included, as in the sciences, not as sensed or described, but as explained. And this will hold true even if some of the descriptive relationships of the things must correspond to their explanatory counterparts if cognition is to advance from description to explanation, from scientific explanation to metaphysics (cf. I, 394b, 514b; cf. UB, 173–175b).

Seventhly, and, most importantly, such a metaphysics would be the "**personal attainment**" (I, 396d) of the reflective, Self-knowing subject (cf. I, 429c).

8. The Method of Metaphysics—The Ontology of Proportionate Being

Lonergan defines in outline the **method** of **metaphysics**. This is the method by which the "latent" metaphysics of the human mind, the integral heuristic structure of proportionate Being, is to be made **explicit**. And if the application of such a method would eliminate disputation from the converse of philosophy, so its use presupposes that the "evidence" for metaphysics has been secured, that its "foundation" has thereby been "laid" and "made fast." But "philosophic evidence" lies:

within the philosopher . . . [herSelf] (I, 429b);

not within easy reach of every indolent mind, but **only** at the term of a long and difficult accumulation of direct and reflective insights (I, 484a, emphases mine).

And our hard-won "evidence" for metaphysics has consisted in the subject's **breakthrough** into Self-affirmation, her **encirclement** of the notion of Being, her **confinement** to the positions within primitive if further differentiable sets of antitheses. But with such "foundations" beyond dispute, the subject: "can proceed rapidly with the [methodical] erection of the integral heuristic structure of proportionate (B)eing" (I, 484c).[1] First, then, by the "lower blade" of metaphysical method, the "data" are prepared and made available. Secondly, the "upper blade" consists in the relevant affirmations implicit in the "minor" and "major" Self-affirmations of the subject. Thirdly, the two "blades" are "closed." Finally, the analytic principle of the isomorphism of human thought and its "object" is used to construct a metaphysics proportionate to objective human cognition of the surrounding world.

In a first step, the Self-knowing subject, adverting to the polymorphism of human consciousness and to the fact of sensitive

---

[1] The interested reader will find three, slightly different accounts of the method of the subject's metaphysical "construction." The reader should consult Insight, pp. 396 ff, 483 ff, 520 ff.

interference with the full tri-fold unfolding of human intelligence, directs his dialectical "criticism" towards:

> the common nonsense [e.g., the bias] that tries to pass for common sense and against the uncritical philosophy [e.g., mechanist determinism] that pretends to be a scientific conclusion (I, 399a).

The result of this critique is the transforming "re-orientation" of "one's common sense and scientific views." This yields the "**secondary minor premise**" of the argument and the "lower blade" of "metaphysical method."

In a second step, the subject recalls her minor **and** major Self-affirmations. These, as the reader recalls, consist of the affirmation of the relatively invariant "structures" and "notions" integrating the dynamic to her own, to any intellectually patterned and sensitively motivated consciousness. With respect to the evidence of her **major** Self-affirmation:

> (t)he simplest of these structures is that every instance of knowing proportionate being consists of a unification of [the] experiencing, understanding, and judging [of the subject] (I, 400a).

Thus, the affirmation of one's Self as a knower is also, simultaneously, an affirmation of the general structure through which any "object" of proportionate (B)eing is known.

With regard to her **minor** Self-affirmation, with respect to the affirmations prepared for by her reflections upon the second level of her advancing consciousness, there is recalled:

A. the quadrate of notions penetrating and structuring the four-fold differentiation of the classical, statistical, genetic, and dialectical methods of the subject (cf. the first subdivision of the Introduction to this chapter, above);

B. the notion of the thing to which she applies the results obtained by his exercise of the methods (cf. the second subdivision of the Introduction);

C. the "structurally unifying" notions of special and emergent probability and of explanatory genera and species (cf. the third subdivision of the Introduction).

And the point to the subject's minor Self-affirmation is that these notions outline and represent in advance the minimal set of formal possibilities necessary for her <u>understanding</u> of "the data."[1] And they constitute a non-reductionistic, explanatory context adequate to house and integrate the results of the modern specializations of the scientific pursuit insofar as they shed light on the nature of her own conscious Being, of "human Being" <u>per se</u>.[2] Thus, the minor <u>affirmation</u> of one's Self as necessarily employing these notions when one "knows," is also, simultaneously, an affirmation of the formal possibilities through which any proportionate being is to be <u>understood</u>. But the minor **and** major Self-affirmations of the subject together yield the "primary minor premise" of the argument and the "upper blade" of metaphysical method.[3]

In a <u>third</u> step, the Self-knowing subject begins to "close the scissors" (<u>I</u>, 523a), to unite the principal and secondary premises. Again, she does this: "much as a physicist unites a differential equation with empiricaly ascertained boundary conditions . . ." (<u>I</u>, 484c). The upshot of the process is the transposition of the dialectically transformed contents of the advancing science and common sense of the subject. They are transposed into the higher integrative setting prescribed and demanded by the now explicit, formal possibilities and basic structures of the cognition of the subject. Such a setting will reflect the power and reach of such general methodological categories as those of: systematic, non-systematic, dynamic and dialectical process; classical, statistical, genetic and dialectical law; thing; emergent probability, etc. Again, the "closing" of the scissors has, in fact, already been provisionally accomplished. It resulted in the specific, seven-tiered heuristic pyramid discussed in "Man and Thing," the concluding Subsection of Section B8, Chapter V, above.

<u>Finally</u>, since by the Self-knowing subject's "encirclement,"

---

[1] Cf. Chapter V, Sections B3, 5, 6-7, 8, 9, 10.

[2] Cf. Chapter V, Subsection B8e.

[3] Cf. <u>Insight</u>, pp. 399e-400a, 484c 5-8, 485b-486a.

Being is identified with the "object" of her sensitively motivated
inquiry and reflection, there follows a "principle of isomorphism."
This principle, when applied in its proportionately restricted context,
constitutes the "major premise" and effects the final step in the "deduction" of explicit metaphysics (cf. I, 552d). On this principle,
since:

> [the] knowing [of the subject] consists of a related set of acts
> and the known is the related set of contents of these acts, then
> the pattern of the relations between the acts is similar in form to
> the pattern of the relations between the contents of the acts.
> This premise is analytic (I, 399d).

But since the known object of human knowledge is Being, then the subject's:

> affirmation of . . . [herSelf] as a knower also is an affirmation
> of the general structure of [and, by way of her minor Self-affirma-
> tion, **the formal possibilities** inherent in] **any proportionate ob-
> ject of human knowledge** (I, 523a).

But, as we have seen, in the fully explanatory knowledge of the subject
there will be distinct but related acts of experiencing, understanding,
and affirmation. And isomorphic with these cognitional elements there
will be the metaphysical elements of, respectively, potency, form, and
act.

> From the different modes of understanding concrete things and ab-
> stract laws, there follows the distinction between central and con-
> jugate forms and, as a corollary, the distinctions between central
> and conjugate acts (I, 486b).

Thus, a "scientific explanation" is:

> a theory verified in instances; as **verified**, it refers to **act**; as
> **theory**, it refers to **form**; as **instances**, it refers to **potency**.
> Again, as a theory of the **classical** type [e.g., as representing a
> classical law], it refers to [conjugate] forms as forms; as a
> theory of the **statistical** type [e.g., as representing a statistical
> law], it refers to forms as setting ideal frequencies from which
> acts do not diverge systematically; as a theory of the **genetic** type
> [e.g., as representing a genetic law], it refers to the conditions
> of the emergence of form from potency [e.g., genetic "form"] (I,
> 432b–433a, emphases mine).[1]

---

[1] This author would add that as a theory of the dialectical type,
it refers to the conditions of the reversal of the failures and refusals of human intellectual, rational, and rational Self-consciousness,
or its products, e.g., a dialectical "form."

Further, from "the structural unification of the methods by generalized emergent probability" there follows the horizontal, vertical and, ultimately, the absolute **"finality" of Being**.[1]

----

[1]Cf. Insight, pp. 486d–487a.

9. Being as Intelligible

Lonergan faces the question of whether the intelligibility represented by the metaphysical, heuristically defined categories of the
subject is extrinsic or intrinsic to surrounding world process. Thus,
he asks whether it represents only the structure of his cognition of
the world or also the structure immanent in the reality of proportionate Being itself.[1]

But, first, the simplest explanation for why the subject's cognition "has its peculiar structure would be that proportionate (B)eing
has a parallel structure" (I, 499b).

Secondly, the notion that it is extrinsic to Being assumes that
the subject's relationship to reality is "prior to [his] asking questions and independent of [his] answers . . ." (I, 499e). It assumes
that knowing is constituted by the sensitively attached "extroversion"
or "introversion" of consciousness towards what is already "out there"
or "in here" now. But these assumptions represent the performative
desertion of basic cognitional, epistemological, and ontological
"positions." On the other hand, reflecting upon his intellectually
patterned performance, the subject may have discovered that Being is
what alone satisfied his intelligence and reasonableness. But, then,
he has already at least implicitly understood and affirmed that Being
could not be "anything apart from the intelligible or beyond it," that
Being is "intrinsically intelligible" (I, 499d). If intelligibility is
intrinsic to Being, it is "not all of a piece, but of different kinds"
(I, 500e). Thus, there is in this world "a formal intelligibility that
makes understanding a necessary component" in the subject's advancing
cognition of Being.[2] There is "a potential intelligibility that makes

---

[1]Cf. Insight, XVI.3.2.

[2]Thus, formal intelligibility "is the content of the insight and
dominant component in the consequent set of concepts" advanced by the
intelligent subject.

experience a necessary component" in his knowing.[1] And there is "an
actual intelligibility that makes judgment a necessary component"[2] (I,
515c) of his cognition.[3]

But then there is to any proportionate Being a tri-fold intelligible unity[4] that makes the experience, understanding and conception,
reflection and judgment of the subject, necessary components of his
advancing cognition (cf. I, 501b-c).

---

[1]Thus, the subject's understanding presupposes the presentations
that are the materials for his inquiry.   This intelligibility of the
materials: "is not formal but potential; . . . it is the intelligibility of the materials in which the idea is emergent, which the idea unifies and relates" (I, 501a).

[2]Thus, the actual intelligibility of Being is "what is known [by
the subject] inasmuch as [he] grasps the virtually unconditioned . . .
. [It is what is] restricted to what in fact is" (I, 501a).

[3]The subject would clarify the character of the distinction between the metaphysical elements, between the different modes of intelligibility "within" a being which they represent.   But, then, he can
advance by reflecting upon the kinds of negative comparative judgments,
e.g., P is not Q, in which he actually brings out the distinctions of
things. Thus, if P and Q are mere objects of his thought or supposition, their distinction is notional. If "P or Q or both have not been
. . . definitively [explained]" by the subject, their distinction is
problematic. If P and Q are both real, if, then, the judgment by which
he properly affirms their distinction reflects his experientially or
consciously motivated intellectual pattern, then their distinction is
real. But a major real distinction obtains between members of different genera, of different species within a genera or different individuals within the same species. Minor real distinctions obtain between
the components or constituents within proportionate being. Thus, for
example, the central and conjugate forms of an Arabian race horse differ with a real minor distinction. Finally, there is an adequate real
distinction between Peter and Paul or between Peter's right and left
hands, but only an inadequate real distinction between Peter and his
hands, between Peter and his central form (cf. I, XVI.1).

[4]Lonergan discusses the unity of the concrete being at length in
Insight, XVI.4.2.

10. The Metaphysical Self-Expression of the Incarnate Subject

In Insight, XVI.4.3, Lonergan resolves the issue of the character[1] of the unity of the incarnate human subject in light of the simultane-ously material and Spiritual dimensions to his activity. Beginning, then, from this latter point, Lonergan notes that if the metaphysical "center" of the subject's operation is differentiated by intellectual conjugates, this activity can effect the higher system of his sensitive living either consciously or unconsciously.[2]

It does so unconsciously in the case of the subject of common sense. He does not understands the full intellectual character of his nature. He does not manifest it to himSelf by conceiving and affirming it. He does not work out the metaphysical structure which it mirrors and, therefore, evidences. He does not opt to adhere to its immanent, normative exigences. He, therefore, grasps and implements only the advancing intelligible systems of immediate relevance to organically motivated practical, artistic, and dramatic activity in the natural and social worlds.

It does so consciously when the subject's deliberately willed activity is so informed and mediated by Self-knowledge. Under this

---

[1] It is important to recall that in the critically grounded meta-physical order that has been advanced, that the human subject, no less than physical, chemical, organic, and sensitive beings, is: individual by his central potency; existent by his central act; one in nature by his central form, where the unity of that form extends to and is dif-ferentiated by the intellectual conjugates of his intentional life (cf. Appendix I, below, and the discussion of the differentiation of the Being of the subject in Subsection B8e of Man and Thing, Chapter V, above). Similarly, the actual understanding of the subject is grounded in conjugate act. His mastery of an intellectual skill or subject mat-ter is grounded in conjugate form. That he is capable of understanding is grounded in conjugate potency; can be said of him by intrinsic denomination, that he is a father by extrinsic denomination, etc.

[2] This author would argue that, in light of the distinctions made in Appendix II, below, that the use of these two terms in their soon to be specified senses is confusing and inopportune to say the least.

circumstance, the subject will be oriented towards "the whole universe of [emergent] (B)eing." He will be aiming at knowing "the objective contents of his experience." His primary concern will not only be "the particular animal I am." Rather, he will be out to integrate his own organic demands as situated within and relevant to the prior, all-encompassing dynamic to the natural and human worlds, etc.[1]

Next, Lonergan advances from a description to an explanation of the grounds of the two-fold character of the subject's higher integration of his sensitive life. In the first place, then, and first, in Section B8, above, the distinction between the potential, formal, and actual intelligibility of proportionate being was framed. But, secondly, the human subject also "is." And insofar as his conscious, intelligent being represents a further differentiation within the all-inclusive horizon of Being, there can be distinguished:

. . . the potential intelligence of . . . [his] detached, disinterested, desire to know;

. . . the formal intelligence that consists in [his] insights [into the objective data] and grounds [his] conceptions [of it];

. . . the actual intelligence . . . [with which he] grasps the unconditioned and posits being as known (I, 516a).

But, finally, then, the subject of our preceding reflections is not only intelligible, is not only an intelligent intelligibility, but he also knows himSelf (cf. I, 516a).

Thus, the "material" can be nominally defined in terms of the non-intelligent intelligibility of surrounding world process. And the "Spiritual" can be similarly defined in terms of the intelligent, Self-knowing, and Self-determining intelligibility of the activity of the subject in the world. But, then, inasmuch as the subject is:

material, . . . [he is] constituted by otherwise coincidental manifolds of conjugate acts that unconsciously and spontaneously are reduced to system by higher conjugate forms.[2] But inasmuch as

---

[1]In this second case, then, the subject is exerting a "conscious intellectual control" (I, 515b 9) over his sensitive interface with the surrounding world.

[2]In the order of Self-"discovery," the subject of the non-conscious, i.e., pre-reflectively advancing, higher integration of his sensitive life is only "potentially" Spiritual since he has not appropropriated and implemented the Spirituality of his own Being.

. . . [he is] spiritual, . . . [he is] orientated towards the universe of (B)eing, know(s) . . . [himSelf] as . . . [a part] within
that universe, and guide(s) . . . [his] living by that knowledge
(I, 516a).

In the second place, insofar as the consciously intelligent subject can and does correctly understand the material universe, there
will be both a "correspondence between the material intelligibility
that is understood [by him] and the (S)piritual intelligibility [e.g.,
the subject himSelf] that is understanding" (I, 516b). There will also
be a difference between these two kinds of intelligibility. But this
difference can be reflectively specified in a precise and explanatory
manner. Thus, in such a case, the direct, experientially motivated
understanding of the intellectual subject:

abstracts from the empirical residue;

[grasps] the universal apart from its instances, the limit apart
from the continuum, the invariant apart from particular places and
times, the ideal frequency apart from the non-systematic divergence
of actual frequencies (I, 516b, emphases mine).

But even as Spiritual intelligibility, therefore, "is apart from
the empirical residue," so it is the case that "material intelligibility is not without it." In this manner, then:

(t)he universal can be thought [by the subject] but cannot be
without the instance; the limit can be thought [by him] but cannot
be without the continuum; the invariant can be considered [by the
subject] but does not exist apart from particular places and times;
ideal frequencies can be formulated [by him] but cannot be verified
apart from actual frequencies. The empirical residue, then, is at
once what (S)piritual intelligibility excludes and what material
intelligibility includes (I, 516b, emphases mine).[1]

And, furthermore, even:

(a) brief consideration of . . . [the] functioning [of subatomic
entities, chemical elements and compounds, plants and animals]

---

[1] Again, if the empirical residue is, indeed, included by material
intelligibility, and since it has previously been identified with prime
potency, it is also, therefore, prime matter.

reveals not merely that it does not occur but even that it could not occur apart from the empirical residue, apart from manifolds of instances in a space-time continuum, and apart from actual frequencies that non-systematically diverge from ideal frequencies (I, 517a, emphases mine).

But on the basis of these reflections, the **material** can be implicitly defined as "whatever is constituted by the empirical residue or is conditioned intrinsically by . . . [it]" (I, 517a, emphases mine).

Granting this, four points must be added. First, the conjugate potencies, forms, and acts of subatomic, chemical, biological, and zoological entities are material. Secondly, central forms are unities differentiated by their conjugate forms. Again, act shares the definition of form. Hence, the corresponding central forms and acts on these levels are material. Thirdly, the **Spiritual** can be similarly defined as what is neither "constituted nor . . . conditioned intrinsically by the empirical residue" (I, 517b). But by his direct insights into data, the intellectual subject abstracts from the residue. By his grasp of the virtually unconditioned, of "fully rational factualness," he transcends the "brute factualness" by which members of a kind differ, by which the continuum is "non-countable because non-ordinable," and by which actual frequencies non-systematically diverge from their ideal. Thus, the intellectual subject's experientially motivated insight and grasp upon the virtually unconditioned differ from the empirical residue. So, also, will "the inquiry and critical reflection that lead [the subject] to them" differ from this residue. And so, also, will his "conception and judgment that result from them and express them" so differ. (I, 517b). Fourthly, in this case, the Spiritual is conditioned "extrinsic(ally)" by the empirical residue" since the inquiry and insight of the intellectual subject "demand something apart from themselves [e.g., sense experience] into which . . . [he can] inquire and attain insight" (I, 518a) and from which he can abstract. Again, the sense experience of the subject conditions his grasp of the virtually unconditioned but is not equivalent to it.

Taking up the **former** point, Lonergan notes that if the subject is material by the conjugates P_i, C_j, O_k, Z_l, and Spiritual by R_m, he is not merely an "assemblage of conjugates." Again, if the **unity** of the

"object" of his cognition is to be accounted for, the subject of inquiry and understanding must be identical with the subject of experience. Again, if he is to be a unity, the subject of rational reflection must be identical with the subject of experience and understanding. Again, this "unity on the side of the [conscious] subject," no
less than the unity of any real being, has "its metaphysical ground in
his central form."

But given his critical appropriation of this fact and its attend-
ants, there is a further, inevitable question for the subject's reflection. The question is whether "the break—down of his organic and sensitive living [is] necessarily . . . the end of his [own] identical
[conscious] existence" (I, 519c). It asks, therefore, whether the central form and metaphysical ground of his conscious unity is "material
or (S)piritual" (I, 518c). If, on the one hand, his approach to this
issue is descriptive, the central form of the subject will seem to be
"the point of transition from the material to the (S)piritual."

> As the centre of [the] sensitive experience [of the subject], it is
> material; as the centre of the transformation of [his] sensitive
> experience by the imposition of an intellectual pattern, and as the
> origin and ground of [his] inquiry and insight, reflection and
> grasp of the unconditioned, . . . [his central form] emerges as
> (S)pirit (I, 519a, emphases mine).

On the other hand, it is only from an **explanatory** perspective that the
claims of reality are properly and fully engaged and discharged.

Again, the subject exists and functions physically, chemically,
organically, sensitively, and intellectually. The material and Spiritual conjugates of his functioning respectively are and are **not** intrinsically conditioned by the empirical residue. Again, because these two
kinds of conjugates cannot both differentiate the central form of his
properly human existence and functioning, the preceding, descriptively
grounded solution is surpassed and eliminated. Again, were the central
form of the subject material, it could not mediate the role and function of his Spiritual reality, could not center his inquiry and insight, etc., could not ground the conjugates of his conscious, intellectual advance. But were his central form Spiritual, it could perform
the role and function of his material reality. As Spiritual, it could
be:

the ground and centre of his physical, chemical, organic, and sensitive conjugates; for the spiritual is comprehensive; what can embrace the whole universe through knowledge, can provide the centre and ground of unity in the material conjugates of a single . . . [human "I"] (I, 520a).[1]

---

[1]The reader may find Appendix IV of some use at this point. It briefly relates the preceding metaphysical reflections on the Being of man to those of Aquinas. It goes on to clarify, from Lonergan's perspective, the relationship between the "person" and "nature" of human Being. Finally, it offers a caution concerning the immediate, metaphysical transposition of merely grammatical, abstract, or merely descriptive elements.

11. Mystery and the Metaphysically Mediated Self-Knowledge of the Subject

In _Insight_, XVII.1, Lonergan specifies the general conditions by which a "correspondence" between the respective "operators" of the "sensitive" and "intelligent" dimensions of the subject can be achieved (cf. I, 532b).

First, as intelligent, the subject anticipates the meaning of Being by the totality of answers she desires. And her further relevant questions condition her transcendence of any limited stage of her intellectual development, towards a "vast" but, nevertheless, "impalpable" "known unknown" (I, 531d–532a). Again, the orientation of the "censorship" determines the sequences of integrations by which neuro-organic demands upon the subject's sensitive life are taken up into affects, images, memories, symbols, sensori-motor schemes, etc. But, then, when the censorship shifts from "alignment" with the biologically pre-set goals of her organism to the "intelligible" goals set by her further relevant questions, the sensitivity of the subject stands in dynamic "correspondence" with her intellectual development. But the virtually universal "affective" dispositions associated with the subject's "Awe," her sense of "Mystery," "Astonishment," etc., effect such a shift of the censorship. Thus, they transpose the character of the subject's relationship to the sensible and to the sensitive. They open and attune the orientation of her feelings, images, responses, gestures, etc., by their higher order correspondence to the "horizon" of Being which the Self-knowing subject affirms.

Thus, they determine the subject's pre-conscious selection and/or rejection of sensitive contents by their relevance to a "cosmic," "hidden," "further reality than meets the eye" (I, 625d, 532b), one which always implicitly pervades and orients the horizon of her common sense living.

These contents, then, are determined by their relationship to the potentially infinite "depths" of Being. But it is "into" these "depths" that the subject's further relevant "**questions**" open out. It is these "depths" which they query and learn to know under the aspect of the "known unknown" and its always outstanding "Horizon" (cf. I, 532a-c).

Thus, they are determined by the subject's advancing cognitional and/or practical relations to the "intelligibility" of a dynamic universe of "emergent probability" (I, 546c 12-14; cf. 625d, 536b).

Again, Lonergan argues that her affective "conversion" to the "Mystery" is only ever fully integrated within the subject's everyday living when it takes place within the context of its **symbolic** expression and evocation. But the meaning of this point must be drawn out in two steps.

First, the structure of the subject's symbolic relationship with the "Mystery" is two-fold. On the one hand, there is the process by which the socio-historical subject creates novel symbolizations of her "Openness" to the "Mystery." On the other, there is the process by which, by exposing herSelf to the relevant historically and socially instituted and selected symbols, her incarnate relation to the "Mystery" is awakened and/or sustained. But by both or either of these complementary processes, the subject's sensitive awareness of and responsiveness to the Mystery is made systematic. Secondly, the intertwining of the subject's: further relevant questions and the "known unknown;" symbolizations and the Mystery, represent complementary literal and symbolic expressions for what the Self-affirming subject "knows." They represent complementary expressions answering to the same question of the authentic meaning and context of her very Being. On the one hand, the subject's every advance towards the more profound literal expression of her Self-knowledge makes possible:

> an increasing consciousness and deliberateness and effectiveness in . . . [her] choice and use of dynamic images . . . [e.g., of the "horizon" of her Being] (I, 548a).

On the other hand, every advance in her symbolization of and symbols for the "Mystery" make more likely and profound her advance in the literal expression of her Self-knowledge.

Secondly, the symbolic adumbration of the "known unknown" is a never eliminable facet of a properly human life. Thus, it will be necessary as long as the subject's further relevant questions remain unanswered. Similarly, the subject's intellectual development involves her venture upon the relations of the things in their relations to each other, her use of the "complex symbols of mathematics, the cumbrous technical terms of science [and intentionality analysis], the bloodless ballet of metaphysical categories" to express the reality it intends. But, then, the "horizon" and language of the subject's intellectual development will increasingly abstract her from:

> the world of [her] poetry and common sense, . . . the flow of . . . [her] sensitive presentations, . . . feelings and emotions, . . . the talking and doing that form the palpable part of . . . [her everyday] living with persons and . . . dealing with things (I, 547a, emphases mine).

They will increasingly abstract her from her common sense and dramatic Self-understanding. But if it converges upon the "things themselves," the subject's intellectual development "does not [therefore] give man a home" (I, 547a 1). But, then, it is through her symbols that the subject brings her intentional abstraction, her withdrawal from the sensitive home. It is through them that she re-immerses herSelf in the sensitive by taking it up in a transposed manner. It is through them that she invests the sensible as well as the sensitive with the higher order significance of the intelligible and intelligent. It is through them that she dwells, incarnate in the sensitive, without destroying the conditions for her higher order development.

Thirdly, in "myth" and its correlative mythic consciousness, the Self-knowledge of the subject is falsified. Thus, the mythic consciousness of the subject is pre-reflective, pre-philosophic. But, then, it fails: (1) to distinguish the positions and counter-positions; (2) to devise adequate criteria for real Being and distinctness; (3) to differentiate the horizons of description and explanation; (4) to devise criteria for effectively anticipating the occurrence of insight. The myth in which such consciousness issues, then, carries the sense of the Self-centred, biological subject in a world of "bodies." It carries the sense of a being-in-the-world at variance with the subject's Self-knowledge, with her participation in a universe of Being. Again, parallel to the dialectic of the positions/counter-positions, there will be the dialectic of the symbolic and mythical consciousness of the subject, of the corresponding symbols and myths in which they issue and to which they respond. Finally, even if for a time the sensitivity of the subject outstrips the discernment of his intelligence and reasonableness, the final interpretant of the latter dialectic must remain the reflectively grounded and, hence, Self-controlled cipher of the subject's explicit Self-knowledge. But, then, the order in which symbols/myths as well as their interpretations emerge and proceed, can be anticipated, in advance, will constitute either a genetic or dialectical system.[1]

Fourthly, then, a general conclusion can be drawn. Thus, for any subject at no matter what the stage or differentiation of her development, her intentional dynamic will represent:

either the proper unfolding of . . . [her] detached and disinterested desire . . . or else . . . [its] distorted unfolding due to the interference of other [e.g., sensitive, organically motivated] desire (I, 548a).

Again, for any subject, the sensitive dynamisms:

from which [her] intellectual contents emerge and in which they are represented, expressed, and applied, either are involved in the mysteries [e.g., the symbols] of the proper unfolding or distort these mysteries [e.g., symbols] into myths (I, 548a).

Thus, the subject's integral human development hinges upon her achievement of the right correspondence of the initial terms specified, respectively, in the preceding two quotations, e.g., intelligence-mystery, detached desire-symbol, of the previous alternatives.

---

[1]Cf. Chapter II, p. 38 n1.

B. Concluding Remarks

The reflections of Chapter VI of this study recover essential aspects of the viewpoint of the philosophically differentiated subject of the intellectual pattern of experience.

The starting point of the chapter is the subject's Self-"understanding" as, minimally, a tri-fold unity of acts of experiencing, understanding, and judgment, etc. And the source of these reflections has been the subject's reflections upon her own performance in the artistic-aesthetic, common sense, dramatic, and scientific patterns to her experience. But the subject's Self-understanding gives way to her Self-affirmation. It is shown on both positive and negative, on both "empirical" and "performative" grounds that this affirmation is certain. It is shown that it represents an invariant which cuts across the "intellectual" development of any human subject, in any relevant pattern to her experience, and describes their "interior," essential unity as human. Finally, the subject's Self-affirmation lays bare the un-evadable, invariant grounds in human consciousness for all of the heuristic, methodological notions which merely expand upon the tri-fold structure of human conscious intentionality. These include the notions of the thing, emergent probability, etc., etc, etc.

On the "basis" of the "position" on human knowing which the Self-affirmation of the subject establishes, further, invariant positions on the "Being"-notion and "objectivity" of the subject are secured. Continuing the expansion upon the initial "base," a method is specified and implemented for rendering the invariant, "integrally heuristic" metaphysical structure of any "object" proportionate to human cognition. One effect of its implementation is the transposition of the methodological notions mentioned in the previous paragraph into their metaphysical equivalents. Again, the nature of the human subject is transposed into metaphysical terms and the "Spirituality" of the "central form" of human Being is established. Finally, the notion of "Mystery," of the correlative symbolic forms, corresponding in the sensitivity of the subject to her higher order intellectual functioning is brought out.

APPENDIX I

The purpose of this appendix is essentially, twofold. First, it will work out systematically and, thereby, clarify, the "implicit" definition of human Being laid down in Section 2, above. Secondly, it will exhibit alternative contexts of expression within which this definition can be equivalently framed and affirmed.

First, as noted, the specification of conditions A through C in Section 2, above, represents Lonergan's "implicit" definition of the knowing, of the distinctive manner of activity, by which the human subject is properly differentiated. Thus, the relations of "presupposed by" (henceforth, "pdb") and "complemented by" (henceforth, "cdb") can be used to fix basic sets of cognitional terms, the basic sets of terms can be used to fix the basic set of relations, and the subject's reflectively gathered Self-understanding, her insight into the data of her own cognitionally engaged consciousness, will then fix the mutual definition of relations and terms. In this way, then, the reflecting subject can, for example, define:

A. 1. "data" and "perceptual images" as what are pdb and cdb "free images;"
   2. "free images" as what are pdb and cdb "utterances;"
   3. the "first level of consciousness" with respect to these terms;
B. 1. "questions for intelligence" as what are pdb and cdb by "insights;"
   2. "insight" as what is pdb and cdb by "formulations;"
   3. the "second level of consciousness" with respect to these terms;
C. 1. "questions for reflection" as what are pdb and cdb "reflection," (cf. I, 274a), etc., etc., etc.;
D. the "first level of consciousness" as what is pdb and cdb the "second level of consciousness;"
E. the "second level of consciousness" as what is pdb and cdb the "third level of consciousness;"
F. human knowing as whatever derives from the subject's proper, integral performance on these three distinct but related levels;
G. the relations of "pdb" and "cdb" in terms of the distinct levels and intra-level terms of consciousness which they relate.

Deepening her reflection, the subject can specify her cognitive nature further as:

H.   differentiated into distinct, definable patterns;
I.   a formally dynamic system (cf. $\underline{C}$1, 223d; Chapter V, Subsection B8a, above);
J.   incomplete as long as anything remains to be known (cf. Chapter VII, below, and Subsection B8e of Chapter V, above, in which the meaning of the implicit definition of human Being is taken up in the context of, respectively, an explicit and implicit reflection upon the "operator" of human development), etc.

Further, the definition specifies the "operations" constitutive of the subject's knowing independently of the "objects" known through their advancing execution. (cf. Method in Theology Institute, file 641, question session #1). Thus, once it has been definitively affirmed, Lonergan can specify the ontological properties and categories of the "contents known" by using the "structure" specified by the "operations" performed (cf. Section 8, above).

Secondly, the specification of these conditions admits equivalent but alternate formulations. First, in metaphysical terms, where something acts there is conjugate form. But informed action of a specifiable kind supervenes upon the actualization of some potentiality or capacity once the appropriate conditions have been fulfilled. But the subject's cognition involves his performance of related sequences of conscious acts. As cognitional, his activity is informed by the relevant sets of explanatory conjugates upon whose implicit definition Lonergan's transcendental method has been converging (cf. conditions A–C, specified in Section 2, above, the initial exposition to this footnote, and definition #4, Subsection "e" of "Man and Thing," above, e.g., $T_r = f(Z_e, R_m)$). Secondly, then, the subject can be defined as:

an individual existing unity differentiated by capacities [e.g., potentialities] to experience [cf. condition A of Section 2, above], to inquire [cf. condition B, above], and to reflect [cf. condition C, above] ($\underline{I}$, 522b, emphasis mine).

Thirdly, since there is always an "awareness immanent in" his object-oriented intentional acts (cf. $\underline{I}$, 322a), the subject can be defined in terms of his being "conscious empirically (cf. condition A, above, etc.), intelligently, and rationally" ($\underline{I}$, 374b, emphasis mine). Finally, the nature of human consciousness is taken up in Appendix II, immediately below.

APPENDIX II

The condition of reflection, of <u>all</u> the reflections recounted in this study, and of the Self-affirmation recounted in Section 3 of this chapter, is the <u>consciousness</u> "of" the subject. On Lonergan's analysis, it is to be understood <u>neither</u> as "some sort of inward look" (<u>I</u>, 320b) upon mental entities "already in here now" <u>nor</u> a merely metabolic, chemical, or mechanical process only mistakenly thought to require irreducible explanatory conjugates of its own. Rather, it is to be understood as an immanent "awareness" (cf. <u>I</u>, 322a), an immanent "quality" (cf. <u>I</u>, 326b 2ff) pervading the unified intentional activity of the subject. It is the "awareness" or "quality" by which the subject is only "open to" her "object" because she is also "present to her-(S)elf" in the unity of her tri-levelled, "object"-oriented acts (<u>UB</u>, 16a 17–18). Thus, the subject is always already elementally if at least <u>implicitly</u> "given" to herSelf, is always open to the "data of consciousness." This is so prior to and independently of her search after, her understanding, description, definition, and her affirmation and "option" for herSelf. And precisely <u>because</u> this is so, it has been possible for the subject to "heighten" this implicit awareness. She has done this by "shifting h(er) attention" <u>away</u> from the objective "contents" of, for example, her science and common sense, <u>to</u> the very intentional acts through which these contents have been, are, or will be known. She has been able, thereby, to thematize and reflectively appropriate this giveness as a further region of data upon which her intentional processes of inquiry and reflection may supervene. She has been able to frame the cognitional Self-understanding abbreviated in conditions A–C set down in Section 2, above (cf. <u>I</u>, 274b 11–13). She has been able to affirm that Self-understanding, employ and, thereby, "reduplicate" the use of the structure set forth in A–C to know his own knowing, to know <u>herSelf</u> (<u>C</u>1, 225a). Again, to test and/or verify some empirical hypothesis, there is required the "reversion" of the subject's focus back to what is sensibly given, e.g., to pointer readings, to, for instance, "visual experiences on the level of merely seeing" (<u>I</u>, 327a). Similarly, to test and/or authenticate her <u>Self</u>-understanding, there must be the subject's "reversal" towards:

what is given consciously. Just as the former reversal is away from the understood as understood, the formulated as formulated, the affirmed as affirmed, and to the merely sensed, so also the latter reversal is from the [Self as] understood, formulated, affirmed as such, to the merely given [within the field of one's own original presence to one's Self] (I, 327b, emphases mine);

[Thus,] . . . the fulfillment of the conditions in consciousness [for the reflexive judgment "I am a knower"] is [only] to be had by reverting from such formulations to the more rudimentary state of the formulated where there is no formulation but merely experience (I, 328a, emphases mine).

Finally, if the consciousness of the subject is the prior condition of, for example, the Self-revelation and -affirmation of the subject set forth, above, that same Self-revelation and -affirmation can clue a deepened understanding of her own, pre-reflectively operative consciousness as a consequence. Thus, working backwards from the key components within them, the subject can sharply frame the different kinds or qualities of consciousness within the pre-reflected, elemental field of her immediate Self-presence. Mediating the immediacy of that presence, then, she can distinguish a(n):

A.   empirical consciousness, e.g., her presence to herSelf as spontaneously open to the surrounding world;

B.   intellectual consciousness, e.g., her presence to herSelf as spontaneously caught up in the pursuit of understanding and its articulation;

C.   rational consciousness, e.g., her presence to herSelf as spontaneously demanding the virtually unconditioned and abstaining from judgment unless the demand is met;

D.   presence to herSelf in the "unity of consciousness" spanning and underlying the triad of his cognitional dynamic and its consciousness (cf. I, 322a–328a, UB, 16–17).

APPENDIX III

The purpose of this appendix is to initiate discussion and clarification of two aspects of Lonergan's "argument" as set forth in Section 3 of this chapter. This is done by relating them to Kant's "metaphysical" and "transcendental" deductions of the "categories" in his Critique of Pure Reason. For Lonergan's longest and most significant articulation of other divergences and affinities between his thought and that of Kant, the reader is referred to Chapter XI, Section 10 of Insight. For their interpretation, she is referred to the entries under Giovanni Sala in the bibliography and Chapter VII, Section 3 of Vincent Potter's The Philosophy of Knowledge.

First, in his "metaphysical deduction" of the categories (cf. KRV, A70/B95-B116), Kant begins by specifying what he takes to be the complete table of the "logical forms" of human judgment. He "argues back" from them to the categories of human understanding as their "conditions of possibility." But Kant thought that these forms had been thoroughly studied by the "science" of formal logic. And the evidence of the latter discipline as well as its relative invariance since the time of Aristotle, led Kant to assume the universal and necessary character of its claims in general, the correctness of its division of logical forms in particular, and its suitability as a basis for his deduction of the a priori categories of "human" understanding.

Again, in his "transcendental deduction" of the categories (cf. KRV, A84/B116-B146), Kant took a second, complementary tack. He tried to show that true judgments about empirical objects are only possible because the categories, as pure, a priori forms of human thought, are also simultaneously the conditions of the possiblity of any phenomenal object of thought being intelligible at all. Deny their operation, and this object of thought would be, literally, unintelligible. Thus, their denial would presuppose their use. Pursuing this line of thought further, Kant argues that the "transcendental ego" unifies the possible experience of the subject according to the a priori forms of human thought. Ultimately, then, the "transcendental ego" accounts for the unity of the (phenomenal) objects thought by the subject.

Secondly, Lonergan's variant on Kant's metaphysical deduction is stated in Chapter XI, Section 9 of Insight. Lonergan begins by recalling the conditions of any possible judgment of fact. What are such conditions? They consist in:

> a concrete unity—identity—whole that experiences some given, that inquires, understands, and formulates, that reflects, grasps the unconditioned, and so affirms or denies (I, 338b).

But this is the concrete human subject engaging the dynamic, three-fold "system" of her intentional operations in some context. Lonergan concludes that "if there is any concrete judgment of fact, no matter what its content, there must be as well the occurrence of its conditions" (I, 338b). But, then, Lonergan is arguing that given any judgment of fact by the subject, he may "argue back" to its "intentional" and not exclusively formal "conditions."

Again, Lonergan's variant on the transcendental deduction is stated in Chapter XI, Section 6 of Insight. His "argument" is that (leaving the issue of objectivity temporarily aside) the three-fold unity of the subject's conscious activity is the condition of knowing anything and, therefore, of anything being knowable by the subject at all. Thus, if any of his claims to know is to be performatively intelligible, then the subject cannot deny the fact of his being a knower, of his being, minimally, a tri-fold intentional unity.

> Am I a knower? . . . . But the answer, No, is incoherent, for if I am not a knower, how could the question be raised and answered by me? No less, the hedging answer, I do not know, is incoherent. For if I know that I do not know, then I am a knower; and if I do not know that I do not know, then I should not answer (I, 329b).

Thirdly, to establish the existence of, respectively, the categories with their transcendental ego and the three-fold unity, Kant and Lonergan have "argued": (1) "back from" the results of their previous applications; (2a) that they are necessary conditions of knowing anything, of anything being humanly knowable at all; (2b) from the unintelligibility" which results given their "denial." The complementary deductions yield, respectively, the formal unity of the transcendental subject and a concrete, socio-historical locus of developing sensitivity, intelligence, rationality and, as we shall see, responsibility. Again, unlike Kant's, Lonergan's "deductions" yield "categories" with "metaphysical" and not merely "phenomenal" relevance only through the mediation of the further arguments traced in Sections 4–8, above.

APPENDIX IV

According to Aquinas, some being P is a person if it is (1) distinct, (2) subsistent, and if it has (3) an intellectual nature (cf. DCC, Section 6). P satisfies condition (2) and is a thing in the proper sense, if it, therefore, possesses its own central act and per se unity. It satisfies condition (1) if there is a real major distinction between it and some other real, subsistent being Q. Again, Aristotle defines a nature as an immanent principle of motion and rest (Physics, II, I, 192b 22). But the questions behind the advancing cognition of the subject are her questions for intelligence, reflection, etc., etc. Since they intend what she is to know "before" she actually knows, they represent the immanent principles or "operators" of the movement of her inquiry. When at the end of each inquiry she arrives at a correct answer, her intention rests. Thus, the questions constitutive of the motion and rest of the inquiry of P determines her nature as intellectual (cf. the "implicit" definition in Section 2, above, etc.) and fulfill condition 3).

Again, the distinction between the **person** and **nature** of the subject distinguishes between P, e.g., the subject and some aspect of P, e.g., her intellectual nature. Thus, they differ by a real, inadequate distinction. Again, the subject's advance towards Self-knowledge began from intentionality analysis, passed through the crucible of Self-affirmation and the positions on Being and objectivity only to, first, derive the components of proportionate being and secondly, a critically grounded if incipient metaphysical account of her own dynamic being, of her own intelligent intelligibility.

Finally, it should at least be pointed out to the reader that if there is a general community of meaning and reference between the metaphysical elements of Being and the true propositions which "represent" Being, that this community is not accessible to logical or grammatical analysis in their present forms. Thus, if it is true that A is similar to B, then it is grammatically and logically correct to say that "similarity to B" is properly predicated of A. But if this is true, it does not follow that "similarity to B" is a metaphysical component of

A, one that is even constitutive of A. Before the "metaphysical equivalents" of the proposition can be assigned, then, it must be
transposed.

> The rule of structural transposition requires a transition from the
> logical subject, A, to two beings, A and B. The predicate, simi-
> larity, has its metaphysical ground in the fact that the difference
> between at least one constitutive component of A and one constitu-
> tive component of B is merely empirical (I, 506a).

Similarly, abstract and descriptive propositions must be translated,
respectively, into concrete and explanatory form before their equivalents can be assigned, their implications worked out, their intrinsic
and extrinsic relations assigned, etc. (cf. I, 503 ff).

CHAPTER VII

EXPANDING THE FOUNDATIONS

In Insight, Lonergan's pre-theological reflections upon the meaning of human Being reach their greatest depths in Chapter XV, Subsection 7.4 and Chapter XVIII. Again, these depths could only be reached because: they further plumb the "foundations," established in Chapter VI, above, for the analyses set forth in Chapters I-V; the bearing of these "foundations" upon the issues of fully human development and action have implications which remain to be worked out. Still, where a complete, lengthy, and profound discussion is necessary, where the "grounds" for it have already been laid, practical considerations dictate only a sketch of its further lines.

First, the purpose of Insight, XV.7.4 is to make the "genetic heuristic notion"[1] applicable to the specific "tri-fold unity" of human organic, sensitive, and intellectual development; thereby set out in advance the set of "heuristic principles" specifically relevant to the study and institution of fully human growth. In what follows we will take up the final three of the five principles which Lonergan lays down.[2]

First, the **"Law of Integration"** starts from the assumption that the initiative for the subject's development can be: (1) organic, e.g., for "loving and begetting [and fending for] children;" (2) sensitive-intersubjective, e.g., for the aesthetic, for the "idle hours with

---

[1] This notion was taken up in the Introduction of Chapter V, Section B9, above.

[2] The interested reader will find the first two of these principles in Insight, pp. 470b-471a.

those with whom one feels at home," etc.; (3) intellectual, e.g., for coming to grips with some scientific, philosophical, or ethical issue; or (4) external, e.g., for meeting some political, economic, technological, or dramatic challenge, etc. It goes on to argue that such development will remain "fragmentary until the principle of correspondence between the [relevant] levels [of his Being] is satisfied" (I, 471b, emphases mine). Thus, for example, the _initiative_ for the subject's further Self-development might be the "conversion" of his intellectual orientation demanded by his Self-affirmation, his discovery of his confinement by the positions, their metaphysical and personal implications, etc. But, in fact, such a re-orientation of the intentional life of the subject will not survive unless: (1) his sensitivity and intersubjectivity are displaced _from_ the immediate organic goals centering his biologically patterned experience _to_ those consistent with his intelligence and reasonableness; (2) his "will" is displaced from the particular "object" of appetite to the good as object of rational choice; (3) the relevant external conditions, e.g., the social, cultural and organic factors which may be needed to conserve and expand his three-fold "conversion," are fulfilled.

Secondly, the law of **"Limitation and Transcendence"** which structures the "finality of Being," generally, is identified in, and its consequences spelled out for, the conscious, _intentional_ Being of the subject. In its human context, then, the law **elementally** marks the opposition between: (1) the intelligence and reasonableness of the subject, e.g., "B," and his sensitivity, e.g., "A;"[1] (2) the linked but mutually opposed orientations of their subject to, respectively, detachment and attachment, "Being"-centredness and "Self"-centredness, inquiry and sensitivity, intelligibility and sensibility. **Concretely,** the opposition works itself out as the "tension" between the sensitively attached "integrator" or "integration" of the subject at some stage of development and the dynamic "operator," e.g., the further relevant

---

[1]The letters in quotation marks represent the same conventions as those which were introduced and applied in Chapter V, Section B10, above.

questions which bring out the limitations of the given stage and which,
if met, would carry him to a higher and further level of integration.
But given his transcendence of these limitations and the re-attachment
of his sensitivity to the further integration it represents, the tension is merely re-instituted from a higher and further starting point
for a future development, etc., etc. Thus, for example, once our inquiry, reflection, and/or deliberation have proximately discharged the
tension by "reach(ing) the truth":

> we are prone to find it unreal and shift from the realm of the in-
> telligible and unconditioned back into the realm of sense, to turn
> away from . . . (B)eing and settle down like good animals in our
> palpable environment (<u>I</u>, 559b).

But this proneness marks every stage of human development, would abso-
lutize what are really its limitations, would mask or exclude the further relevant "issues" which bring them out and foster their overcoming. Thus, the subject's every Self-achievement always eventually
faces him with the further issue of Self-transcendence, of a "lesser"
Self, a "past" to be sacrificed, a "greater" Self, a "future" Self to
be won. Again, it commits him perpetually and without release to patterns of growth, to meeting successively the re-irruption of the tension into his conscious Being at each successive stage of his genesis.

Thirdly, there is the "**Law of Genuineness.**" This law pertains to
the subject as conscious. It demands that he **meet** the tension between
limitation and transcendence. And the demand it places is "analogous."
Thus, the demand <u>may</u> possibly be met by the pre-reflective subject.
But, at some point issues will arise which even a genuine but "naive"
subject cannot discharge. Thus, in its highest and most mature form
the demand is taken up by the **Self**-knowing subject's reflective mediation of his own becoming. In the latter case, then, the subject guides
his **own** Self-development by his reflectively, Self-affirmed, and metaphysically appropriated fidelity to: (1) the advancing demands of intelligence and reasonableness; (2) the "positions" on Being and objectivity which they imply; (3) the project of repeatedly transcending the
limitations with which his living tasks him; (4) the <u>specific</u> situation
of his Self-transcendence within the "finality," within the "Horizon"
of emergent human and natural Being.

Thus, the "authentic" subject sets himSelf, without fugitive Self-concealments and without deliberate illusion, squarely within the "tension" of existence. As such, he:

> does not brush questions aside, smother doubts, push problems down, escape to activity, to chatter, to passive entertainment, to sleep, to narcotics. [He] . . . confronts issues, inspects them, studies their many aspects, works out their various implications, contemplates their concrete consequences in . . . [his] own life and in the lives of others. If [he] . . . respects inertial tendencies as necessary conservative forces, [he] . . . does not conclude that a defective routine is to be maintained because [he] has grown accustomed to it. Though [he] . . . fears [e.g., is "anxious" over] the cold plunge into becoming other than [he] . . . is, [he] . . . does not dodge the issue, nor pretend bravery, nor act out of bravado. [He] . . . is capable of assurance and confidence, not only in what [he] . . . has tried and found successful, but also in what is yet to be tried. [He] . . . grows weary with the perpetual renewal of questions to be faced, [he] . . . longs for rest, [he] . . . falters and fails, but [he] . . . knows [himSelf, his] . . . weakness[1] and [his] failures and . . . [he] does not try to rationalize them (I, 477b);

identifies himSelf with the "operator," the "pure desire" of his "intellectual" development;[2] repeatedly "operates" upon the "integrators" of his own Being. Furthermore, the manifold to the subject's patterns of experience represents differentiations "within" the unity of his conscious Being. But if this is so, then, the implications of his achievement of genuineness will ramify throughout the manifold. In its highest and most mature form, such genuineness would involve the subject's (1) reflective mediation of the immediacy of his presence in the patterns (cf. Chapters I-V, above); (2) his Self-affirmation and metaphysically mediated Self-knowledge (cf. Chapter VI, above); (3) his critical affirmation of the laws of integration, limitation and transcendence, genuineness, etc. But such a critical affirmation would entail: his identification with his own integrated, intelligent development within the aesthetic, common sense, dramatic and scientific patterns of his conscious Being in the surrounding world; his achievement of a "second immediacy," a higher spontaneity in carrying out this

---

[1] Cf. Insight, p. 627b.

[2] Cf. Insight, p. 561b 22-25.

identification. But this point is best explored by concentrating on its inverse. Thus, for the subject ultimately to **fail** in his achievement of such genuineness is **not** for him to: "**escape** but only to **displace** the tension between [his own] limitation and transcendence" ($\underline{I}$, 478c, emphases mine). But such failure, such displacement, is:

> the root of the **dialectical** phenomena of scotosis in the [dramatic pattern to the everyday life of the] individual, of the [individual, group, and general] bias of [his, of his community's] common sense, of basic philosophical differences [e.g., between the positions and counterpositions], and of their prolongation in natural and human science, in morals and religion, in educational theory and history ($\underline{I}$, 478c, emphasis mine).

But, then, the mature subject's achievement of genuineness must **ultimately** commit him to: (1) implementing his **critical** Self-knowledge; (2) developing the "positions" but also reversing the, his "counterpositions" in all their forms; (3) identifying himSelf with the knowledge and prosecution of the full range of intelligibility upon which the four-fold battery of his classical, statistical, genetic, but also his **dialectical methods** converge;[1] (4) doing so with an ease and integral virtuosity associated with his spontaneity.[2]

Finally, as noted, the preceding laws engage heuristic anticipations which are always necessary to make sense of the "development" of the human subject. Again, they must also be thought of as interior implications of the Self-affirmation of the subject in its full sweep. As such, then, they: (1) pertain to the structure, the "nature" of the conscious Being of $\underline{any}$ human subject; (2) are also simultaneously the laws "ruling" any of its students.

Secondly, Chapter XVIII of $\underline{Insight}$ is entitled the "Possibility

---

[1]Cf. Chapter V, Section B10, above.

[2]"Humour" and "satire" have proper functions within the integral dialectic of the subject. The former "keeps the positions in contact with human limitations and human infirmity." The latter "would depict the counter-positions . . . [and, thereby] hurry them to their destiny of bringing about their own reversal" ($\underline{I}$, 626b).

of Ethics." Its presupposition is the subject who has so grown in Self-knowledge, that (1) she has been able to appropriate, minimally, the expanding series of conclusions set forth in the preceding six and one half chapters, e.g., Chapters I-XVII of Insight; (2) the limitations of the preceding analyses have become apparent to her. Thus, the question of her own "responsible freedom" has become an issue for her. Again, Chapter VII of Insight (cf. Chapter III, Division B, above) and XVIII are both written from the attitude of reflection. Both take up the issue of human practise in the socio-historical world. But the analyses of Chapter VII were well beyond the limited "viewpoint" and reflective capacities of the common sense subject and, consequently, well exceeded her powers to understand, affirm, or apply. But this is not so of the unrestricted viewpoint, the critically grounded, and metaphysically set Self-knowledge of the subject of Chapter XVIII.[1] Finally, Chapter XVIII takes up the question of the fact and meaning of the cognitionally Self-appropriated subject's freedom as the question of whether the normative science of ethics can be conceived "along the same lines of metaphysics" (UB, 277a), i.e., along the same lines as the previous cognitional implementation of the "integral heuristic structure" of proportionate Being.[2] But these issues lead back to, find their ultimate "foundations" in, the further issue of the "fundamental option" with which freedom always tasks its human subject.

First, Lonergan evidences the subject's always already at least latent possibility of responsible freedom by thematizing its inverse. Thus, the following phenomena are not only all-pervasive, but manifest the implicit recognition that one "could" because one "ought" to have acted better or otherwise. The subject, then:

    (1) flees rational "Self"-consciousness for "idle talk," "keeping busy," "going through the motions," etc.;

---

[1] Thus, the analyses of Chapter XVIII pertain to the subject who is reflecting on her own conscious Being in her specific knowledge of her situation "within" a universe of emergent probability, within the "finality" of proportionate human and natural Being.

[2] Cf. Chapter VI, Sections 6 ff, above.

(2) <u>rationalizes</u> whatever she has in <u>fact</u> done into virtue;

(3) <u>renounces the moral</u> and, therefore, the effort to extend her "knowledge" into action (cf. <u>I</u>, p. 599b).

Again, in such cases the subject is fleeing, rationalizing, and renouncing the claim of the "ought," of the "good" upon her conscious Being.

Secondly, in Chapter III, Division B, above, the human "good," what has now emerged as the "ought" or "imperative" upon the subject's responsible freedom, was defined heuristically in terms of the since established "invariant" structure of human "sensitivity," "intelligence," and "reasonableness." Thus, the "particular good" was identified with the "object of desire." The "good of order" was identified with the "intelligible possibilities" of individual or collective action grasped by conscientious, deliberative practical <u>intelligence</u>. "Value" was identified with the "intelligible orders and their contents" that are or would, consequently, be "<u>rationally</u> **chosen**."

Thirdly, then, values are "true" insofar as the choice which implements them: (1) does **not** reflect the "flight from rational Self-consciousness," "rationalization" or "moral renunciation" described in the penultimate paragraph, above; (2) meets the "imperative," the "exigence" defined proximately by the judgment of her intelligence and reasonableness and, remotely, by the self-correcting process guided by her pure desire (cf. <u>I</u>, 601b, 602a 1-16);[1] (3) is, therefore, consistent with the "positions;" (4) springs from the option of the fully "genuine" subject described in the first part of this chapter. But, then, values are "false" when they: (1) <u>do</u> reflect the "flight from rational Self-consciousness," etc., etc.; (2) violate their consistency with the exigence; (3) are, therefore, consistent with the "counter-positions;" (4) spring from the "inauthenticity" of the subject and the mere "seeming" that results from the counter-positions in all their forms (cf. <u>I</u>, 602a 16-21).

---

[1]Cf. Chapter V, Section B10.4-5.

Fourthly, then, a "normative" science of ethics is possible by implementing "dialectical method" in the realm of human practise. And its presupposition is that: (1) the intelligent and reasonable components of given facets of human living and institutions can be discerned; (2) in each case, the positions (i.e., "true" values) are to be developed and the counter-positions (i.e., false values) reversed; (3) the "foundations" recollected in Chapter VI, above, are, indeed, transculturally "secure."

Fifthly, as noted, the "horizon" of Chapter XVIII of Insight is set by the integral heuristic structure of proportionate Being and its principal metaphysical elements of "potency," "form," "act," and "finality." In such a context, then, the "free acts" of the subject are her acts of **"willing."** The regular recurrence of free acts of various kinds presupposes the subject's already established **"willingness"** to perform them. She develops such a "personal differentiation" or "character" in her choices by her gradual "persuasion" by "reasons" and her actual engagement of acts of the given kind. Once such an "habitual orientation" is formed:

> when the occasion for [the subject's] doing arises . . . [she] will not have to be persuaded to act [i.e., her act will follow with a "second" spontaneity] (UB, 283a, emphases mine).

Again, the subject's **"will"** is an "appetite" which, when not interfered with, follows intelligence and reasonableness. But, then, the subject's **"will"** corresponds to conjugate "potency," her **"willingness"** to conjugate "form," and her actual choice, her **"willing"** to conjugate act. But, from the first two numbered paragraphs of the second part of this chapter it follows that:

> knowledge of itself [e.g., of what is and is not intelligent and reasonable in the given case], does not settle [e.g.,[1] the subject's] . . . course of action (UB, 279b, emphasis mine).[1]

Thus, in her options for false values, her failures to opt for the true, her periods of "drift," etc., the subject evidences a further

---

[1] Lonergan's point is that the phenomena run counter to the rationalist identification of knowledge and virtue, cf. Plato's Meno, 77a-79e. Cf. The Collected Dialogues of Plato (Pantheon Books: Bollingen Series LXXI, 1961), pp. 360-362.

distinct capacity, operation, or habituation of her conscious Being be-yond the cognitional. The subject, then, becomes "**rationally Self-con-scious**" when: (1) what she is to "make of herSelf" has become an issue for her; (2) her concern shifts from "objects of appetite" to the ques-tion "What am I to do?," to understanding, to, thus, uncovering the relevant intelligible "possibility" which answers to her question.[1] But such a shift also involves the turning of her concern toward: (1) the "reasons" for the possible act she has grasped; (2) "achieving" consistency between her knowing and doing. But the moral "conversion" or "re-orientation" of her choices, of her willingness, etc., from the criteria of "false" to "true" values is never accomplished once and for all. Consequently, the relation between her "knowing" and "doing" is only contingent. Thus, the matter of her "responsible" freedom is al-ways an issue for her, always something to be won and/or lost, achieved and/or defaulted upon. Finally, then, the subject is always already "**essentially**" free to "will," to decide for the intelligent and reason-able. But given the antecedent character of her "willingness," of what she has made of herSelf, she may not be "**effectively**" free to do so.[2]

Sixthly, the reader is asked to recall the argument of Chapter VI, above. It advanced, for example, from the subject's Self-affirma-tion to the notion of Being. It proceeded from the division of posi-tions and counter-positions to the construction of a heuristic meta-physics. It argued from the notions of the "intelligibility" and "fi-nality" of Being to the identification of the latter notion with the methodological precept of "emergent probability," etc. Again, as noted in the third preceding paragraph, the tri-fold notion of the "human good" expands upon and shares in the same invariant, Self-affirmed "base" as the preceding metaphysical corollaries. Finally, as "intel-ligent" and "rational" in their choices, the subject, the given

---

[1] Cf. Understanding and Being, p. 281a 1-2.

[2] Cf. Insight, pp. 619-622a.

community of subjects:

> originates **orders** that are parallel [in structure] to the intelligibilities that are investigated by empirical scientists (I, 618b).[1]

But taking this latter point as a clue and the preceding recollections as a "base," the subject's notion of the "human good" can be expanded into a heuristic, "metaphysical" account of the good per se. Thus, Lonergan proposes to regard:

(1) the "potential **good**" as identical to "potential **intelligibility**" "within" the horizon of Being and, therefore, as including the "particular good" or "object of desire" as one of its cases;

(2) the "formal **good**" as identical to the "formal **intelligibility**" "within" surrounding world process and, therefore, as including the "good of order" as one of its cases;

(3) the "actual **good**" as identical to the "actual **intelligibility**" "within" the horizon of Being and, therefore, as including the "values" involved in choosing such orders and their contents as one of its cases.

But he justifies the proposed expansion of his regard in three brief steps. First, the "objects" of the subject's desire:

> are bound inextricably through natural laws and actual frequencies with the total manifold of the universe of proportionate (B)eing. If objects of desire are instances of the good because of the satisfactions they yield, then the rest of the manifold of existents and events ["within" Being] also are good, because desires are satisfied not in some dreamland but only in the concrete universe (I, 605b).

Secondly, the "intelligible possibilities" which when grasped and instituted by human practise constitute the dynamic "good of order":

> are but further exploitations of prehuman, intelligible orders ["within" Being]; moreover, they fall within the universal order of generalized emergent probability [e.g., of "finality"], both as consequents of its fertility, and as ruled by its more inclusive sweep. If the intelligible orders of human invention are good because they systematically assure the satisfaction of [the

---

[1]Cf. Chapter III, Section B2, above.

subject's, her community's] desires, then so also are the intelligible orders ["within" that "finality"] that underlie, condition, precede, and include man's invention (I, 605b).

Thirdly, if intelligible orders and their manifold contents are "possible objects of rational choice" they are "values." But as said, the all-encompassing "order" of emergent probability "underpins" and "over-arches" every "particular order" as well as every "actual intelligibility" within the "finality" to the procession of Being. But it would be irrational for the subject to opt for and even implement some actually intelligible order, e.g., the "human good of order," and reject: (1) its conditions; (2) the "whole" within which it is merely a dynamic "part;" (3) its "antecedents," e.g., the "intelligibility" of Being, etc.

> Accordingly, since [the subject, her community, etc.] . . . is [always already] involved in choosing [human values and their "orders"] and since every [one of her, its consistent] choice(s), at least implicitly, is a choice of [the] universal order [of emergent Being], the realization of the universal order [in which she, they play some small but, minimally, "significant" part] is a <u>true value</u> (I, 605b).

But, the normative, "dialectical" science of ethics, described above, was a corollary of the subject's reflective appropriation of the invariant structure of her own conscious Being. And in light of the argument, immediately above, "ethics" can be regarded in its practical import as the "implementation" in the realm of human affairs of the integrally heuristic notion of "Being," of the integrally heuristic notion of the "Good" with which it is convertible.

Seventhly, the subject as intelligent and rational not only grasps and affirms the facts immanent in the surrounding world but also grasps, affirms and implements its intelligible possibilities. But the reflections which can now be said to "ground" and situate the preceding remark are, potentially, functions of the naive, pre-reflective subject's validated pursuit of Self-understanding, her appropriation of the tri-fold structure of her Being as conscious. But the second part of this chapter has augmented her cognitional Self-knowledge with a notion of a "freedom" which, if it is to respect the dynamic, "intelligent and rational" "nature" of the subject, must be responsible, must represent a "'rational' Self-consciousness." But this augmenting includes the subject's grasp and judgment of value upon a new "practical possibility." This possibility consists in the dialectical or genetic transformation of her "own spontaneous living." For her naive "living" within the community of emergent Being:

> exhibits an otherwise coincidental manifold into which [the subject] can introduce a higher [dynamic-dialectical] system [e.g., "herSelf" as intelligent, reasonable, and responsibly free] by . . . [her] own understanding of . . . [herself] [cf. Chapters I-VII, above] and . . . [her] own deliberate [radical] choices (I, 599a).

To such an end, then, was the subject's implicit Self-option, her pre-reflective "choice" to understand, to know herSelf in her intelligent, intelligible, responsible "nature." Again, then, the sum of the preceding reflections has been to the end of issuing to the subject, e.g., the reader, "an invitation to a personal, a decisive act" (I, xixb); tasking her with a "fundamental option." We have seen that the conditioned, intelligent and rational consciousness of the subject freely grounds her own actions and their products. So, in a fundamental sense, would the only implicitly and irregularly intelligent and rational subject, now having come to know herSelf, freely ground the "making of herSelf" as her first and foremost "existential" possibility of authentic human Being. The prospect of such a foundational Self-choice, then, challenges the subject with the possibility of: a fundamental option in behalf of her own intelligence and responsibility, the correlative "intelligibility" of Being in all its forms; the "founding" of all her consequent relative options upon this resolute "fundament;" being so much more than what she has actually made himSelf. It challenges her with the possibility of: achieving and implementing an integral "genuineness" in all the relevant patterns and interactions of her experience; a "moral conversion" of her "will" to effect, preserve, and re-coup such genuineness. Again, it challenges her with the prospect of opting fundamentally and from the critical-dialectical but also "existential" perspective this study has now achieved to break the "duality" immanent in the position/counter-position split, the linked

but opposed Self-implementations this split implies,[1] and in full knowledge of the individual, social, and historical consequences a failure
of such practical Self-institution holds out, a success makes possible.
Again, it challenges her with the awe-ful prospect of her own "rational
(S)elf consciousness clearly and distinctly taking possession of it-
(S)elf as rational (S)elf-consciousness" (I, xviiib). Finally, then,
the institution of such a prospect is the condition of the ongoing construction, recognition, and institution of an ethics; service to, recognition and institution of the "intelligibility" of Being.

Eighthly, by the "principle of integration," above, it follows
that the intellectual and moral "re-orientations" implicit in the subject's achievement of rational Self-consciousness will "remain fragmentary" and that the latter achievement will eventually breakdown unless

---

[1]Three points should be made here.

First, corresponding to the position/counter-position split is a
corresponding duality in the Self-knowledge of the subject. Thus, the
biologically patterned Self-"knowledge" of the subject corresponds to
an embodied centre of "power and (S)elf-satisfaction." (The dialectically opposed counter-position to the preceding Self-conception would
approximate to the dis-embodied, res cogitans of the rationalist tradition.) Its "intellectual" counterpart corresponds to a Spiritual
center of acts of empirically motivated intelligence, reasonableness,
responsibility. But the extension of the subject's Self-"knowledge"
into action leads to linked but opposed implementations of her own
Being. To have said this, however, is to have presupposed the achievement of a "critical" and, therefore, "dialectical" perspective upon
one's own freedom, to have set the stage for a fundamental "breaking"
of the duality, an institution of the genetic-dialectical intelligibility of one's authentic Self. Finally, the full "existential" implications of the subject's Self-choice were taken up in Chapter V, Section
B10, above, but the analysis context of human responsible freedom, of a
fundamental option had not as yet been reached.

Secondly, Lonergan does not speak of a "fundamental option" in
Insight. But it is impossible to make complete sense of the cited
texts without invoking it. Again, this notion corresponds to his notion of a "vertical exercise" of liberty in, for example, Method in
Theology (cf. MT, 40, 122, 237-238, 240, 269).

Finally, the "existential" dimension of the Self-choice of the
subject comes strongly to the fore in "The Subject," (Milwaukee:
Marquette University Press, 1968). It is reprinted in A Second Collection, edited by William F.J. Ryan and Bernard J. Tyrrell (Philadelphia:
The Westminster Press, 1974), pp. 69-86.

further conditions are fulfilled. This will include her further achievement of a symbolically mediated "openness to the 'Mystery'" to sustain the "dynamic correspondence" of the psycho—neural and the procession to its higher integrations. This will include the securing of the necessary intersubjective, social, interpersonal and organic conditions that happen to be necessary in order to preserve the tri-fold intellectual, volitional, and affective "re—orientations."

Finally, then, the prospect of such a triply integral, rational Self—consciousness is the condition of the subject's ongoing achievement of a fully "effective freedom." It is a condition, then, of a freedom which is able to: actually implement its fundamental option in all the ongoing contexts within which it becomes an issue; successively transcend the limitations with which her situated being in a developing world faces her; avoid the flight from Self—knowledge, from Self—choice; implement human Being as an "originating value."[1] It is a hard won achievement. Again, "the key point":

> is to reach a willingness to persuade oneself and to submit to the persuasion of others. For then one can be persuaded to a universal willingness; so one becomes antecedently willing to learn all there is to be learnt about willing and learning and about the enlargement of one's freedom from external and psychoneural interferences (I, 623e—624a).

But it has been to the persuasion of such a willingness that this study, in fidelity to the thinking of Lonergan's Insight, to the Self—exploration it charts and would re—activate, has offered its service.

---

[1]Cf. Insight, p. 601b 5—9. Also cf. Method in Theology, p. 51b 11 and p. 51b 3—7.

APPENDIX I

As noted, Lonergan defines terminal values heuristically as the "objects" of the (effectively free) subject's possible choice. He indicates that these values are ordered hierarchically. However, in Insight he neither determines these values nor their relative positions within a hierarchy. Finally, he claims that the hierarchy, together with the division of values into those which are true and false, terminal and original, etc.:

> reveal how the dynamic exigence of . . . [the effectively free subject] for [performative] self-consistency [between his value judgments and actions] unfolds into a body of moral precepts concretely operative in moral consciousness ($\underline{I}$, 601d).

But what might such a "hierarchy" of values be when it has a nontrivial and even, possibly, a "foundational" significance? What could its justification be? How would it fit into the critical, "foundation" expanding problematic which has been the implicit theme of the preceding chapter of our study? And even if such a hierarchy could be specified and justified, how would it admit application in concrete situations? But the stage has been set for at least attempting tentative answers to these questions.

First, Chapter V, Section 10, above, defines heuristically the "hierarchy" of intelligible orders constitutive of the "nature" of the human subject. The hierarchy was neo-classical since: (1) it was consistent with the viewpoint of emergent probability; (2) it admitted successive, distinct, interlocking levels; (3) predecessor were to proximate, successive strata as conditioning to conditioned, etc. But recall the human subject of that hierarchy as specified by definition III, i.e., $T_r = f(B_k, Z_e, R_m)$. From the higher vantage point won by adding Chapters IV-VII to Chapter III of this study, we can say that he stands: (1) under such laws of human development as those of integration, limitation and transcendence, genuineness, and those of dialectical process generally, etc.; (2) within human community and history conceived along the lines of emergent probability. Again, "R_m" specifies the fully intentional, "natural" strata of human Being and development in a heuristic and explanatory manner. But there are three "aspects" to the intentionality of human Being which we must familiarly abbreviate by intelligence, e.g., inquiry and insight, rationality, e.g., reflection and judgment, and responsibility, e.g., deliberation and choice. Again, B_k and Z_e similary specify the underlying neuro-organic and sensitive strata of his being. Finally, precisely because definition III correctly describes the Being of the subject, the three-fold "conversion" of intentional process described in the Chapter VII, above, is de facto necessary if effective freedom is to be achieved.

Secondly, under what conditions would a neo-classical values hierarchy command the positive affectve response, the intellectual assent, and deliberate option of the effectively free subject? By using available clues we can say that it would do so were it to: (1) share the invariance of the three-fold structure of his conscious life; (2) represent the conditions and ultimate terms of his "development" as faithful to the structure's proceeding exigences; (3) offer some kind of guidance to his activity in community with the other and in history. But definition III merely represents that three-fold structure in conjunction with its underlying and communal-historical conditions.

But, thirdly, then, we must attempt the following specification of the general lines of the sought for hierarchy.

Corresponding, then, to the "sensitivity" of the practical subject in both his individual and communal dimensions (cf. stratum B_k and Z_e in definition III), there would be a cluster of "vital values." Again, corresponding to them there would be the proceeding "habits" of schematic performance which activate their pursuit in successively transposed contexts. Among these, there would be the "physical values" by which the organic strength and virtuosity of the incarnate subject are sustained and advanced. Among them also would be included "aesthetic," "artistic," "intersubjective," "dramatic," and "symbolic" values. Their function would be to renew and enhance the incarnate subject's dynamic openess to the Mystery generally and to the Mystery of the Other; his implicit or explicit, sensitive correspondence to the exigencies of higher level, dynamic functions.

Corresponding to the "intelligence" of the practical subject in both his individual and communal dimensions (cf. a first aspect of stratum R_m in definition III), there would be a cluster of "social values" and associated, developing "habits" . . . . Among these would be the technical, economic, and political values constitutive of the "social life" of the subject and his community, the subject's contributions to and receipts from the ongoing good of order.

Corresponding to the "rationality" of the practical subject in both his individual and communal dimensions (cf. a second aspect of stratum R_m), there would be a cluster of "cultural values" and associated, developing "habits" . . . . To these would correspond values locally constitutive and/or reflective of: (1) the great, historical achievements of art and literature, philosophy and science, politics and religion, etc. insofar as these (a) shape or spring from human activity and (b) awaken concrete, historical subjects in community to (c) the "dignity" of their being as human and the "intelligibility" of their world; (2) the critical/creative spirit which these achievements presuppose and imply; (3) the reflectively grounded, developing "controls" on meaning and value which these higher achievements represent, etc.

Corresponding to the "responsibility" of the practical subject in both his individual and communal dimensions (cf. a third aspect of R_m), there would be a cluster of "personal values." To these, perhaps, would correspond those values constitutive and/or expressive of: (1) the subject's engagement or reflectively appropriated realization of his own functions of sensitivity, intelligence, rationality, and rational choice; (2) his openness to the other as a locus of similar, ongoing possibilities of similar realization and activity.

But, fourthly, then, the relations of the fundamental levels of value correspond to those informing the intelligible strata specified in definition III.

Fifthly, from the vantage point of the preceding remarks and those of Chapters IV–VII, the reflections of Chapter III, above, can be better understood and situated. Thus, it is the genuine, effectively free and, at the limit, the fully self-appropriated subject who will be able to discern: which contributions to the good of order "are similar;" how, therefore, to "apply" the "principle of the good of order;" how to "apply" and, in certain cases, re-order the values hierarchy so that it is relevant to the concrete situation or the situation of human Being generally; when further learning is or is not necessary before action is taken or corrected, specific value judgments re-affirmed or revised, etc., etc.[1] Thus, near the term of our reflections, and in a thoroughly transformed context, we find Lonergan in agreement with Aristotle. For each locates both a proximate and remote answer to the fundamental question "what is to be done?" in the powers of judgment and decision of the "good," effectively free human subject who is also "familiar with" the concrete situation at hand.

Sixthly, some approximation to the stated hierarchy of values is worthy of the explicit rational choice of the subject. But this is because it: (1) implicitly transposes the fruits of the reflective analyses of the three-fold structure of human conscious Being set forth in Chapters I-XVII of Insight into their practical, option worthy context; (2) prolongs the subject's self-affirmation of that structure and, therefore, definition III into that context. But precisely because it does so, the fundamental lines of the values-hierarchy will share in the relative, trans-cultural invariance of that structure, that definition.

Seventhly, we have found that the full intelligibility and value of Being are coextensive. But precisely for this reason, it is not surprising that: (1) the values hierarchy is "founded" on the Being of the human; (2) it does no more than sum up the existential conditions and termini of the flourishing of that Being; (3) it, therefore, enjoins the development of the positions and the reversal of the counter-positions in all their forms and all the patterns and contexts in which they arise, etc. But, then, only the subject's fundamental option for that hierarchy makes ultimate sense, is ultimately intelligible. Again, that hierarchy is implicit in any of the subject's rational choices. Thus, "all thing being equal," the subject's fundamental or proximate options which are in conflict with the concrete demands of that hierarchy would be performatively inconsistent with the terms and conditions of their own engagement.

---

[1]Cf. above, pp. 88 n, 61b ff, 92d ff, Chapter V, Section B10d.

And the same arguments will apply when what is at issue is the "object" of the subject's option, e.g., a social system; a lower order system of values for determining specific choices in specific contexts, etc.

Finally, as noted in Chapter VI, Section 11, above, the "affective" dimensions of human consiousness can proceed in actual or anticipatory correspondence with the subject's higher level openess to what is. Again, suppose such correspondence in a given case and recall the recent argument to the convertibility of the value and the intelligibility of Being. But, then, there will also be the case of anticipatory correspondence in which the subject's affections apprehend and motivate his responses to and decisions for values even when the intellectual developments necessary for their explicit recognition and engagement are as yet unformed or distorted. The case may pertain to either proximate or fundamental options. And such a case may tend to be pervasive and chronologically prior to the one in which appropriate intellectual and reflective development have taken place. Again, the point would require further development if we were to acknowledge the "L_1" stratum of human Being sketched in definition VI, of Chapter V, Section 8, above (Cf. I, XX, MT, II, esp. pp. 31c–41a).

GENERAL CONCLUSION

To bring this text, finally, to a close, we would make, essentially, four brief points. The first of the four specifies characteristics of the philosophical anthropology whose possibility and grounds this study has been relating. The second offers some clarification of the order of the exposition of which this study has availed itself. The third accentuates the essentially heuristic character of what has been achieved. And a fourth briefly underscores the fundamental limitation under which this study has labored.

First, then, on the basis of the preceding analyses, the possibility of a philosophical anthropology that is (1) methodical, (2) dialectical, (3) comprehensive, (4) non-reductionistic, (5) contemporary without merely abandoning the old, (6) oriented toward "existence" and transformative "praxis," and (7) "Being"-centred, has been established.

It is (1) "methodical" because it has been arrived at by a "generalized empirical" or "transcendental" "**method**." Thus, by pursuing an appropriate, ordered set of reflections upon her own intentional performance, the "pure" definition and performative corollaries of human Being can be validated in the personal experience of any "sufficiently cultured" reader. Again, the "full" definition can be presumptively validated by adding, minimally, the heuristic notion of emergent probability and further premisses that are empirically verifiable.

It is (2) "dialectical" through its distinction between, minimally, the performatively opposed "biological" and "pure" Self-conceptions of the subject. The reflectively evidenced ground of this distinction consists in, respectively, the material contradiction or consistency of proffered Self-understanding with the intentional fact that in being posited and acted upon, it is being intelligently grasped, reasonably affirmed, and responsibly taken up by its subject. Again, through such an anthropology's acceptance of the viewpoint of

398

emergent probability, the fruits of chemical, physical, neural, sociological, cultural and other studies can be integrated into or with a "full" definition of human Being. And such an integration is possible without acceding to but only recognizing mechanist determinism or other forms of the counter-position. Finally, the basic dialectic of position/counter-position admits further determination. Thus, we have introduced and exemplified but not developed the notion of "dialectically opposed" anthropological "counter-positions," etc.

It is (3) "comprehensive" because in its "pure" form its operative account of human Being is trans-socially and -culturally invariant and can, furthermore, expand along the minor but significant lines which signify further contemporary developments in Self-understanding. Again, its "full" form is presumptively invariant since it can assimilate the results and even revolutionary developments of any of the relevant extant empirical sciences of "man" or non-human nature whether these pertain to the non-conscious, pre-conscious, or conscious dimensions of human Being. Furthermore, the main lines of such a "full" form could remain essentially intact while it expands to incorporate the science of even a newly discovered "stratum" of intelligible data, e.g., that "between" the chemical (non-living) and organic (living) dimensions of Being in general, of human Being in particular, etc.

It is (4) "non-reductionistic" because it would assimilate the complete explanation of the sensitivity, affectivity, intelligence, rationality and/or rational Self-consciousness of the subject to neither neuro-organic nor purely sensitive conjugates nor the latter to the laws of physics and/or chemistry.

It meets the exigences of (5) "contemporary" thinking and this in a number of ways. Thus, it can accomodate the "scientific" exigence in its contemporary expression while retaining its consistency with the fruits of its methodical application. It has adapted the modern "turn to the subject" or "critical" exigence and the phenomenological method of Self-reflection without concluding to an immanentism, a skepticism, a repudiation of an authentic sense of "objectivity," community, etc. It can underscore the sense in which human Being, human community and meaning, and even non-human nature are radically temporal and historical without falling into the mistaken and even performatively Self-contradictory equation of Being with time. Again, if it meets these contemporary exigences, it retains a certain continuity with the old. For example, then, Lonergan's notion of the, minimally, "'tri-levelled unity' of the development of the human subject" "transposes" the Thomistic-Aristotelian notions of the unicity of substantial form, the tri-partate division of organic, sensitive, and intellective functions of the rational soul, etc. into their contemporary, explanatory context.

Again, the centrality of a "fundamental option" or "resolution" to the authentic Self-constitution of the subject; "dialectic" to the Being and community of the subject so opted for, establishes the relationship of Lonergan's reflections to contemporary (6) existential and transformative "theorists" of praxis.

Finally, we must recall in order to accent: (a) the notion of human Being as "Being's executor;" (b) the subject's reflective discovery of herSelf as a locus of and, therefore, both appropriated and called to deliberately discharge "the tension" which irrupts within and wracks Being in its proportionate totality; (c) the subject's reflective conclusion to the "primacy" of Being over human Being and community generally, etc. But (a)-(c) undercut any easy, pre-reflective identification of Lonergan's "word on man" with a (7) Being-forgetful "philosophy" of "subjectivity."

Secondly, we have addressed the theme of Lonergan's notion of human Being by (1) assuming, exemplifying and, then, only later definitively establishing the invariance of the tri-levelled structure of human consciousness; (2) ordering the materials of Insight in terms of Lonergan's notion of "patterns of experience;" (3) thus arguing that because the tri-fold structure which attaches to the conscious Being of the subject is invariant that, therefore, it admits the previously articulated series of patterns. But these patterns can be construed in two ways.

On the one hand, they represent the related, intelligible sets of relationships which can be discerned and verified in the conscious activity of any "sufficiently cultured" human subject.

On the other hand, these related intelligible sets represent "differentiations" within the **process** by which the human subject becomes "sufficiently cultured."

Given this, and the fact that our table of contents diverges from Lonergan's, the question arises of the principle(s) by which our exposition of these patterns was ordered.

But unlike the primarily pedagogical intent of Insight,[1] the ordering principle of this study has been to bring both the genetic and dialectical dimensions of human Being centrally to the fore, as befits the subject at hand. We will explain and, perhaps, justify this procedure, briefly, by expanding upon the recently accentuated notion of the "differentiations" of human consciousness.[2]

First (1), then, the child's engagement of and development in the attitude of common sense involve his transcendence of the "world of immediacy" and, therefore, the biological pattern to which he, as an infant, had been confined. This Self-transcendence is "into" the world "mediated" by the fruits and the fact of his family's and, therefore, his local community's experience, understanding, judging, and action. It involves, not the exclusion, but the unification and mediation of his psychic and intersubjective life by reference to functions on,

---

[1] Cf. Insight, pp. xxvia–xxviib.

[2] Two points should be made here.
First, for the following development of the notion of the differentiations of human consciousness I have relied upon Doctrinal Pluralism, pp. 13b–22a and Method and Theology, pp. 27b–30a, 257b–265b, etc. For the explanatory locus of the discussion see Insight, p. 452e and, therefore, Chapter V, p. 265b #5, above.
Secondly, I have deviated from Lonergan's handling of the issue in several respects.
First, I have not included all the differentiations that Lonergan cites. For example, then, by prior resolve, I have not treated the "scholarly" differentiation of human consciousness (Cf. DP, 19c and I, XVII.3, etc.).
Secondly, I have listed the dramatic pattern and the achieved, rational Self-consciousness of the subject as differentiations of human consciousness. My justification for doing this in the former case is Lonergan's inclusion of the aesthetic pattern of experience as a proper differentiation of consciousness (cf. DP, 56c). My justification for doing this in the latter case is that it seemed eminently sensible if not, in other contexts, completely necessary to do so (cf. S, 27c–28a).

minimally, the second and third levels of consciousness. Again, if relative to the biological, the common sense attitude of the subject is "differentiated," relative to further possible developments it is "undifferentiated consciousness," exclusively at home within its local variety of common sense.

Secondly (2), the young adult's engagement of and development in the "scientific attitude" involve, not the negation, but the unification and mediation of his common sense functions on a higher intentional level. This higher unification-mediation of his activity implements such operations as experimentation, theorizing, and controlled verification. It involves or anticipates his ability to perform logical operations upon abstractions, discover and affirm universal principles that sustain properties of invariance and equivalence, and empirically verify his convergence upon the relations of the things "to each other," etc.

Thirdly (3), the adult subject's engagement and development of the "contemporary" "philosophic differentiation" of consciousness involve not the exclusion but the unification and mediation of, minimally, his common sense and scientific levels of intentional operation. This higher unification-mediation proceeds when query turns reflective; discovers and verifies (a) a basic nest of terms and relations and (b) the dynamic structure which, together, define the unity of his intentional performance; expands this discovery into a dialectically grounded epistemology, metaphysics, and account of the relations and proper functions of the manifold differentiations and patterns of human experience, etc.

Fourthly (4), the subject's engagement and development of a fully "ethical differentiation" of consciousness does not interfere with but only preserves, perfects, and expands the field of relevance of his philosophically mediated Self-knowledge.[1] Again, the expansion is "into" the sphere of his and/or his community's reflectively mediated practise. Thus, it represents the "sublation" of his achievement of Self-knowledge into the project of a critically controlled

---

[1] Cf. The Subject, pp. 27c-28a, etc.

implementation of true values within a universe of emergent Being. And it subsumes the project of cognitional Self-appropriation within the higher, dynamic context of the subject's deliberations, evaluations, and relative and fundamental options.

But, fifthly (5), some principle "B" "sublates" some other principle "A," if and only if "B" "goes beyond" "A." But "B" "goes beyond" "A" just in case it "unifies" "A" on a higher level, introduces "something new" to "A," makes the new element a "new base of [higher] operations" and does this without interfering with or negating its lower order principle.[1] For example, then, if "B" and "A" represent viewpoints, and "B" is proximately "higher" than "A," then "B" "sublates" "A." Again, if "B" and "A" represent a series of successively higher viewpoints, then the succession is an instance of "genesis." But the scientific differentiation of human consciousness "sublates" that of common sense. The philosophic "sublates" those of science and common sense. And the ethical differentiation "sublates" those of science, philosophy and common sense, etc., etc. Thus, minimally, the "structure" linking the contents of, respectively, Chapters III, V, VI, and VII of this study is genetic in character and accounts for their order of exposition.

Sixthly (6), the subject's procession through the succession of higher differentations described, above, has at least two conditions.

The first consists in the occurrence of a "shift" in the "sensitivity" of the subject towards some approximation to the aesthetic pattern and/or its implicit sense of Mystery. Again, that occurrence is necessary to free human sensitivity from the routines imposed by previous patterns of development; for openness to and cooperation with a "next" higher form of differentiated operation. Again, such an aesthetic differentiation would be incipient in the infant on the threshold of achieving the attitude of common sense. And for this reason, we have made discussion of this pattern the second

---

[1]The cited phrases are to be found in The Subject, pp. 20b–22b and 27c–28a. Still, if "A" is "retained, preserved, yet transcended and completed by" "B," "B" does not reconcile, in the Hegelian manner, a "logical" "contradiction" in "A." Cf. The Subject, p. 21b n11.

chapter of this study.   Again, such differentiation would find mature form only later and under further sets of appropriate conditions.

Again, the aesthetic "shifting" of the sensitivity of the subject (a) can be "combined" with the common sense "differentiation" of the consciousness of the child; (b) can itself be shifted towards an elemental concern that the artistry and virtuosity of one's own manner of Being in the world be promptly recognized and responded to by others. The child's family community would be the initial site of this combining and shifting.   Again, the latter combination can itself combine with the inevitable, spontaneous need for (c) "graceful" negotiation of underlying neural demands to ensure the integration of psychic life with its higher intentional dynamic. But the combination signified by (a)-(c) effects the child's opening to and heads him for the full negotiation of a properly "dramatic" differentiation of conscious development. Again, such a differentiation would seem to be contemporaneous with or to succeed that of common sense.   It would seem, furthermore, to sublate it, and to be necessary if the subject is to sustain the manner of everyday living in which higher stages of development are achieved and partially, intermittently, but appropriately sustained.   Thus, we have made discussion of the dramatic differentiation of human consciousness the fourth chapter of this study.

But, seventhly (7), the development of the subject is at risk in any pattern or at any relevant level of differentiation or undifferentiation.   But this would be so because of (a) the ineradicable, sensitive component of human conscious Being; (b) the possible interference of its attached, biological motivation with the implicit, Self-differentiating intentionality inherent in its tri-fold structure; (c) the uncritical philosophical assumption that biologically patterned subjectivity is properly and adequately revelatory of and, therefore, normative in matters pertaining to the essence or practise of human Being.

Consequently, the development of the mature subject is at risk within (a) the common sense pattern; (b) the dramatic pattern; (c) the scientific pattern; (d) the philosophical pattern and (e) its further, ethical differentiation. Again, the differentiation of the developing subject is at risk as he (a) shifts from the world of immediacy to the world mediated by meaning; (b) mounts from the world mediated by common sense to those mediated by scientific, philosophic, and ethical meanings and values; (c) consciously shifts from one "world" to another once differentiation is attained, etc.

But in keeping with the preceding analyses, Chapters I and II of this study, above, introduced, respectively, the linked but opposed biological and aesthetic orientations of the "first" or "sensitive" stratum of the consciousness of the subject. Chapters I and VI set forth the reflective "grounds" for the counter–position/ position, and Mystery/myth divisions. And Chapter V, Section B10 worked out the dialectical implications of the division at each relevant further level of the differentiation or patterning of the subject. Again, Chapter VII distinguished human authenticity from its inverse and true from false values, etc. But in these senses and these respects, the ordering principle of this study has been Self–consciously dialectical in character.

Again, eighthly (8), from the "principle of integration,"[1] it has been concluded that the condition of the subject's appropriation of his fully effective freedom is a triply compounded "conversion" of his conscious life. But in Chapter XVII, Section 2.2.5 of Insight, Lonergan analyzes the nature of the human "appropriation" of "truth." He argues that such appropriation is intellectual, volitional, and affective. But Insight is a method for calling forth the subject's appropriation of the truth "of" **his own conscious Being**. And that appropriation is, as we have seen, minimally, three–fold. Thus, the reader is asked to "learn" about himSelf.[2] He is helped critically to "identify" his own intelligent, reasonable and reponsible acts and to "distinguish" them from their performative contraries.[3] He is taught

---

[1]Cf. Chapter VII, pp. 379c and 391b ff, above.

[2]Cf. Insight, p. 558d.

[3]Cf. Ibid., p. 558e–559a.

the "re-orientation" of his attitude towards truth which his embrace of the "positions" involves.[1] He learns of the consequent "affective" **and** "volitional" re-orientations[2] which are required to make his judgments effective, to preserve the orientation within which he will correct his errors, transcend the limitations of his viewpoints, learn.   But, finally, the three dimensions of the subject's appropriation of the truth are, ultimately, "solidary,"[3] e.g., they presuppose and imply **each other.**   Thus, if the responsible choice of the subject springs from his genuineness, his achievement of genuineness springs from his responsible choice. Again, neither his responsibility nor genuineness can be properly initiated or ultimately sustained without the properly dramatic, symbolically mediated, and Mystery-opened "aesthetic" orientation of his sensitivity and daily living, etc. etc.   But one of the implications of this fact is that the subject's pursuit of Self-appropriation can take its start from **any** of the three dimensions of human Being under consideration. And the point is that if its achievement is to be integral, it must finally engage the other two and this, ultimately in a critical manner.

But, then, the genetic/dialectical order of successively higher differentiations of consciousness which has informed the exposition of this study is not necessarily the order in which human differentiation concretely works itself out. Thus, the subject's path to full and integral Self-differentiation admits, minimally, a minor flexibility.[4] Thus, for example, some approximation to the full ethical differentiation of human consciousness may, in fact, precede the differentiations of philosophy and science. Again, assuming the achievement of undifferentiated consciousness, there are multiple possibilites of "further" differentiation that are, respectively, onefold, twofold, threefold, fourfold, fivefold and this at some stage

---

[1] Cf. Insight, p. 559b.

[2] Ibid., p. 561b–562a.

[3] Ibid., p. 561b.

[4] Cf. Insight, p. 453b; Chapter V, p. 266b #6, above.

of a given subject's development or at its term in the individual case.[1] Further possibilities of differentiation would have to be specified were we to add scholarly or other differentiations of consciousness to our account.

But, ninthly (9), then, what the subject _is_ at any given stage or level of differentiation has been set out heuristically, e.g., will be some function of the implicitly defined, genetically–dialectically related "categories" we have been setting forth and grounding in the above study, etc. Again, the **unity** of differentiated consciousness consists in the subject's **critical** Self-knowledge, and Self-implementation on that "basis."

Thirdly, the continuity of _Insight_'s concern with the "conversion" of human consciousness, with the subject's appropriation of the essential, genetic–dialectical terms, relations and implications of her, minimally, tri-fold intentional Being, with, therefore, her "existence" as a human subject, has already been touched upon in the preceding chapter. But we now hasten to add that:

> there has been for millenia a vast multitude of individuals in whom the basic nest of [conscious] terms and relations can be verified: for they too attend, understand, judge, decide. Moreover, they do so not in isolation but in social groups and as such groups develop and progress and decline, there is not only society but history (MT, 286b).

But on the basis of the analyses offered in the preceding study, the grounds have been established by which, within the relevant experience and living of any of these individuals, and despite the level of their culture, society, etc., there can be distinguished: (1) the different kinds and levels of conscious operations they perform; (2) the different patterns of experience and their relevant levels and combinations of differentiation; (3) the manifold, variously linked "horizons" of human biology, common sense, science, philosophy, etc.; (4) the presence or anticipation of the presence of the four-fold battery of heuristic structures, the integrally heuristic conception of Being, etc., etc.; (5) the distinction between the intersubjective, civil, and cultural communities of the subject; (6) the particular

---

[1]As the reader has surmised, this point has significant implications for socio-cultural analyses.

good, good of order, and value; (7) true and false, originating and terminal, hierarchically ordered values; (8) essential and effective freedom; (9) the positions and counter-positions in their full, dialectically opposed anthropological conceptions; (10) the tension between limitation and transcendence; (11) the contrary pulls of authenticity and inauthenticity, rational choice and bias and, therefore, the springs of human progress and decline, etc.; (12) the presence or absence of conversion; (13) metaphysical and intentional accounts of the realtiy of the human subject, etc., etc., etc.[1]

But such differentiations afford the primitive, heuristic and implicitly defined "categories" for an empirical anthropology, for historical, socio-cultural research, for tracing historical patterns of individual, social, cultural, and civilizational advance and regression, etc. And, again, their advantage is that they are reflectivley identifiable within the consciousness of the given subject and have their essential "grounds" in its invariant, transcultural structure.

Finally, if the critically appropriated genuiness, universal willingness, and "Mystery"-opened affectivity of the subject are necessary conditions of her integral effective freedom, such conditions, given the tension of the positions and counter-positions, will always, actually and inevitably, either be achieved only to suffer decline, or not be achieved, or find only partial achievement. Thus, the subject's "natural" development faces the subject with a further "limitation," a further "incapacity" for "sustained development." But, this further, de facto limitation of the subject's Self-transcendence points to a still higher integration of human Being and doing. This further dimension corresponds to the "religious" dimension of human Being in its individual, social, cutural and, therefore, historical and dialectical bearings. And from this dimension this study has been forced to abstract.[2]

---

[1] Cf. Method in Theology, pp. 285c-288a.

[2] Cf. Insight, Chapters XX and the Epilogue, and also Chapter XIX.

BIBLIOGRAPHY

PUBLISHED BOOKS AND IMPORTANT UNPUBLISHED

WORKS BY LONERGAN

C1 Collection. Edited by Fred Crowe. New York: Herder and Herder, 1967.

C2 A Second Collection. Edited by F. Ryan and B. Tyrrell. Philadelphia: Westminster Press, 1974.

C3 A Third Collection. Edited by Fred Crowe. New York: Paulist Press and Geoffrey Chapman: New York/Mahwah and London, 1985.

CM Caring about Meaning. A transcript of six conversations with Lonergan, edited by Pierre Lambert, Charlotte Tansey, Cathleen Going. Montreal: Thomas More Institue, 1982.

DCC De Constitutione Christi Ontologica et Psychologica. Rome: Gregorian University Press, 1956.

DT De Deo Trino: Pars Analytica. Rome: Gregorian University, 1961.

DP Doctrinal Pluralism. Milwaukee: Marquette University Press, 1971.

DT1 De Deo Trino: Vol. I, Pars Dogmatica, 2nd revised edition. Rome: Gregorian University Press, 1964.

DT2 De Deo Trino: Vol. II, Pars Systematica, 2nd revised edition. Rome: Gregorian University Press, 1964.

DuL Dublin Lectures on Method in Theology. Presented in August, 1971. Available at The Lonergan Research Insitute, Regis College, Toronto, Ontario.

ESA An Essay in Circulation Analysis. The original manuscript dates from 1944. It is available at the Lonergan Institute. It underwent successive revisions in 1978, 1980, 1982, and 1983. A transcript of the final (1983) version has been compiled by Pat Byrne and Charles Hefling and is available at The Lonergan Center, Boston College, Chestnut Hill, Massachusetts.

GF Grace and Freedom. Edited by J. Burns. New York: Herder and Herder, 1971. The original introduction to this work has only recently been published and is cited, separately, below. The contents of Grace and Freedom were previously published as "St. Thomas' Thought on Gratia Operans," in a series of four articles in Theological Studies:

in Theological Studies:

"Introduction" and "The General Movement of Aquinas' Thought," TS 2 (1941): 289–324;

"Habitual Grace as Operans and Cooperans," TS 3 (1942): 69–88;

"St. Thomas' Theory of Operation," TS 3 (1942): 375–402;

an untitled section followed by "Actual Grace as Operans and Cooperans," TS 3 (1942): 533–78.

GFI "The Gratia Operans Dissertation: Preface and Introduction." Method 3 (1985): 9–46.

HE Hermeneutics. This is an unpublished lecture delivered in 1962. Available at The Lonergan Research Insitute.

I1 Insight. London: Longmans, Green, and Co., 1957. First edition. The original preface to this work has only recently become available and been published. It is cited, separately, below.

I Insight. London: Longmans, Green, and Co., revised student edition, 1958.

IM De Intellectu et Methodo. This is an unpublished lecture delivered in Rome at the Gregorian University in 1956 and reconstructed from student notes. It is available at The Lonergan Research Institute.

IR Intelligence and Reality. This is a set of notes made by Lonergan for his course at Thomas More Institute, Montreal, 1950–51. They are available at The Lonergan Research Institute.

IP "The Original Preface." Method 3 (1985): 3–8. This is the unpublished preface of Insight.

LE Lectures on Existentialism. These are unpublished and were delivered in 1957. A transcript made by Nicholas Graham as well as Lonergan's own notes are available at The Lonergan Research Institute.

LED Lectures on Education. This is the anticipated publication title for Lonergan's Institute on Philosophy of Education. It was held in Cincinnati at Xavier University in 1959. A revised transcript is available at The Lonergan Research Institute.

LM Lectures on Mathematical Logic. These are unpublished and were delivered in 1957. They are available at The Lonergan Research Institute.

MT Method in Theology. New York: Herder and Herder, 1972.

MTH De Methodo Theologiae. This is an unpublished lecture delivered in Rome at the Gregorian University in 1962 and reconstructed from student notes. It is available at The Lonergan Research Institute.

MOT   The Method of Theology. These are the notes of an an institute held at Regis College in 1962. They are available at the The Lonergan Research Institute.

NS   De Notione Structurae. This is an unpublished lecture delivered at the Aloisianum in Gallarate, Italy in 1964. Available at The Lonergan Research Institute.

PGT   Philosophy of God and Theology. Philadelphia: The Westminster Press, 1973.

RTH   The Redemption, Time and Meaning, and Healing and Creating in History. Edited by R. O'Connor. Montreal: Thomas More Institute, 1975. These lectures were delivered in the late 1950's.

S   The Subject. Milwaukee: Marquette University Press, 1971. Reprinted in C2, pp. 69–86.

SP   Supplementum Schematicum de Praedestinatione: De Scientia et Voluntate Dei. This is a set of notes to a course given in 1950. It is unpublished but available at The Lonergan Research Institute.

UB   Understanding and Being. Edited by E. and M. Morelli. New York: Edwin Mullin Press, 1980. This is a publication of Lonergan's Halifax Lectures given on Insight in 1958.

V   Verbum. Edited by D. Burrell. Notre Dame: University of Notre Dame Press, 1967. The chapters of this book originally appeared in Theological Studies, 7 (1946): 349–92; 8 (1947): 35–79, 404–44; 10 (1949): 3–40, 359–93.

VI   De Verbo Incarnato. Rome: Gregorian University Press, 1964.

WN   The Way to Nicea. Translated and edited by Conn O'Donovan from the Pars Dogmatica (17–112) of De Deo Trino. Philadelphia: The Westminster Press, 1976.

RECENT AND SELECTED EARLIER ARTICLES BY LONERGAN[1]

AT   "Aquinas Today: Tradition and Innovation."   C3, pp. 35–54. Previously published in The Journal of Religion 55 (1975): 165–85.

B   "Bernard Lonergan Responds." In The Foundations of Theology: Papers from the International Lonergan Congress, pp. 223–34. Edited by Phil McShane. Notre Dame: University of Notre Dame Press, 1971.

BT   "Belief: Today's Issue." C2, pp. 87–100.

CS   "Cognitional Structure." C1, pp. 221–39.

CT   "Christology Today: Methodological Reflections." C3, pp. 74–99. Previously published in Le Christ Hier, Aujourd'hui et Demain, pp. 45–65. Edited by R. LaFlamme & Michel Gervais. Quebec: Les Presses de L'Universite Laval, 1976.

DA   "Dialectic of Authority." C3, pp. 5–12. Previously published in Boston Studies in Philosophy 3. The Hague: Martinus Nijhoff, 1973, pp. 24–30.

FL   "Finality Love and Marriage." C1, pp. 16–53.

FS   "Functional Specialties in Theology." Gregorianum 50 (1969): 485–504. This is reprinted as the fifth chapter of Method in Theology.

H   "Horizon." Unpublished paper, delivered in 1963. Available in The Lonergan Research Institute.

HG   "The Human Good." Humanitas 13 (1979): 113–26. Subsequently published as the second chapter of Method in Theology.

IN   "An Interview with Fr. Bernard Lonergan, S.J." C2, pp. 209–30. Reprinted in Clergy Review 56 (1971): 412–31.

IR   "Insight Revisited." C2, pp. 263–78.

MA   "Medalist's Address: Philosophy and Theology." Journal of the American Catholic Philosophical Association 43–44 (1969–1970): 19–30.

M   "Merging Horizons: System, Common Sense, Scholarship." Cultural Hermeneutics 1 (1973): 87–99.

MH   "Metaphysics as Horizon." C1, pp. 202–20.

---

[1]Alternate sources will only be specified for Lonergan's recent articles.

MV   "Method: Trend and Variations." C3, pp. 13–22.

MS   "Mission and the Spirit." C3, pp. 23–34.   Previously   published
      in Concilium 10 (1976): 69–78.

NHR   "Natural Right and Historical Mindedness."   C3, pp. 169–83.
      Previouly published in American Catholic Philosophical Association
      15 (1977): 132–43.

NPT   "A New Pastoral Theology." Unpublished lecture, 1973.   Available
      at The Lonergan Research Institute.

OGM   "The Ongoing Genesis of Methods." C3, pp. 146–65.   Previously
      published in Sciences Religieuse/Studies in Religion 6 (1976–77):
      341–55.

OR   "Openness and Religious Experience." C1, pp. 198–201.

PT   "Philosophy and Theology." C2, pp. 193–208.

P   "Pope John's Intention." C3, pp. 224–38.

PH   "A Post–Hegelian Philosophy of Religion."   C3, p. 202–223.
      Previously published in Lonergan Workshop 3 (1982): 179–99.

PSE   "Prolegomena to the Study of the Emerging Religious Consciousness
      of our Time." C3, pp. 55–73. Previously published in Studies in
      Religion 9 (1980): 3–13.

Q   "Questions with regard to Method: History and Economics."   In
      Dialogues in Celebration, pp. 286–314.   Edited by Cathleen M.
      Going.

R   "Response." Proceedings of the American Catholic Philosophical
      Association 41–2 (1967–68): 254–59.

RC   "Religious Commitment." In The Pilgrim People: A Vision of Hope,
      vol. 4, pp. 45–69. Edited by J. Papin.   Villanova: The Villanova
      University Press, 1970.

RE   "Religious Experience." C3, pp. 113–28. Previously published in
      Trinification of the World, pp. 71–83.   Edited by T.A. Dunne & J.
      Laporte. Toronto: Regis College Press, 1978.

RK   "Religious Knowledge." C3, pp. 129–45.   Previously published in
      Lonergan Workshop 1 (1978): 309–27.

RMS   "Reality, Myth and Symbol." In Myth, Symbol and Reality, 31–37.
      Edited by Alan M. Olson.   Notre Dame and London: University of
      Notre Dame Press, 1980.

RU   "The Role of a Catholic University in the Modern World."   C1, pp.
      114–20.

SS   "Sacralization and Secularization." Delivered at Yale University, New Haven, 1974.

TC   "Theology in its New Context." C2, pp. 55–67.

TP   "Theology and Praxis." C3, pp. 184–201. Previously published in The Catholic Theological Society of America: Proceedings 32 (1977): 1–16.

T   "The Transition from a Classicist World–View to Historical–Mindedness." C2, pp. 1–9.

U   "Unity and Plurality." C3, pp. 239–50.

SECONDARY LITERATURE ON OR REFERRED TO BY LONERGAN

Ashead, S.A.M. "Buddhist Scholasticism and Transcendental Thomism." The Downside Review 95 (1977): 297–305.

Barden, Garrett. "Aristotle's Notion of **Epieikeia**." In Creativity and Method: Studies in Honor of Rev. Bernard Lonergan, pp. 353–66. Edited by Matthew Lamb.

Bauer, Carl. "Lonergan's Philosophy of Science and Empirical Studies of Leadership–Group Dynamics and Organizational Behaviour." Unpublished paper prepared for the International Lonergan Conference of 1970. Available at the Lonergan Center, University of Santa Clara, Santa Clara, California.

Boyle, J.P. "Faith and Community in the Ethical Theory of K. Rahner and B. Lonergan." Ph.D. dissertation. Fordham University, 1972.

_____. "Lonergan's Method in Theology and Objectivity in Moral Theology." Thomist 37 (1973): 589–601.

Braxton, E.K. "Bernard Lonergan's Hermeneutic of the Symbol." The Irish Theological Quarterly 43 (1976): 186–97.

Brennan, Ann Marie. "Bernard Lonergan's World View: Emergent Probability and the God–World Relation." Ph.D. dissertation. Columbia University, 1973.

Butler, B.C. "Bernard Lonergan and Conversion." Worship 49 (1975): 329–36.

Byrne, Pat. "The Question of Development: The Rise of the Methodological Approach in the Thought of Bernard Lonergan." Masters thesis. Boston College, 1972.

_____. "Einstein's Quest for the Foundations of Science." Ph.D. dissertation. State University of New York at Stony Brook, 1978.

_____. "The Thomist Sources of Lonergan's Dynamic World View." Thomist 46 (1982): 108–45.

_____. "Mathematics and Mystery." Boston: Lonergan Workshop, 1981.

_____. "Relativity and Indeterminism." Foundation of Physics 2 (1981): 913–32.

_____. "God and the Statistical Universe." Zygon 16 (1981): 345–62.

_____. "Lonergan and the Foundations of the Theories of Relativity." In Creativity and Method: Studies in Honor of Rev. Bernard Lonergan, pp. 477–94. Edited by Matthew Lamb.

_____. "The Significance of Voeglin's Work for the Philosophy of Science." In The Beginning of the Beyond: Papers from the Gadamer and Voeglin Conferences, pp. 93-6. Edited by Fred Lawrence.

_____. "The Fabric of Lonergan's Thought." Lonergan Workshop 6 (1986): 1-84.

_____. "Economic Transformations: The Role of Conversions and Culture in the Transformation of Economics." In Religion and Culture: Essays in Honor of Bernard Lonergan, S.J., pp. 327-48. Edited by Timothy Fallon and Boo Riley.

_____. "Insight and the Retrieval of Nature." Paper delivered at the Lonergan Workshop, Boston College, summer 1987.

Byrne, Pat & Keeley, Richard. "LeCorbusier's Finger and Jacobs' Thought: The Loss and Recovery of the Subject in the City." In Communicating a Dangerous Memory, pp. 63-108. Edited by Fred Lawrence.

Cahill, P.J. "Myth and Meaning: Demythologizing Revisited." In No Famine in the Land: Studies in Honor of John L. McKenzie, pp. 275-91. Edited by J.W. Flanagan and A.W. Robinson. Missoula, Montana: Scholars Press, 1975.

Calabretta, Rose B. "The Intellectual Origins of the Problem of 'Value Free' Sociology." Ph.D. dissertation. Fordham University, 1980.

Carmody, John. "The Biblical Foundation and Conclusion of Lonergan's De Verbo Incarnato." Andover Newton Quarterly (1974): 124-36.

_____. "Lonergan's Latin Theology: Resume and Critique." Princeton Seminary Bulletin 68 (1975): 81-9.

_____. "Lonergan's Trinitarian Insight." In Philosophy of Religion and Theology: 1975 Proceedings, reprinted papers compiled by J.M. McClendon, pp. 161-76.

_____. "Lonergan's Trinitarian Insight." In Philosophy of Religion and Theology: 1975 Proceedings, American Academy of Religion. Compiled by J. McClendon, pp. 161-76.

Clarke, Norris. "Insight: A Book Review." Theological Studies 18 (1958): 629-32.

Colleron, K.J. "Bernard Lonergan on Conversion." The Dunwoodie Review 11 (1971): 3-23.

Conn, Walter. "Primitive Consciousness." American Catholic Philosophical Association 45-46 (1971-1972): 147-57.

_____. "Conscience and Self-Transcendence." Ph.D. dissertation. Columbia University, 1975.

_____. "Bernard Lonergan on Value." Thomist 40 (1976): 243–57.

_____. "Bernard Lonergan's Analysis of Conversion." Angelicum 53 (1976): 362–404.

_____. "Moral Development as Self–Transcendence." Horizons 4 (1977): 189–205.

_____. "The Ontogenetic Ground of Value." Theological Studies 39 (1978): 313–35.

_____. "Bernard Lonergan and Authenticity: The Search for a Valid Criterion of the Moral Life." The American Benedictine Review 30 (1979): 301–21.

_____. "Ethical Style for the Creative Conscience." Louvain Studies 7 (1979): 183–94.

_____. Conscience and Self–Transcendence. Birmingham, Alabama: Religious Education Press, 1981. This work is a revised version of his doctoral dissertation.

_____. "Moral Development: Is Conversion Necessary." In Creativity and Method: Studies in Honor of Rev. Bernard Lonergan, pp. 307–24. Edited by Matthew Lamb.

_____. "Affective Conversion: The Transformation of Desire." In Religion and Culture: Essays in Honor of Bernard Lonergan, S.J., pp. 261–76 Edited by Timothy Fallon and Boo Riley.

Crowe, Fred. "The Origin and Scope of Bernard Lonergan's Insight." Sciences Ecclesiastiques 9 (1957–58): 263–95.

_____. "St. Thomas and the Isomorphism of Human Knowing and its Proper Object." Sciences Ecclesiastiques 13 (1961): 169–90.

_____. "How Inflexible is Catholic Dogma?" Crosslight 2 (1961): 14–26.

_____, ed. Spirit as Inquiry. Chicago: St. Xavier College, 1964.

_____. "The Exigent Mind." In Spirit as Inquiry, pp. 16–33.

_____. "Neither Jew nor Greek, but One Human Nature and Operation in All." Philippine Studies 13 (1965): 546–71.

_____, ed. Collection. New York: Herder and Herder, 1967.

_____. "Dogma versus the Self–correcting Process of Learning." In Foundations of Theology, pp. 22–40. Edited by Phil McShane.

_____. "Christologies: how up–to–date is yours?" Theological Studies 29 (1968): 87–101.

_____. "Pull of the Future and Link with the Past: On the Need for Theological Method." Continuum 7 (1969): 30–49.

_____. "But is there a Fault in the Very Foundations." Continuum 7 (1969): 323–31.

_____. "Eschaton and Wordly Mission in the Mind and Heart of Jesus." In The Eschaton: A Community of Love V, pp. 105–44. Edited by J. Papin. Villanova: Villanova University Press, 1971.

_____. "The Conscience of the Theologian with reference to the Encyclical." In Conscience, pp. 312–32. Edited by W.C. Bier. New York: Fordham University Press, 1971.

_____. "On the Method of Theology." Theological Studies 23 (1962): 637–42.

_____. "Early Jottings on Bernard Lonergan's Method in Theology." Science et Esprit 25 (1973): 121–58.

_____. "Development of Doctrine: Aid or Barrier to Christian Unity." CTSA: Proceedings 21 (1966): 1–20.

_____. Theology of the Christian Word. New York: Paulist Press, 1976.

_____. "Doctrines and Historicity in the Context of Lonergan's Method." Theological Studies 38 (1977) 115–24.

_____. "An Exploration of Lonergan's New Notion of Value." Science et Esprit 29 (1977): 123–43. Reprinted in Lonergan Workshop 3 (1982): 1–25.

_____. "Dialectic and the Ignatian Spiritual Exercises." Lonergan Workshop 1 (1978): 1–26.

_____. "The Mind and Jesus." In Trinification of the World, pps. 71–83. Edited by T.A. Dunne and J. Laporte.

_____. ""Interiority" Going Forward?" In Dialogues in Celebration, pp. 260–85. Edited by Cathleen M. Going.

_____. The Lonergan Enterprise. Cambridge, Mass.: Cowley Publications, 1980.

_____. "Christology Tomorrow." Paper delivered at Lonergan Workshop, Boston College, summer 1981.

_____. Lonergan's Early Use of Analogy." Method 1 (1983): 31–46.

_____. "Transcendental Deduction: A Lonerganian Meaning and Use." Method 2 (1984): 21–40.

_____. "The Human Mind and Ultimate Reality: A Lonerganian Comment on Dr. Leaky." Ultimate Reality and Meaning 7 (1984): 67-74.

_____. Old Things and New: The Strategy for Education. Atlanta: Scholars Press, 1985.

_____. "A Note on Lonergan's Dissertation and its Introductory Pages." Method 3 (1985): 1-8.

_____. "A Note on the Prefaces of Insight." Method 3 (1985): 1-2.

_____, ed. A Third Collection. New York: Paulist Press and Geoffrey Chapman: New York/Mahwah and London, 1985.

_____. "Son and Spirit: Tension in the Divine Missions?" Lonergan Workshop 5 (1985): 1-22.

_____. "From Kerygma to Inculturation." Paper delivered at the Lonergan Workshop, Boston College, summer 1986.

_____. "The Task of Interpreting Lonergan." In Religion and Culture: Essays in Honor of Bernard Lonergan, S.J., pp. 3-16. Edited by Timothy Fallon and Boo Riley.

_____. "Bernard Lonergan as Pastoral Theologian." Gregorianum 67 (1986): 451-70.

_____. "Bernard Lonergan and Liberation Theology." In The Third World and Bernard Lonergan, pp. 1-15. Edited by Walter L. Ysaac.

_____. ""The Role of a Catholic University in the Modern World"— An Update." In Communicating a Dangerous Memory, pp. 1-16. Edited by Fred Lawrence.

_____. "Insight: Genesis and Ongoing History." Paper delivered at the Lonergan Workshop, Boston College, summer 1987.

Dawson, Christopher. "The Study of Christian Culture." Thought 35 (1960): 485-91.

Donahey, Mary Ellen. "The Knowing-Believing Relation in the Works of Bernard Lonergan and Leslie Dewart." Ph.D. dissertation. Columbia University, 1974.

Donceel, J. "On Transcendental Thomism." Continuum 7 (1969): 164-68.

Doran, Robert. "Paul Ricoeur: Toward the Restoration of Meaning." Anglican Theological Review 55 (1973): 443-58.

_____. "Aesthetics and the Opposites." Thought 52 (1977): 117-33.

_____. "Psychic Conversion." Thomist 41 (1977): 200-36.

_____. "Subject, Psyche and Theology's Foundations." Journal of

Religion 67 (1977): 267-87.

_____. "Christ and the Psyche." In Trinification of the World, pp. 112-43. Edited by T.A. Dunne and J. Laporte.

_____. "The Theologian's Psyche." Lonergan Workshop 1 (1978): 93-142.

_____. "Metaphysics, Psychology, and Praxis." Unpublished article. Written in 1978 and available at the Lonergan Institute.

_____. "Jungian Psychology and Christian Spirituality." Review for Religious 38 (1979): 497-510, 742-52, 857-66.

_____. "Psyche, Evil and Grace." Communio 6 (1979): 192-211.

_____. "Aesthetic Subjectivity and Generalized Empirical Method." Thomist 43 (1979): 257-57.

_____. "To Find the Significant Questions in and beyond Psychology." In Dialogues in Celebration, pp. 129-57.

_____. ""Be Attentive" in Jung and in Lonergan." In Dialogues in Celebration, pp. 158-84. Edited by Cathleen M. Going.

_____. "Theology's Situation: Questions to Eric Voeglin." In The Beginning of the Beyond: Papers from the Gadamer and Voeglin Conferences, pp. 69-92. Edited by Fred Lawrence.

_____. "Theological Grounds for a World-Historical Humanity." In Creativity and Method: Studies in Honor of Rev. Bernard Lonergan, pp. 105-22. Edited by Matthew Lamb.

_____. Subject and Psyche. Landam, Md.: University Press of Ann Arbor, 1980.

_____. "Dramatic Artistry in the Third Stage of Meaning." Lonergan Workshop 2 (1981): 147-200.

_____. "Education for Cosmopolis." Method 1 (1983): 137-57.

_____. "Theology's Situation: Questions to Eric Voeglin." In The Beginning of the Beyond: Papers from the Gadamer and Voeglin Conferences, pp. 93-6. Supplementary issue of Lonergan Workshop 4, Chico, California: Scholars Press, 1984. Edited by Fred Lawrence.

_____. "Suffering Servanthood and the Scale of Values." Lonergan Workshop 4 (1983): 41-68.

_____. "Primary Process and the 'Spiritual Unconscious.'" Lonergan Workshop 5 (1985): 23-48.

_____. "From Psychic Conversion to the Dialectic of Community."

Lonergan Workshop 6 (1986): 85–108.

_____ . "Duality and Dialectic." Delivered at the Lonergan Workshop, Boston College, summer 1986.

_____ . "Insight and the Ontology of Meaning." Delivered at the Lonergan Workshop, Boston College, summer 1987.

_____ . The Analogy of Dialectic. Publication pending in January of 1988 as a supplementary volume of the Lonergan Workshop.

D'Souza, Lisbert. "Lonergan's Metaphysics of Proportionate Being." Thomist 32 (1968): 509–27.

Dunne, T.A. "Lonergan on Social Progress and Community: A Developmental Study." Ph.D. dissertation. University of St. Michael's College, 1975.

_____ . Trinification of the World. Ed. with Jean-Marc Laporte. Toronto: Regis College Press, 1978.

_____ . Community and Redemption. Lectures given at the Toronto School for Theology, spring semester, 1979.

_____ . "Consciousness in Christian Community." In Creativity and Method: Studies in Honor of Rev. Bernard Lonergan, pp. 291–303. Edited by Matthew Lamb.

_____ . "Faith, Charity, Hope." Lonergan Workshop 5 (1985): 49–70.

_____ . "What Makes a Story Interesting." In Religion and Culture: Essays in Honor of Bernard Lonergan, S.J., pp. 221–36. Edited by Timothy Fallon and Boo Riley.

Ellis, Marc. "The Mystery of God's Presence in an Age of Holocaust." Delivered at Lonergan Workshop, Boston, 1981.

Fallon, Timothy and Riley, Boo, eds. Religion and Culture: Essays in Honor of Bernard Lonergan, S.J. Includes an anticipated supplementary volume. Albany: State University of New York Press, 1986.

Fallon, Timothy, ed. and Rosselli, Dennis, co-ed. Combined Lonergan Indices. Santa Clara: Lonergan Center, 1987.

Fitzpatrick, J. "Lonergan and Poetry." New Blackfriars 59 (1978): 441–51 and 517–26.

_____ . "Lonergan and Hume I: Epistemology (1)." New Blackfriars 63 (1982): 122–70.

_____ . "Lonergan and Hume II: Epistemology (2)." New Blackfriars 63 (1982): 219–28.

_____ . "Lonergan and Hume III: Critique of Religion (1)." New

Blackfriars 63 (1982): 275–86.

_____. "Lonergan and Hume IV: Critique of Religion (2)." _New Blackfriars_ 364–72.

_____. "Lonergan's Notion of Belief." _Method_ 1 (1983): 101–13.

Flanagan, Joseph. "Knowing and Language in the Thought of Bernard Lonergan." In _Language, Truth and Meaning_, pp. 49–78. Edited by Phil McShane.

_____. "Lonergan's Epistemology." _Thomist_ 36 (1972): 75–97.

_____. "Literary Criticism of the Bible." In _Trinification of the World_, pp. 219–40. Edited by T.A. Dunne and J. Laporte.

_____. "Transcendental Dialectic of Desire and Fear." _Lonergan Workshop_, 1 (1978): 69–92.

_____. "Culture and Morality." _Lonergan Workshop_, 2 (1981): 109–46.

_____. "Psychic and Intellectual Conversion." A paper delivered at Lonergan Workshop, Boston, 1981.

_____. "From Body to Thing." In _Creativity and Method: Studies in Honor of Rev. Bernard Lonergan_, pp. 495–508. Edited by Matthew Lamb.

_____. "The Self-Causing Subject: Intrinsic and Extrinsic Knowing." _Lonergan Workshop_ 3 (1982): 33–52.

_____. "Symbolic Modes of Meaning." Paper delivered at the Lonergan Workshop, Boston College, summer 1986.

_____. "Insight: Chapters I–V." Paper delivered at the Lonergan Workshop, Boston College, summer 1987.

_____. "Schemes of Recurrence." Paper delivered at the _Lonergan Workshop_, Boston College, summer 1987.

Frings, Manfred S. "Insight—Logos—Love." _Philosophy Today_ 14 (1970): 106–15.

Gadamer, Hans–Georg. "Articulating transcendence." In _The Beginning of the Beyond: Papers from the Gadamer and Voeglin Conferences_, pp. 1–12. Edited by Fred Lawrence.

Gibbons, Michael. "To Find the Relevant Questions in Biotechnology." In _Dialogues in Celebration_, pp. 23–48. Edited by Cathleen M. Going.

_____. "Insight and Emergence." In _Creativity and Method: Studies in Honor of Rev. Bernard Lonergan_, pp. 529–42. Edited by Matthew

Lamb.

_____. "Economic Theorizing in Lonergan and Keynes." In Religion and Culture: Essays in Honor of Bernard Lonergan, S.J., pp. 313–25. Edited by Timothy Fallon and Boo Riley.

Gilbert, A. and Roy, L. "La Structure Ethique de la Conversation Religieuse D'Apres B. Lonergan." Science et Esprit 32 (1980): 347–60.

Going, Cathleen. "Persons: A Study in Communication." Unpublished paper prepared for the International Lonergan Conference of 1970. Available at the Lonergan Center, University of Santa Clara, Santa Clara, California.

_____. ed. Dialogues in Celebration. Montreal: Perry Printing Limited, 1980.

_____. "Theological Anthropology." CTSA: Proceedings 36 (1981): 174–78.

_____. "'Persons as Originating Values': A Primer (Reader) from Lonergan's Thought on the Topic of Value." Lonergan Workshop 3 (1982): 1–24.

Harding, Thomas. "Moral Education in Adulthood." Ph.D dissertation. University of Toronto, 1975.

Haughton, Rosemary. The Transformation of Man: A Study of Conversion. Springfield, Ill.: Templegate, 1967.

_____. Tales of Eternity. New York: Seabury Press, 1973.

Hefling, Charles C. Why Doctrines? United States of America: Cowley Publications, 1984.

_____. "On Understanding Salvation History." Unpublished paper.

Hepburn, R.W. "Method and Insight." Philosophy 48 (1973): 153–60.

Helmeniak, Daniel A. "Four Viewpoints on the Human: A Conceptual Schema for Interdisciplinary Studies: I." The Heythrop Journal 27 (1987): 420–37.

_____. "Four Viewpoints on the Human: A Conceptual Schema for Interdisciplinary Studies: II." The Heythrop Journal 28 (1987): 1–15.

Hosinki, Thomas. "Lonergan and a Process Understanding of God." In Religion and Culture: Essays in Honor of Bernard Lonergan, S.J., pp. 63–78. Edited by Timothy Fallon and Boo Riley.

Johnson, D.H. "Lonergan and the Redoing of Ethics." Continuum 5 (1967–1968): 211–20.

Keefe, D. J. "A Methodological Critique of Lonergan's Theological Method." Thomist 50 (1986): 28-65.

Lamb, Matthew. "Lonergan on Aquinas." Continuum 5 (1967): 425-31.

_____. "An Interview with Fr. Bernard Lonergan." Clergy Review 56 (1971): 412-31.

_____. History, Method and Theology: A Dialectical Comparison of Historical Reason and Bernard Lonergan's Meta-Methodology. Ph.D. dissertation. Westphalian Wilhelms University of Munster, 1974. Later published. California: Scholars Press, 1978.

_____. "Wilhelm Dilthey's Critique of Historical Reason and Bernard Lonergan's Meta-Methodology." In Language, Truth and Meaning, pp. 115-66. Edited by Phil McShane.

_____. "The Theory-Praxis Relationship in Contemporary Christian Theologies." CTSA: Proceedings 31 (1976): 149-78.

_____. "Theology and Praxis: A Response (II) to Bernard Lonergan." CTSA: Proceedings 32 (1977): 22-30.

_____. "The Production Process and Exponential Growth: A Study in Socio-Economics and Theology." Lonergan Workshop 1 (1978): pp. 257-308.

_____. "The Exigences of Meaning and Metascience." In Trinification of the World, pp. 15-45. Edited by T.A. Dunne and J. Laporte.

_____. "Dogma, Experience and Political Theology." In Revelation and Experience, pp. 79-90. Edited by E. Schillebeichx and B. van Iersel. New York: The Seabury Press, 1979.

_____. "Education and Change in Social Structures." In Dialogues in Celebration, pp. 234-59. Edited by Cathleen M. Going.

_____. "The Challenge of Critical Theory." In Sociology and Human Destiny, pp. 182-231. Edited by Gregory Baum. New York: The Seabury Press, 1980.

_____. "Orthopraxis and Theological Method in Bernard Lonergan." CTSA: Proceedings 35 (1980): 66-87.

_____. "Methodology, Metascience, and Political Theology." In Lonergan Workshop, 2 (1981): 281-403.

_____. "A Distorted Interpretation of Latin American Liberation Theology." Horizons 8 (1981): 352-64.

_____, ed. Creativity and Method: Studies in Honor of Rev. Bernard Lonergan. Milwaukee: Marquette University Press, 1981.

425

_____. "Generalized Empirical Method and Praxis." In Creativity and Method: Studies in Honor of Rev. Bernard Lonergan, pp. 53–78.

_____. "Power in Liberation Theology—Thesis 3." CTSA: Proceedings 37 (134–6).

_____. "Christian Spirituality and Social Justice." Horizons 10 (1983): 32–49.

_____. "Moral Conversion in the Nuclear Age." Ecumenist 22 (1984): 44–6.

_____. Solidarity with Victims: Toward a Theory of Social Transformation. New York: The Crossroads Press, 1985.

_____. "The Dialectics of Theory and Praxis within Paradigm Analysis." Lonergan Workshop 5 (1985): 71–114.

Lardner, Mary Denis. "The Notion of Person as Self–Transcendence in Bernard Lonergan's Philosophy." Ph.D. dissertation. Boston College, 1970.

Lauer, Quentin. "Review of Insight." Philosophy and Phenomenological Research 18 (1957–58): 548–49.

Lawrence, Fred. "Self–Knowledge in History in Gadamer and Lonergan." In Language Truth and Meaning, pp. 167–17. Edited by Phil McShane.

_____. "Responses to 'Hermeneutics and Social Science.'" Cultural Hermeneutics 2 (1975): 321–25.

_____. "A Response (II) to Gerald McCool." CTSA: Proceedings 32 (1977): 90–7.

_____. "The Horizon of Political Theology." In Trinification of the World, pp. 46–70. Edited by T.A. Dunne and J. Laporte.

_____, ed. Lonergan Workshop, vols. 1–6. Boston: Scholars Press, Boston College, 1978 through 1988.

_____. "Political Theology and 'The Longer Cycle of Decline.'" Lonergan Workshop 1 (1978): 223–56.

_____. "Questioning the Culture: Liberal Education?" In Dialogues in Celebration, pp. 185–209. Edited by Cathleen M. Going.

_____. "Gadamer and Lonergan: A Dialectical Comparison." IPQ 20 (1980): 25–47.

_____. "'The Modern Philosophic Differentiation of Consciousness' or 'What is the Enlightenment?.'" Lonergan Workshop 2 (1981): 231–80.

_____. "Method and Theology as Hermeneutical." In Creativity and Method: Studies in Honor of Rev. Bernard Lonergan, pp. 79-104. Edited by Matthew Lamb.

_____, "Language as Horizon?" In The Beginning and the Beyond: Papers from the Gadamer and Voeglin Conferences, pp. 13-34.

_____. "On "The Meditative Origin of the Philosophical Knowledge of Order." In The Beginning of the Beyond: Papers from the Gadamer and Voeglin Conferences, pp. 53-68.

_____. "Basic Christian Community: An Issue of the Mind and Mystery of Christ." Lonergan Workshop 5 (1985): 263-88.

_____. "Transcendence as Interruption: Theology in a Political Mode." In Transcendence and the Sacred, pp. 208-25. Edited by A. Olson and L. Rounier, Manchester, New Hampshire: Notre Dame Press, 1981.

_____. "Lonergan as Political Theologian." Paper delivered at the Lonergan Workshop, Boston College, summer 1985.

_____. "Elements of Basic Communication." Lonergan Workshop 6 (1986): 127-42.

_____. ed. Communicating a Dangerous Memory: Soundings in Political Theology. Supplementary Issue of the Lonergan Workshop, vol. 6, 1987.

_____. "Dangerous Memory and the Pedagogy of the Oppressed." In Communicating a Dangerous Memory, pp. 17-36. Edited by Fred Lawrence.

Loewe, William P. "Lonergan and the Law of the Cross: A Universalist View of Salvation." Anglican Theological Review 59 (1977): 162-74.

_____. "Dialectics of Sin: Lonergan's Insight and the Critical Theory of Max Horkheimer." Anglican Theological Review 41 (1979): 224-45.

_____. "Toward the Critical Mediation of Theology: A Development of the Soteriological Theme in the Work of B. Lonergan." Ph.D. dissertation. Marquette University, 1974.

Manning, Paul. "A Descriptive Exposition of the Mathematics Used by Bernard Lonergan in the Development of his Philosophical-Theological System." Ph.D. dissertation. New York University, 1983.

Marasigan, Vicente. "A Banahaw Prophecy of Cosmopolis." In The Third World and Bernard Lonergan, pp. 56-60. Edited by Walter L. Ysaac.

_____. "On Surmounting the Economic Surd." In The Third World and Bernard Lonergan, pp. 61-8. Edited by Walter L. Ysaac.

Marsh, James. "Review of Method in Theology." The Modern Schoolman 50 (1972-1973): 390-93.

_____. "Lonergan's Mediation of Subjectivity and Objectivity." Modern Schoolman 52 (1975): 249-61.

_____. "The Paradox of Perception." Modern Schoolman 54 (1976-77): 379-84.

_____. "An Inconsistency in Husserl's Cartesian Meditations." New Scholasticism 52 (1979): 460-74.

_____. "Perception and Reflection." Modern Schoolman 58 (1981): 237-48.

_____. "Collins and Gadamer: On Interpretation." Unpublished article.

_____. "Objectivity, Alienation, and Reflection." IPQ 22 (1982): 131-39.

_____. Post-Cartesian Meditations: An Essay in Dialectical Phenomenology. Manuscript accepted by Fordham University Press for an anticipated, 1988 publication.

Mathews, William. "Personal Histories and Theories of Knowledge." Milltown Institute of Theology and Philosophy 8 (1981): 58-74.

_____. "On Journalling Self-Appropriation." Milltown Studies 7 (1981): 96-134.

_____. "Personal Histories and Theories of Knowledge." Milltown Studies 8 (1981): 58-73.

_____. "Method and the Social Appropriation of Reality." In Creativity and Method: Studies in Honor of Rev. Bernard Lonergan, pp. 425-43. Edited by Matthew Lamb.

_____. "Lonergan's Economics." Method 3 (1985): 9-30.

_____. "Intellectual Conversion and Science Education." Lonergan Workshop 5 (1985): 115-44.

_____. "Explanation in Social Science." In Religion and Culture: Essays in Honor of Bernard Lonergan, S.J., pp. 245-60. Edited by Timothy Fallon and Boo Riley.

McCool, Gerald. "Philosophical Pluralism and an Evolving Thomism." Continuum 2 (1964): 3-16.

_____. "Social Authority in Transcendental Thomism." ACPA:

428

Proceedings 49 (1975): 13–23.

_____. "Duty and Reason in Thomistic Social Ethics." In Freedom and Value, pp. 137–60. Edited by Robert Johann. New York: Fordham University Press, 1976.

_____. Catholic Theology in the Nineteenth Century: The Quest for a Unitary Method. New York: The Seabury Press, 1977.

_____. "Theology and Philosophy." CTSA: Proceedings 32 (1977): 1–16.

_____. "How Can There Be Such A Thing As A Christian Philosophy." ACPA: Proceedings 54 (1982): 126–34.

_____. "History, Insight and Judgment in Thomism." JPA: Proceedings (1985): 37–68.

_____. "History, Insight, and Judgment in Thomism." 107 IPQ (1987): 299–313.

_____. "Neo–Thomism and the Tradition of St. Thomas." 62 Thought (1987): 131–46.

McKelvey, Charles. "The Problem of Objectivity in Sociology: The Implication of the Cognitional Theory of Bernard Lonergan." Ph.D. dissertation. Fordham University, 1979.

McKinney, Ronald. "Lonergan on Dialectic." Ph.D. dissertation. Fordham University, 1980.

_____. "Lonergan's Notion of Dialectic." The Thomist 46 (1982): 221–41.

_____. "Marxist and Lonerganian Dialectic: A Comparative Study." Unpublished paper.

_____. "The Origins of Modern Dialectic." Unpublished paper.

_____. "The Hermeneutical Theory of Bernard Lonergan." IPQ 23 (1983): 277–90.

_____. "The Role of Conversion" in Lonergan's Insight." The Irish Theological Quarterly 52 (1986): 268–78.

_____. "Beyond Objectivism and Relativism." The Modern Schoolman 64 (1987): 97–110.

McPartland, Thomas. "Historicity and Philosophy." In Religion and Culture: Essays in Honor of Bernard Lonergan, S.J., pp. 107–22. Edited by Timothy Fallon and Boo Riley.

_____. "Meaning, Mystery, and the Speculative Philosophy of History." Paper delivered at the Lonergan Workshop, Boston

College, summer, 1986.

McShane, Phil. "The Foundations of Mathematics." The Modern Schoolman 40 (1963): 373–87.

_____. "Insight and the Strategy of Biology." In Spirit as Inquiry, pp. 74–88. Edited by Fred Crowe.

_____, ed. Language, Truth and Meaning. Notre Dame, Indiana: University of Notre Dame Press, 1969.

_____. Randomness, Statistics and Emergence. Notre Dame, Indiana: University of Notre Dame Press, 1970.

_____, ed. Foundations of Theology. Notre Dame, Indiana: University of Notre Dame Press, 1972.

_____, ed. Introducing the Thought of Bernard Lonergan. London: Darton, Ligner and Todd, 1973.

_____. Wealth of Self and Wealth of Nations: Self–Axis of the Great Ascent. Washington, D.C.: University Press of America, 1975.

_____. The Shaping of the Foundations. Washington, D.C.: University Press of American, 1976.

_____. Music that is Soundless: An Introduction to God for the Graduate. Washington, D.C.: University Press of America, 1977.

_____. "The Psychological Present of the Academic Community." Lonergan Workshop 1 (1978): 27–68.

_____. Lonergan's Challenge to the University and Economy. Washington D.C.: University Press of America, 1980.

_____. Generalized Empirical Method and the Actual Context of Economics." In Creativity and Method: Studies in Honor of Rev. Bernard Lonergan, pp. 543–71. Edited by Matthew Lamb.

_____. "An Improbable Christian Vision and the Economic Rhythms of the Second Million Years." Lonergan Workshop 3 (1982): 53–82.

_____, ed. Searching for Cultural Foundations. Lantham, New York, and London: University Press of America, 1984.

_____. "Preface: Distant Probabilities of Persons Presently Going Home Together in Transcendental Process." In Searching for Cultural Foundations, pp. i–xxi.

_____. "Middle Kingdom: Middle Man." In Searching for Cultural Foundations," pp. 1–43.

_____. "Systematics, Communications, Actual Contexts." Lonergan

Workshop 6 (1986): 143–74.

_____. "Towards the Transposition of Hermeneutics." Paper circulated for discussion purposes at the Lonergan Workshop, Boston College, summer 1986.

McShane, Phil & Barden, Garret. Towards Self-Meaning. New York: Herder and Herder, 1969.

Melchin, Kenneth. "Military Deterrence Strategy and the 'Dialectic of Community.'" In Religion and Culture: Essays in Honor of Bernard Lonergan, S.J., pp. 293–309. Edited by Timothy Fallon and Boo Riley.

_____. History, Ethics and Emergent Probability. Lanham, Maryland: University of America Press, 1987.

_____. "Ethic in Insight." Paper delivered at the Lonergan Workshop, Boston College, summer 1987.

Metz, J.B. "Communicating a Dangerous Memory." In Communicating a Dangerous Memory, pp. 37–54. Edited by Fred Lawrence.

Meynell, Hugo. "Lonergan's Theory of Knowledge and the Social Sciences." New Blackfriars 56 (1975): 388–98.

_____. "Science, the Truth and Thomas Kuhn." Mind 84 (1975): 333.

_____. An Introduction to the Philosophy of Bernard Lonergan. London: The Macmillian Press, 1976.

_____. "On the Aims of Education." Proceedings of the Philosophy of Education Society of Great Britain 10 (1976): 79–97.

_____. Freud, Marx, and Morals. Totowa, New Jersey: Barnes and Nobles Books, 1981.

_____. "Lonergan, Wittgenstein, and Where Language Hooks onto the World." In Creativity and Method: Studies in Honor of Rev. Bernard Lonergan, pp. 369–82. Edited by Matthew Lamb.

_____. The Intelligible Universe. Totowa, New Jersey: Barnes and Nobles Books, 1982.

_____. "Two Directions for Pneumatology." Religious Studies Bulletin 2 (1982): 101–17.

_____. "Where the Philosophy of Science Should Go From Here." The Heythrop Journal 23 (1982): 123–38.

_____. "Analytic Philosophy and the Critique of Culture." Method 1 (1983): 74–81.

_____. "Foundations of Empiricism: An Exercise in Dialectic."

Method 1 (1983): 174–94.

_____. "A Note on Cosmological Argument." New Blackfriars 64 (1983): 287–91.

_____. "Reversing Rorty." Method 3 (1985): 31–49.

_____. "A Pseudo-Problem of Communication and Understanding." Lonergan Workshop 6 (1986): 175–94.

_____. The Nature of Aesthetic Value. Albany: State University of New York Press, 1986.

_____. "Wilfred Sellars: A Thomist Estimate." Thomist 50 (1986): 223–37.

_____. "How Right Plato Was." Paper delivered at the Lonergan Workshop, Boston College, summer 1987.

Moore, Sebastian. "The Discovery of Metaphysics—One Man's War." In Spirit as Inquiry, pp. 120–24. Edited by Fred Crowe.

_____. "Word of God: Kerygma and Theorem, a Note." Heythrop Journal 5 (1964): 268–75.

_____. "Christian Self-Discovery." Lonergan Workshop 1 (1978): 187–222.

_____. "Created, Alienated, Redeemed." Delivered at Lonergan Workshop, Boston College, summer 1981.

_____. "For a Soteriology of the Existential Subject." In Creativity and Method: Studies in Honor of Rev. Bernard Lonergan, pp. 229–248. Edited by Matthew Lamb.

_____. "The Language of Love." Lonergan Workshop 3 (1982): 83–106.

_____. "Original Sin, Sex, Resurrection and Trinity." Lonergan Workshop 4 (1983): 85–98.

_____. "The New Life." Lonergan Workshop 5 (1985): 145–62.

_____. "The Communication of a Dangerous Memory." In Religion and Culture: Essays in Honor of Bernard Lonergan, S.J., pp. 237–41. Edited by Timothy Fallon and Boo Riley. Also in Communicating a Dangerous Memory, pp. 55–62. Edited by Fred Lawrence.

_____. "The Forming and Transforming of Ego: An Explanatory Concept in Soteriology." Paper delivered at the Lonergan Workshop, Boston College, summer 1987.

Moore, Sebastion & Hughes, Glenn. "Hamlet and the Affective Roots of Decision: A Dramatic Specification of Bernard Lonergan." Paper delivered at the Lonergan Workshop, Boston College, summer 1986.

Morelli, Elizabeth. "The Sixth Stage of Moral Development." Journal of Moral Education 7 (1977-78): 97-108.

_____. "The Feeling of Freedom." In Religion and Culture: Essays in Honor of Bernard Lonergan, S.J., pp. 95-106. Edited by Timothy Fallon and Boo Riley.

Morelli, Mark. "Horizonal Diplomacy." In Creativity and Method: Studies in Honor of Rev. Bernard Lonergan, pp. 459-74. Edited by Matthew Lamb.

_____. "Reversing the Counter-Position: The Argumentum ad Hominem in Philosophic Dialogue." Lonergan Workshop 6 (1986): 195-230.

Nilson, Jon. "Transcendent Knowledge in Insight: A Closer Look." Thomist 37 (1973): 366-77.

_____. Hegel's Phenomenology and Lonergan's Insight. Meisenheim: Verlag Anton Hain, 1980.

O'Callaghan, Michael C. Unity in Theology: Lonergan's Framework for Theology in it New Context. Ph.D. Dissertation. Tubingen University, 1978. Later published. Washington: University Press of America, 1980.

_____. "Resurrection: The Healing of Mind." Delivered at Lonergan Workshop, Boston, 1981.

_____. "Rahner and Lonergan on Foundational Theology." In Creativity and Method: Studies in Honor of Rev. Bernard Lonergan, pp. 123-40. Edited by Matthew Lamb.

_____. "The Theologian and the Truth." In Religion and Culture: Essays in Honor of Bernard Lonergan, S.J., pp. 135-47. Edited by Timothy Fallon and Boo Riley.

O'Connell, Matthew. "St. Thomas and the Verbum: An Interpretation." The Modern Schoolman 24 (1947) 224-34.

O'Connor, Eric. "Towards an Articulation in Education of Transcendental Method." Unpublished paper prepared for the International Lonergan Conference of 1970. Available at the Lonergan Center, University of Santa Clara, Santa Clara, California.

_____. "A Dialogue on Learning Mathematics." In Creativity and Method: Studies in Honor of Rev. Bernard Lonergan, pp. 509-25. Edited by Matthew Lamb.

O'Grady, D.W. "The Notion of the Good in Bernard Lonergan's Insight and Method in Theology." M.A. thesis. University College, 1980.

Keefe, Donald J. "A Methodological Critique of Lonergan's Theological Method." Thomist 50 (1986): 28-65.

Potter, Vincent. "The Irrelevance of Philosophy." Thought 49 (1974): 145–55.

_____. "Lonergan and Peirce on Objective Chance." Unpublished paper delivered at the First International Lonergan Congress, Florida, 1970.

_____. "Foundations: Lonergan and Peirce." In the anticipated supplementary volume of Religion and Culture: Essays in Honor of Bernard Lonergan, S.J. Edited by Timothy Fallon and Boo Riley.

_____. "Metaphysics as Open to God: Insight, Chapters XII–XVIII." Paper delivered at the Lonergan Workshop, Boston, summer 1987.

Price, Geoffrey. "The Nuclear Issue and the Human Sciences." In Religion and Culture: Essays in Honor of Bernard Lonergan, S.J., 277–91. Edited by Timothy Fallon and Boo Riley.

_____. "Politics and Self–Acceptance." In Creativity and Method: Studies in Honor of Rev. Bernard Lonergan, pp. 443–58. Edited by Matthew Lamb.

Quesnell, Quentin. "Beliefs and Authenticity." In Creativity and Method: Studies in Honor of Rev. Bernard Lonergan, pp. 173–85. Edited by Matthew Lamb.

_____. "Pinning Down the Meaning." Paper delivered at the Lonergan Workshop, Boston College, summer 1986.

_____. "On Not Neglecting the Self in the Structure of Theological Revolutions," pp. 125–33. In Religion and Culture: Essays in Honor of Bernard Lonergan, S.J. Edited by Timothy Fallon and Boo Riley.

_____. "What Kind of Proof is Insight XIX?" Paper delivered at the Lonergan Workshop, Boston College, summer 1987.

Raymaker, John Anthony. Theory–Praxis of Social Ethics: The Complementarity Between Bernard Lonergan's and Gibson Winter's Theological Foundations. Ph.D. dissertation. Marquette University, 1977.

_____. "The Theory and Praxis of Social Ethics." In Creativity and Method: Studies in Honor of Rev. Bernard Lonergan, pp. 339–52. Edited by Matthew Lamb.

Reichman, James. "The Transcendental Method and the Psychogenesis of Being." Thomist 32 (1968): 449–508.

Reiser, William E. "Ethics and Biological Man: An Essay on Ethical Method." Studies in Religion 2 (1972–1973): 50–62.

Ring, Nancy. "The Symbolic Function of Religious Doctrine as

Revelatory of the Mind and Mystery of Christ: A Feminist Perspective." Delivered at Lonergan Workshop, Boston College, summer 1981.

Roach, Richard Russell. "Fidelity: The Faith of Responsible Love." Ph.D. dissertation. Yale University, 1974.

_____. "Nature and Praxis." Communio: International Catholic Review 5 (1978): 252-74.

Robert, Pierre. "Theologie et Vie Spirituelle: Recontre avec Bernard Lonergan." Science et Esprit, XXXVIII (1986): 331-41.

Roy, David. "Bioethics as Anamnesis." In Creativity and Method: Studies in Honor of Rev. Bernard Lonergan, pp. 325-39. Edited by Matthew Lamb.

Rulla, L.M. "The Discernment of Spirit and Christian Anthropology." Gregorianum 59 (1978): 537-69.

Ryan, William. "Intentionality in Edmund Husserl and Bernard Lonergan: The Perspective of Intuitive-Constitution and Affirmation." Unpublished paper. Available at the Lonergan Center, University of Santa Clara, Santa Clara, California.

_____. "The Transcendental Reduction according to Husserl and Intellectual Conversion according to Lonergan," pp. 79-93. In Creativity and Method: Studies in Honor of Rev. Bernard Lonergan, pp. 401-10. Edited by Matthew Lamb.

_____. "Victor Frankl's Notion of Intentionality." In Religion and Culture: Essays in Honor of Bernard Lonergan, S.J. Edited by Timothy Fallon and Boo Riley.

Sala, Giovanni. Das Apriori in der menschlichen Erkenntnis. Eine Studie uber Kants Kritik der reinen Vernunft und Lonergans Insight. Meisenheim am Glan: Verlag Anton Hain, 1971.

_____. "L'Evoluzione della Intelligenze Morali." Concilium: Revisita Internazionale di Teologia (1976): 63(1685)-78(1672).

_____. "The A Priori in Human Knowledge: Kant's Critique of Pure Reason and Lonergan's Insight." Thomist 60 (1976): 179-221.

_____. "Kants Lehre von der menschlichen Erkenntnis: eine sensualistiche Version des Intuitionismus." Theologie und Philosophie 57 (1982): 202-24, and 321-47.

Schuchman, Paul. "Aristotle's Phronesis and Transcendental Thinking: The View of Bernard Lonergan." Appendix I of Aristotle and the Problem of Moral Discernment, pp. 113-47. Bern, Switzerland: P. Lang, 1980.

_____. "Bernard Lonergan and the Question of Moral Value."

Philosophy Today 25 (1981): 252-61.

_____. "The Concept of the Unrestricted in the Thought of Bernard Lonergan: Abstract." ACPA: Proceedings 55 (1981): 169. Presented in St. Louis at the fifty-fifth annual meeting of the American Catholic Philosophic Association, April 3-5, 1981, under the title "The Human Subject in the Later Thinking of Bernard Lonergan." This paper and its complete, unpublished abstract are available at the The Lonergan Research Institute.

Shea, William M. "The Stance and Task of the Foundational Theologian." The Heythrop Journal 17 (1976): 273-92.

_____. "The Subjectivity of the Theologian." Thomist 45 (1981): 194-218.

Swanston, Hamisch. "On First Reading Insight." Paper delivered at the Lonergan Workshop, Boston College, summer 1987.

Toulmin, Stephen. "Pluralism and Authority." In Religion and Culture: Essays in Honor of Bernard Lonergan, S.J., pp. 17-29. Edited by Timothy Fallon and Boo Riley.

Tracy, David. "Horizon Analysis and Eschatology." Continuum 6 (1968): 166-79.

_____. The Achievement of Bernard Lonergan. New York: Herder and Herder, 1970.

_____. "Lonergan's Foundational Theology: an Interpretation and a Critique." In Foundations of Theology, pp. 197-222. Edited by Phil McShane.

_____. "Review of Method in Theology." Journal of the American Academy of Religion 43 (1975): 380-81.

_____. "Theological Models: An Exercise in Dialectics." Lonergan Workshop 2 (1981): 83-108.

_____. "Theologies of Praxis." In Creativity and Method: Studies in Honor of Rev. Bernard Lonergan, pp. 35-53. Edited by Matthew Lamb.

Turner, John Boyd. "Lonergan's Practical Political Transformative Understanding: The Example of Development in the Province of Northern Samar." In Communicating a Dangerous Memory, pp. 109-241. Edited by Fred Lawrence.

Tyrrell, Bernard. "The New Context of the Philosophy of God in Lonergan and Rahner." In Language, Truth and Meaning, pp. 284-305. Edited by Phil McShane.

_____. "Bernard Lonergan's Philosophy of God." Ph.D. dissertation, Fordham University, 1972. Published in 1974, shortened and revised. Indiana: Notre Dame Press, Notre Dame, 1974.

_____. Christotherapy: Healing through Enlightenment. New York: Seabury Press, 1975.

_____. "Christotherapy and the Healing of Neurosis." In Trinification of the World, 144-74. Edited by T.A. Dunne and J. Laporte.

_____. "On the Possibility and Desireability of a Christian Psychotherapy." Lonergan Workshop, 1 (1978): 143-86.

_____. "Christotherapy and the Healing/Transformation of Communal Consciousness with Special Reference to the American Consciousness." Lonergan Workshop 2 (1981): 201-30.

_____. "Passages and Conversion." In Creativity and Method: Studies in Honor of Rev. Bernard Lonergan, pp. 35-53. Edited by Matthew Lamb.

_____. "'Dynamics of Christotherapy' and the Issue of De Jure Psychotherapeutic Pluralism." Lonergan Workshop 3 (1982): 125-48.

_____. "Christian Imagination and Christian Prayer." Lonergan Workshop 4 (1983): 167-85.

_____. "Feelings as Apprehensive-Intentional Responses to Values." Paper delivered to the Lonergan Workshop, Boston College, summer 1985.

_____. "Psychological Conversion, Methods of Healing, and Communication." Lonergan Workshop 6 (1986): 239-60.

Van Roo, William. "Lonergan's Method in Theology." Gregorianum 55 (1974): 99-151.

Vertin, Michael. "Immateriality, Phenomenology and Man." ACPA: Proceedings 52 (1978): 52-60.

_____. "Towards the Emergence of Foundational Questions." In Dialogues in Celebration, pp. 210-33. Edited by Cathleen M. Going.

_____. "Philosophy of God, Theology and the Problems of Evil." Laval Theologique et Philosophique 37 (1981): 15-32.

_____. "Marechal, Lonergan and the Phenomenology of Knowing." In Creativity and Method: Studies in Honor of Rev. Bernard Lonergan, pp. 411-22. Edited by Matthew Lamb.

_____. "Seminar on the Nature and Method of Theology: Toward a Theology of Evil." CTSA: Proceedings 39 (1984): 166-69.

_____. "Seminar on the Nature and Method of Theology: The Ressurrection, Reconstructive Hermeneutics, and Foundational

Theology." CTSA: Proceedings 40 (1985): 181–84.

_____. "Dialectically Opposed Phenomenologies of Knowing: A Pedagogical Elaboration of Basic Ideal Types." Lonergan Workshop 4 (1983): 1–26.

_____. "Lonergan's 'Three Basis Questions' and a Philosophy of Philosophies." Paper delivered at the Lonergan Workshop, Boston College, summer 1986.

_____. "Is God in Process?" In Religion and Culture: Essays in Honor of Bernard Lonergan, S.J., pp. 45–62. Edited by Timothy Fallon and Boo Riley.

_____. ""Knowing," "Objectivity," and "Reality": Insight and Beyond." Paper delivered at the Lonergan Workshop, Boston College, summer 1987.

Voeglin, Eric. "The Gospel and Culture." In Jesus and Man's Hope 2, pp. 59–102. Ed. by D.G. Miller and D.X. Hadidan. Pittsburgh: Pittsburgh Theological Seminary, 1971.

_____. "The Meditative Origin of the Philosophical Knowledge of Order." In The Beginning and the Beyond: Papers from the Gadamer and Voeglin Conferences, pp. 43–52. Edited by Fred Lawrence.

_____. "Responses at the Panel Discussion of "The Beginning of the Beginning."" In The Beginning and the Beyond: Papers from the Gadamer and Voeglin Conferences, pps. 97–110. Edited by Fred Lawrence.

_____. "Autobiographical Statement at Age Eighty-Two." In The Beginning and the Beyond: Papers from the Gadamer and Voeglin Conferences, pp. 111–31. Edited by Fred Lawrence.

Vokey, D.J. "Bernard J.F. Lonergan on the Objectivity of Judgments of Value." M.A. thesis. Carleton University, 1980.

Von Hildebrand, Dietrich. The Sacred Heart. Baltimore: Helicon, 1965.

_____. The Art of Living. Chicago: Franciscan Herald Press, 1965.

_____. Ethics. Chicago: Franciscan Herald Press, 1953.

Wilhelmsen, Frederic. "The Priority of Judgment over Question: Reflection on Transcendental Thomism." IPQ 14 (1974): 475–93.

Wilson, Patricia. "Human Knowledge of God's Existence in the Theology of Bernard Lonergan." Thomist 35 (1971): 259–75.

Winter, Gibson. Love and Conflict. New York: Doubleday Dolphin Book, 1958.

Ysaac, Walter L. The Third World and Bernard Lonergan. Manila:

Cardinal Bea Institute, 1986.

_____. "Inculturation as Praxis and Method of Radical Solidarity with the People." In The Third World and Bernard Lonergan, pp. 16-55.

SELECTED BIBLIOGRAPHY

Aristotle. The Basic Works of Aristotle. Edited by Richard McKeon. New York: Random House, 1944.

Bunge, Mario. Scientific Research I. New York: Springer Verlag, 1967.

Cassirer, Ernst. An Essay on Man. New Haven: Yale University Press, 1944.

Clarke, W. Norris. The Philosophical Approach to God. North Carolina: Wake Forest University, 1979.

_____. "To Be is to be Self-Communicative: St. Thomas' View of Personal Being." Theology Digest 33 (1986): 441-54.

Heelan, Patrick. Quantum Mechanics and Objectivity. The Hague: Martinus Nijhoff, 1965.

Heidegger, Martin. "Letter on Humanism." Translated by Edgar Lohner in Philosophy in the Twentieth Century. Edited by William Barret and H.D. Aiken. New York: Random House, 1962, vol. III, pp. 270-302. Reprinted in The Existentialist Tradition. Edited by N. Langiuli. Garden City: Doubleday-Anchor, 1971, pp. 204-48. Retranslated by F.A. Capuzzi and J.G. Glenn in Martin Heidegger: Basic Writings. Edited by D.F. Krell. New York: Harper and Row, 1977, pp. 193-246.

Hilbert, David. The Foundation of Geometry. Translated by E.J. Townsend. La Salle: Open Court, 1947.

Holmes, Sandra. Outline of Plant Classification. New York: Longman, 1983.

Idhe, D. Listening and Voice: A Phenomenology of Sound Athens: Ohio University Press, 1976.

Kant, Immanuel. The Citique of Pure Reason. Translated by Norman Kemp Smith. New York: St. Martin's Press, 1965.

Kuhn, Thomas S. The Copernican Revolution. New York: Vintage Books, 1957.

_____. The Structure of Scientific Revolutions, Second edition, enlarged. Chicago: The University of Chicago Press, 1970.

Lindsay, Robert B. and Margenau, Henry. Foundations of Physics. New York: Dover Publications, 1956.

Locke, John. Two Treatises of Government. New York: Hafner Publishing Company, 1947.

Maslow, Abraham. Motivation and Personality. New York: Harper & Row,

1954, 1970.

_____. The Psychology of Science. Chicago: Henry Regnery Co., 1966.

_____. Toward a Psychology of Being. New York: D. Van Nostrand, 1962, 1968.

_____. The Farthest Reaches of Human Nature. New York: Viking Compass Book, 1971.

Marx, Karl. Economic and Political Manuscripts of 1844. Edited by Struck, Dirk J. and translated by Milligan, Martin. New York: International Publishing Company, 1964.

Newman, John H. An Essay in Aid of a Grammar of Assent. Indiana: University of Notre Dame Press, 1979.

Peirce, Charles Sanders. Collected Papers of Charles Sanders Peirce, 1-6. Edited by Charles Hartshorne and Paul Weiss. Cambridge: Harvard University Press, 931-35. 7-8, edited by Arthur W. Burks. Cambridge: Harvard University Press, 1958.

Pellegrin, Pierre. Aristotle's Classification of Animals. Trans. by Anthony Preus. Berkeley: University of California Press, 1982.

Pico Della Mirandola, Giovanni. Oratione de Hominis Dignitate. Translated by Elizabeth L. Forbes. Lexington, Kentucky: Anvil Press, 1953.

Plato. The Collected Dialogues. Ed. by Edith Hamilton and Huntington Cairns. New York: Pantheon Books, 1963.

Potter, Vincent G. Charles S. Peirce: On Norms and Ideals. Amherst: The University of Massachusetts Press, 1967.

_____. Philosophy of Knowledge. New York: Fordham University Press, 1987.

Sartre, Jean-Paul. Being and Nothingness. Trans. by Hazel E. Barnes. New York: Philosophical Library, 1956.

Sorokin, Pitirim. Social and Cultural Dynamics. 4 vols. New York: American Book Company, 1937-41.

Struik, D.J. A Concise History of Mathematics, 3rd ed. New York: Dover Publishing, 1967.

Sullivan, H.S. The Interpersonal Theory of Psychiatry. New York: The Norton Library, 1953.

_____. "The Illusion of Unique Individuality." Psychiatry 13 (1950): 317-32. Reprinted in The Fusion of Psychiatry and Social Science, pp. 198-216. New York: The Norton Library, 1964.

Toynbee, Arnold. _A Study of History_. 12 vols. New York and London: Oxford University Press, 1939–1961.

Wilks, Samuel S. _Elementary Statistical Analysis_. New Jersey: Princeton University Press, 1952.